THE NINE YEARS WAR, 1593–1603

The Nine Years War, 1593–1603

O'Neill, Mountjoy and the Military Revolution

JAMES O'NEILL

FOUR COURTS PRESS

Typeset in 10.5 pt on 13.5 pt CaslonPro by
Carrigboy Typesetting Services for
FOUR COURTS PRESS LTD
7 Malpas Street, Dublin 8, Ireland
www.fourcourtspress.ie
and in North America for
FOUR COURTS PRESS
c/o ISBS, 920 NE 58th Avenue, Suite 300, Portland, OR 97213.

A catalogue record for this title is available
from the British Library.

ISBN 978–1–84682–636–8

SPECIAL ACKNOWLEDGMENT

This publication has been aided by a support from the College of Arts,
Celtic Studies and Social Sciences, University College Cork.

Coláiste na hOllscoile Corcaigh, Éire
University College Cork, Ireland

Printed in England
by CPI Antony Rowe, Chippenham, Wilts.

To Amanda, James and Katie

Contents

Illustrations

Preface

IT IS NO UNDERSTATEMENT TO SAY this book has been long in the coming. It is occasionally pointed out by a friend or family member that I have been researching this conflict for longer than it lasted, surely I must be done with it by now? Now at last I can wave something under their collective noses with cries of 'look here, see what I have been up to all these years'. However, it has been no simple matter of gathering together every piece of evidence or work on the Nine Years War, give it some due consideration, then disgorge my ruminations to all and sundry in print. My task was not a simple one as I was confronted with the fundamental question of who was I writing this for? Was it for my academic peers, whose demand for an in-depth scholarly monograph called for much historiographical analysis and penetrating observations of the minutiae of the conflict? To paraphrase Prof. Mary O'Dowd's advice to me may years ago, don't tell me what, tell me why and why I should care. I felt that I had an obligation to history enthusiasts, who as yet had no publication addressing the entire course of the Nine Years War, and very much wanted to know the what's and where's, as well as the why's. Therefore to attend to both I have written a somewhat chimeric work. The initial chapter sets out the historiography of the subjects and identifies the major questions concerning the study of the war, an absolute must in academic research. Yet with these formalities aside I jump straight into the narrative coupled with pauses for scrutiny of key events of the separate phases of the war. The last two chapters provide some overarching analysis of the events discussed in the preceding chapters. I hope you find the balance a suitable compromise.

As a matter of good housekeeping I will get some initial points out of the way. The term 'confederate' has been used to describe the alliance of Tyrone and other Irish lords in opposition to the crown. It was used by crown officials during the war to describe the association between those in rebellion. The term was also frequently used by Philip O'Sullivan Beare to describe Tyrone's coalition of Irish chiefs. Consequently, it will be used in this regard throughout. The expression 'Old English' refers to the descendants of the Anglo-Norman settlers. It defines Palesmen or Anglo-Irish. They often intermarried with the local Irish elite, and they remained Catholic which set them apart from the New English of the latter half of the sixteenth century who were increasingly Protestants. Contemporary spelling is updated to modern English where appropriate, and the currency referred to is sterling unless otherwise stated.

Though my name is on the front of this book, I would have some neck on me to suggest it was in any way a solo achievement. Many individuals and institutions have supported, guided and given advice freely and unselfishly to ensure that this work lives up to the faith and expectations of those who have invested in many years of my scholarly investigations into the Nine Years War. If there are failings, mistakes or glaring oversights to be found it is purely down to my thick-headedness and no one else. First among many to be thanked must be my own personal Dalai Lama and friend, Dr Hiram Morgan of University College Cork. His unstinting support and encouragement has ensured my long-in-the-making work is something fit for human consumption. Moreover, his wealth of knowledge of the period prevented more than a few howlers making it into print. I am grateful to Dr David Edwards also of UCC for his insightful observations of this work, all of which were much-needed and gratefully received. Thanks to Dr Ruth Canning for her collaboration during the two-year period when this book was written. Her knowledge of the Old English community of this period allowed me to plumb scholarly depths that my own research had only skimmed over. Thanks must go to Prof. Sean Connolly and Prof. Mary O'Dowd of Queen's University Belfast who diligently and with great patience supervised my original research on the Nine Years War. I cannot forget Dr John Lynch with whom I studied at undergraduate level. I also need to thank Prof. Peter Gray who many years ago listened patiently to an overly-effusive graduate ranting about the lack of a definitive history of the Nine Years War; he recommended I should do something about it. I'm not saying this book is definitive, but I hope it makes good on our meeting back in 2008. This work would never have seen the light of day if it were not for the financial support of the Irish Research Council, whose two years post-doctoral research fellowship at UCC under the mentorship of Dr Hiram Morgan allowed me to devote the time to craft a coherent and hopefully enjoyable monograph. Also, to University College Cork School of History where I held the fellowship for providing me the facilities in which to work – scrivening away on research while others had to go out and teach. I am grateful to my many friends whose advice and patience has been invaluable: Helen Murphy, Rhonda Robinson, Michael MacDonagh, Ruairi O'Baoill, Tim Watt, Leanne Calvert and Erica Doherty; they have aided my endeavours more than they know. Finally, I have to thank my family, my wife Amanda and my children James and Katie, who have endured absences and foul moods brought about by this work. They are my rock on which this is all founded, and they continually remind me that this is, after all, only work. Last but not least my parents May and Jim, who always said all that reading would come to some use.

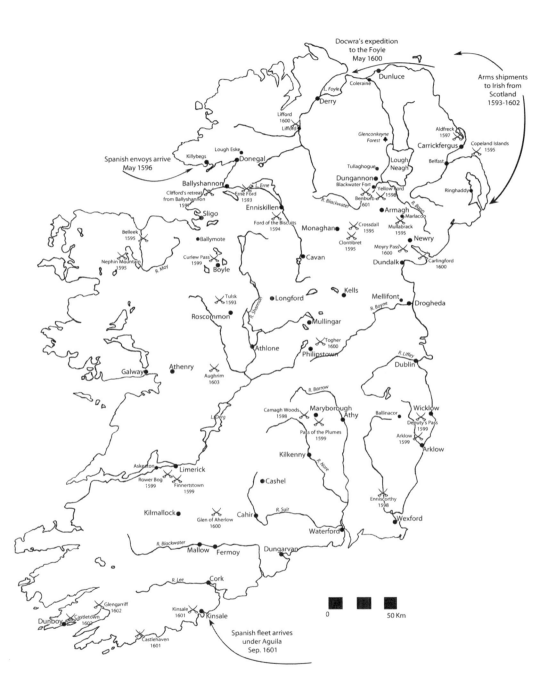

Docwra's expedition
to the Foyle
May 1600

Arms shipments
to Irish from
Scotland
1593–1602

Dunluce

Coleraine

L. Foyle

Derry

Lifford
1600
Lifford

Aldfreck
1597

Carrickfergus

Copeland Islands
1595

*Glenconkeyne
Forest*

Belfast

Lough
Neagh

Killybegs

Lough Eske

Spanish envoys arrive
May 1596

Donegal

Tullaghogue

Dungannon
Blackwater Fort

Yellow Ford
1598

Ringhaddy

Ballyshannon

L. Erne

Erne Ford
1593

Clifford's retreat
from Ballyshannon
159?

Benburb
1601

Marlacoo

Sligo

Enniskillen

Armagh

R. Blackwater

R. Bann

Ford of the Biscuits
1594

Crossdall
1595

Mullabrack
1595

Belleek
1595

Ballymote

Monaghan

Clontibret
1595

Newry

Moyry Pass
1600

Nephin Mountain
1595

R. Moy

Curlew Pass
1599

Boyle

Cavan

Dundalk

Carlingford
1600

Tulsk
1593

Longford

Kells

Mellifont

R. Boyne

Drogheda

Roscommon

R. Shannon

Mullingar

Athlone

Togher
1600

Philipstown

R. Liffey

Dublin

Galway

Athenry

Aughrim
1603

L. Derg

R. Barrow

Carnagh Woods
1598

Maryborough

Athy

Ballinacor

Wicklow

Deputy's Pass
1599

Pass of the Plumes
1599

Arklow
1599

Arklow

Kilkenny

R. Nore

Askeaton

Limerick

Cashel

Rower Bog
1599

Finnertstown
1599

Enniscorthy
1598

Kilmallock

Cahir

R. Suir

Glen of Aherlow
1600

Wexford

R. Blackwater

Mallow

Fermoy

Dungarvan

Waterford

R. Lee

Cork

0   50 Km

Glengarriff
1602

Kinsale
1601

Dunboy

Castletown
1602

Kinsale

Castlehaven
1601

Spanish fleet arrives
under Aguila
Sep. 1601

1 Ireland and the Nine Years War, 1593–1603

Introduction

As DAWN BROKE OVER Armagh on 14 August 1598, Sir Henry Bagenal must have been beset by conflicting emotions. On the one hand he would have had a degree of trepidation, familiar to any soldier who had experienced combat. Apprehension was common before a battle, but Bagenal had seen enough action to know that this would fade as the business of organizing his regiments and issuing orders to his officers displaced any distracting anxieties. Bagenal had fought in the Glens of Antrim, seen Lord Grey's army destroyed at Glenmalure in Wicklow in 1580, routed Maguire at Belleek in 1593 and resisted Tyrone's exertions to break his army at Clontibret in 1595. Battles could be won and lost, but Bagenal had been through victory and defeat without serious injury. Therefore the prospect of combat held few mysteries to unsettle him. Furthermore, Bagenal may have been genuinely excited at the prospect of engaging with his most hated adversary, Hugh O'Neill, second earl of Tyrone. Tyrone had betrayed the trust of his sovereign, Queen Elizabeth of England. Rebellion put Tyrone and his cohorts outside the customs of war, but Bagenal's animosity was also personal. His sister Mabel had eloped with Tyrone in 1591, but Tyrone had been anything but a devoted husband. Bagenal did everything he could to prove the marriage was invalid but to no avail. However, he could and did withhold Mabel's £1,000 dowry. Tyrone had assailed Bagenal's army at Clontibret in 1595, burnt and devastated Bagenal's estates and defied all attempts to bring him to heel, but circumstance had placed Bagenal at the head of the largest and best-equipped army yet fielded by the crown in Ireland, and with it he would smash the Irish rebels.

Tyrone had besieged the English garrison in the Blackwater fort since the start of June. An army of almost 4,000 men had been assembled to force its way through to resupply the garrison. Tyrone had the advantage at Clontibret because the English army there was less than 2,000 strong and poorly supplied with officers and munitions. This time Bagenal's men were well equipped and commanded by some of the crown's finest and most experienced officers. In the early hours of the summer morning, the noise and commotion of an army organizing for war would have resounded through the chill air. The Marshal ordered his 3,500 infantry into six regiments with armoured pikemen at their core surrounded by ranks of shot. The acrid smell of their smouldering match would have filled the air as thousands of firearms were prepared for combat. In support were 350 horsemen. Armed with lance, sword and pistols, and armoured with steel cuirass and helmet, the English horse were rightly feared and avoided by the Irish. Tyrone had developed pike units to counter the English cavalry, but Bagenal had brought four artillery pieces that could plough bloody furrows through the Irish pike blocks if they attempted to deploy. As the regiments marched out of the camp at eight in the morning, Bagenal expected Tyrone to attack; he may even have hoped for it. Everything was in place to ensure that the crown army would prevail; Bagenal had no reason to believe otherwise.

Eight hours later the army returned to Armagh a blasted remnant of the force that left that morning. Bagenal was dead, as were fourteen senior officers and 1,200 of his men. Hundreds more were wounded, but the retreating English managed to throw a defensive cordon around the ecclesiastic buildings at Armagh. Tyrone had given Bagenal the fight he wanted, but Irish firepower and manoeuvrability had outfought and overthrown the English. Nothing stood between Tyrone and Dublin, and a sense of panic gripped the crown's officials who realized that they had nothing to stop Tyrone if he chose to march south. In five years of warfare Tyrone and his allies had brought the power of the English crown in Ireland to the point of utter collapse. They had prevailed in almost all significant military engagements and no one in the establishment in Dublin knew how to stop what appeared to be the irresistible advance of Irish military power.

Less than four years later an English lord deputy marched over the same ground. Tyrone was a fugitive, forced to hide in the forests of Glenconkeyne. The earl's confederation of Irish lords was destroyed, and Ulster lay in ashes. The Irish in the fastness of the Wicklow Mountains, which had been a constant thorn in the side of the administration, had now submitted to English law. Indeed, native Irish power throughout the island was broken. Lord Mountjoy and his regional commanders had little left to do apart from some local mopping-up operations in south Cork and Fermanagh. The social order of Gaelic Ireland was on the eve of its extinction, and the Tudor monarch's armies had almost completed the final conquest of Ireland. The change in fortunes over such a small space of time could not be more dramatic, but how could this happen?

In ten years Tyrone and his allies had forged native Irish armies that prevailed time and again against every English force sent against them. They were faster and more mobile than their enemies, their discipline better and weapons skills superior. For seven years Tyrone's men marched from one victory to another, but from 1600 onwards they met with little else but defeat and failure. The greatest of these was the calamitous reverse at Kinsale on Christmas Eve 1601. Though outnumbered three-to-one, Mountjoy's haggard and sickly English army routed Tyrone. How could an army that had fought so successfully for so long suddenly stop winning, then continually lose until their final defeat three years later? This sudden reversal of fortune and the catastrophic effect it had on Tyrone's confederation was more than enough to pique my interest in this period of Irish history, but all attempts to obtain a comprehensive analysis of the course of the war were thwarted by an unusual scarcity of secondary literature.

Historiography of the 'Nine' Years War

The conflict that has become known as the Nine Years War is paradoxical in Irish history, as some aspects have been studied in great detail and others relatively ignored. Certain issues, such as the events and politics behind the rise to power of Tyrone and his later surrender and exile, have all been thoroughly researched.[1] The brutality and destructiveness of the war have also drawn much recent attention, but while scholarly investigations have shed light on many facets of the war, resulting in much revision and debate, other aspects have remained largely untouched. Most of the narrative and academic analyses of the military characteristics of the war are over sixty years old.[2] The seminal and oft-quoted works are those by Richard Bagwell, Cyril Falls and G.A. Hayes-McCoy.[3] Later publications have focused on specific events that occurred during the war, most notably the defeat of Tyrone and his allies at the battle of Kinsale at the end of 1601.[4] There is also a significant number of publications dealing with major figures of the war; unsurprisingly, Tyrone features highly.[5] The foremost of these is Hiram Morgan's influential book *Tyrone's rebellion: the outbreak of the Nine Years War in Ireland*. Morgan covered much of the period before the war, but his analysis tantalizingly stops in 1596, just as the war was gathering momentum. Prominent individuals such as Feagh MacHugh O'Byrne, Sir Henry Docwra, Sir Arthur Chichester, Lord Mountjoy, Hugh Roe O'Donnell and Robert Devereux, second earl of Essex, have all received attention, but these works have naturally focused on the events surrounding their protagonists.[6]

Over the last quarter of a century there have been various studies published in monographs, edited collections and in journals, which have addressed elements of the war, but to date, there has been no examination of its entirety or any corresponding revision of the narrative based on new research.[7] Even the starting date of the war has not been agreed on. Tyrone himself termed it the eleven years' war in a letter to Philip III in 1607.[8] Philip O'Sullivan Beare called it the 'fifteen years' war' commencing in 1588 at the time of the wreck of the Spanish Armada, and Standish O'Grady, who coined the term 'Nine Years War', believed the war started in 1594.[9] Of the more recent commentators, Morgan ascribed the beginning of the war to April 1593; Colm Lennon has opted for 1594 and Mary Ann Lyons chose February 1595.[10] This lack of consensus over a basic detail of a war that witnessed the zenith and eventual collapse of native Irish military and political power is puzzling. Technically speaking the expression 'Nine Years War' would only be correct if one believed the war began in 1594. 'Tyrone's rebellion' has been used to describe the conflict, but the term does not adequately describe the involvement of people such as Hugh Roe O'Donnell, Hugh Maguire, Feagh MacHugh O'Byrne or the influence of Spain. While there is evidence that the crown considered the war to have started in 1593, I have no desire to rebrand the conflict as the 'Ten Years War'.[11]

While the subject attracts academic study with regards to political and social history, the absence of any comprehensive analysis of the martial element of the war appears to be a curious academic lacuna. One possible explanation for this is a belief that the work of Hayes-McCoy et al. has adequately answered all the questions regarding the war and no further examination is required. Some years ago an august and well-respected scholar of early modern Ireland told me that there was little left to cover on the Nine Years War, apart from some analysis of naval activity on Lough Neagh. Another problem is the reluctance of Irish academia to study the fundamentals of warfare. An open admission to researching military history on the conference circuit is usually the cue for furtive sideways glances, polite smiles and rapid changing of the subject. In conversation, some have suggested that academic military history is essentially a form of re-enactment by those who like guns and dressing up as soldiers. Ian Beckett referred to the tenuous acceptability of military history in academic circles due, in many ways, to the old-style 'drum-and-trumpet' approach to military history.[12] In this regard, the Irish academy should not feel too bad as it only mirrors attitudes frequently found elsewhere.

Throughout international academia, there have been suspicions that those who study war in some ways seek to condone or glorify it.[13] Given that the brutality of war is repugnant to all people of a normal disposition, would it not be wise to avoid those who actively pursue scholarly knowledge of events which facilitate humanity's basest acts and emotions? Circumspection is not wholly unwarranted, as many popular publications have readily embraced triumphalism, lionized military leaders or worse still, sought to hyprotize their readers with military hardware pornography.[14] The popularity of this type of work is demonstrated by bookshops and television channels overflowing with military history of variable quality. Consequently, to retain academic legitimacy and distance themselves from the drum-and-bugle-brigade, many academics have quarantined the realities of warfare and focused on events before and after combat. Tedious details of strategic decision making, operational manoeuvre, logistics and the violence of the battlefield are brushed over as they appear unconnected to anything outside warfare.[15] To be fair, the detailing of troop movements, generals and the recounting of battles without any higher goal than mere historical voyeurism has probably had its day, but that does not mean that exhaustive examination of military events cannot provide evidence and shed new light on broader questions of historiographical debate.

A key aspect of research has been the debate on the nature and extent of violence in early modern Ireland. The historiography of Tudor Ireland has generated a startling divergence of opinion on violence and government reform in Ireland. Before the 1970s, Irish historians tended to avoid dealing with atrocity and the horror of war in early modern Ireland, preferring a 'soft-focus view' of the violence that appeared endemic during the period.[16] Brendan Bradshaw castigated the trend of revisionism in the Irish academy for its evasion of the issue of violence as a central feature of the early modern Irish experience.[17] Nicholas Canny argued that the attitude of the Elizabethans to their governance of the Irish was heavily influenced by an ideology that viewed the native Irish as irredeemably barbarian who could only be subdued by force.[18] The Tudor emphasis on law and process was replaced by unrestrained savagery by the crown's officers.[19]

Contrary to the idea of reformation by fire and sword, Ciaran Brady contended that the policies of the viceroys in Ireland in the second half of the sixteenth century were aimed at recovering control by gradual legal reform and assimilation of the native Irish polity.[20] Brady hit back at any suggestion of an institutionalized English penchant for conquest and brutality, arguing that the crown's recourse to extreme acts of war, such as scorched earth strategies, were only used in times of crisis.[21] Contrary to the government's gradualist reforms, it was greedy self-interest on the part of New English adventurers, not crown policy, that led to the failure of peaceful reform and the rise of violent colonization.[22] This concurred with Steven Ellis' view that the crown's programme to create a civil society within the Gaelic lordships was based upon persuasion and education. Where private plantations were attempted only the Irish elite were to be removed, leaving the native husbandmen to work the land to the profit of their new English masters.[23] Outside times of war the crown's army was quickly reduced and limited to regional peacekeeping duties.

The debate on crown brutality has recently been reignited by David Edwards in his discussion of the increase in violence and atrocity in Ireland during the latter half of the sixteenth century.[24] He claimed that rather than using military force sparingly, the crown repeatedly resorted to acts of military aggression in Ireland, unlike anywhere else in the Tudor realm.[25] Edwards rejected the suggestion of a reform-orientated policy, and concluded that conquest was the preferred means to subjugate Ireland, and was prosecuted in a way that would have been unconscionable in England. Vincent Carey has gone further still, suggesting that the crown's campaign to defeat Tyrone and his allies bore all the characteristics of genocide.[26] Rory Rapple has taken an alternative approach and looked at the perpetrators of much of the violence – the Elizabethan captains and military men.[27] He believed that a micro-contextual method of examination shows that the rising levels of violence inflicted on the Irish by the English were more a result of individuals' personal frustrations with the *status quo* in England, and their burning ambitions to turn healthy profits. In a kingdom where micro-diplomacy mattered more than grand design, brutality was guided more by the whims of crown officials than by any overarching policy.[28]

With the renewal of the debate on levels of brutality, closer scrutiny of interpersonal violence during the Nine Years War is required. Much of the analysis of the violence of this period has cited occasions of undeniable brutality, but most have avoided a comprehensive examination of hostility throughout the episodes of warfare during the years 1593–1603. There has been a focus on the English campaigns in Ulster at the closing stages of the war, but little has been said on the behaviour of the belligerents throughout the conflict. The concept of escalating and unrestrained English brutality in Ulster has proliferated in recent years through other related genres of historical studies, such as *Blood and Soil*, in which Ben Kiernan uncritically replicated much of Carey's interpretation.[29] Correspondingly, it is essential to re-evaluate patterns of activity within the crucible of open warfare, with the aim of clarifying the nature of violent (or non-violent) behaviour, whether based on necessity, frustration, reciprocity, policy, and religious or gender antagonism. Furthermore, causative factors of atrocity can be found in the psychological impact of low-intensity or partisan warfare on the troops involved. Comparison with contemporary violence outside Ireland will help determine if the experience of warfare in Ireland during the Nine Years War was exceptional, or if it was a mere portend to the devastation soon to visit continental Europe during the Thirty Years War.

Modernization of native Irish society?

There may be still some out there who will question the value of research on military history for informing broader discussions on the nature of Irish society. Is warfare not an extreme experience and therefore not representative

of peacetime values or behaviour? Possibly, but the stresses of war may force
society to develop or display characteristics that would have been difficult if
not impossible to identify outside warfare. Before the Second World War, who
could have anticipated that strategic bombing of population centres could
stiffen, not weaken national resolve? Concerning the Nine Years War, the
campaign of the Irish confederation led by Tyrone was far more sophisticated
on strategic, operational and tactical levels than anything that had gone before.
This transformation is directly relevant to the ongoing historiographical
debate concerning the openness of Gaelic society to change, the extent of
modernizing influences, and the degree to which the Irish rejected or
embraced these impulses at the end of the sixteenth century.

Before the 1970s, Gaelic society was viewed by historians as conservative
and introverted with no real capacity to change in response to outside
influences, typified by A.L. Rowse who described Irish civilization as 'part
medieval, in part pre-medieval ... in a stage of rapid social decomposition'.[30]
This notion was restated by Richard Berleth in *The twilight lords*, which
became the subject of Bradshaw's sharp rejoinder.[31] Bradshaw promoted the
concept of Irish flexibility and openness to change as reflected in
contemporary native literature.[32] A subsequent study by Michelle O'Riordan
suggested that Gaelic verse composed during and after the period of the Tudor
conquest exhibited a remarkable acceptance of the *fait accompli* of the Gaels'
military defeat.[33] Native culture would go to great lengths to adapt to the new
political values of the victors, thereby demonstrating an extraordinary cultural
flexibility. Nerys Patterson proposed similar ideas for the adaptability of Irish
legal traditions.[34] However, Mary O'Dowd suggested that the transformations
in Irish society at this time should not be overstated.[35] She has noted that rates
of change varied dramatically depending on the character and effect of the
changes. Numerous Irish lords readily adopted alterations in the nature of title
to land and inheritance rights. However, the progressiveness cannot be
interpreted as evidence for a wholesale restructuring of the Gaelic mind-set;
their motives were founded on conservative ideas aimed at maintaining their
local independence. Katharine Simms also noted that modernizing trends
were used to consolidate power within the Irish lordships.[36]

Where does military transformation fit into this debate? A reappraisal of
the improvements in native Irish military methods serves several purposes. At
its most basic level, the degree to which methods and technology of the Gaelic
military were improved can be established. Additionally, the rate of change
speaks directly to the willingness of the Irish soldiery to engage in the
modernizing process. Beyond the role of the individual soldiers, to what degree
did the Irish nobility and society as a whole accept the transformations

required to maintain a modernized army? A modern army had to be paid, clothed, equipped, and given adequate shelter and medical care. It needed to be well-led and be responsive to operational and strategic objectives that required regional collaboration; no mean feat in a country where even local co-operation between Irish lords could be difficult to achieve. The native economy would have to transform to support the new military organization, as troops needed to be equipped with expensive firearms and sustained with munitions, much of which had to be imported. Tyrone and his confederates made these changes in less than ten years; the degree to which it was realized shall be discovered in the coming chapters.

The Nine Years War occurred during a period of transformation and development of military techniques and technology in Europe known as the military revolution. The concept of the military revolution was first raised at my *alma mater*, Queen's University Belfast, in 1955 by Michael Roberts.[37] He claimed that in the century after 1560 European warfare was transformed by a revolution in tactics, army size and operational strategy, with a corresponding accentuation of the impact of warfare on society. Since then the debate has become vigorous and contentious.[38] Geoffrey Parker argued that the origin of the military revolution was during the fifteenth century, when gunpowder artillery obliged a rethink on defensive architecture; squat, angular structures of the *trace italienne* design replaced tall medieval walls.[39] Artillery and small arms firepower allowed infantry to eclipse the power of heavy cavalry. Furthermore, Parker claimed that the revolution that evolved in the sixteenth century with bastioned fortresses, disciplined firepower-centric armies, and ocean-going broadside armed sailing ships was the beginning of the military dominance of Europeans over non-Europeans.[40] Clifford Rogers placed the date of the most important military changes as early as the start of the fourteenth century, with steady improvement over time, punctuated by separate 'revolutions' in infantry, artillery, and then fortifications.[41] Jeremy Black contended that innovation was not concentrated during the sixteenth century, rather at the end of the fifteenth and again in the late seventeenth century.[42] There were requests for the debate to move beyond the concept of a distinct revolutionary event occupying a singular moment in historical time, but claim, counter-claim and reworking of opinions and chronology are likely to rumble on for some time yet.[43]

It has been suggested that part of the reason why the experience of warfare in Ireland has been marginalized by historians was the misconception that Irish wars were primitive and therefore had little to contribute to the wider military revolution debate.[44] Furthermore, others claimed that apart from a few isolated examples, Ireland was scarcely touched by the effects of the European reforms.[45] Presumptions that the Irish could not fight in a modern manner ignored the paradoxical appearance of Irish pike and shot units and sophisticated field fortifications. There appeared to be a fundamental flaw in the understanding of the military history of this period. Therefore it is understandable that Eoin Ó Néill called for a root-and-branch rethink on the study and analysis of the Nine Years War, more specifically its military aspects.[46] The current history of the war has a battle-centric focus. This view of the conflict is too narrow, as fighting was only a part of a war in which the most mundane elements, such as logistics, deception, irregular warfare and negotiation, played an equal, if not more important, role.

The kindling of war

The confederation of Irish lords presented the greatest threat to English domination in Ireland since the Norman Conquest, but it must also be recognized that the crown was extremely unlucky to have to contend with them in the first place. The imbalance of power between the Elizabethan state and the north Irish lords may have made the concept of a general revolt against English rule in Ireland seem remote. The population of England dwarfed that of Ireland, perhaps four to five times that of all of Ireland, never mind that of Ulster.[47] Moreover, English economic capacity and ability to generate revenue dwarfed the resources available to Tyrone and his allies. The idea that the Ulster chiefs could challenge the crown, let alone bring it to the point of collapse in Ireland, would have appeared ridiculous.

The flash point that occurred in 1593 was at a confluence of issues, the removal of any one of which might have prevented regional disquiet from exploding into open war. The first was the destruction of the Spanish ships along the coasts of Ulster and Connacht in 1588. From this disaster (for the Spanish at least) political bonds were forged between Spain and the Irish lords who needed the economic and military assistance of Europe's premier military power. This support gave them the confidence to believe they could prevail against England and give legitimacy to Irish attempts to abjure the sovereignty of Queen Elizabeth in Ireland. After all, the Irish were not seeking a republic but attempting to substitute their English monarch for a Spanish one. The arrival of the Spanish along the Irish coast coincided with disaffection of northern Irish lords, the most powerful (and ambitious) being Hugh O'Neill and Hugh Roe O'Donnell.

Hugh O'Neill may have been the central figure of the Nine Years War, but his childhood and upbringing did little to mark him out for greatness. Born around 1550, he was the second son of Matthew O'Neill, first baron of

2 Hugh O'Neill, 2nd earl of Tyrone

Dungannon, who found himself, along with his brother Brian, on the losing side of a dynastic dispute with Shane O'Neill, which ended with Matthew's assassination in 1558. Hugh O'Neill and his brother became wards of the state and were fostered by the Hovenden family in the Pale. Turlough Luineach had Brian murdered in 1562, but the young O'Neill remained to be raised and educated until he sued out his livery, becoming the baron of Dungannon in 1567. Sir Henry Sidney hoped to use him as a counter to the growing power of Turlough Luineach, but O'Neill was not content to be a mere foil to Turlough's ambition. He developed a network of alliances and contacts that spanned Gaelic, Old English, New English settlers and English society. Hugh served faithfully for two years in Ulster under Walter Devereux, first earl of Essex, and with Lord Deputy Arthur Grey in Munster during 1580. However, an indication of O'Neill's aspirations came March 1583, when it appeared that Turlough Luineach had died. O'Neill raced to the inauguration site at Tullaghogue to assume the title of 'the O'Neill', but news of Turlough's demise was premature, as he regained consciousness after a twenty-four-hour drink-induced coma.

O'Neill's power continued to grow, and in 1587 he was made the second earl of Tyrone, but efforts by the lord deputy, Sir John Perrot, to curb the new earl's influence led to Tyrone's alliance with Hugh O'Donnell, with whom he attacked Turlough Luineach in 1588, but was defeated at Carricklea. Tyrone reaffirmed his fidelity to the crown when part of Philip II's Spanish Armada foundered along the north and west coast of Ireland. Though he saved individual Spanish officers, he ordered the slaughter of hundreds of Spanish survivors. The collusion between Turlough Luineach and the MacShanes led to another round of conflict, but their aspirations were truncated when Tyrone hanged Hugh Gavelach MacShane from a thorn tree. Notwithstanding Tyrone's ability to prosper in spite of resistance from English and Irish enemies, the tide of English reform ebbed closer. Strong as he was, Tyrone depended on his web of alliances to resist English encroachment on his patrimony. The most powerful of his allies was Hugh Roe O'Donnell, lord of Tirconnell.

Hugh Roe was the eldest son of Sir Hugh O'Donnell and the formidable Fiona MacDonnell, also known as Iníon Dubh, whose Scottish contacts enabled a ready supply of mercenaries. He was set to become the successor to the Tirconnell lordship and correspondingly was betrothed to Rose O'Neill, Tyrone's daughter. This union threatened to create a dangerously powerful political and military alliance in Ulster, therefore in 1587 Lord Deputy Perrot had him kidnapped and imprisoned in Dublin castle. His first escape attempt in 1591 failed but the second succeeded with the aid of a silk rope and well-placed bribes by Tyrone. In Hugh Roe's absence, predatory attacks by English freebooters and competitors for the O'Donnell title had convulsed Tirconnell. However, Iníon Dubh paved the way for O'Donnell's return, ruthlessly deploying her Scottish 'redshanks' to kill Hugh Roe's rivals. O'Donnell's father stood down, making way for Hugh's inauguration as the O'Donnell in April 1592. He received official government recognition when he formally submitted to the lord deputy in July 1592, during which O'Donnell made all assurances that he would be a faithful and obliging subject, none of which was true. O'Donnell harboured a loathing for the English, therefore when the first hint of foreign intrigue appeared in 1592, in the shape of the Archbishop Edmund Magauran, O'Donnell enthusiastically encouraged Spanish intervention in Ireland.

Tyrone and O'Donnell were the most powerful lords opposing the crown, but they were allied with others who also saw the threat of English reform and armed encroachment. Hugh Maguire, lord of Fermanagh, was Tyrone's son-in-law and was mindful of the break-up of the neighbouring MacMahon lordship in Monaghan. Fitzwilliam's appointment of Captain Humphrey Willis as sheriff of Fermanagh exacerbated Maguire's disquiet. Willis' reputation for rapacious activities in Tirconnell suggested that Fitzwilliam had unwelcome intentions for Maguire's lordship. The Ulster lords were also closely tied to Feagh MacHugh O'Byrne. He was the most powerful Gaelic leader in Leinster and had long been a thorn in the side of the Dublin establishment. O'Byrne fought in the first Desmond revolt and was again in action against the crown during the Baltinglass revolt, during which he routed Lord Grey de Wilton's army at Glenmalure in August 1580. Feagh was complicit in O'Donnell's jailbreak from Dublin castle that Tyrone had facilitated, and by the time Tyrone finally broke with the crown it was clear that O'Byrne was deeply involved in the northern lord's machinations. These were all prominent figures in the growing network of alliances that would mature into a confederation of Irish lords stretching from the north coast of Antrim to the Beara peninsula in Cork. However, the central figure was always Tyrone. It was to him they corresponded with, or looked to for assistance, military aid and supplies. Tyrone had the strongest economic base of any Irish lord, and it was from his household that the first large-scale and sustainable formations of modernized Irish soldiers emerged. As *primus inter pares*, Tyrone prepared to challenge the power of the crown, meanwhile the queen's officers obliged by providing every pretext for war.[48]

To this volatile mix was added Lord Deputy William Fitzwilliam. He had been viceroy from 1571 to 1575, and was reappointed in 1588, replacing Sir John Perrot, who was later convicted of treason and sentenced to death on Fitzwilliam's decidedly dubious evidence. Rather than solve the thorny issues of reforming the government in Ireland, Fitzwilliam instead concentrated on getting rich.[49] Allegations of corruption beset his deputyship, and Fitzwilliam's minimalist approach to government gave rapacious local officers, such as Sir Richard Bingham in Connacht and Sir Henry Bagenal in Ulster, free rein to aggrandize and enrich themselves at the expense of the native Irish. This was not the sort of governor Elizabeth needed to calm Irish concerns or promote stability. Five years into his second term as viceroy, native discontent reached a flashpoint in the Fermanagh lake lands. No one could have guessed that Ireland would soon be wracked by unprecedented levels of warfare, destruction and human misery, bringing the English economy to the point of ruin, extinguishing the last vestiges of native Irish political culture, and completing the English conquest of Ireland.

CHAPTER I

Tyrone's proxy war, 1593–4

L IES, INSINUATION AND OBFUSCATION clouded the opening phases
of what has become known as the Nine Years War or Tyrone's Rebellion.
Look at the start of almost any war, and one finds deception, deceit and lies
predicated on strategic and operational necessity. However, the evasion and
chicanery have propagated differing opinions in the modern historiography of
the war. Canny suggested that Tyrone was unwillingly pushed into rebellion
to prevent his followers defecting to his brother, Cormac MacBaron.[1]
Alternatively, Morgan has represented Tyrone as an arch-schemer and
complicit in the war from the very start.[2] Tyrone was indeed intrinsically
connected to the events in Fermanagh and Connacht during 1593–4. The
actions of Maguire, O'Donnell and others were part of a proxy war to deceive
the English into committing resources in the west, leaving the crown's allies in
the rest of Ulster unsupported. This diversion enabled Tyrone to forge
alliances, intimidate, and where necessary assassinate, those who stood in the
way of cementing his domination of Ulster.

In retrospect, Tyrone's planning for open conflict with the crown could be
observed in the preparations he made during the proxy war period. The earl
misled Bagenal and Fitzwilliam into believing their campaign against Maguire
was successful, when in fact it had no real effect. Raiding spread Tyrone's
influence from east Ulster to north Connacht. Tyrone's soldiers blockaded
garrisons and routed English armies; all without retaliation against the earl
from Dublin. While the crown wrestled to control what it believed to be a
localized and containable revolt, Tyrone dramatically expanded his army,
stockpiled munitions and established gunpowder and arms manufacturing at
Dungannon. By the time the queen's officers in Dublin realized Tyrone's
involvement, the Irish confederates were in a position to challenge English
authority in Ireland.

Maguire's revolt: a precursor to Tyrone's war

The opening shots of the Nine Years War initially appeared minor and of
little consequence. Lord Deputy William Fitzwilliam appointed Captain
Humphrey Willis as sheriff of Fermanagh in spring 1593. Marching north

into Fermanagh at the head of one hundred soldiers, Willis quickly set about spoiling Hugh Maguire's lands. The sheriff's men were accompanied by their dependants, 'all which lived on the spoil of the country'.[3] Willis was well known for this behaviour and had acted in a similar fashion in Donegal, until Hugh Roe O'Donnell drove him out in February 1592.[4] Willis had no legal justification for targeting Maguire, but the expedition was most likely an attempt by Fitzwilliam to suppress a major client of Tyrone's at a time when the earl was cementing his power in Ulster.[5] Nonetheless, Maguire was initially unable to oppose Willis with the troops at his immediate disposal.

The arrival of reinforcements of shot, pikes and Scots bowmen led by Tyrone's brother, Cormac MacBaron, and then shot under the commands of Donnall and Donough O'Hagan, allowed Maguire to take the offensive. Now seriously overmatched, Willis and his men were compelled to seek safety in a church for almost a week until Tyrone negotiated their safe conduct out of Fermanagh.[6] After Willis had retreated, both O'Hagans remained *buannacht* in Fermanagh.[7] According to the deposition of Morris O'Scanlon, Maguire took the opportunity to place them upon the lands of Connor Roe Maguire, his rival and a valuable ally for the Dublin authorities in the region.[8]

Few would have guessed that sparks of localized discontent in Fermanagh during the spring of 1593 would be the opening act of a war that would lead to the final overthrow of the Gaelic social order in Ireland, and nearly bankrupt the English state. Almost ten years of war would result in many thousands of military and civilian deaths, and visit unprecedented levels of destruction upon the island. The depredations of a petty official in Fermanagh and the hostile reaction of Maguire may appear minor, but it was in the context of attacks on native structures of lordship, the encroachment of English laws, extra-legal freebooting by crown officers and native Irish conspiracy with foreign powers.

The fears of the northern lords were not without reason; Lord Deputy Fitzwilliam's actions in Monaghan were a cause of much Irish concern. After the death of Sir Ross MacMahon in 1589, Fitzwilliam initially supported Hugh Roe MacMahon's (the late chief's brother) claim to succession. Hugh Roe marched into Monaghan backed by 400 English troops, but Brian MacHugh Óg, the old chief's *tánaiste*, defeated them.[9] By the end of the year, the lord deputy had switched his support to Brian MacHugh Óg. Fitzwilliam's *volte-face* may have been caused by Hugh Roe's failure to deliver a bribe of 800 cows. Hugh Roe was imprisoned on charges of treason, which allowed the crown to confiscate his lands.[10] He was executed in autumn 1590, and the lordship was broken up into five demesnes, with hundreds of smaller tenants receiving freeholds that paid rent to the local lord but held their lands from the crown.[11] The settlement of Monaghan was a direct assault on the class structure of Gaelic society. As a model for dealing with the rest of the Irish lordships, no one was immune to the imposition of English laws and institutions.

The crown recognized the growing power of Tyrone and plans were developed to curtail his influence in Ulster. In June 1590, Tyrone was forced to agree to twenty-five articles which included the shiring of his territory in Ulster, the imposition of composition payments as seen in Connacht and the delivery of pledges [political hostages] as sureties for his loyalty.[12] The articles constraining Tyrone were seen as a blueprint for reforming the rest of the Ulster lords, but Tyrone had little intention of adhering to the agreement.[13] However, the success of the settlement of Monaghan emboldened the authorities in Dublin to attempt to dissect Tyrone's lordship. Initial plans came to nothing, but the naming of Sir Henry Bagenal as chief commissioner of Ulster in 1591 was a direct challenge to Tyrone's authority. Tyrone and Bagenal were bitter enemies, made worse after Tyrone eloped with Mabel, Bagenal's sister, in August 1591. Tyrone protested in the strongest terms to the privy council, asking that Bagenal not be given authority in Ulster 'whereof he reigns as a little king, and overcrows me, whose wrongs done to me, are such as I cannot well bear'.[14] The privy council exempted Tyrone's territory from Bagenal's commission, but it was clear that the regional ambitions of the two were on a collision course.

Fitzwilliam's corrupt administration encouraged others to make inroads into areas traditionally under Irish domination. When Bagenal was named chief commissioner in Ulster, Fitzwilliam granted him a title that was of little use unless it had a sufficient financial foundation. For this to happen, Bagenal's gain would have to be at Tyrone's expense. Unsurprisingly, Bagenal advocated the methods employed to fragment the MacMahon lordship in Monaghan.[15] Bagenal sent troops to abduct an expert in canon law from Armagh to prove that Tyrone's marriage to Mabel was invalid. The mission proved futile, but it demonstrated that Bagenal was willing to use force against Tyrone.

In the west, Sir Richard Bingham, the chief commissioner of Connacht, was rapidly undermining the authority of the native Irish lords. A veteran soldier, with experience campaigning in Scotland, France and the Low Countries, Bingham fought against the Turks at the battle of Lepanto (1572) and had seen action in Ireland during the second Desmond rebellion (1579–83). He had acted with brutal efficiency and showed no mercy to those washed ashore from the ill-fated Spanish Armada in 1588, nor to the Irish who aided the Spaniards. Bingham forced Sir Brian O'Rourke to flee West Breifne. O'Rourke escaped to Scotland but was handed over by James VI and executed in London. In 1590, Bingham engaged in a campaign of spoiling and repression in northern Connacht, with allegations that he exploited martial law for his personal enrichment.[16] Superior military strength allowed Bingham to monopolize positions of power at the expense of the regional Irish. Moreover, Bingham eyed the lordships in Tirconnell and Fermanagh with the aim to extend his influence into Ulster.

Tensions were raised further with the arrival of Edmund Magauran, archbishop of Armagh, at the end of 1592. During his audience with Philip II of Spain in September 1592, the king expressed his intention to assist a rising against the English if requisite support was found among the Irish lords.[17] Along with James O'Hely, archbishop of Tuam, and other bishops, Magauran met with Hugh Maguire, Hugh Roe O'Donnell and Brian O'Rourke at Enniskillen castle on 8 May where letters were drafted to the king of Spain and to Irish exiles requesting military aid to overthrow English rule.[18] O'Hely returned to Spain, arriving at the Spanish court in September 1593. Sir Richard Bingham was alarmed at the activities of the Irish primates, noting that their interference had the potential to incite rebellion in the Ulster lords with promises of Spanish support.[19] As English power impinged further on Irish territory, the Irish lords now had alternatives other than submission, and the promise of Spanish military aid may have emboldened those Irish lords to believe that war was a viable option.

Maguire on the offensive

At the end of May 1593, Hugh Maguire responded to Willis' provocation with a raid into Sligo. Approximately 1,100 men including MacSweeny gallowglass and O'Hagan shot, under the leadership of Shane and Donough Óg Maguire, entered Sligo and proceeded to Ballymote, burning the town to the very gates of the medieval castle, then held by Sir George Bingham.[20] Maguire's attack into Sligo did not stop at Ballymote castle. Half his men blockaded Bingham, while the rest scoured the neighbouring districts. The surrounding countryside was thoroughly pillaged, where 'there was not much of that country which he [Maguire] did not plunder ... also burned on that day thirteen villages on every side'.[21] Maguire fired Ballymote town and withdrew to Fermanagh with 7–800 stolen cattle. No doubt buoyed by the success of his first raid Maguire launched a much more ambitious attack into Roscommon in June, but this time he met stiffer resistance.

Taking the lead of 120 horse and 1,000 foot, Maguire moved south along the western shores of Lough Allen and, passing through Boyle, continued south. As he approached Tulsk on the morning of 23 June 1593, Maguire encountered cavalry led by Sir Richard Bingham. Bingham had positioned himself and his men on a hill outside the town, most likely the ancient inauguration site at Rathcroghan.[22] Fog shrouded the hillsides, blinding Bingham and Maguire. In the gloom, Bingham's scouts blundered into the Irish cavalry and were compelled to beat a rapid retreat to Bingham's position, losing several men to the closely pursuing Irish horsemen.[23] On joining the main force of 80 horse, Bingham counter-charged putting the attacking Irish to flight.[24] The Irish horse retreated until they reached their supporting infantry.[25] When the English horse came into view of the Irish foot, several volleys of shot checked the English advance.

Bingham realized his force was overmatched. Therefore he broke contact and extricated his small force under cover of the surrounding mist. Losses on both sides were relatively slight, but during the confused melee Archbishop Magauran (champion of the Irish cause in the Spanish court) was separated from the main Irish force. He was attacked by several English horsemen and killed while attempting to escape.[26] Maguire and his men continued their raid through Annally, after which they returned north with their spoils, but the death of Magauran was a bitter blow to the Irish cause.

The Connacht–Ulster borderlands were not the only areas of concern during the spring/summer of 1593. As war was escalating in the west, other footholds of the English presence in Ulster came under pressure. Tyrone's nephews, Art MacBaron's sons, engaged in a campaign of spoiling in east Ulster, which focused upon the crown's Irish allies. In concert with Eoin MacHugh O'Neill, they descended upon Killultagh, South Clandeboye, the Great Ards and Lecale, prompting urgent pleas for assistance to be sent north.[27] On 14 May, Phelim MacTurlough O'Neill was assassinated by the O'Hagans and his lands spoiled.[28] During July the government's important outpost at the Blackwater was harassed by Brian MacArt MacBaron, who denied the garrison access to local markets to restock their stores.[29] Negotiations throughout the summer between the lord deputy, Maguire and Tyrone were fruitless. Fitzwilliam's patience was answered by Maguire's irruption into Monaghan and Farney in September, where he preyed as far as Castle Ring on the Louth border. Maguire attacked the garrison in the abbey at Monaghan on his return journey, but was reportedly beaten back with some loss.[30]

Maguire's depredations finally provoked a large-scale military expedition under the joint command of Sir Henry Bagenal and Tyrone. Bagenal received his commission on 11 September and was soon making his way to Fermanagh at the head of 144 horse, 763 foot and 118 kerne. Tyrone was to rendezvous with him in Fermanagh with a further 200 horse and 1,200 foot.[31] Bagenal's army paused briefly to attack the demesne lands of Brian MacHugh Óg MacMahon near Rooskey Lough (Co. Monaghan), but by 24 September he reached Enniskillen. Tyrone joined him two days later, but with only half the troops promised to the lord deputy. Bagenal did not have the forces to assault Maguire's stronghold at Enniskillen, nor could he cross the river, as Maguire's men occupied robust earthwork defences on the ford at Lisgoole abbey.

Unable to force the crossing, Bagenal broke camp on 7 October and marched north towards the ford at Belleek. The combined forces of Bagenal and Tyrone approached the ford on 10 October 1593 and got their first view of Maguire's positions. The defences were described by Bagenal as, 'fortified in front and flank for their own defence and our annoyance in the best sort they could devise'.[32] A mixed force of gallowglass, Scots and shot manned the fortifications.[33] The attacking army was split into two battles of infantry, with one leading the assault, the other seconding it from the southern bank. Sleeves of loose shot were dispatched to the left and right to support the advance by pouring fire into the flanks of the Irish position. Armed with heavy, large-bore muskets, they easily overmatched the short range bows and calivers available to the defenders. Utilizing the cover provided by woods on the right flank and rocks on the left, the English shot assailed Irish trenches without fear of effective return fire. Irish sources recorded that 'the gunners were able from a wood which adjoined the river bank to attack with impunity the Catholics'.[34]

An illustration drawn by John Thomas complimented the accounts. Identified as an English soldier, Thomas illustrated the crossing in great detail, showing the formations of the troops and the main officers involved.[35] The assaulting infantry entered the water led by Captains Lee and Dowdall. The water level at the ford was high, as the infantry waded 'through to the arm holes with their shot to approach the fort'.[36] Though deep, the ford was discovered sufficient to accommodate a simultaneous crossing by elements of the horse. As they crossed, the assault column received several ineffectual volleys of gunfire, but their resolution to take the far bank inclined the defenders to abandon their defences and retreat. The Irish withdrawal was initially orderly as they decamped in troops, but the horse made landfall first and rapidly put them to flight.[37] Casualties for the attackers were exceptionally slight given the difficult crossing and prepared defences, with only three soldiers killed and six wounded, including Tyrone who sustained a wound to his leg from a horseman's staff, and Bagenal whose shin was bruised with the flat of a gallowglass axe.[38]

Tyrone provided most of the horse, some 200 men, and all the accounts of the battle from both English and Irish sources noted that it was the cavalry

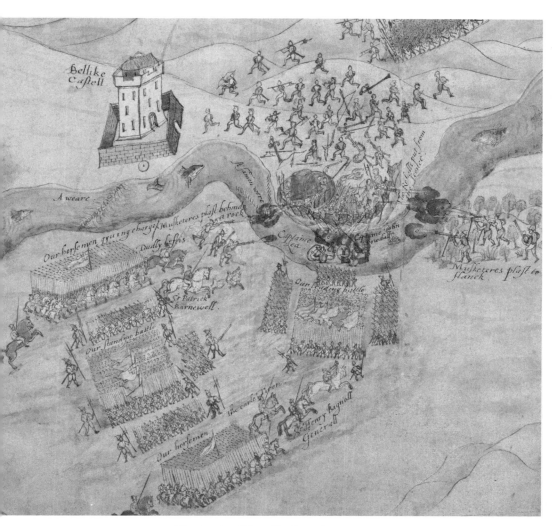

3 The battle of Erne Ford, 10 Oct. 1593
(British Library, Cottonian MS Augustus I. ii, f. 38)

that caused the majority of Maguire's losses.[39] In his journal, Bagenal wrote that the horsemen 'had the chase and killing of them with our horsemen above five miles', and his scoutmaster later counted over 300 dead.[40] An account which took a slightly differing view, yet originated from an Englishman, was from Captain John Parker. He arrived in Bagenal's camp on 6 October and was placed under the earl's command. Parker reported to the lord deputy that at no time did he leave Tyrone's company during the campaign. He wrote that

he [Tyrone] did so valiantly behave himself in that conflict, as he hath
confirmed at full the report made of him to his great honour, and that
if his horsemen had answered him accordingly the overthrow had been
far greater than it was. Which slackness of theirs he reproved them for
at their return to the camp … as not one of them durst after came in his
sight.[41]

O'Sullivan Beare claimed that Tyrone was in command of the cavalry that day
and it was he who led the charge that routed Maguire's men, but that the
pursuit was much shorter than the four to seven miles recorded in the state
papers.[42] The follow-up of the cavalry may not have been as vigorous as
Bagenal and Tyrone claimed. Sir Philip Holles described the chase as
'reasonable', a description which somewhat lacks the dash and drama of
Bagenal's claims of a rout.[43] Tyrone returned to Dungannon for treatment
while Bagenal remained to spoil along the western shore of Lower Lough
Erne. Even though Bagenal had not directly engaged Maguire's main force,
Fitzwilliam was content that Maguire's revolt was broken.[44] After leaving a
garrison of 300 foot under Captain John Dowdall at Castle Skea (now the site
of Castle Balfour, Lisnaskea, Co. Fermanagh), Bagenal marched to Clones
where he dispersed his men to their respective garrisons.

Bagenal victorious?

The modern historiography of the Nine Years War has paid little attention to
the military aspects of Bagenal and Tyrone's campaign against Maguire.
Tyrone's role has been interpreted as compliant to Fitzwilliam's demands,
though with greater or lesser degrees of enthusiasm.[45] When looked at in
isolation, the punitive expedition appeared to achieve most of its objectives.
Bagenal burned and spoiled the MacMahon's territory, Maguire was chased
out of Fermanagh, and Conor Roe Maguire had been reinforced with a strong
garrison at Castle Skea. These successes cost the English few casualties, but a
closer analysis of the campaign suggests that the victory claimed by Bagenal
was illusory. Moreover, he was deceived into believing that the forces of
Maguire were archaic, disorganized and the rebellion in decline; in reality, the
opposite was true.

Many of the incidents during Bagenal's Fermanagh expedition appear
incongruous when viewed in context with the approach of the Irish to the
conflict during 1593 and beyond. Indeed, it is possible to interpret the entire
episode as a sophisticated deception to divert the crown's military resources in
an ineffective campaign, and prolong Tyrone's façade of loyalty. The lead up to

the assault at Belleek was interesting, as a combination of actions by Maguire and Tyrone obliged Bagenal to march north and induced him to storm the Irish fortifications. Bagenal did little after he reached the ford at Lisgoole. The strongly-held Irish defences prevented Bagenal from making his crossing south of Enniskillen, as he lacked artillery and other 'implements to win the place'.[46] The troops occupying the Lisgoole position were described as Maguire's full strength and the trenches were manned 'wherein they had placed all their shot'.[47] Bagenal formulated two plans to break the impasse. He proposed splitting the army, sending part of his force south to flank Maguire at Lisgoole via a circuitous march around Upper Lough Erne, but Tyrone refused to hold the northern shore citing the weakness of the forces that would be left behind. Bagenal then requested that the earl convoy reinforcements from Clones while Bagenal fronted Maguire at Lisgoole. Meanwhile, he would send a detached unit to flank the Irish at the abbey; again Tyrone refused to co-operate.[48] Out of options, Bagenal broke camp and marched north towards Belleek on 7 October.

Two weeks later Bagenal and Tyrone were again confronted with stout earthwork defences on a ford occupied by a sizable enemy force, but the tactical situation was unlike that at Lisgoole. Maguire did not deploy the same forces that had previously checked Bagenal. He primarily used gallowglass and Scots mercenaries rather than pike and shot. Opting to use old-style troops rather than modernized forces found at Lisgoole must have been a deliberate decision by Maguire. Throughout the war, Irish units maintained superior operational mobility to their English adversaries. If Maguire had wished it, the troops blocking the ford at Lisgoole could have easily reached Belleek before Bagenal. In the event, Maguire was nearby during the assault, but the modernized forces of Cormac MacBaron and the O'Hagans were nowhere to be seen. The weak defence at Belleek appears premeditated.

The Irish position at Belleek could have been significantly stronger if they had been reinforced out of Donegal by Hugh Roe O'Donnell, but he only sent small numbers of men led by an officer who had proven troublesome in the past. Hugh Roe was nearby in Ballyshannon with the majority of his forces, but was ordered by Tyrone not to reinforce the position in person.[49] O'Donnell did send 60 horse, 60 targets (swordsmen) and 100 gallowglass under the command of Niall Garbh O'Donnell.[50] Niall Garbh was, until very recently, a rival of Hugh Roe, whose submission was secured by intimidation.[51] Therefore it seems odd that O'Donnell would appoint an officer of questionable loyalty to such an important task at a moment of crisis. Niall Garbh's continued truculence caused O'Donnell to have him detained during February 1594 and only released when O'Donnell received Niall's brother as a pledge of good behaviour.[52] It is possible that O'Donnell dispatched the reinforcements to Belleek with the understanding that they were to be sacrificed to maintain the strategic deception of Tyrone's continued loyalty. Niall Garbh's death would not have damaged O'Donnell's cause and would have removed an uncertain ally – suspicions that were proven well-founded when he defected to the crown in 1600.[53]

That the battle happened at all is suspicious. For much of the war, the Irish could choose when and where engagements occurred. Captain Nicholas Dawtrey noted that the Irish would 'observe time, place and opportunity, and the natural disposition of their enemies' before engaging on the most advantageous ground.[54] Furthermore, they could rapidly break contact if the tactical situation became unfavourable.[55] This had long been the case in Ireland, as John Zouche noted in 1580 that 'we shall never fight with them unless they have a will to fight with us first'.[56] The war to that point had demonstrated that the crown's officers usually only managed to engage the Irish by accident or when small parties were encumbered by the baggage and spoils gathered during a raid. Bingham encountered Maguire at Tulsk because he had discovered that the ancient inauguration site at Rathcroghan was a rendezvous point for the spoiling parties.[57] Maguire's horse ran into Bingham's men as a thick fog hid them from view. Bagenal's expedition managed to spoil MacMahon's country and burn stores on crannogs, but he had not been able to make contact with any large units until Maguire blocked the ford at Lisgoole. While Bagenal camped opposite Lisgoole, he appeared more apprehensive about Tyrone than of the likelihood of encountering Maguire.

Bagenal had received intelligence that Tyrone advised Maguire to avoid engaging Bagenal until his army had been dispersed.[58] Any correspondence by Bagenal about Tyrone has to be viewed with caution, but irrespective of his efforts to implicate Tyrone, the policy of Irish avoidance corresponded well with how Bagenal's campaign was frustrated. Maguire's tactic of deliberate avoidance was highlighted by the journey of Sir Richard Bingham, who marched unmolested from Boyle abbey to Ballyshannon by 12 October 1593, with a tiny force of only 48 horse and 92 foot.[59] While there is no doubting that hundreds of Irish troops fell during the rout at Belleek, few if any of Maguire's main force were killed or wounded. An examination of the list of the dead at Belleek suggests that the majority were MacSweeny Fanad gallowglass and Scots mercenaries.[60] They were not the troops employed by Maguire during his summer campaign, and their loss had no real effect on the military strength of the Irish lords.[61] Sir Ralph Lane confirmed this when he reported that by 4 December 1593, Maguire 'hath gathered again a head of 1,000, having indeed lost very few of his own followers at the passage of

Belleek'.[62] It was a departure for the Maguires to be so closely involved with large numbers of Scots mercenaries, and their slaughter at the hands of Tyrone and Bagenal may have gone unlamented, as the expense of maintaining them may have begun to rankle with Maguire's followers.[63] Maguire's main striking force of horse, pike and shot remained intact, despite claims by the crown's officers of a great victory.

The march on the ford at Belleek neutralized the English campaign and facilitated a powerful strategic deception in both military and political terms. Tyrone was suspected of providing aid and even directing the actions of Maguire. Intelligence reports claimed that Tyrone had taken delivery of Maguire's creaghts (herds of cattle) for safekeeping and had secret meetings with Maguire and O'Donnell.[64] What better way could Tyrone demonstrate his loyalty to the authorities in Dublin, than shedding prodigious quantities of Irish blood in the queen's name? The wound sustained by Tyrone, though undoubtedly unintended, served to underpin his assertions of loyalty. Tyrone made sure to emphasize his injury in a letter to the privy council on 5 November, 'being glad though my hurt was sore, that for a testimony of my loyalty and faithfulness to serve Her Majesty it was my chance to have a print in my body of this day's service'.[65] Ó Clérigh recorded that Tyrone 'was pleased therat, so that the English should not have any suspicion of him'.[66]

In military terms, the battle brought the autumn campaign to a satisfactory conclusion for Bagenal and Fitzwilliam. In their reports to the privy council in London, the Irish rebels had been demonstrably defeated and ensuing intelligence supported their belief that Maguire's power was broken and his forces dwindling.[67] They had shown the rebel forces to be disorganized, relatively primitive and liable to flight when confronted with the disciplined pike and shot formations deployed by the crown. However, the Ulster confederates had complied with a guiding principle of military deception by shaping Bagenal's perception of his battlefield. In doing so, they not only made him believe that he had defeated Maguire, but had also constructed the ruse to conform to what Bagenal had hoped to achieve at the outset of the campaign.[68] What had been accomplished was minimal in strategic military terms.

Bagenal's army was skilfully manipulated into an operational cul-de-sac. By moving north (something Bagenal never intended to do) he had been forced into a no-win situation. If the English marched into Donegal, Bagenal would have to engage O'Donnell on his home ground against forces of an unknown quantity with Maguire to his rear; a prospect that none of his senior officers would countenance. If Bagenal moved south to finish off Maguire, he would leave O'Donnell threatening behind him. Both options would have left his lines of supply exposed and over-extended. Bagenal's only viable option was to move to the south-east along the southern shore of lower Lough Erne, in effect a retreat to Clones. Maguire and O'Donnell could not have achieved this by clever manoeuvring alone.

Bagenal's original plan to circuit the upper lough would have kept Maguire and his allies to the north and maintained his waterborne lines of supply, and in turn this might have permitted a winter campaign, which Dowdall later prosecuted during January and February 1594. The advance and assault on the ford (which Tyrone claimed he suggested, and ensured by providing fresh supplies) placed Bagenal's army in an operational vice, extraction from which could only be achieved by withdrawal. Bagenal and Fitzwilliam thought they had scored a great victory and that the conflict was on the wane, but this was very far from the truth.

The conflict widens

No sooner was the campaign over than a bitter row erupted over credit and due appreciation for services to the crown, with Tyrone complaining about a perceived lack of sufficient rewards or praise.[69] As the war of words raged in Dublin, hostilities continued unabated. Captain John Dowdall, commanding the garrison at Castle Skea, fought a riverine campaign of ambush and skirmish. However, on 24 January he landed infantry and artillery to invest Maguire's stronghold of Enniskillen.[70] The siege lasted nine days culminating in an amphibious assault which forced a breach in the curtain wall and burnt the water gate. On gaining entry, all the occupants were put to the sword or drowned in the moat.[71]

The end of February marked a dramatic escalation of spoiling by the Irish. Farney was preyed and soon after the Irish attacked Monaghan, Iveagh and Kilwarlin.[72] Carrickfergus and the greater Ards were raided at the beginning of March, with depredations reported in Louth, Meath and Farney on 9 March. Raiding reached new levels during April, with widespread burning and spoiling across Ulster. Beginning on 16 April, lands belonging to the English, their tenants and Irish allies were burnt, and their goods carried off. First targeted was Connor Roe Maguire in Fermanagh, who was so thoroughly spoiled that Sir Henry Duke wrote that 'Ulster doth daily prepare themselves for rebellion … which in my simple judgement is already partly manifested by the late accidents in burning, preying and killing of Her Majesty's subjects in Fermanagh'.[73] Clones was plundered on 23 April, and Monaghan, Dartry and Fermanagh all on 26 April.[74] On 27 April, the districts surrounding Carrickfergus were spoiled, and in the days following Clandeboye, Dufferin, Kilwarlin and Lecale were all attacked in turn.[75]

4 The siege and capture of Enniskillen by Captain John Dowdall, 2 Feb. 1594
(British Library, Cottonian MS Augustus I. ii, f. 39)

The security situation deteriorated in east and south Ulster to the point
that many isolated English wards could not venture into the countryside for
fear of ambush. The Monaghan garrison was bloodied in skirmishes with
Conn Mac an Íarla, Tyrone's bastard son, and Captain Robert Bethell's men
were roughly handled in Castlereagh when they attempted to counter a raid
by Brian MacArt MacBaron.[76] At the end of May, the constable of
Enniskillen castle reported that a large force had entered Fermanagh with the
intention of taking the castle.[77] Furthermore, reports suggested that Hugh Roe
O'Donnell, lord of Tirconnell, had now taken the field.[78] There had been doubts
about his loyalty and O'Donnell had provided some support to Maguire, but now
he was directly engaged in besieging the ward in Enniskillen.

The castle was closely blockaded by 11 June, and by the end of July, many
of the ward were ill due to privation, food shortages and exhaustion brought

on by incessant skirmishing.[79] A relief expedition was organized under the joint command of Sir Henry Duke and Sir Edward Herbert, who planned to march from Cavan to Enniskillen, break the siege and resupply the castle. Though attended by experienced officers, they were unconvinced they had sufficient forces to complete the mission.[80] Fitzwilliam sent an additional 200 foot from Dublin, but unaware of the reinforcements Duke and Herbert set out from Cavan on 4 August with 600 foot and 46 horse.[81] They were due to arrive at the castle on 7 August, but Maguire and Cormac MacBaron's troops held the ford on the Arney river. Intense gunfire checked the convoy at the crossing, five miles short of their destination.[82] Attacks on the rear and flanks of the column shattered the English formations. Duke's relief force was routed and fell back in confusion to Sligo. The army's baggage and supplies intended for the castle were abandoned at the ford, giving rise to the battle's better-known name, *Bel-atha-na-mBriosgadh* or the Ford of the Biscuits.[83]

The new lord deputy, Sir William Russell, was met by news of the defeat on his arrival in Dublin, where he promptly decided to launch a second relief expedition.[84] While Russell assembled his force, Tyrone made the startlingly bold move of arriving unheralded in Dublin, 'without standing on any terms for his security', promising loyalty and offering his services to the lord deputy.[85] Tyrone was no fool, as he had assurances of his safety from the Irish council and the word of the lord deputy. His appearance before Russell allowed the earl to repudiate Bagenal's allegations and assuage Russell's desire to find a military solution to the conflict. At the very least Tyrone bought time to allow the harvest to be brought in without interference from the crown.[86] Russell led the new relief force north on 19 August and arrived without incident at Enniskillen twelve days later.[87] Russell was new to Ireland, so it did not seem untoward that not one of his scouts returned to him during his march to Enniskillen, or that the ward in the castle was ignorant of Russell's advance until he came within view.[88] During his stay at Enniskillen Russell received letters requesting pardon and protection for Maguire and O'Donnell.[89] The untroubled march to Enniskillen and letters from Maguire and O'Donnell may have convinced Russell that the crisis was waning. Though he was suspicious of Tyrone, Russell chose not to call on reinforcements from England. In fact, he discharged 600 of the troops raised by Fitzwilliam and committed only three foot companies to guard the Ulster borders.[90]

In the subsequent months, prevarication by Tyrone, allegations of his complicity in the destruction of the first Enniskillen supply column, and the landing of munitions from Scotland convinced Russell that Tyrone and his allies would have to be dealt with by force.[91] Russell requested additional troops from England; meanwhile the lord deputy turned his attention to one

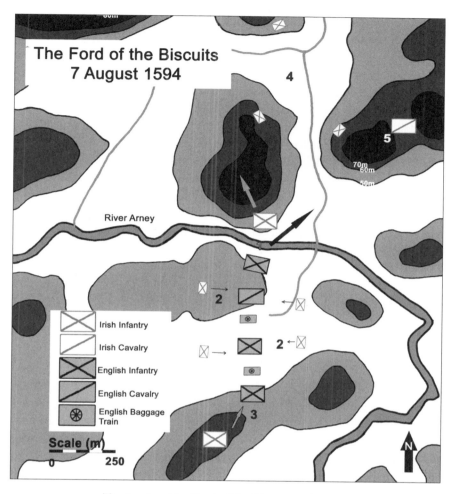

5 The battle of the Ford of the Biscuits, 7 Aug. 1594
1: Irish shot stop the column but eventually forced back. 2: Flank attacks disordered
English infantry. 3: Irish pike charge disordered English pushing the rear and main
battle towards river. 4: English make it to low ground, counter-attack south but
forced to cross further upstream. 5: Irish horse play no part in battle.

of Tyrone's suspected allies, Feagh MacHugh O'Byrne, lord of *Crioch
Raghnuill*. Suspicions had long been harboured about the loyalty of Feagh
MacHugh. In May 1594, Sir Ralph Lane reported that O'Byrne was rearming
his gallowglass with modern weapons.[92] At the start of August, Fitzwilliam
claimed that O'Byrne had been providing intelligence to the rebels and
intended to revolt when the time was right.[93] Russell did not wait for
provocation as he was wary that O'Byrne might receive reinforcements from

Tyrone. Consequently, he launched a pre-emptive strike into O'Byrne's mountain fastness in the Wicklow Mountains on 16 January 1595.

The surprise attack in the early hours of the morning would have taken O'Byrne's entire household but for a precipitate assault by one of the English captains, which alerted the occupants and enabled their escape.[94] While Russell maintained the pressure in Wicklow, Tyrone requested a meeting at Dundalk and protections for the rebel lords, including Feagh MacHugh. Unmoved, Russell dismissed this as an attempt to distract him from the job at hand in Wicklow.[95] Moreover, it served to confirm O'Byrne's connection to Tyrone and his confederates. Russell's suspicion was corroborated by James Fitzgerald, who confessed that two days after Russell proclaimed Feagh MacHugh a traitor (19 January), O'Byrne dispatched a messenger north requesting Tyrone to send 'for aid or at least burn and spoil the Pale'.[96] Tyrone did not ignore his Wicklow ally. On the morning of 16 February, the same day chosen by the northern lords to meet Russell's commissioners at Dundalk, forces led by Art MacBaron O'Neill assaulted and took the Blackwater fort on the Armagh–Tyrone border.[97] Tyrone attended in person to see the bridge over the Blackwater broken; he was now in open conflict with the crown.[98]

The strategy of proxy war

Relatively small-scale engagements and the disconcerting, but not disastrous, defeat at the battle of the Ford of the Biscuits, suggests that while there was an escalation in the quantities of forces deployed, the fighting had not seriously affected the military strength of the crown. Clinical tabulation of the cost of the war and physical impact of the fighting implied this was a localized affair which expanded into a regional conflict in 1595, but war was (and remains) about more than just combat. However, Fitzwilliam and others did not recognize this throughout 1593–4, which allowed Tyrone to smother English influence in Ulster without eliciting any response from the authorities in Dublin; the war in Fermanagh was a hugely successful deception. While Bagenal futilely attempted to engage Maguire in 1593 and attention was focused on the plight of the Enniskillen garrison in 1594, Tyrone cajoled, coerced, assaulted and assassinated the queen's Irish allies in Ulster.

The distraction caused by Maguire focused the attention of the government to the west, while more telling strategic advances were made by Tyrone and his associates in the east. The harnessing of military power to oppose Maguire left the crown's Gaelic clients dangerously exposed and ultimately failed to provide support or protection when they and their lands came under attack. Concurrent to Maguire's depredations in Connacht, the crown's Irish allies in Ulster were spoiled and pressurized to join the confederation of Irish lords under the leadership of Tyrone. In Ards, Niall MacBrian Fertagh O'Neill's lands were raided. Connor Roe Maguire, the crown's staunchest supporter in Fermanagh, was spoiled by Tyrone, even as the earl was ostensibly leading an expedition to put down Hugh Maguire's revolt. Though the raids damaged the economic infrastructure of loyal Gaelic chiefs, they also undermined their faith in government assurances of military assistance in the future. Sir Robert Wilbraham, the solicitor-general for Ireland, recognized the need to protect the loyal Irish in Ulster when he advised Burghley that their Irish allies 'showed obedience so long as they be defended from outrage of their stronger neighbors'.[99]

When persuasion, threats and intimidation proved ineffective, Tyrone had intransigent Irish lords assassinated. The strategic district of Killetra fell to Tyrone's domination after Phelim MacTurlough O'Neill was murdered. Tyrone had previously tried to replace Phelim with one of the O'Hagans, but Phelim killed Tyrone's man. Bagenal arranged a pardon and safe conduct for Phelim and Tyrone was later compelled to guarantee his safety.[100] The idea of a client of Bagenal's occupying a critical position on the Bann must have proved intolerable, and his elimination coincided with Maguire's raids in Connacht. On 14 May 1593, Phelim met with Tyrone at Toome, but when the earl was 'not twenty score from his house' Phelim was set upon by several O'Hagans and was killed along with three or four of his men.[101] The following year, a similar fate befell Ever MacRory Magennis, captain of Kilwarlin. He was driven out of Ulster because he refused to join Tyrone. When Magennis tried to return home he was murdered.[102]

The defences of the key military positions at Monaghan, and more importantly the Blackwater fort, were successfully probed without eliciting any significant response from the authorities in Dublin. The Blackwater garrison comprised twenty-four warders and was commanded by Edward Keyes. On 8 July 1593, Keyes reported that Brian MacArt O'Neill was preventing the garrison from procuring supplies from the local market town, and those previously willing to provide victuals to the fort were reluctant to attempt what had become a loose blockade. Keyes approached the earl to remedy the matter but Tyrone prevaricated, claiming he would require a notice of protection from the lord deputy before he could intervene.[103] On attempting to secure fresh supplies, one of the ward was detained and not released until a hefty ransom was paid. Efforts were made to make off with the garrison's stock of cattle, but on both occasions, they were recovered without loss. The garrison's stores of food steadily dwindled, forcing Keyes to request 'some imprest considering our great need'.[104] This action appears to have been to test the garrison's response to pressure, while at the same time critically weakening its ability to resist an attack or siege. Direct action would have focused the government's attention on mid-Ulster and would have been difficult for Tyrone to deny any knowledge. The illusion of English strength on the Blackwater was maintained, but the fort was weak and could be swiftly neutralized.

When the attacks were renewed the following year, they were on a much larger scale, more co-ordinated and ultimately forced the crown's few northern allies to join Tyrone's growing confederation. All the client or allied lords of the English authorities in Ulster were preyed. A frequent victim of spoiling in 1593–4 was Niall MacBrian Fertagh, who wrote to the lord deputy on 4 June 1594 that the earl of Tyrone had threatened to take his lands if he would not swear allegiance.[105] Niall was briefly removed from power but was restored after submitting to Tyrone.[106] The same was true for all those who initially remained loyal to the crown. As the strength of the Ulster confederates grew, the O'Hanlons of Orior, Magennises in Iveagh and even Connor Roe Maguire in Fermanagh acquiesced to Tyrone's demands of fealty. Bagenal noted how 'the O'Hanlons, and the Magennises have combined with the earl, but not for any love they bear him'.[107]

By the time Tyrone openly joined Maguire and O'Donnell, the northern lords had consolidated their strategic position, to the extent that the Irish had pushed most the military and economic assets of the Dublin authorities south of the lakeland and drumlin-belt barrier that geographically isolated the north. It was this barrier that would later trammel manoeuvre options for successive English military incursions into the north, with access by land into Ulster limited to the fords around Ballyshannon in the west and the Moyry Pass in the east.[108] Of the five outposts remaining in crown possession at the start of 1595, Enniskillen, Monaghan, the Blackwater fort, Newry and Carrickfergus, all but the last two, with their formidable defences and coastal communications, were quickly eliminated before the year was out.

Tyrone implicated?

Tyrone's involvement in the first two years of the war has been subject to divergent interpretations. Though there is no evidence directly linking Tyrone with the direction of the raids or leading attacks against government troops, examination of the opening two seasons of depredations in 1593 and 1594 provide circumstantial evidence for Tyrone's involvement. Aside from the wholesale participation by members of his household and family, gatherings of key northern lords and their followers preceded the outbreak of spoiling and unrest in both years. The sheriff of Monaghan wrote of a meeting of northern lords late in April 1593, at which Tyrone was present. Irrespective of the veracity of the allegations of the swearing of treasonous oaths, Tyrone was in attendance.[109] Just over two weeks later Captain Willis was expelled from Fermanagh by Maguire and forces from Tyrone's household.

Tyrone met with Maguire and others between 9 and 14 May 1593; within two weeks Maguire had burned around Sligo, and Eoin MacHugh O'Neill had preyed the Ards. According to Captain Eggerton in Carrickfergus, the destabilizing influence of Tyrone was to blame for Niall MacHugh O'Neill's truculence. Eggerton noted that 'M'Hugh M'Phelim hath been with him [Tyrone]. Since which conference with the earl I find him nothing the man he seemed before ... with scornful speeches, but also desirous rather of wars than peace'.[110] Tyrone met with Maguire in early August 1593, after which he advised Fitzwilliam that Maguire had dispersed his forces in his presence, but within weeks Maguire launched penetrating raids into Monaghan that reached the borders of Louth and hazarded the garrison in Monaghan town.[111]

The following year, from 16 to 18 February 1594, there was another meeting of Tyrone's followers at Dungannon at which Maguire's household was also present, and Brian MacHugh Óg MacMahon was nearby. Two weeks later, Farney, Monaghan, Meath, Carrickfergus and the Ards were all subjected to raiding. From 8-15 March 1594, the key leaders of Tyrone's lordships surrounded him at his meeting with the commissioners near Dundalk. Four days later the nearby lands of Tyrone's hated rival, Sir Henry Bagenal, were ablaze. The synchronicity of the late April raids which, in a ten-day period, targeted Carrickfergus, Ards, Lecale, Dufferin, Dartry, Fermanagh (twice), Clones and Monaghan, suggested a level of direction and coordination beyond the possibility of coincidence. Tyrone was the only person in Ulster with province-wide power and influence able to orchestrate an action on this scale. In early May, soon after making off with the horses from around Monaghan, Brian MacHugh Óg MacMahon was back at Tyrone's house in Dungannon.[112] If the earl had no hand in the raiding, what business did MacMahon have at Dungannon so soon after successful series of attacks?

During 1594 there were several allegations that Tyrone was actively directing the attacks. Sir Edward Herbert and Captain Humphrey Willis claimed that Tyrone was ordering the raids. They described how Tyrone had been giving instructions to those spoiling the borders, when;

> the earl would often come with himself a dozen horsemen from Dungannon and meet those forces by the way and go with them to the

mountain called Slieve Beagh [Cos. Fermanagh and Monaghan] …
and there the earl would give those forces directions which way each
company should go and what to do, and so to return back again himself
as to be said he came from hunting.[113]

Later in the year, there was a first-hand account of Tyrone's complicity.
Joan Kelly testified to the presence of the earl at Liscallaghan (modern
Fivemiletown, Co. Tyrone). She recounted how Tyrone had instructed Art
MacBaron, Henry Óg and Turlough Breasalach O'Neill that 'they should do
the uttermost in burning and praying the Breanie [Breifne], and the borders
of the Pale adjoining' while Tyrone was visiting the lord deputy.[114] It was many
years later when Tyrone was in exile in Rome when he came close to admitting
personal culpability for the attack on Duke and Herbert's army at the battle
of the Ford of the Biscuits. Writing to Philip III of Spain in 1616, Tyrone
mentioned that Pedro Blanco, a survivor of the 1588 Spanish Armada and one
of his closest associates, was present at the battle on the Arney river. Moreover,
Tyrone described the Irish engaged that day as 'my captains'.[115]

Tyrone's belligerency during 1593–4 was underpinned by the development
and expansion of his economic and, more importantly, military assets.
Throughout the period of Tyrone's supposed loyalty, he took steps to increase
the numbers of trained soldiers within his territory. Tyrone had been allowed
to retain 50 horse and 100 foot, who were trained by English officers.
However, it was later claimed that Tyrone used this agreement to train far
more than was permitted.[116] It was suggested that he repeatedly dismissed
trained soldiers and replaced them with new recruits, enabling Tyrone to build
up a large reserve of well-trained troops in Ulster.[117] However, just having large
numbers of soldiers did not automatically confer military strength; Tyrone
needed a sustainable supply of arms and munitions.

When Tyrone entered the war against the crown, it quickly became
apparent that his infantry was principally armed with firearms. Prolonged
engagements could expend prodigious quantities of gunpowder; therefore
Tyrone had to secure considerable stores to maintain his war effort. With
hindsight, Tyrone's intentions become evident as he took measures to stockpile
gunpowder and lead during 1594. During October, Tyrone landed a shipment
of gunpowder, lead and firearms from Scotland worth £300.[118] Four months
later a further shipment worth £500 was delivered.[119] Tyrone also took
deliveries of lead. It is difficult to estimate how much powder was bought, but
the price of gunpowder at the Tower of London was 10 pence per pound in
August 1594. At these rates £500 could buy 12,000 pounds.[120] Even if the
price was inflated due to costs incurred importing the powder from the Baltic,

or that the practice was illegal in Scotland, this still represented a substantial quantity of gunpowder.

By the end of 1594, Sir Geffrey Fenton was uneasy that Tyrone had amassed large stores of powder over the preceding year and distributed it to several of his houses. Fenton was concerned that there were no crown garrisons at the sites and that a subject could 'engross so great a proportion of powder into his own hands, especially in this tottering state'.[121] Tyrone also took advantage of his licence to import lead. The crown allowed Tyrone to acquire six tonnes of lead to weatherproof his new hall in Dungannon, but none of it made its way onto Tyrone's roof. Instead, the earl melted the lead into bullets for his shot.[122] Worse still, Tyrone was making gunpowder at Dungannon. Reference to Tyrone's capacity to manufacture gunpowder came in an unsigned intelligence report in August 1594. It noted that 'as for powder there is enough made in the earl's own country'.[123] Peter Lombard may have been referring to this when he wrote that 'they [the Irish] were particularly anxious to discover how gunpowder may be made, and having learnt this, they began themselves to make it, for this country possessed plenty of material thereof'.[124]

While the levels of manufacturing at Dungannon would have been relatively small and wholly unable to provide the thousands of pounds of gunpowder needed to meet the needs of Tyrone's troops and those of his allies, establishing facilities for manufacturing munitions suggests a hostile intent on Tyrone's part. The financial outlay to make gunpowder would have been great. Investment in an infrastructure that could produce viable quantities of gunpowder suggested that Tyrone was developing an industry that could support or at least partially maintain a war effort. Furthermore, establishing clandestine gunpowder production can hardly be construed as the activity of a loyal subject trapped by circumstance.

A comparison of Irish strategic behaviour from 1595 may allow some inferences to be drawn regarding the involvement of Tyrone in the military campaigns of 1593-4. The defining feature of confederate operations from 1595-8 was strategic deception and misdirection of enemy forces. With Tyrone directing the strategy, diversionary or dislocating manoeuvres were precursors to successful actions elsewhere.[125] Examination of the military activity in Ulster during 1593-4 reveals similarities with later doctrine. Maguire's actions facilitated a wider objective of domination in Ulster and the suppression of English allies. This shows an early and effective use of deception by the Ulster leaders. Though Tyrone had not declared open hostilities during 1593-4, the distinguishing qualities of his strategic direction were unmistakeable.

CHAPTER 2

The war for the north, 1595–6

Tyrone's open break with the crown at the start of 1595 finally caused the scales to fall away from English eyes. Clearly, the earl was at the apex of the Irish conspiracy. His presence at the demolition of the Blackwater fort put this beyond all doubt. As the military power of the English was focused on maintaining their forts in south Ulster, Irish raids plunged deep into Connacht and ravaged north Leinster and the Ulster borderlands. Many hoped that a negotiated settlement could bring the conflict to a satisfactory conclusion, but English optimism was shaken as Tyrone inflicted a stunning reverse at the battle of Clontibret in May 1595. Tyrone displayed the full strength of his modernized troops as his well-ordered pike and shot with support from their cavalry almost succeeded in overwhelming Bagenal's men. Despite Irish success earlier in the war, some believed that a show of force would soon bring the intractable Irish lords to book. However, the crown's army only escaped annihilation by the narrowest of margins.

English operations centred on Sir John Norreys in Ulster and Russell in Wicklow, but in the west O'Donnell ran roughshod over Bingham. All the while Tyrone solidified his contacts with Spain. Tyrone completed his rise as the preeminent power in Ulster with the death of Turlough Luineach, after which the earl was inaugurated as 'the O'Neill'. A ceasefire in September gave some glimmer of hope that the war could be concluded without further loss, but to Tyrone and his allies the cessation was just another tool of war not an avenue to peace. During the cessation the power of the Irish lords continued to grow. The forces under Norreys and Russell appeared to have little to no impact on Tyrone's confederation. Norreys soon discovered this war was nothing like the rebellions of Shane O'Neill or the Desmonds of Munster.

Storm on the Blackwater

The Blackwater fort had been a provocative eyesore at the heart of the Ulster lordships for almost twenty years. It was established to curb the growing power of Turlough Luineach O'Neill and provide support to the 'enterprise of Ulster' by Walter Devereux, first earl of Essex, and Sir Thomas Smith. That attempt at plantation failed, but an outpost of military strength on the border of Co.

Tyrone helped secure the crown's new ally in the region, Hugh O'Neill, baron of Dungannon.[1] The fort was square in plan, 'twelve score yards in circuit' and reinforced with two bulwarks.[2] A wooden bridge spanned the river Blackwater, and a stone tower commanded the Tyrone side, which acted as a gateway onto the bridge. The position was later improved with a wooden tower raised to overlook the Armagh side of the bridge.[3] Despite O'Neill's offer to maintain (and thereby command) the ward, the crown was careful to keep the garrison under English control.

In 1588 the fort had 50 troops but could accommodate 200, and the building of houses outside the fort allowed the garrison to be increased to 400 if needed.[4] Over the years both Turlough Luineach and Hugh O'Neill aspired to take control of the fort, but it remained under the command of Captain Edward Keyes. The ward slowly dwindled until there were only twenty-six warders and their dependants by 1594. When trouble flared in the summer of 1593, several of Keyes' men were killed in a skirmish with Art MacBaron O'Neill and a loose blockade ensured that when the attack came in February 1595, the warders within the fort were not prepared for a determined assault.

At eight o'clock in the morning on 16 February, Art MacBaron approached the fort from Armagh with 40 to 50 soldiers and two 'prisoners'. As they crossed the bridge, a guard noticed that the Irish were preparing for combat as the matchcords on their firearms were lit, and they had bullets in their mouths, ready to load. The Irish firearms were matchlocks, which needed a smouldering cords of match to be applied to the powder charge in the barrel of the gun to make it fire. The alarm was raised, giving warders in the stone tower time to lock their doors, thereby preventing the Irish from gaining entry to the upper stories. Thwarted in their initial attack, MacBaron's men overran the earthen ramparts of the fort and opened up a sustained fire upon the wooden castle.[5] The ward put up stubborn resistance from the stone and wooden towers, but a shortage of ammunition and MacBaron's threat to burn the wooden tower forced them to surrender. MacBaron's capture of the Blackwater fort was a setback for Russell, but of far more significance than the loss of the fort was the presence of Tyrone when the fort and bridge were subsequently demolished.[6]

The situation on the Ulster borders rapidly deteriorated as the town of Cavan was burned, and the surrounding country spoiled. Louth was preyed on the 17 February, and after burning all the churches in Farney to prevent their use as garrisons, the local Gaelic leaders (Ever MacCon Uladh MacMahon's sons) took charge of troops from Tyrone near Ardee.[7] The garrisons at Enniskillen and Monaghan were isolated; the former had already almost been lost at the start of January when its outer walls were overrun, and the latter was

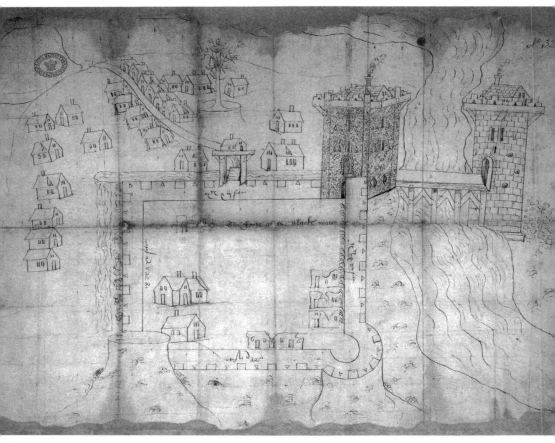

6 The first Blackwater fort, 1587 (The National Archives, Kew, MPF 1/99)

under threat of betrayal by some of the garrison.[8] Despite the developments in Ulster, Russell harboured a burning hatred for Feagh MacHugh, and he would not be distracted from his campaign in the Wicklow mountains. Russell persevered in Wicklow until 24 February when he returned to Dublin. The forces at Russell's disposal received a welcome boost with the arrival of the long-awaited Brittany veterans in Waterford on 19 March, led by the highly acclaimed Sir John Norreys. He was a veteran of almost thirty years of military service and was one of the finest officers available to the queen, but he did not arrive in Ireland until 4 May, and it was left to his brother, Sir Henry Norreys, to march them to Dublin, where he mustered 1,300 men on 2 April 1595.[9]

The crown was at last taking steps to reinforce the army in Ireland, but events did not wait for the English. Early in March, Hugh Roe O'Donnell marched south into Connacht and took substantial preys, spoiling north Roscommon. Sir Richard Bingham attempted to cut off O'Donnell and his men on their return north, but rather than return via Boyle, O'Donnell crossed the Shannon into Leitrim. Though Bingham's men managed to skirmish with O'Donnell's rear-guard, the main body escaped unharmed.[10] Bingham was sure O'Donnell would return; he was correct, as this was only the first of three major incursions by O'Donnell during 1595.[11] O'Donnell remained in Leitrim to celebrate Easter, then on 21 April (Easter Monday) he launched his forces into Annaly.

The castle of Longford was assaulted and burned, and the constable, Christopher Brown, taken prisoner. O'Donnell encountered little resistance as he entered Co. Cavan and ravaged the districts surrounding the fort at Cavan town, but left the garrison unmolested due to the strength of their defences.[12] Burdened with plunder, O'Donnell and his men returned northwards into Donegal. This raid was especially successful. Sir Geoffrey Fenton reported that Longford was a wealthy county and that around 10,000 cattle had been taken. He commented that 'the rebels of Ulster will be able by so great a quantity of cattle to feed themselves and their hired Scots a long time'.[13] Ill tidings continued to pour in from the north when on 17 May, Russell received news that the stronghold at Enniskillen had been retaken by the Irish.[14]

Things were no better for the government's position in the east. As O'Donnell drove into Roscommon in March, Tyrone's men were burning in Louth, the barony of Slane and in Sir Henry Bagenal's estates in Mourne.[15] Monaghan was beleaguered, and though Russell preferred to abandon both Enniskillen and Monaghan at the start of the year, the arrival of the troops from Brittany may have steeled his determination to re-victual Monaghan after Enniskillen fell.[16] Still engrossed with his pursuit of Feagh MacHugh in Wicklow, Russell tasked Bagenal with command of the relief force.

The shock at Clontibret

Bagenal assembled his army at Newry, totalling 1,500 foot and 250 horse. Though this was a sizable force to be concentrated for one resupply mission, there were indications that some were not taking the prospect of confronting the Irish as seriously as they should. Before the expedition set out, a Brittany captain voiced concern over the limited supply of ammunition. Russell dismissed his fears; 'captain, you are deceived, you are not now in France or the Low Countries, for you shall not be put here to fight as there'.[17] If it was so safe why assemble such as large army to resupply the fort? 'To give countenance to the service' replied Russell, who clearly believed that he need only show up to overawe the Irish.[18] Russell's blasé attitude ignored the fact that an almost identical operation to resupply the garrison at Enniskillen castle had been routed on the Arney river only nine months previously.

Bagenal and his men marched out on 25 May, covering eight miles before halting for the night. It was at this time that Tyrone appeared in person, leading a troop of one hundred horse to reconnoitre Bagenal's camp.[19] The following day, the English army dislodged from camp and marched a further eight miles until the lead elements fell into an intense skirmish with Tyrone's shot at Crossdall on the border of Cos. Monaghan and Armagh. Initially, there was confusion as the van of the column lacked a senior officer in charge. Captain Richard Cuney took command and drew out 150 shot and pike to counter the Irish advance. An attack by Cuney's men pushed the Irish back, and he ordered them to take up positions in the woods and rocky terrain, which provided good cover from Irish gunfire.[20] Cuney and his men held the passage for four hours until the column passed through to Monaghan, then decamped towards Monaghan with the rear of the army.[21]

The Irish blockading Monaghan withdrew as Bagenal's force approached. The garrison at Monaghan was replaced with a fresh company of troops and their stores replenished. Bagenal ordered his army for their return journey to Newry the following morning. To avoid the hazards of the previous day and for the safety of the women and children in the column, an alternative route was chosen via the church at Clontibret. The army started to leave Monaghan around ten o'clock in the morning. Though Bagenal had elected to make a more southerly route home, Tyrone had managed to place troops on both sides of the English line of march. However, unknown to Bagenal, Tyrone was not able to deploy the full strength of the Ulster army against him. An amphibious raid by Sir George Bingham in Tirconnell caused O'Donnell to march into north-west Ulster.[22]

Tyrone sent Cormac MacBaron with 300 shot supported by pikes to occupy a hill (almost certainly Crossaghy Hill, Co. Monaghan) on the column's right flank. A bog to the English left held a body of Irish shot and Tyrone held back to assail the rear of the column at the first opportunity. However, Bagenal was not so foolish as to blunder into an ambush without taking precautions. He organized his men into three units; the van, the main battle and the rearward. Bagenal took command at the front in the van, Sir John Chichester and Captain Brett led the main battle and Captains Richard Cuney and Thomas Maria Wingfield had charge of the rear. The soldiers of the van, battle and rear formed into infantry squares or battles. The square or oblong formations acted as combined arms teams enabling co-operation between the two main types of infantry deployed by the English, pike and shot.

English foot companies were made up of shot, armed with firearms and pikemen in a ratio of one to one or two to one favouring the shot.[23] Pikemen formed the core of these units. They were armed with long spears called pikes, ten to fifteen feet long, and provided the defensive strength of the infantry. Compared to other infantry they were heavily armoured with helmets, breast-plate or a cuirass and occasionally steel tassets that protected their upper thighs. Pike could be used as shock troops if ordered to charge, but they were also the primary defence against cavalry. A hedge of pikes could present an impenetrable barrier to even the heaviest armoured cavalry. Furthermore, the slow-firing shot could shelter under the pike hedge if threatened by enemy cavalry.[24]

The majority of the English shot were armed with calivers, but possibly one-third carried muskets.[25] Muskets were large-bore firearms weighing up to twenty pounds and had to be braced on a forked rest to fire. They were effective to one hundred metres and could easily penetrate armour, but muskets were heavy, had a slow rate-of-fire and were unsuited to fast-paced skirmishing. Musketeers stayed with the pike and were usually deployed in a sleeve along the flanks and front of the close-order pike block. The caliver weighed half as much as a musket and fired smaller calibre bullets. Correspondingly, the effective range was little over fifty metres, but its ease of handling and ability to carry more ammunition meant that it was ideally suited for skirmishing.[26] The calivermen were put into loose sleeves and detached from the main body of the formation. This allowed them to skirmish with an enemy and protect the densely packed main body of pike and musketeers from close-range gunfire. Bagenal also had 250 cavalry at his disposal. The English cavalry were 'light horse' armed with a lance, sword and sometimes pistols. They were heavily armoured in comparison to the Irish horse, wearing a helmet, cuirass/breastplate, a horseman's coat and possibly tassets.[27] They were one of the most feared arms of the English military in Ireland. Throughout the war, the Irish always put significant effort into protecting their troops from enemy cavalry and isolating English infantry from their cavalry support.

After passing the church at Clontibret, the column was attacked from all sides. As Bagenal's force approached a narrow pass, Cormac MacBaron assailed the van, Tyrone the rear, and the Irish shot played along the English left and right flanks. Tyrone's shot were seconded by their horse and stands of pike. This kept the English cavalry at bay and pushed Bagenal's skirmishers back, enabling the Irish to open fire from just thirty metres away. The English supplies of ammunition ran critically low, and units of pike were forced to charge, compelling Tyrone's shot to keep their distance.[28] The fighting was intense and in three hours Bagenal's men only advanced a quarter of a mile. As Tyrone's cavalry massed to exploit the gaps torn in the English ranks by Irish gunfire, a heroic but doomed counterattack was made by forty English horse. A cornet from the Pale named Sedgreve pulled Tyrone to the ground but quick action by one of the O'Cahans severed Sedgreve's arm, and Tyrone finished the matter with his knife. The cavalry were mauled, but the attack gave the English the space they needed to break through the pass.

The battle lasted eight hours, but exhausted powder supplies made Tyrone draw back his troops, allowing Bagenal's men to make camp for the night.[29] Munitions were short in the English camp, but a daring night march from Newry by Captain John Audley brought enough ammunition to enable the army to reach Newry the next day.[30] Losses were put at 31 dead and 103 wounded by the muster master Sir Ralph Lane, who later declared that there were far more killed and wounded than was 'thought fit to be given forth upon the first advertisement'.[31] The battered relief force was hemmed into Newry as the Irish held the passes south, but the danger receded when Tyrone retired north.[32]

More troubling for the lord deputy and the future conduct of operations were the modern arms and disciplined conduct of Tyrone's troops. In a letter to the privy council, Russell noted the Irish skilful use of pike and musket, their experienced leaders and discipline on the battlefield.[33] The renowned veteran of continental warfare, Sir John Norreys, was unambiguous in his report to Burghley. He wrote

> the state of the northern rebels is far different from that it is well wont to be; their number greater, their arms better, and munition more plenty with them whereof there can be no greater proof than that, there being at this present 1,700 of the best footmen in Ireland at the Newry, and near 300 horse with them they dare not undertake to march thence to Dundalk, which is but eight miles … but that they are fain to be sent for by water … a thing never before heard that such a troop should not be able to make their own way in Ireland.[34]

These were clearly not the sort of Irish soldiers Norreys had expected to fight. The latter half of the sixteenth century in Ireland had been a turbulent time, when soldiers and officers had ample opportunities to gain experience fighting the truculent Irish lords and their native hosts. Throughout this period the Irish deployed four types of troops: cavalry, kerne, the gallowglass and mercenary redshanks from Scotland.

The Irish horse represented the cream of Gaelic society. Their numbers were drawn from the wealthier members of the lord's *gairm slua*, and were commonly relatives.[35] John Dymmock described them as clad in mail, riding on a pillion without stirrups and using a lance overhand, which for the time would have appeared antiquated.[36] Kerne were light infantry and typically fought unarmoured. They carried a range of weapons that could include swords, shields, large knives, bows and javelins, known locally as darts. Dymmock noted how the kerne would throw their darts 'with a wonderful facility and nearness, a weapon more noisome to the enemy, especially horsemen, than it is deadly'.[37] Dymmock also described the armoured core of traditional Irish armies, the gallowglass. They were heavy infantry, protected by steel helmets, mail coats and armed with great swords or ferocious long-handled axes. The axe was six foot long and had a blade so keen 'the stroke whereof is deadly where it lighted'.[38] Gallowglass were the shock arm of Irish armies and fought in brutal close combat until their enemy broke and ran. Dymmock failed to mention the seasonal Scots mercenary forces that were hired and brought to Ireland as needed. Known as redshanks, they were unarmoured and fought with swords, axes and bows. Though primitively armed, the Scots could be hired in large numbers to provide armies numbering several thousand on relatively short notice.[39]

At the near-disaster at Clontibret, most of the traditional elements of the Irish armies were present. Scots redshanks and kerne were spotted, and the Irish cavalry played a crucial role in protecting Tyrone's skirmishers, but it was the disciplined and co-ordinated actions of Tyrone's pike, shot and cavalry that caused the most anxiety. Furthermore, the gallowglass, which had for so many years been the cornerstone of Irish strength on the battlefield, were absent.[40] Tyrone had raised an army that was hitherto unseen by the English. The defeat of Sir Henry Duke at the battle of the Ford of the Biscuits was a taste of the new skills of Tyrone's infantry; at Clontibret Tyrone demonstrated the full capability of his new formations. Russell wrote of Tyrone's men, 'their arms and weapons, their skill and practice therein far exceeding their wonted usage, having not only great force of pikes and muskets, but also many trained and experienced leaders as appeared by their manner of coming to the fight, and their orderly carriage therein'.[41] Tyrone's forces deployed pike and shot, as used by the English, but firearms were the dominant weapon as firepower replaced melee attacks. Firepower coupled with their superior tactical mobility enabled Tyrone's infantry to dominate their English opponents, who appeared ponderous in comparison.[42]

Impasse in Ulster

The government's woes continued to mount when news arrived of the murder of Sir George Bingham by the ward of Sligo and their subsequent surrender to the Irish.[43] Russell's efforts in Wicklow reduced Feagh MacHugh to the point where he was no longer regarded a threat, therefore anxious to engage with Tyrone, Russell struck north from Dundalk on 24 June.[44] The army encountered little resistance, reaching Armagh on 29 June. A fort was erected around the surprisingly intact Armagh cathedral and occupied by two foot companies. The day after Russell's arrival at Armagh, word came that Tyrone had destroyed his castle at Dungannon and all those of his principal leaders. Over the next two weeks, supplies were shuttled from Newry to Monaghan and the newly established garrison in Armagh. While the crown strengthened Armagh and Monaghan, Tyrone attacked targets on the eastern side of the river Bann, preying Sir Hugh Magennis' lands in Iveagh, and laying waste to Sir Henry Bagenal's holdings around Newry.[45] Russell had intended to fortify and erect a bridge on the river Blackwater, but torrential rains and flooding frustrated his plans.[46]

Russell had achieved all he could, and his supplies were running short, therefore the lord deputy returned to Newry on 11 July. Despite some minor skirmishes near the Moyry Pass, Russell's first journey into Armagh failed to provoke a major engagement.[47] The army was dispersed to its garrisons and Russell returned to Dublin by 18 July. Six days later, Sir John Norreys was formally commissioned to take charge of the prosecution of the war in Ulster.[48] The maintenance of the new fort at Armagh was his primary concern, as shortages of supplies meant it could not last for long unsupported. Consequently, Norreys set out for the north again on 22 August.[49]

The journey was incident-free saving the receipt of letters from Tyrone, touching on the possibility of submissions and pardons, but Norreys dismissed these as distracting ploys to enable the Irish to bring in the harvest.[50] While Tyrone parleyed with Norreys in Armagh, O'Donnell pushed south into Connacht for his third, and most ambitious raid of the year. His men preyed Co. Galway as far south as Tuam.[51] Sir Richard Bingham saw this as O'Donnell's main effort to win Cos. Galway and Clare for the Irish confederates, which remained the only unaffected areas of Connacht.[52] Bingham attempted to cut off O'Donnell during the return leg of the raid, but O'Donnell evaded him and made the crossing at Sligo two or three hours ahead of Bingham's men.[53] Bingham was again thwarted when his assault on Sligo was repulsed at the start of September.

It was not all bad news for the crown in Ulster though. At the end of July Captain George Thornton with ships out of Carrickfergus managed to corner a large fleet of Scots galleys, reportedly carrying 3,000 men. On 27 July Thornton received word that the Scots had landed on the Ards peninsula. Consequently, the next day he took the ships *Popinjay* and *Charles* to the bay at the Copeland Islands. Thornton found the Scots army camped on the island with their galleys pulled up to the high water mark. After brief negotiations, during which Angus and Donnell Gorme MacDonnell claimed they wished to serve the crown, Thornton attacked. The English ships pummelled the Scots' fleet with their heavy guns, and engaged the men on the shore with musket fire until six o'clock in the evening when the Scots called for a truce.[54] Twelve of the scots galleys were damaged and fourteen soldiers killed, but little damage could be caused to the troops on the island as they retired out of sight during the attack. Nevertheless, the Scots had nothing to counter English firepower and after repairing their ships, the MacDonnells withdrew. For the rest of the war, Scottish soldiers were not seen in the same numbers.

Events in September bore witness to two critical fractures in Tyrone's relationship with the crown. The first of these was occasioned by the death of Turlough Luineach O'Neill in Strabane. Tyrone travelled to Tullaghogue and was inaugurated 'O'Neill', thereafter signing his correspondence in preference of his new Gaelic title.[55] The second was the interception of letters addressed to Philip II of Spain and others in the Spanish court. In return for military aid, Tyrone and O'Donnell offered the kingdom of Ireland to Philip as well as the restoration of the dominance of the Catholic faith.[56] Though it had been long suspected in Dublin that Tyrone was in contact with Spain, this was the government's first piece of tangible evidence.

The convoys in August to Armagh had not solved the supply problems of the garrison. Norreys again marched into Ulster on 1 September and reached the fort the next day. He continued to reinforce the fort, and his working parties were harassed as they cut timber in the neighbouring woods, but the Irish never threatened to take the position. With the garrison resupplied Norreys broke camp on 5 September, but this time Tyrone was not inclined to let Norreys' men march south in peace. The Irish shadowed the English as they marched south-west towards Newry. After eight or nine miles, Tyrone made his move.

Norreys believed that Tyrone intended to cut off his retreat at a river ford, most likely at the Cusher river, Co. Armagh. Therefore he concentrated his baggage in the vanguard and passed them over the ford before the Irish arrived.[57] Tyrone's cavalry threatened the rear of the column, but a charge by the English horse forced them to retreat, only to reform nearby. The Irish shot and Scots bowmen took up positions in a bog and wood along the English left flank. Norreys ordered his infantry to force the Irish back, but after two hours of skirmishing Tyrone's troops remained. The English shot ran low on ammunition, but reinforcement from the vanguard enabled a renewed assault by the English horse and pike. The English advance forced the Irish back, but whenever Norreys' horse and pike halted, the Irish resumed their fire. Norreys' men had great difficulty coming to grips with the Irish, as the superior mobility of both the Irish horse and infantry meant they could rapidly withdraw when threatened by the English counterattacks. The English army eventually broke contact and retreated south over the river.

Norreys and his officers claimed a great victory over Tyrone, but the casualty list of senior officers suggested English success was less than clear-cut. Reports of the English losses varied between 9 to 25 killed, and 30 wounded; the list of casualties included many officers. Norreys was shot twice, Sir Thomas Norreys shot in the thigh, Captain Richard Wingfield shot in the elbow, a gentleman volunteer received an arrow to the forehead, and Captain Collier shot in the back.[58] Norreys had fought in Ireland in the 1570s but admitted that this was not the kind of war he had seen in Ulster over twenty years previously. In a letter to Burghley, he wrote 'All those that have formerly seen the wars in this country do confess they have not accustomably been acquainted with the like fight'.[59] Moreover, the muster-master Sir Ralph Lane later suggested that the English had narrowly avoided a catastrophe. He claimed that the new soldiers supplied from England lacked training and discipline and that it was only the prompt action by the Brittany companies (and the protection of God over Norreys) that prevented a disaster.[60]

Though small in scale compared to Clontibret, the battle was reported in Spain and Rome as a momentous victory by the Irish over Elizabeth's premier general. Regardless of this, Norreys had more pressing issues in Ireland. The crown's army was beset by manpower and supply shortages, to the extent that Norreys threatened to stand down as commander in a letter to Russell on 16 September.[61] The pressure was relieved when overtures of submission, with an accompanying ceasefire to accommodate negotiations, were sent by Tyrone late in September.[62] Norreys' precarious supply situation and rising food prices, due to two failed harvests, compelled him to secure a truce. The extent of food shortages for the English can be discerned by the four clauses of the ceasefire that address food and foraging issues.[63] Tyrone signed the cessation of arms on 27 October 1595. Initially, the crown set down detailed conditions for Tyrone's submission, but as time wore on the queen relented to securing the peace at almost any cost.[64] By January 1596, Russell and Norreys were advised to offer a free pardon to Tyrone and all his allies on the sole condition that they submit in person 'for the speedy conclusion of a general quiet, you may ratify whatever may effect the same'.[65]

A phoney peace: the war in Connacht

While Tyrone made peaceable overtures to Russell and Norreys in Ulster, the war continued unabated in the west. Tyrone was obliged to observe the cessation, but as had been seen during 1593-4, he did not have to take the field to continue the war. On 3 October, the provost of Connacht, Captain Robert Fowle was sent to relieve the ward in Belleek (Co. Mayo), with eight companies of foot and fifty horse.[66] Theobald Burke's forces, who had recently been reinforced by O'Donnell, set upon the English north of the Ballylahan ford on the Moy river. Fowle was killed when the Irish attacked the baggage train, scattering the pack horses and cattle held within it.[67] The column continued into Tirawley but turned back after hearing that the ward at Belleek had been taken. Three days later Burke again attacked the retreating army at Nephin Mountain, where the hapless English were engaged for six to ten hours. The beleaguered companies ran out of bullets and resorted to shooting stones and buttons at the Irish.[68] Also, the ineptitude of the new troops from England was painfully demonstrated. They had so little training with their firearms that they were unable to use them. Consequently, their officers were forced to disarm them and give their weapons to the Irish shot in English pay. Bingham later noted that it was his Irish troops who 'stood us in best stead that day'.[69] Ralph Lane railed that the 'utter overthrow' in Connacht was due to the new soldier's lack of training;[70] Norreys described the defeat as 'shameful'.[71]

Bingham claimed that the setback in Connacht had cost the army 20 dead, including Captain Joshua Mynce, but they had inflicted a satisfactory 80 Irish killed in return.[72] On face value, this appeared to be a positive outcome for the English with the Irish losing four times as many men, but this did not correlate with Lane's claim that the attack by Burke led to the 'utter overthrow' of the English infantry. The truth of the incident was not revealed until four years later when John Bingham admitted that the army sustained 60 killed and 100 wounded.[73] This was an example of a common occurrence during the war; minimizing one's losses while exaggerating the enemy's. This practice was openly admitted to by Sir Ralph Lane after that battle of Clontibret.[74] He did not elaborate with full details of the actual casualty figures, but Lane's description of one of the foot companies gives some idea. He stated that he saw eighteen wounded men from Captain Mansell's company in the churchyard in Newry who were too severely injured to be moved. Furthermore, they were all armoured men (therefore pikemen) from the main stand. Mansell's company had been raised in Lancashire and was composed of 40 pikes, 50 musketeers and four halberdiers.[75] Lane's account claimed that almost 50 per cent of Mansell's pike were incapacitated. This report did not address those who were walking wounded or indeed killed. If this is extrapolated to the shot, then Mansell's company was devastated at Clontibret. In the official report, Bagenal claimed that Mansell's company (mistakenly noted as Captain Mansfield) had taken just seven wounded during the engagement.[76]

The misreporting and overemphasis of enemy casualties was a regular occurrence throughout the war, yet English officers were not alone in overstating success and minimizing reports of combat deaths. The Irish accounts were quite willing to record vastly inflated victories. O'Sullivan Beare claimed that Sir John Norreys was defeated with the loss of 600 men at Mullabrack in September 1595.[77] Furthermore, he reported that 400 English were killed at Nephin Mountain.[78] Given that the English only fielded 408 men this claim was vastly overblown.[79] Circumspection is warranted when the description of tactical predicaments ran contrary to the reported casualties. Casualties were frequently misreported during Lord Mountjoy's campaign in southern Ulster in the autumn of 1600. Throughout the fighting in the Moyry Pass in September–October and the retreat to Carlingford in November, his men were attacked by the Irish from elevated and fortified positions. Mountjoy's men were exposed on both flanks in the Moyry Pass, and enfiladed by Irish gunfire as they marched along the beach to Carlingford. In all his reports Mountjoy consistently placed the Irish losses at three-to-four and once ten times his own. After the engagement north of Carlingford, Mountjoy had claimed he lost ten killed, including his secretary George Cranmer. Again it was Sir Ralph Lane who chose to pierce the bubble of the English battlefield durability. He contradicted Mountjoy's figures in a letter to Sir Robert Cecil, commenting that the army had lost 'some 10 special men of mark, and of 80 others'.[80] Consequently, as a rule, caution should be used when citing casualty figures during the war, especially when the reports were by an officer in command of the forces engaged.

English power in Connacht was dealt a severe blow with the murder of Captain William Fildrew in October. Killed by his own soldiers, his galley was then commandeered. Killing Fildrew removed Bingham's key naval asset in the west, as he was described by Bingham as 'our chief captain for the service by sea' and was likely the means by which George Bingham raided Tirconnell in May. This strike demonstrated the effectiveness of amphibious forces, as Bingham's attack drew O'Donnell north just when Tyrone could have used him against Bagenal at Clontibret. Fildrew was murdered 'that he might not serve against them [the Irish] by sea', and his death removed a threat to the Ulster lords' vulnerable coastline.[81]

The disturbances in Connacht finally caused Russell to conclude that the rebellion in Connacht was not due to personal grievances between Sir Richard Bingham and the local lords, but brought about by an unprecedented alliance with the earl of Tyrone. In a letter to Burghley, Russell wrote 'they hold one course with Tyrone, and though they pretend many grievances through the extreme or hard courses used towards them by the governor [Sir Richard Bingham] … yet will they neither accept peace, nor pursue war but as he [Tyrone] will direct'.[82] Bingham reinforced this message in a letter to the queen, in which he advised that the conflicts in Ulster and Connacht were one and the same. Bingham noted how those in action in Connacht termed themselves 'the pope's and Tyrone's men'.[83]

Despite the 'cessation' trouble continued to flare. There were reports of a conspiracy by Ulick Burke and O'Donnell to kidnap the earl of Clanricard's only daughter in December. Anthony Brabazon suggested this was to marry her to O'Donnell, but since Hugh Roe was already married to Tyrone's daughter, she was more likely to be held captive to limit the actions of Clanricard who had remained stalwartly loyal to the crown.[84] Without firing a shot Tyrone's power continued to grow, as at the end of December news came of the loss of the English fort at Monaghan. The garrison of 100 foot surrendered without resistance to the sheriff, Patrick MacArt Moile MacMahon who had defected to Tyrone.[85] They were allowed to retreat and 'set in a place of safety with bag and baggage'.[86] This loss caused some concern in Dublin as the garrison was from Captain John Dowdall's company, which was composed of mostly Englishmen. There was no want of supplies or ammunition, but both Dowdall and his lieutenant were absent, with only a sergeant left in command of the fort. Fenton blamed it on the ongoing ceasefire and Russell demanded that it be returned, as its capture ran contrary to the 'tenor of the cessation'.[87] Unsurprisingly, Tyrone ignored this request.

With the passing of the New Year, the danger continued to grow in Connacht. Six small garrisons were likely to be lost if not relieved while other castles in Cavan fell to the Irish.[88] Bingham warned that Tyrone and O'Donnell's influence spread further south as all the Irish septs in Breifne were 'loose in their obedience' where Tyrone 'extended his strength and greatness further than before, so likewise O'Donnell' who was making advances in Connacht with the 'Burkes and others of their faction'.[89] An attack on Athlone was repulsed, but Bingham was well aware that he had insufficient forces or supplies to put up much resistance.[90] Russell feared the effect Sir Brian O'Rourke (lord of Breifne and the son of Brian executed in 1591): would have as he could disturb the Pale and play 'Robin Hood' if left at large, even if Tyrone and O'Donnell were observing the ceasefire. He was right to worry. By the end of January O'Rourke was on the borders of the Pale inciting the O'Reillys to revolt, and extorting goods from those still loyal to the crown.[91] On 11 February, Burkes from Connacht embarked on a campaign of spoiling that swept southwards, preying along the line of the Shannon as far as Meelick.[92] They had entered Offaly and Laois by mid-March, threatening a link-up with Feagh MacHugh O'Byrne in Wicklow.[93]

The lengthy duration of the truce was working to the advantage of Tyrone's Irish lords. Perrot wrote that the Irish used the time to husband their cattle, replenish munitions and acquire other necessary imports.[94] Russell and Norreys were well aware of this and used the truce to request reinforcements of horse and foot from England.[95] Tyrone's strength grew as he attracted new adherents, such as the O'Reillys in Cavan, the O'Farrells of Longford and also some members of the Nugents and the Plunketts who were Old English marcher families from the Pale.[96] Cavan castle fell to the Irish at the end of February after the chief warder was murdered. It was claimed that John O'Reilly held it for Tyrone, but the earl refuted this. Moreover, Tyrone (somewhat sardonically) claimed he would have prevented it if he could, and would take it upon himself to build a better castle if it would please the queen.[97] Meanwhile, in Connacht and parts of the Pale raiding and spoiling escalated.

An attempt by Bingham to resupply the Boyle garrison was intercepted. The conveyor William O'Comyn mounted a passport on a stick, outlining the articles allowing victualing of the queen's garrisons. This administrative nicety did not impress the sons of Dowaltagh O'Connor, who confiscated the supplies of biscuit and the pack-horses carrying them.[98] The events unfolding around the ward at Ballymote during February and March demonstrated that the Irish lords had no regard for the cessation. The ward was attacked while out gathering firewood, though collecting fuel was permitted within the terms of the truce. Most were killed, but a small number remained to hold the castle.[99] Bingham marched north to resupply the ward, but his force was attacked in the Curlew Mountains by troops led by Brian O'Rourke. Bingham claimed to have fought his way through with the loss of 8 or 9 killed and 12 hurt; Sir John Norreys was more scathing of the affair.[100] He reported that three of the veteran Brittany companies had taken 35 casualties, including 5 officers, during the operation as they had been abandoned by the other 10 (possibly 12) foot companies. Norreys disdainfully added 'neither do I hear that the others ever stayed to know what became of their fellows till they were past the mountain, but I am sure they left the bodies of those that were slain at the devotion of the rebel'.[101]

The cessation of 1595–6 was characterized by submissions of Irish grievances, negotiation, offer and counter-offer that both raised and dashed

7 Ballymote castle

hopes of a peaceful end to the war. Russell was convinced that the continuation of the cessation by Tyrone and O'Donnell was just a ploy to win time for the arrival of Spanish aid in May. He was correct, but the lord deputy had little option but to agree to an extension of the truce due to the weakness of his forces.[102] There was no concrete evidence linking Tyrone to the disturbances outside Ulster, so it must have rankled Russell to receive a letter from Tyrone demanding strict compliance with the terms of the cessation, with demands for restitution for any breaches.[103] Tyrone's audacity appeared to have few limits when he appropriated a supply convoy destined for the garrison at Armagh at the end of February. The earl had helpfully provided troops to protect the convoy, but the seventy-eight garrans (pack horses) laden with biscuit, wine and munition were waylaid by Tyrone's son Conn and taken to Marlacoo, which was one of Tyrone's principal storehouses in Co. Armagh.[104] Tyrone claimed it was in reparation for damages done to him during the cessation.

During April there was some indication that peace was possible. Hugh Maguire and others made personal submissions to Norreys, and Tyrone gave assurances that he would go to explain himself to the queen, and send his sons to be raised in England. Fenton implied that the worst was over in his letter to Burghley, writing 'the whole realm is glad of this conclusion, and the people do wonderfully honour Her Majesty by this peace she has vouchsafed'.[105] Extended negotiations to work out the basis of a peace treaty and submission of the Irish lords were almost complete by May 1596. As far as the crown commissioners were concerned, the only elements to be completed were the granting of the queen's pardon and oaths of fealty by Tyrone, O'Donnell and their allies.[106] However, the delicate diplomacy was undone by the appearance of three Spanish ships in Donegal at the start of May. The first brought Alonso Cobos, who met with the northern leaders in Lifford. Here he convinced the Irish lords to dispense with the crown's peace offers and continue the war, by promising military aid and the prospect of a Spanish landing.[107] Two other ships later landed carrying more ambassadors from Spain, but also munitions.[108] The ramifications of the arrival of Spanish envoys were clear. Russell urgently requested troops from England, adding that since the shipment of arms and ammunition out of Spain, Ireland was 'standing in so doubtful a balance, uncertain whether peace or war may be expected'.[109]

Ostensibly all was still set for the conclusion of peace, as Tyrone and O'Donnell's letter of 6 May to Norreys apparently confirmed.[110] Norreys entered Connacht in June with the intention of taking the submissions and pledges of the local Irish lords and relieving the garrison in Boyle abbey, but English expectations were met with Irish prevarication. Unhappy at having to depend on his enemies for victuals, impending exhaustion of his supplies forced Norreys to disband his army into dispersed garrisons.[111] Norreys may have been attempting to deal in good faith, but for the Irish the charade with Norreys was 'but to spy, circumvent, and decoy each other, if they could'.[112] Henry Hovenden confirmed this, when alluding to the activities of O'Donnell, he wrote to Tyrone that 'all the delays that could possibly be used for prolonging the causes here have not been omitted'.[113] Tyrone refused to supply cattle to the fort at Armagh at the end of May, and by July the road south was blocked by his son, Conn.[114] During June, tenants of Thomas Butler, tenth earl of Ormond, were spoiled in Nenagh (Co. Tipperary), and one month later a letter was dispatched by Tyrone and O'Donnell into Munster; their goal to incite an uprising in support of 'Christ's Catholic religion'.[115] It appeared that Tyrone not only intended to continue the fighting, but wished to expand the scope of the war into previously quiescent regions. This was no longer a war for the north; it was a war for Ireland.

CHAPTER 3

The war for Ireland, 1596–8

THE COLLAPSE OF THE CEASEFIRE in 1596 marked a defining
moment in the course of the war. Tyrone's expansion of the war in
Leinster and Connacht, and his efforts to incite the Munster lords to join him
against the crown made it clear that the Irish lords' ambition had moved
beyond localized goals. Tyrone's strategy became aggressive after he made
substantive contacts with the Spanish, and received firm assurances of an
impending Spanish military expedition. Expulsion of English authority from
Ireland became the ultimate goal of Irish strategy. Changes in confederate
military posture were not piecemeal or sporadic but implemented throughout
the territory under confederate control. The focus of Irish operations moved
from the Ulster borderlands to the Irish midlands along the peripheries of the
Pale. Tyrone's confederation threatened English rule as never before, as he
created a network of alliances, employing synchronized campaigns of large and
small units that constantly outpaced and out-fought their English adversaries.
The Irish lords' ability to execute a coordinated strategic shift suggests that
Tyrone orchestrated their actions according to an overarching strategy.
Tyrone's letter to the Munster lords was clearly intended to widen the war and
expand his network of alliances into an all-Ireland confederation of Irish
lords.[1] Furthermore, combat was only one tool for fighting the war. Tyrone
used ceasefires and cessations to achieve his objectives as much as open
warfare. Raiding brought the war to virtually every corner of Ireland,
confirming (if any doubted it) that Tyrone could project his influence and
military power throughout the island.

The arrival of the Spanish envoys triggered a swift response. The O'Mores
embarked on a series of raids in Cos. Offaly and Laois at the end of May. This
marked the beginning six months of attacks that visited levels of burning,
preying and devastation hitherto unseen during the war.[2] Meath and Louth
were intensively spoiled, and Lecale was devastated to deny supplies to crown
garrisons.[3] Despite the apparent breakdown of the ceasefire, Tyrone fed
English hopes with an illusion that a peaceful solution was imminent.[4] The
earl's honeyed words were all part of the deception, as he clandestinely bought
arms and munitions for the next stage of the war. Dowdall reported that
Tyrone was purchasing 'munition and implements of war even by the

63

merchants of every town of this kingdom'.[5] The earl imported large quantities of gunpowder from Scotland, receiving regular shipments from Glasgow during May 1596.[6] Two months later Tyrone was said to have stockpiled £2,000 of arms and ammunition at Dungannon.[7] Tyrone was unquestionably broadening the scope of the war, but he was not doing this alone. The earl anticipated the arrival of a Spanish army, whose power would enable him to eradicate the last vestiges of English authority in Ireland.

A Spanish expeditionary force was raised to aid the Irish confederates. Philip II had decided to send an army in April, moreover the capture of Cadiz by the English at the end of June sharpened the Spanish king's appetite for invasion. The Spanish army for Ireland was immense when compared to the numbers of troops deployed by both the Irish and English in Ireland. In Lisbon, 84 ships and boats of all sizes carried 10,790 men. A further 2,500 troops were carried on 30 flyboats from Seville, and in Vigo 6,000 troops waited to go.[8] Combined with their Irish allies, an army of this size would have vastly overmatched the queen's army in Ireland, which had little over 6,000 horse and foot in arms at the time.[9] The armada was scheduled to sail at the beginning of October 1596; intelligence in Ireland appeared to concur.[10] With confidence that a large Spanish landing was at hand, Tyrone and his allies made their move in September 1596.

Feagh MacHugh O'Byrne had been in regular contact with Tyrone during the summer, heightening English uncertainty about his intentions.[11] Consequently, Russell maintained the fort at Ballinacor in Wicklow 'til it may be seen what Feagh's loyalty will be'.[12] O'Byrne received reinforcements from the north in June, but Feagh's letter to Tyrone in August suggested that the earl would support the resumption of the war in Wicklow with a company of shot from Connacht.[13] O'Byrne's aims became apparent on 9 September when his men stormed and took the English fort at Ballinacor, named 'Mount Russell' after the lord deputy.[14] According to Russell, the shot deployed by O'Byrne were sent by Tyrone.[15] The loss prompted Russell to strike south from Dublin, retaking Ballinacor and establishing a new fort at Rathdrum. O'Byrne withdrew into his mountain fastness, causing Russell to spend over two months campaigning, in a vain attempt to run Feagh to ground; meanwhile, the northern counties of the Pale burned.[16] Spoliation was rife outside Russell's area of operations, with raids and burning in Laois, Kilkenny, Carlow, Wexford and even along the Wicklow coast between Newcastle and Arklow. Sir Geffrey Fenton noted that while Russell was pursuing Feagh MacHugh, Laois and Carlow were wasted, moreover Offaly, Kilkenny and Wexford could also fall into ruin.[17]

Concurrent with O'Byrne's actions in Wicklow, Tyrone marched a large force into Connacht. Sir Edward Moore claimed Tyrone's expedition had four key objectives: constrain Norreys' army in the province; resupply the earl's allies; prevent the rebuilding of Sligo castle; link up with a landing force from Spain.[18] Tyrone succeeded in the first three, but with regards to the Spanish landing, Tyrone was disappointed. The Spanish arrived in Tirconnell at the end September, but it was only three ships bringing munitions and further promises of aid.[19] Subsequently, there were reports that both Tyrone and O'Donnell were stockpiling supplies and gathering pack horses to service the expected Spanish landing. Captain Rice ap Hugh was informed that O'Donnell had set aside '10,000 beeves, 10,000 porks and 10,000 muttons for vittles, and for carriage 2,000 garrans'.[20] In the meantime, Tyrone intensified the blockade of Armagh.

Tyrone made it clear that he would isolate Armagh as long as the drive against O'Byrne continued.[21] His men attacked and overran a supply convoy outside the town.[22] The garrison sallied out to rescue the convoy, but they charged straight into a trap.[23] Conn O'Neill's men ambushed the garrison from the cover of the nearby friary, killing 20–30 men and forcing the rest to retreat pell-mell into the town.[24] Regardless, Russell would not be distracted from his obsessive pursuit of O'Byrne.[25] Tyrone was not prepared to leave Feagh MacHugh to engage Russell alone; therefore weekly reinforcements were sent from Ulster.[26] Tyrone's aid proved sufficient, as Russell returned to Dublin on 29 November with little to show for two months in the Wicklow Mountains.

Tyrone's efforts to stockpile supplies for the Spanish were for nothing though, as his hopes of a significant Spanish landing in 1596 were not realized. Everything was set for a new Spanish armada at the start of October, but in a startling change of heart, Philip II ordered the fleet to sail for Brittany to seize the port of Brest. The force sailed at the end of October, but a sudden storm scattered the fleet, sinking fourteen ships and claiming over 3,000 lives.[27] The long-promised Spanish army would not come in 1596.

Though Russell had withdrawn to Dublin, Tyrone maintained his stranglehold on the garrison in Armagh. Norreys met with Tyrone at the start of January 1597 to negotiate for the relief of the men there, but his march to the Ulster borders left Connacht unguarded. O'Donnell swept south burning and spoiling to the gates of Galway town.[28] Galway had remained relatively untouched to that point; therefore the pickings were especially rich.[29] The devastation of Connacht coincided with the arrival of the new chief commissioner, Sir Conyers Clifford.[30] He replaced Bingham, who had fled to England to escape charges of corruption.[31] Clifford decided to take the offensive and wrest the initiative from Tyrone and O'Donnell. He set out on 8 February, and in little over two weeks had relieved the garrisons in Tulsk,

Boyle and Ballymote while taking submissions from many of the Connacht lords then in rebellion.[32] Shortage of supplies forced the English to disperse into garrisons, but by 17 March Clifford had retaken Sligo.[33] He secured the defections of Donough O'Connor Sligo and Theobald Burke, enabling the expulsion of Tibbott MacWilliam Burke from Mayo.[34] O'Donnell made efforts to reinstate MacWilliam Burke, but these were undone by Clifford as soon as O'Donnell returned north.[35]

The decision to replace Russell as viceroy with Lord Thomas Burgh was made in December 1596.[36] Russell had little desire to stay, but this did not lessen his hatred for Feagh MacHugh O'Byrne, and he made one last effort to extirpate his elusive enemy.[37] His single-mindedness finally paid dividends when on 8 May, an early morning foray out of Dublin surprised O'Byrne. When O'Byrne attempted to escape the encircling troops, one of Captain Thomas Lee's sergeants caught O'Byrne and executed him out of hand.[38] While the English offensives focused on Connacht and Wicklow, Tyrone preyed east Ulster and the midlands.[39] The Irish burned Mullingar at the end of May, but the arrival of the new lord deputy, Lord Thomas Burgh, galvanized English strategy.[40] Burgh planned to take the war to Tyrone's heartland.

Burgh's assault on Ulster

Burgh was a veteran of the wars in the Low Countries and been the governor of Brill in Flanders before ill-health made him return to England at the start of 1596. He landed near Bray on 15 May and was sworn in as lord deputy one week later. The new lord deputy had a decidedly more aggressive attitude to prosecuting the war, noting that 'there is no other course to be held with Tyrone, than to take him down with force'.[41] Burgh's plan called for a two-pronged attack into Ulster, the first led by himself into Armagh at the start of July, followed by Conyers Clifford's thrust into Tirconnell later that month. Burgh intended to resupply the fort at Armagh, cross the Blackwater and devastate his way through Tyrone to the Foyle. Clifford was to join him there, where they would be met by four provision ships.[42]

Burgh marched north from Newry on 12 July and took two days to reach Armagh. The following morning he led 1,200 foot and 300 horse to the river Blackwater, where Burgh discovered Tyrone had fortified the crossing. The Irish fort was described as a 'straight entrenchment, and plain curtain without flank, excepting two, one at the one end and the like at the other of their defences'.[43] A deep trench and palisade 'of great stakes, hard and wattled, at least four score long and two men's height' protected the rampart along the riverbank.[44] However, the position was poorly sited as attacking troops were

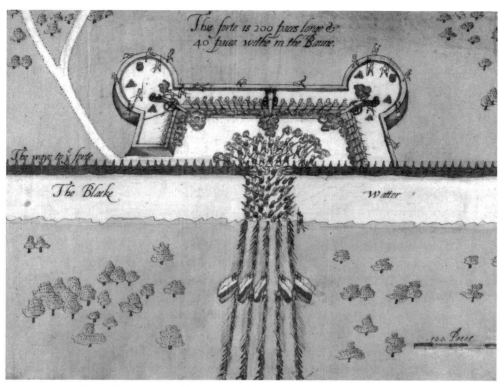

The forte is 200 paces longe &
40 paces withe in the Baune.

The way to ye forte

The Blacke   Watter

.100. Paces

8 Lord Deputy Burgh's assault on Tyrone's Blackwater fort, July 1597
(Trinity College Dublin, MS 1209/34)

safe from most of the defensive fire once they were half way across the river.[45] Consequently, the assault by the English infantry quickly put the Irish defenders from their position, but heavy skirmishing during the following days brought the deaths and injury of many gentleman volunteers and officers who were 'greedy of service'.[46] Burgh did achieve one notable success when a daring night attack, led by the newly defected Turlough MacHenry O'Neill, succeeded in burning part of Dungannon, destroying the great hall and Tyrone's mills.[47]

Burgh ordered a fort built on the Tyrone bank of the river.[48] The English fought with Tyrone's men daily during the two weeks it took to construct the new Blackwater fort, but the fighting did not go as Burgh hoped. Something more deadly than the 'vagabond assembly' expected by the lord deputy checked all Burgh's attempts to advance, and Burgh confessed that 'the hurt has not been to Tyrone as the writer desired'.[49] Setbacks in the midlands also vexed the lord deputy. The rising out of Meath, and the Kells garrison were routed by Captain Richard Tyrrell (one of Tyrone's most trusted and skilful officers), convincing Burgh that an advance to the Foyle was now impossible.[50] Captain Thomas Williams took command of the new Blackwater fort; however, Burgh withdrew the garrison at Armagh when the army marched south for Newry on 3 August.[51] He planned to build a second fort on the Armagh bank of the Blackwater, but a lack of supplies and the threat to the Pale from Tyrrell forced Burgh to order his army into Monaghan and Cavan.[52]

In the west, Clifford's advance was meeting similarly active resistance. He forced the crossing of the Erne with little difficulty on 30 July, then attacked Ballyshannon castle, supported by cannon landed from a ship near Asseroe abbey.[53] Clifford's infantry assaulted breaches in the defences made by the artillery, but despite several determined attacks, ferocious close-range gunfire forced the English to retreat.[54] Maguire and O'Rourke joined O'Donnell, but when Clifford was informed that Burgh had pulled back, he knew that the full weight of the Ulster armies would soon be upon him and his men. Clifford broke camp and headed south for the relative safety of Boyle, but the Irish reinforced with Cormac MacBaron's shot caught up with his army as it marched along the coast between Ballyshannon and Bunduff. The sleeves of English shot struggled to keep the Irish infantry away from the left flank of the main body, but after six hours of skirmishing Clifford's shot fell back on the column, their ammunition spent.[55] Fortunately for the English, at their moment of greatest vulnerability, a sudden rainstorm extinguished the match of every firearm on the field, enabling the English to use their pikemen to deter further Irish attacks. The Irish withdrew, as it was evident there was no possibility of breaking the English ranks. Clifford and his men crossed the river Drowse into Leitrim and reached Sligo by nightfall.[56] Though fortunate to have escaped, Clifford knew that the best chance of success against the Ulster confederates that year was gone.[57]

The raising of a new fort on Tyrone's doorstep may have given the illusion of progress, but as Tyrone was well aware, the garrison needed to be supplied and reinforced by 10 October.[58] Hence Tyrone launched a *coup de main* to take the position on 2 October. Troops with scaling ladders assailed the ramparts under heavy fire from the defending shot and artillery.[59] The assault was a bloody affair where the attackers 'stood they right manfully to it', but the resolve of Williams' men and point-blank cannon fire forced the Irish to retire, leaving 120 of their number dead around the fort.[60] Burgh marched to Armagh on 5 October and resupplied the Blackwater fort the following day, meeting little resistance. However, the lord deputy fell sick with the 'Irish ague'. Burgh was carried on a litter back to Newry, where he died on 13 October.[61] The lord justices took over civil affairs and Ormond assumed overall command of the army.[62] Tyrone exploited the vacuum in English leadership, sending troops to the O'Mores and O'Byrnes, expanding the war in Leinster where, by the end of the month, 'almost no part of it [the Pale] is free from their burning, preying and spoiling'.[63]

Burgh's death meant that the immediate threat to the south Ulster borderlands receded. Consequently, Tyrone turned his attention northwards to deal with the persistent irritation that was the garrison in Carrickfergus and its commander, Sir John Chichester. Chichester had some local success against Tyrone's allies in Antrim while Tyrone dealt with Burgh and Clifford, and had even captured the castle at Edenduffcarrick (modern Shane's castle, Co. Antrim).[64] Tyrone met with James MacSorley MacDonnell on 1 November, where the earl promised MacDonnell his daughter's hand in marriage and provided him with much-needed reinforcements of Irish shot.[65] MacDonnell then set about spoiling the districts around Carrickfergus, taking 'three preys near Carrickfergus, two from the Island Magee and one from Kilroot'.[66] Chichester requested a parley to discuss the recent attacks to which MacDonnell agreed. The two sides met north of Carrickfergus (the battle is known locally as Aldfreck), but some of Chichester's officers took umbrage with the Scots' haughty demeanour, feeling shame that 'we should suffer a sort of beggars to brave us'.[67] The English charged the Scots, forcing them to fall back, but MacDonnell drew the English into an ambush. Volleys of fire poured into Chichester's men from shot concealed on scrub ground, shattering the English units. Chichester was shot in the head and killed, and a charge by the Scots routed the remnants of the English force.[68] Over half the garrison perished in the battle; one estimate put the figure at 220 of the foot and 60 locally raised kern.[69] Chichester's head was packed in a barrel and sent to Tyrone, much to the earl's great satisfaction. Over the next few days, survivors trickled into the castle, but Tyrone had neutralized the threat from Carrickfergus for the time being.

Quite unexpectedly, Tyrone sent letters to Dublin requesting a truce to facilitate peace negotiations. The earl professed to crave the queen's 'gracious favour', and sent orders to his allies in Leinster to forbear attacking English interests.[70] On 8 December, Ormond travelled to Dundalk to discuss terms with Tyrone, but the miserable condition of the English troops appalled the lord general when he arrived. Ormond could only gather 500 serviceable troops from the eighteen foot companies present, leaving the rest behind in Dundalk 'being ashamed to draw them forth where the enemy might see them'.[71] The contrast with Tyrone's forces could not be starker. Ormond's scouts reported that Tyrone had 1,200 shot, 200 pike and 200 horse, all 'strong and well furnished'.[72] Ormond had left Dublin with an extensive list of punitive conditions for Tyrone's pardon, which stipulated that Tyrone make his submission on his knees, disband his army and abjure his alliances.[73] However, with the English forces in disrepair, Ormond was in no position to make demands of Tyrone. The best he could get was an eight-week ceasefire and the withdrawal of some of Tyrone's troops from the Pale. This was the second time Tyrone had sanctioned a ceasefire, but it was not out of any feeling of compassion, war weariness or desire for peace. Cessations were just another tool to gain advantage for the next stage of the war.

Cessations, ceasefires and truces

Combat, confrontation and military manoeuvring were obvious aspects of the war, but a crucial commodity for both sides in the war was time. Time allowed Tyrone and the crown to reinforce troops, import vital war materials, negotiate and formulate plans. Mutually agreed ceasefires secured this. Tyrone's approach at the end of 1597 started yet another round of ostensibly fruitless negotiations. Ormond noted that Tyrone was also keen to agree on a cessation, and would have agreed a longer term of truce, a year or two if possible.[74] However, Ormond was also eager to secure a treaty as the English army in Ireland was in no state to fight Tyrone and his allies, never mind deal with a potential Spanish invasion. Ormond received instructions to make some cessation; consequently, he concluded a truce that lasted until May of 1598.[75] The cessations patently served both belligerent's needs, but an absence of fighting was not peace; the war continued even if there were no overt military actions.

The Irish made use of the periods of truce to reinforce and resupply their forces. Clauses within the articles of cessation allowed free movement and access to the market towns without hindrance by English garrisons. The Irish took advantage of this freedom. They entered the Pale to buy arms, armour and food supplies, whereby the increase in demand caused inflation in commodity prices.[76] Cessations also allowed Tyrone to address agricultural concerns. He returned cattle to grazing pastures that had been previously threatened by garrisons and could release men from their military obligations to get the harvest brought in.[77]

Though Tyrone resupplied troops from his stores, there were frequent complaints that ceasefires allowed the Irish to cess troops on crown subjects. Spoiling was prohibited under the terms of cessation, but this was frequently ignored, indeed exploited as reduced interference from crown garrisons made spoiling easier.[78] Bingham complained about the repeated breaches of the peace in Connacht, to the extent that he believed the cessation was not operating in the province at all.[79] There were frequent violations of truces by both sides throughout the war, but neither belligerent could afford a return to open warfare while they attempted to reinforce threatened positions or relocate troops for the next round of hostilities.[80]

The Irish gained a military advantage at operational levels using cessations. In asking for truces, Tyrone and his allies were able to demand delays that either displaced English forces, creating exploitable regional weaknesses, or forced their enemies' troops to consume the limited supplies held in their baggage. Even a short delay could compel English field forces to break camp and return to their garrisons for resupply. This occurred in Connacht during 1596 when O'Donnell engaged in facile negotiations with Sir John Norreys. O'Donnell temporized long enough for Norreys' army to exhaust their victuals, forcing them to withdraw.[81] With their encampments facing each other on the river Robe, both sides used this opportunity to gather intelligence.[82]

It was evident to many English commentators that the cessations were highly damaging to the English cause. Captain Dawtrey reported that peace did not weaken the Irish but made them 'better able to maintain it [the war], than they were before such peace was made'.[83] Hugh Collier considered the cessations to be to the advantage of the enemy, expensive to the crown and impoverishing to the Pale.[84] Russell was highly critical of cessations and Burgh rejected them out of hand, but limited military resources forced the queen's officers to temporize with the Irish.[85] Orders dispatched to the earl of Ormond in 1597 were clear that he was to do his utmost to secure a ceasefire, even if he could not secure a submission or even pledges from Tyrone.[86] The primary motivating factor behind this was the weakness of the English army in Ireland. Breathing space was needed to reinforce and resupply their forces. The inadequacy of the crown's army was a major factor in deciding the approach of government officials during the negotiations with Tyrone at the start of 1596. One of the reasons compelling Russell to seek a ceasefire in 1596 was the constant harassing of his supply columns.[87] Russell reminded the commissioners of 'how slenderly we are furnished for war', and asked them to sue for two further months of cessation or as much as they could get.[88]

While a respite to rebuild their forces was a significant element in the desire for cessations, there were other more subtle plans running concurrently. Tyrone used periods of truce, and the resulting freedom of travel, to coerce uncommitted lords to ally with him against the crown. Russell commented in 1596 that Tyrone had sent out messengers to the Pale and elsewhere during the truce 'to sound out how every man stood'.[89] The cessations were later condemned because they had enabled Tyrone to 'increase his combination and to arm himself both in foreign parts and at home'.[90] Thomas Lee observed that the Irish used the peace to strengthen their alliances. Furthermore, he noted that the Irish sent communications between regional leaders to prepare plans for a renewal of the war.[91]

Though cessations may have curtailed the fighting, the crown still needed to feed its troops. Onerous demands on the loyal subjects in the Pale led some to side with the northern lords. The crown cessed many of the garrison forces in the Pale, as supplies frequently ran short due to their limited logistical infrastructure. The cess, or purveyance, had a long history of raising disquiet in the Pale.[92] For some, government demands to supply troops who were incapable of protecting them from Irish attacks proved intolerable. Sir Henry Wallop noted that it was this burden, upon the otherwise loyal subjects, that drove many into rebellion.[93]

During the early stages of the war, some hoped that a period of peace with negotiation could return the Ulster lords to their loyalty to the queen, using offers of free pardons and guarantees of life, lands and goods.[94] Sir John Norreys believed that a ceasefire was the best way to reduce Tyrone. In a letter to Cecil, he opined that a cessation was the best way to 'cut his [Tyrone's] own throat', by drawing away adherents, whose allegiance to Tyrone was only secured by force and hostages.[95] Norreys anticipated that the expense of maintaining troops throughout the duration of a ceasefire would force Tyrone's allies to dismiss their men. Tyrone worked to ensure that this would not happen, and later in the war Tyrone authorized his allies in Leinster to take covert 'snatches' of supplies during a ceasefire if it enabled them to pay their soldiers.[96]

The 1597–8 cessation: a prelude to disaster

In contrast to the ceasefire of 1595–6, the 1597–8 cessation was mostly observed by both sides, though local instances of spoiling did result in clashes.[97] Tyrone dispatched orders to the midlands for Tyrrell and his allies to stand down, meanwhile in Ulster, the beleaguered English garrisons in Carrickfergus and the Blackwater fort were resupplied and reinforced.[98] The situation in Connacht appeared settled enough for Clifford to report that the majority of the Irish in the province 'are most willing to live again under the obedience of her majesty's laws'.[99] Tyrone was content to temporize, but Ormond also needed the time to rebuild the decayed remnants of the crown's Irish army, bringing in shipments of troops, money and munitions.[100] Negotiations continued between Tyrone and the crown, but the meetings were just as fruitless as all those before them. Tyrone's contact with James VI of Scotland and plans to foment rebellion in Munster dispelled any illusions that the war could be ended peacefully.[101]

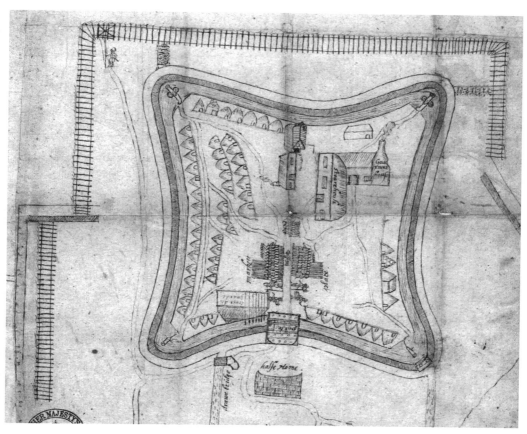

9 Lord Deputy Burgh's new Blackwater fort, 1598
(The National Archive, Kew, MPF 1/311)

It had taken five years of defeat and frustration, but finally the government
in Dublin recognized that their strategy to defeat Tyrone was fundamentally
flawed. Incursions into Ulster with large armies had only succeeded in
consuming men, money and more than a few reputations. Therefore the long-
recommended but unconsummated plan to land an English army on the river
Foyle, deep in Tyrone's rear areas was given the go-ahead. A landing in north
Ulster could draw disaffected Irish lords away from Tyrone and would be a
constant bridle on the Ulster lords' southern operations.[102] An expedition of
1,000 foot (later increased to 2,000) and 100 horse was to sail directly from
England. By the start of May, it was apparent that Tyrone knew about the
English scheme.[103] Breaches in the cessation became more frequent as summer
grew nearer. The Irish spoiled in Offaly and Laois, and in Wexford two
companies of veteran infantry from Picardy and the Enniscorthy garrison were

destroyed attempting to recover preys.[104] Tyrone cast aside any pretensions of peace when the cessation expired at the start of June.

While reinforcements for Tyrone's Leinster allies gathered along the Ulster borders, Irish forces cut off all access to the garrisons in Cavan and the Blackwater fort.[105] At Carrickfergus, 800 Scots kept the garrison shut in behind their earthen ramparts and the English outpost at Belfast was closely besieged.[106] The deceptive peace in Connacht collapsed when Sir Brian O'Rourke declared for Tyrone after reconciling with O'Donnell. Clifford's optimistic reports were exposed as entirely misguided when Ballymote castle was betrayed.[107] Ormond marched to counter the raids in the midlands, whereas Bagenal held the Ulster borders against Tyrone.[108] The lord justices wanted to abandon the Blackwater fort, as they had barely enough troops to defend the territory still in government hands. Moreover, there was a genuine fear that sending the army to revictual the fort would court 'such a disaster as we shall be sorry for'.[109] The crown's military resources were thinly spread. Ormond pleaded for reinforcements from England, advising Cecil that 'our army here is so dispersed … we shall not be able to encounter their [Irish] main force'.[110] Ormond scored a local victory when his men defeated Brian Riabhach O'More in a bloody encounter just west of Maryborough (modern Portlaoise, Co. Laois) in Camagh Woods on 6 July. O'More was fatally wounded and died four days later.[111] Nevertheless, small success could not address the plight of Williams and his men ensconced on the Blackwater, but reinforcements and shipments of money and munitions during July emboldened the regime in Dublin. Bagenal's command was reinforced with the new levies from England, and he was given orders to break through to the embattled garrison.

Bagenal moved north into Ulster with a formidable army, almost 3,500 infantry and 350 horse, reaching Armagh on 13 August.[112] Four cannon augmented the army's firepower, the heaviest being a saker that could fire a six-pound iron ball over 2,000 yards. Early the next day, the infantry and horse mustered into the respective battalia and squadrons. The foot were divided into the van, battle and rear, each of which was sub-divided into two regiments. Intervals of 100–120 yards separated each regiment as they deployed for the march in full battle array. The regiments' central core of pikes were protected by musketeers, then sleeves of loose shot, who deployed 30–40 yards to either side of the column to protect the densely packed infantry from close range gunfire. Bagenal's horsemen were split into two squadrons to support the van and the rear.[113] Baggage and artillery were placed with Bagenal's regiment in the rear of the van. At eight o'clock, the head of the army started north; four miles separated them from the river Blackwater. This army was the largest English army yet fielded against Tyrone and over-confidence may have been a problem. One account claimed that the English soldiers marched with little fear 'as if they would win the goal in a match at football'.[114] Captains Leigh and Turner who had command of the forlorn hope (a detached troop at the head of the column, taken from the Dutch *verloren hoop* or 'lost troop') at the point of the column casually smoked their pipes as they strolled to meet Tyrone's men.

Tyrone had gathered the bulk of his Ulster army and was joined by troops from Connacht.[115] Somewhere between 4,000 to 5,000 foot and 600 horse were secreted along Bagenal's line-of-march.[116] Tyrone knew the route the English must take. Therefore he prepared the battlefield to give his men every advantage. Pits and trenches were cut into the 'common highway' to the Blackwater, forcing Bagenal's column to march to the right of the road along the tops of the drumlins.[117] Though the heights provided clear fields of fire on both flanks, bogs to the left and right canalized the English, greatly limiting their freedom to manoeuvre.

The army came under fire soon after leaving Armagh. Irish calivermen emerged from the scrub lining the lower slopes of the hills to skirmish with the English loose shot. Bagenal's men returned fire, but there was no resistance to their front, so the army pushed on to the Callan river. Gunfire from the Irish was continuous as the English crossed the Callan; fresh Irish units relieved those already engaged. The impetuosity of the lead regiment under Sir Richard Percy began to create a dangerous gap between it and the rest of the army. The saker with Bagenal exacerbated the problem. It was a field piece common to European battlefields, but in Ireland, it was a dangerous liability. Weighing approximately 2,500–3,000 pounds, it kept bogging down in the soft earth, forcing Bagenal to halt while his men recovered it.[118] The delays irritated Percy, who churlishly commented after the battle that the fault was with the rest of the army for not keeping pace with him.[119] Rather than maintain contact Percy pressed ahead over a boggy ford then on to a second hill, below which ran an earthen rampart and trench, cutting across his advance. The Irish poured fire into the first regiment as they waited for Bagenal, causing Percy to quit his position and press ahead over the earthwork. It was five feet high and topped with thorns, and ran for almost a mile through the landscape. The lead regiment clambered over the defence and moved onto a third and final hill that overlooked the Blackwater. No one thought it odd that the Irish should raise an extensive work only to leave it undefended.

Cresting the last hill, Percy caught sight of the fort less than a mile away. The garrison cheered with joy when they saw the colours of the lead regiment. Thinking their relief had finally come, they threw their caps in the air 'hoping

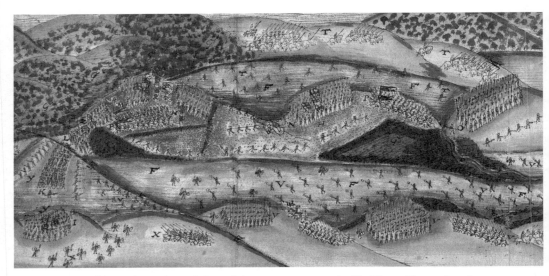

10 Tyrone's crushing defeat of the crown army under Sir Henry Bagenal at the battle of the Yellow Ford, 15 Aug. 1598 (Trinity College Dublin, MS 1209/35)

to have a better supper than the dinner they had that day', but their optimism was short-lived.[120] Unknown to Percy, the rear under Billings and Cuney had been stopped in its tracks at the Callan, and the rest of the army was stalled on the hill before the trench and at the bog ford. Worryingly, Tyrone's horse and foot appeared in ever greater numbers, threatening to cut off Percy's retreat. Beyond the immediate help of the army, Percy received orders to withdraw and link up with Bagenal. Their ammunition spent, Percy's wings of loose shot were forced back to his main body of pikes, allowing the Irish shot to rake the English with extremely close-range gunfire, possibly within ten to fifteen metres. As the English wheeled about their battalia became disordered, allowing Irish targeteers and horse to charge into the gaps, stabbing and slashing at the panicking English infantry.[121] All order was lost as Percy's regiment broke and fled. The powerful contingent of English horse could not come to their aid, as Tyrone's mile-long trench barred their way. Moreover, the barricade impeded the fugitive soldiers escape as 'falling over one another they filled the dyke and were trodden down where they fell'.[122] Isolated and without support, Percy's men were slaughtered.

The carnage at the trench was played out in full view of Bagenal. Tyrone's defences had neutralized the English cavalry. The marshal led his regiment to the trench to rescue the shattered remnants of Percy's unit, but on this day fate favoured the Irish. Descending the hill, Bagenal raised his visor to get a better view. A bullet struck the marshal on the forehead, killing him instantly. The attack continued under Captain Evans, but the English were badly mauled and sent spilling back over the trench. The English predicament got worse. One of the English shot decided to replenish his ammunition direct from the baggage train. Distracted by the mayhem around him, the soldier 'thrust his hand for a handful of powder having a lit match in the same hand'.[123] An explosion ripped through the crowded English position on the hill, killing and wounding scores of men, with many suffering horrendous burns. Cloying smoke enveloped the hill as the Irish came on, encouraged by English misfortune.[124]

Sir Thomas Maria-Wingfield, Bagenal's second-in-command, realized the position was hopeless. The rear had broken through the Irish at the river Callan to join the rest of the army, but the loss of so many soldiers and the devastation of the baggage meant retreat to Armagh was the only viable option. What had been the rear now led the way, Wingfield had charge of the battle, and Captain Cosby brought up the rear with his regiment and the vestiges of Bagenal's and Percy's units. However, for reasons still unclear Cosby ignored his orders and initiated a counterattack across the trench. Tyrone's response was quick and deadly. The Irish crushed Cosby's futile assault. Only the timely intervention by Wingfield and the English horse saved 500 soldiers from annihilation. Cosby, however, was taken prisoner.

Wingfield stabilized the situation at the rear, but the army was still in grave danger. Tyrone attempted to check the withdrawal at the river Callan by sending his cavalry to hold the high ground overlooking the crossing, but English cannon fire gave pause to their advance; the narrow corridor to Armagh stayed open. Fortunately for the English, the Irish gunfire slackened. Just as at Clontibret in 1595, Tyrone's men had exhausted their supply of gunpowder. Cuney was in no doubt that if it was not for this, no Englishmen would have survived to report the disaster. He noted that if the Irish had charged his men 'seeing our distress, I think not any of us should have hardly lived'.[125] The battered army took full advantage of the respite, marching to Armagh with little hindrance from Tyrone. Just over half of the Bagenal's once proud army limped back to Armagh; 300 defected to Tyrone (including two English recruits), the rest lay dead or dying on the hills and bogs north of the town.[126] Tyrone had routed the English, but the victory came at a price, with one estimate placing Irish losses at around 200 killed.[127]

Wingfield's battered and dispirited army was trapped in Armagh. He claimed to have 2,400 men, but almost 700 were unarmed and 400 were wounded, many with severe burns.[128] Tyrone offered terms for their withdrawal south but tied these to the capitulation of the Blackwater fort's garrison. The governor of the fort, Captain Williams, received a letter from the officers in Armagh asking him to surrender the position to Tyrone, 'professing that all their safety depended on his yielding the fort'.[129] Williams was a tough and capable officer, but he would not needlessly sacrifice the lives of thousands of men on a point of honour for a fort that was no longer tenable. After three days Tyrone allowed the troops in the Blackwater fort and those in Armagh to march south stripped of their arms, artillery and supplies.

News of Tyrone's victory reverberated through the corridors of power in Dublin. Panic gripped the queen's Irish councillors, who dispatched a letter appealing to Tyrone's honour to release the defeated army from Armagh unharmed.[130] There was little to stop Tyrone marching on Dublin, and a general advance into Leinster was thought imminent, but the attack never came. Though the Irish had routed the main English field force, the possibility of an English amphibious landing on the Foyle remained. Tyrone could not commit the bulk of his troops to an advance south while the threat persisted.[131] Unknown to Tyrone, the 2,000 men destined for the Foyle were redirected to protect the Pale and the seat of government in Dublin within two days of the defeat.[132]

The punishing losses of men and equipment at the Blackwater threw the queen's army on the defensive until reinforcements could arrive from England, but of more significance was the effect on Irish morale and confidence. Sir Conyers Clifford noted that 'the enemy are since in great pride, the soldiers and subjects much discouraged', and later that the defeat had 'so puffed the minds of these fickle people that all Ireland this day is in actual rebellion'.[133] O'Donnell reasserted his control in Connacht in September, re-establishing MacWilliam and rapidly securing Sligo and Mayo.[134] With limited forces at his disposal, Clifford watched as his hold on the province dissolved. The O'Connors of Roscommon were brought back into the confederate fold, and the placing of a new chief of the O'Briens to oppose the earl of Thomond precipitated a widespread revolt in Co. Clare.[135]

Irish Strategy: defensive or offensive?

Tyrone brought the English administration to its knees in 1598. Crown authority only extended to the precincts of the walled towns and the immediate vicinity of the garrisons. Even then, many of the soldiers within walls or ramparts feared to stray too far from the safety of their fortifications. How could this happen in a war that has been interpreted as defensive?[136] If Tyrone's strategy was solely focused on becoming the leading power in Ulster, why did his confederation come to dominate almost the entire island by the start of 1600? Irish strategic goals shifted from defensive to offensive early in the war.

The ceasefire of September 1595 accommodated negotiations to bring the war to a peaceful end. However, the arrival of Spanish envoys with assurances of Spanish aid put paid to any chance of peace.[137] The pattern of Irish raids moved south and escalated to unprecedented levels, coinciding with a build-up of Spanish ships and troops in Lisbon. Concurrent aggressive action by Tyrone and the gathering of a Spanish amphibious force suggests that the sustained attacks on the Pale may have been in preparation for Spanish landings.

Tyrone frequently utilized deception or operational feints to mislead the English or cause them to draw their attention away from the crucial theatres. As in 1593–4, the most active districts were not the ones in which Tyrone intended to make his advance. In this case, Tyrone wanted Russell looking at the eastern counties while Connacht was to be the location of the Spanish landing. But the hoped-for Spanish troops did not arrive in the autumn of 1596, exasperating Tyrone and his allies. When the Spanish envoy arrived in March 1597, O'Donnell rounded on them for their failure to live up to their side of the bargain. He claimed the Spanish had 'cosened them of Ireland for that they had purchased them to continue in disobedience towards their prince, making many promises that the king of Spain would support and bear them out … yet they have received nothing from him but a little powder'.[138]

In concert with military advances, the confederate leaders made their first efforts to widen the war by making overtures to the nobles in Munster. In a letter laden with strong religious overtones, the northern leaders asked any and all in Munster to join them in assisting 'Christ's Catholic religion', and to make war 'aiding God's just cause'.[139] The critical change in strategic thinking came with the landing of Cobos in May 1596. Before the truce of 1595–6, the confederate military posture outside Ulster was one of defence and containment. Tyrone's strategy changed from defence to one of offence only after he had made substantive contacts with the Spanish, and received firm assurances of an imminent military expedition from Spain.

The pattern of engagements and the switch from defensive to offensive warfare suggests that there was a shift in the political aims of Tyrone and his allies. Until the arrival of the Spanish in 1596, the Confederate campaigns focused primarily on Ulster or consolidation of the Ulster borderlands. The concentration of much of the open warfare in Ulster suggested that defending Ulster was Tyrone's main objective. This implied the earl was aiming to secure greater jurisdiction over his lordship in Ulster during ensuing peace negotiations. Nevertheless, Tyrone's recruitment of new allies in Connacht and Leinster and the corresponding widening of the war during early 1596 indicated that the goals of the northern lords were grander than protecting their power bases in Ulster. The O'Kellys of Roscommon, the O'Farrells of Longford and the O'Reillys of Cavan all sided with Tyrone in January 1596.[140] Raids were already being launched into Offaly and Laois before the Spanish arrival in May. After Tyrone repudiated the crown's offer of pardon his forces devastated Louth and Meath. These attacks did not suggest that Tyrone had limited goals; rather it indicates that he was actively preparing to continue the war into the rest of Ireland during the 1595–6 cessation.

Deceptive offence

Irish resistance to English incursions into Ulster leading to major engagements caused the war in the 1593–9 period to appear strategically defensive, but the reality was quite the reverse. On at least four occasions (Enniskillen 1594, Armagh and Monaghan 1595, Norreys during January 1597 and the Blackwater in 1598), drawing the English field army into Ulster by Tyrone served wider goals. The Irish use of deception and displacement supported Tyrone's broader strategic needs. When Tyrone blockaded the garrison in Armagh during the closing months of 1596, he destroyed a supply convoy sent north, causing a critical shortage of supplies within the fort.[141] Tyrone then concentrated his forces north of Newry, compelling the lord deputy to gather his field army at Dundalk, where they could march to Armagh under the leadership of Sir John Norreys.[142] As battle appeared imminent, Tyrone relented and allowed the victualing of the fort.[143] With the government forces now concentrated in the east, O'Donnell embarked on raids targeting Clanricard, Athlone and Athenry, and burnt the suburbs of Galway town.[144] Only when it was too late did it become apparent that Norreys had been deliberately drawn away, to allow O'Donnell free rein in the west.[145]

Tyrone's greatest success on the battlefield at the Yellow Ford had strategic objectives beyond destroying the English field army. During May 1598, Tyrone and O'Donnell were informed of English plans to send an amphibious force to the Foyle; therefore they met to discuss how to thwart any landing.[146] Tyrone immediately sent forces to cut off the Blackwater fort at the start of June when the cessation expired.[147] The Irish comprehensively defeated the relieving army under Bagenal. Though the stunning overthrow resulted in the loss of up to 2,000 men and the Blackwater fort's capture, Tyrone's victory had more profound strategic implications. With Dublin vulnerable to attack from the north, the authorities redirected the Foyle expedition to defend the Pale.[148] For Tyrone, the crucial issue was not destroying Bagenal's army or taking the fort, but preventing the Foyle landings. When the crown managed to land an army on the Foyle two years later, it played a decisive role in the subjugation of Ulster.[149]

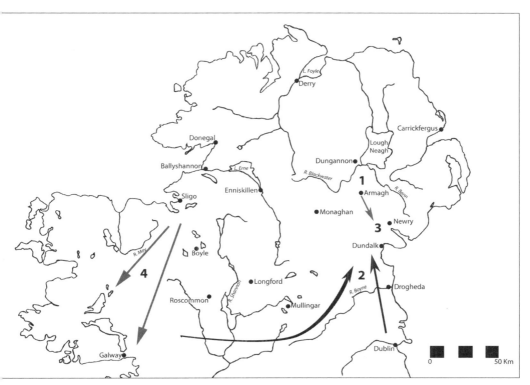

11 Tyrone's deception of Sir John Norreys, Jan. 1597. 1: Tyrone cuts off the Armagh
garrison from supply. 2: Norreys drawn out of Connacht and forces concentrated to
force supply convoy through to Armagh. 3: Tyrone allows convoy to pass unhindered.
4: O'Donnell invades Connacht while crown forces are concentrated in the east.

The engagements described were not truly defensive, as Tyrone required
the English to attack for his broader plan to succeed. The core strategy at the
outset of the war was securing Ulster, by pushing English military and political
influence south of the natural defences of the Ulster borderlands. After 1595,
Irish expectation of Spanish intervention caused Tyrone to focus on eliciting
support and garnering the agricultural wealth of the land while denying both
to the crown. To achieve this, the confederate leaders displayed the ability to
coordinate actions by forces in different regions, which kept the English off
balance, and retained, for the most part, the strategic initiative. The raids of
1594 (east Ulster), 1595 (north Connacht), 1596 (north and south Leinster
and the midlands), and 1597 (south Connacht) were all achieved by successful
feints or tactical diversions to draw garrisons away from the target areas. From
1595, the confederate forces managed to achieve a degree of operational
synchronization that substantially influenced military fortunes elsewhere.

Historically, regional co-operation was rarely (if ever) a feature of Gaelic warfare. However, Tyrone's capture of the Blackwater fort in 1595 served to draw English forces away from Feagh MacHugh O'Byrne in Co. Wicklow. Russell received a letter from Tyrone offering submissions from the northern lords and Feagh MacHugh, but the lord deputy dismissed these as an attempt to divert his attention.[150] On 16 February, the same day Tyrone had requested to meet with Russell, Art MacBaron took the Blackwater fort.[151] Irish forces raided Louth the next day and Tyrone's troops were reported near Ardee.[152] These attacks were precisely what Feagh MacHugh had asked Tyrone to do.[153]

O'Byrne reciprocated Tyrone's assistance the following year when in September 1596 he attacked and took the fort at Ballinacor.[154] Russell harboured a burning animosity towards Feagh MacHugh. Therefore it was predictable, and possibly essential, that Russell's fit of pique kept him engaged in a pointless pursuit of O'Byrne, while elsewhere the Pale was ravaged. The lord deputy's preoccupation in Wicklow earned a rebuke from Norreys and forced Sir Geoffrey Fenton to ask Burghley to have the campaign against O'Byrne halted.[155] Clearly, regional co-operation between the Irish lords was now a reality

Perhaps one of the most finely balanced examples of Irish operational co-ordination was the defeat of Lord Deputy Burgh's summer offensive in 1597. As noted earlier, Burgh's plan called for a two-pronged attack into Ulster through Cos. Armagh and Donegal, with the two armies converging at the Foyle. Tyrone checked Burgh on the Blackwater and Clifford at Ballyshannon. Local supply shortages brought on by the devastation around Newry and Lecale, and Irish threats to the Pale, caused the lord deputy to pull the army back into Monaghan and Cavan.[156] Burgh's withdrawal released Tyrone's forces who streamed westwards and almost succeeded in cutting off Clifford's hasty retreat.[157] This campaign was an example of co-ordinated action between at least three distinct confederate forces. Tyrrell's victory in Meath could be argued as opportunistic, but it was still achieved against a background of spoliation designed to draw Burgh out of Ulster; regional coordination produced dramatic operational success.

Munster in flames

In October 1598, as the scale of the defeat at the Yellow Ford sank in, Clifford realized that his optimism of the summer was misplaced, noting that 'the time wherein I declared the recovery of this revolted province had changed unto the contrary'.[158] Possibly awaiting contact from the Irish of Munster, Owny O'More and Tyrrell delayed their entry into Munster until 29 September, when they invaded Tipperary.[159] The lord president of Munster, Sir Thomas Norreys, gathered the provincial rising out to oppose the incursion, but faulty reports of the size of the Irish army caused him disperse the country forces, with orders to defend themselves and their homes as best they could.[160] Extension of the war to Munster received provincial endorsement when James Fitzthomas, claimant to the vacant earldom of Desmond, joined the rebellion on 10 October by accepting the title of earl of Desmond from Tyrone.[161] The irruption into Munster encouraged many Irish nobles in the province to join with Tyrone; perhaps more than even the confederate leaders expected.[162]

The rising in Munster gained a momentum of its own, and soon English holdings across the province were ablaze as the Irish peasantry turned on the newcomers. Though Ormond's intervention stiffened resistance in Mallow, Kilmallock, Cork and the coastal towns, most English abandoned their settlements without contest. Ormond condemned the undertaker's cowardice as many did not attempt to defend their holdings, and in Kerry the English fled before any Irish forces appeared.[163] Nevertheless, armed civilians were not soldiers. Ormond could not have expected small isolated bands to resist the Irish onslaught without firm leadership. Refugees flooded into the towns to escape the general revolt of their tenants. Operating outside any structures of command, the Munster insurgents engaged in crimes and atrocities that had not been a feature of the war to that point.[164] Though many of the more affluent English reached the towns, others, mostly the poorer settlers, could not escape, leading to outrages which saw defenceless men, women and children put to the sword. It is hard to quantify how many were murdered in cold blood, as it is difficult to differentiate between settlers who were killed and those who were robbed. The vivid yet possibly hyperbolic polemic *The supplication of the blood of the English* makes this task harder still, but it is clear that many hundreds may have been slain.[165] The Irish chroniclers were unequivocal in their assessment of the Munster rebellion, writing that 'in the course of seventeen days they left not within the length or breath of the country … a single son of a Saxon whom they did not either kill or expel'.[166]

With their goals achieved, O'More crossed back into Laois on 19 October, but Captain Tyrrell remained behind to train Desmond's inexperienced troops.[167] The situation appeared bleak in Dublin, where it was thought necessary to bring 3,000 fresh troops into Ireland just to re-assert control in Leinster and Munster. Counties Offaly and Laois were thought lost to the Irish, apart from the forts at Philipstown (now Daingean, Co. Offaly) and Maryborough.[168] Security in the Pale had decayed to the point that Dunboyne, only six miles from Dublin, could be pillaged and burnt in daylight without provoking any effort to impede the raiders.[169] Sir Richard Bingham was rushed back to Ireland to take over the vacant position of marshal, but wrote with some pessimism of Connacht and Munster that 'there is no great cause to write anything of them, for the countries are possessed by the rebels, and few holds left for us to defend'.[170] With three provinces lost and security of the Pale on a knife-edge, this was surely Elizabeth's darkest hour in Ireland.

CHAPTER 4

A kingdom near lost, 1599

IRISH VICEROYS HAVE RARELY been dealt with sympathetically by modern historians, and the last Elizabethan deputies were no exception. Sir William Fitzwilliam has been portrayed as irredeemably corrupt, and the deputyship of Sir William Russell was regarded a military disaster.[1] It is perhaps Robert Devereux, the second earl of Essex, who has attracted most criticism. Bagwell considered Essex's failure against Tyrone a humiliating disgrace, while Falls and Hayes-McCoy were equally harsh.[2] Some have attempted to rehabilitate Essex's reputation, but it is clear that Devereux was out of his depth in Ireland.[3] He squandered the queen's investment in the most powerful army yet deployed to Ireland. Essex's view of war was determined by a need for martial glory that led to ritualized posturing and acts of grandiose bravery aimed at enhancing his reputation.[4]

Though the English were reeling from successive defeats, Tyrone's power was not just the arms and skill of his troops; it was also the systems of command, supply and logistical support developed to deliver orders and supply armies in the field. The Irish confederation was held together by a network of alliances fostered by Tyrone, and underpinned by military, financial and economic aid to bolster the strength and ensure the loyalty of regional lords. This support was enabled by Tyrone's ability to harness the wealth of the territories under confederate control. Revenue enabled the Irish to continue the war with arms, munitions and supplies bought in Ireland and imported from England and Scotland. However, financing and sourcing war materials still did not explain Irish success. Arms, ammunition and supplies had to reach Tyrone's field forces. Therefore the Irish developed a system of logistics that ensured that their troops were fed, clothed and armed. When Tyrone's men met the queen's army at the sharp end of the war, they had everything they needed to prevail.

Essex and Ireland: Icarus undone

The closing months of 1598 in Ireland were ones of fear and uncertainty for the crown. Its most potent striking force was destroyed at the Yellow Ford, and it took little effort by Tyrone and his allies to precipitate a collapse of English rule in Munster. There was no clear leadership from Dublin as there was still no lord deputy in overall control. One of the key figures in maintaining crown resistance was the earl of Ormond. He had been castigated by the queen for not commanding the relief force to the Blackwater in person, as he held the overall command of the army as lieutenant general of Ireland, writing 'it was strange to us, when almost the whole forces of our kingdom were drawn to head, and a main blow like to be stroken for our honour against the capital rebel, that you … should employ yourself in an action of less importance'.[5] Ormond protested his case, but in the meantime he moved with what little forces were available to the northern Pale in an attempt to dissuade Tyrone from making a general assault into Leinster. With the arrival of the reinforcements under Sir Samuel Bagenal, Ormond took charge of the placement of troops along the borderlands between Ulster and the Pale and for the defence of Leinster as a whole.[6] He marched south in response to Irish raids on his lands in Kilkenny and Tipperary, but the conflict in Munster was escalating rapidly.

With the assistance of Sir Thomas Norreys, Ormond did his utmost to bolster the resistance of the walled towns in Munster. Prompt action by Ormond denied both Mallow and Kilmallock to the insurgents at the start of October. His efforts secured the coastal towns, but with so few resources at hand little could be done to save the rural estates of the English plantation. Most of the English undertakers fled to the protection of the walled towns, abandoning their tenants and farms to the approaching Irish. Ormond was scathing of them, noting that 'the most part of the undertakers had most shamefully quitted and forsaken their castles of strength before even the traitors came near them, leaving all to their spoils'.[7] Without question it was Ormond who helped retain what little remained of organized English resistance in Munster.[8] After reinforcing Cork, Kinsale and Youghal, Ormond returned to Kilkenny to deal with his relatives Thomas Butler, second Baron Cahir, and Edmund Butler, second Viscount Mountgarrett, who had sided with Tyrone.[9]

The English position in Ireland was perilous at the beginning of 1599. The disasters of 1598 shook the Tudor government to its core. In response Queen Elizabeth looked to the hero of Cadiz and her court favourite, Robert Devereux, second earl of Essex. Essex had experience of continental warfare both on land and sea. He accompanied the earl of Leicester to the Low Countries in 1585–6, but witnessed little fighting until he took part in a near-suicidal cavalry charge at Zutphen.[10] The positional nature of the war in the Low Countries meant that large-scale actions usually took the form of sieges. The more prosaic, day-to-day soldiering involved raids, skirmishes and attacks on convoys.[11] When Essex marched his men to the gates of Lisbon during the expedition to Portugal in 1589, he saw how an army could wither when an enemy refused to fight.[12] Essex commanded forces in Normandy in 1591, but this proved a military failure. Reproach from the queen and her demand that he return home caused him to fall into a fit of despair.[13] The success of the venture to Cadiz in 1596 was by far Essex's most recognized triumph. The city was sacked and two Spanish galleons captured, but Essex's continuous quest for glory imperilled the whole mission. He was furious that the initial infantry landings had been cancelled, heedless that his small boats were vulnerable to attack by nearby Spanish galleys, and that the beach was strongly defended.[14]

Though Essex's military record was mixed his reputation grew, and his influence increased in domestic military issues. Essex demonstrated his talent for planning and organization when he developed innovative plans for a blockade upon Spain and the creation of smaller, highly trained and motivated land forces.[15] He had no direct experience of warfare in Ireland before his arrival in 1599, but Essex had a preconceived idea that it was 'miserable beggarly ... war'.[16] Despite the urging of Francis Bacon, Essex viewed Ireland as no place to make a name or improve his position in court.[17] He despised the war in Ireland but had made a point of criticizing the previous attempts to subdue Tyrone. His self-aggrandisement as England's greatest soldier meant that when the opportunity arose to command the queen's new army for Ireland, Essex could not decline, even if this made him vulnerable to his enemies at court.[18]

The queen confirmed Essex as lord lieutenant of Ireland on 30 December 1598, but he did not land in Dublin until 14 April 1599. Essex was well aware at the outset of his campaign that the Irish could not be defeated by purely military means. As well as engaging their armies, Essex needed to attack the Irish politically and economically. In a letter to the queen, Essex noted that war solely by military aggression would be lengthy and costly.[19] He suggested that the Irish could be subdued by promoting faction among Tyrone's allies. Essex maintained that spoliation of the land, utilization of the navy to cut off foreign supplies to the Irish, and playing to English military strengths such as command, supply, order and discipline, would procure final victory. The liberal employment of former rebels was advocated by Essex, as he believed this would lighten the burden from his English soldiers, and when one rebel was used against another it would make a 'riddance of either side'.[20] Essex was conscious of what it would take to win in Ireland, as the above points were key ingredients to Lord Deputy Mountjoy's eventual victory in 1603. Furthermore, the resources allocated to Essex's renewed campaign were far greater than in previous military commitments in Ireland.

12 Robert Devereux, 2nd earl of Essex, by Marcus Gheeraerts
the younger (National Portrait Gallery, London)

The appointment of Essex as viceroy was accompanied by an expansion of
the army list in Ireland to 16,000 foot and 1,300 horse, with an annual cost of
£228,246 and £31,408 respectively.[21] Additional levies were made to ensure
that Essex would receive another 3,300 foot by the end of the summer.
Essex was also accompanied by many gentleman volunteers – enthusiastic
contemporaries who were eager to make a name for themselves against the
Irish. In addition to men, the renewed English effort was supported by a
massive increase in supplies. Essex brought with him 120 lasts (approximately
240,000 pounds) of gunpowder, 21,000 suits of apparel and ready money for
three months.[22]

Essex set out towards Munster on 9 May 1599, where he got his first taste
of Irish warfare after relieving the fort at Maryborough. While marching south
Essex's army was attacked at the pass of Cashel on 17 May, but it was secured

13 Cahir castle was never mentioned as a key goal until Essex decided to attack it in May 1599.

with few losses. He continued into Munster where, after a short siege, he captured Cahir castle. At the start of June the army turned north-west and marched towards Limerick. Throughout this time, Essex's men were galled by the elusive Irish, who refused to leave the protection of their woods and bogs.[23] His relief mission to Askeaton on 9 June was attacked by Desmond at Rower Bog, just east of Adare. The Irish 'discharged into their eyes the fire and smoke of their black powder, and showers of balls from straightly-aimed guns'.[24] Two days later Essex's army was again engaged, this time at Finnertstown on the way to Croom. The earl gave few details of the attack, but O'Sullivan Beare reported that the fighting lasted from 'nine in the forenoon until five in the afternoon'.[25] The army marched south, arriving in Fermoy on 15 June. As supplies were beginning to run short, Essex turned the army towards Waterford, reaching Dungarvan by 20 June. His men spoiled the surrounding districts as they marched north through Wexford where the O'Byrnes skirmished with him near Arklow on 30 June.

The lord lieutenant returned to Dublin on 2 July; some felt that his Munster campaign had cost much but achieved little.[26] Over the course of his march, Essex acted contrary to his advice to others. Spoliation as a method to encourage submissions was not consistently implemented by Essex, even though it had been a goal at the start of the campaign. He encouraged the lord president of Munster, Sir Thomas Norreys, to burn all that could not be defended, but on his march through Munster, Essex restricted spoliation to encourage Irish defections. Sir John Brooke deemed this to be a mistake, writing that Essex's mild approach caused few men of note to submit.[27] Essex's warning to Norreys not to take submissions lightly ran contrary to his later acceptance of Lord Roche's, who reneged on his submission after Essex left Munster.[28] The submissions of Mountgarrett and Cahir were seen as inconsequential by Carew, who considered to have done little damage while in rebellion and were of little help to the state while loyal.[29] Matters were made worse for Essex as the queen shared these sentiments. In a highly critical letter, the queen reprimanded Essex for his squandering of time and resources, and his failure to prosecute Tyrone whom she deemed the focal point of the rebellion.[30] During Essex's journey through Munster and his ensuing sojourn in Dublin, military defeat and setback dogged the crown's efforts. News from the north indicated that an attempt by Sir Samuel Bagenal to move out of the safety of Newry was roughly handled.[31] Elsewhere, Sir Henry Harrington's men suffered a severe defeat at the hands of the O'Byrnes on 29 May.[32] The Philipstown garrison, which numbered almost 750 soldiers, was severely beaten with the loss of 50 men.[33] A fourth and more disastrous defeat occurred in Connacht during August.

Sir Conyers Clifford had been chief commissioner then president in Connacht since the start of 1597, and had made progress countering O'Donnell in northern Connacht. He was an able commander who understood that winning the war did not solely hinge on military success, but also regional alliances. Clifford was one of the few English officers at the time to realize that desertion could hurt an enemy far more than battle casualties. Demonstrating the queen's clemency could gain the loyalty of regional Irish leaders faster than English guns.[34] Despite his best efforts, much of what Clifford had gained unravelled after the destruction of Bagenal's army at the Yellow Ford in 1598. One of the few allies he had left in Connacht was Sir Donough O'Connor Sligo, but he was besieged within Collooney castle (Co. Sligo).

An army of 1,496 foot and 200 horse was gathered to break the siege and resupply O'Connor Sligo.[35] Clifford intended to march from Boyle through the Curlew Pass over two miles to the north, then on to Collooney. The horse and baggage were ordered to remain behind while the foot secured the pass.

14 The Curlew Pass today looking south-east

Clifford divided the army into three components; the van, the main battle and the rear. The van was led by Sir Alexander Radcliffe, who had substantial experience of fighting in the Low Countries. Lord Dunkellin commanded the battle, and Sir Arthur Savage led the rear. Pushing into the pass Clifford found it blocked by a 'barri[ca]do with double flanks'.[36] The defences were held by around 400 Irish shot, who fired into the advancing column, but quickly withdrew as the English closed on their position. Clifford opened a gap in the Irish defences and placed infantry on both flanks to ensure the road remained open, presumably for the horse and baggage to pass through once the road was secured.[37] The army pushed on to the crest of the hill where they discovered a broad bog at Bellaghboy on their left and woods on their right. O'Donnell's main force was not immediately on hand to stop them. He had placed his troops over two miles away at the wider of the two roads that crossed the Curlew Mountains. Therefore it was the MacSweeny and O'Gallagher shot who checked the English advance.[38] A protracted skirmish began between the

Irish and Radcliffe's regiment. Sir Henry Harrington claimed that the firefight lasted an hour-and-a-half.[39] The continual firing caused the English shot in the van to run low on ammunition, causing Radcliffe to prepare to charge the Irish, despite his being shot in the face. He was struck down by a bullet to his leg though, and when two of his men tried to drag him to safety, he died 'after being shot through the body with a bullet'.[40] The head of the column fell into disorder, and, as it wheeled about, the sudden arrival of fresh troops under Sir Brian O'Rourke precipitated a general rout of the van.[41]

The panic of the van spread to the main battle as both fell back. Clifford attempted to reform his men, but the collapse was complete as panic gripped the rear regiment. Nonetheless, Clifford tried to impose some order but was soon exhausted. Two of his Irish officers attempted to carry him to safety but Clifford refused to leave, and returning to the fray was killed by a pike thrust.[42] The English fugitives were hotly pursued by the Irish, but Sir Griffith Markham's cavalry held the Irish back long enough for most of the army to make it back to the relative safety of Boyle abbey, though this was at a cost. A gunshot broke Markham's arm and his troop lost seven or eight horsemen and 'several proper men'.[43] Markham's attack stalled the Irish pursuit, but O'Rourke rallied the Irish and forced the cavalry to follow the English infantry back to Boyle.[44] Clifford lay dead out in the pass with 240 of his men. When O'Rourke found Clifford's corpse, he cut off the head and sent it to O'Donnell.[45] Grisly as this seems, Clifford's mutilation served a practical purpose. O'Donnell marched to Collooney to demand O'Connor Sligo's surrender of the castle and his fealty. Both were promptly agreed to when O'Connor Sligo was presented Clifford's severed head.[46]

These defeats inflicted significant material losses but were also telling blows to the English soldiers' spirits; the disaster in the Curlews resulted in a near collapse of morale. Troops deserted in large numbers or made themselves sick to avoid service.[47] Clifford's death caused many formerly loyal Irish to side with Tyrone and O'Donnell. As chief commissioner in Connacht, Clifford had been generous with enticements to secure Irish allies. Gerrott Comerford related how Clifford had used 'fair means to draw to obedience the inhabitants thereof, but hath not only bestowed divers gifts and rewards upon them, but made captains of diverse of them'.[48] With Clifford now gone many Irish troops who had been trained and employed by him defected to the confederates, compounding the loss by reinforcing the Irish ranks, becoming what Comerford called 'the strongest strength they have against us'.[49] Essex sent orders to Lord Dunkellin and Sir Arthur Savage to make assurances with Irish lords dependent on Clifford's favour and money, that their needs would still be met by Essex. He was eager that O'Connor Sligo and Theobald Burke

(Tibbott-na-Long) would remain crown allies.[50] However, Essex's efforts were in vain. Burke and O'Connor Sligo, however unwillingly, submitted to O'Donnell within the month.[51] Rather than taking any remedial measures to reinforce the flagging morale of his troops, Essex removed the majority from the field by placing them in garrisons. He wrote disdainfully to Burke and Savage, ordering them to send men to Mullingar to guard the walls 'since they do so cowardly and basely in the field'.[52]

To compound matters, Essex received word that two of his most senior commanders in Munster had died. Sir Thomas Norreys had been appointed lord president of Munster in September 1597 after the death of his brother Sir John. Norreys was aided by his brother Henry, who had arrived in Ireland in 1595 as captain of one of the foot companies from Brittany and was later the lieutenant of the horse in Munster. Sir Thomas was wounded in the face in a skirmish near Kilmallock during June.[53] The Irish annals recorded that Norreys 'received a violent and venomous thrust of a pike where the jaw-bone joins the upper part of the neck'.[54] Grievously wounded he was carried back to Kilmallock. Several days later as Essex marched to relieve the ward at Askeaton, Sir Henry Norreys was shot in the leg, warranting its amputation.[55] The Norreys brothers survived the immediate effects of their injuries, but both succumbed to their wounds within days of each other in mid-August.[56]

The lord lieutenant finally made his advance towards Ulster at the end of August. Many of his officers believed that an attack into Ulster could serve no purpose. Moreover, the morale of the troops was at a low ebb after the defeat in Connacht. Without an amphibious landing on the Foyle, Tyrone and his allies could concentrate 6,000 troops to oppose Essex, who could muster at most 4,000 men, of which only 2,000 carried a firearm. If Essex did manage to place a garrison at the Blackwater or Armagh, it would only repeat the mistakes of previous deputies, whose efforts got bogged down in a cycle of fruitless resupply convoys.[57] However, pressure from England was such that Essex had to march north. Essex blustered in a letter to the privy council that 'if he [Tyrone] has as much courage as he pretendeth, we will on one side or the other end the war'.[58] Despite his apparent confidence (though a willingness to risk the outcome of the entire war on a single engagement should have been ringing alarm bells), Essex fretted over the safety of the Pale in his absence. Therefore he forbade any active prosecution of the war in Leinster while he was in the north.[59]

Essex left Dublin on 28 August, riding north to Ardbraccan, just outside Navan, Co. Meath. His field force of 3,200 foot and 360 horse assembled near Kells. The initial plan called for the army to capture and garrison Cavan town, but the danger of overland resupply persuaded Essex that Kells was more appropriate as a frontier garrison.[60] The army marched north into Louth, but the passes into Ulster had been fortified causing Essex to hesitate. Tyrone was nearby in force and Essex would not risk his men in an assault on Tyrone's fastness, noting that 'our army, being far less in strength, was not to attempt trenches and to fight upon such infinite disadvantage'; a strong garrison in Louth seemed a better solution.[61] An envoy from Tyrone arrived in the camp on 5 September requesting a parley. Essex refused, but let Tyrone know where he planned to deploy his forces the following day. With a degree of bombast not untypical of Essex, he challenged Tyrone to meet him in single combat 'where we will parlay in that fashion which best becometh soldiers'.[62] On 6 September, Essex marshalled his soldiers, but Tyrone would not be drawn into battle.[63] Tyrone asked for another meeting but not between two armies, adding that he could not be forced to fight or leave his defences. Again Essex refused, but on 7 September Tyrone sent word that he 'desired her majesties mercy'.[64] Possibly unable to resist the prospect of bringing the war to a conclusion without having to fight, Essex agreed and met Tyrone alone at the ford of Bellaclynthe. They talked for half-an-hour in private, and then each was joined by six senior officers. The next day a ceasefire was agreed. Though the initial cessation was just six weeks, it was expected to continue through to the start of May 1600.[65] Just like his predecessors (apart from Burgh), Essex had fallen for Tyrone's use of ceasefires and dissimulation to neutralize the crown's military strength.

The queen was highly critical of Essex's truce and the secretive nature of his meeting with Tyrone. Furthermore, she chastized Essex for his inaction and lack of progress against the Irish, and caustically suggested that Essex would never get round to winning the war as 'surely we must conclude that none of the four quarters of the year will be season enough for you'.[66] Essex had been beguiled by Tyrone's delaying tactics, as 'the same rebels held a like course with others that preceded you'.[67] However, the queen was more agitated by the secretive nature of Essex's first encounter with Tyrone, writing that 'far from mistrusting you with a traitor, yet both for comeliness, example, and your own discharge, we marvel you would carry it no better'.[68] She noted that Essex had only reported the duration of his first conference with Tyrone and not the detail of what passed between them. Tyrone later claimed that he had convinced Essex to join him against the queen, but Essex reneged on the agreement.[69] The queen was scathing of Essex's efforts, and added that after all the expense lavished on his campaign 'you do but piece up a hollow peace, and so in the end prove worse than the beginning'.[70] Disturbed by Elizabeth's tone and fearful of the interference of her advisors in court, Essex sailed for England on 24 September, leaving the government of Ireland in the hands of the Irish council. Essex never returned as an abortive coup led to his execution in February 1601.

The failure of English leadership

If Essex had a clear idea of what needed to be done and was in command of the largest English army deployed during the war, why did he fail to make headway against Tyrone and his allies? Before embarking on his first campaign in Ireland, Essex rid himself of some of his best and most experienced field officers. He cashiered many of the colonels and captains of the army defeated at the Blackwater the previous year. Among those dismissed was Captain Richard Cuney, who had seen extensive service since 1595 and had played a major role during the battle of Clontibret in 1595. Veteran officers from the Brittany companies were discharged, such as Captain Lancelot Alford and Sir Thomas Maria Wingfield. Wingfield was Bagenal's second-in-command at the Blackwater and was largely responsible for saving half the queen's field army from destruction. Essex looked with disfavour upon those whom he saw as having failed in the queen's service; few received commands in his army.[71] Writing many years after the war, John Pooley recorded how Essex summoned the Yellow Ford captains, 'reproved them very sharply', then cashiered their companies.[72] This was borne out in a book of cheques for the armed forces in Ireland covering Essex's tenure, in which scores of officers were recorded as being discharged, including almost all the Blackwater captains.[73] Sir James Perrot suggested that Essex may have used this as an excuse to select officers from his entourage newly arrived out of England, though Perrot could not be sure whether this was the truth, or simply the grumblings of the aggrieved captains.[74]

Essex lacked confidence in the forces at his disposal. He was disdainful of the fighting abilities of the field army under his command, and the usefulness of the garrison troops in keeping order or suppressing the rebellion in the areas in which they were quartered. During the relief of Askeaton, Essex reproached his troops when they displayed timidity in the face of the enemy.[75] In a letter to the privy council on 14 August, he described the troops in garrisons as his 'degenerate countrymen' who feigned sickness to excuse service.[76] Essex's remedy for the cowardice of the army was that 'these base clowns must be taught to fight again'.[77] Though highly critical of his troops' abilities, Essex took no positive steps to improve their efficiency. This lack of faith in his men was compounded by subsequent military failures.

Those intent on rehabilitating Essex's reputation in Ireland have relied upon several claims and assumptions to explain or excuse his strategic decisions. Some have suggested that the council in England had hobbled Essex's army.[78] Though underprovided in carriage horses and shipping, Essex's march south secured Munster from invasion.[79] It has been suggested that the perilous condition of the provinces other than Ulster, and the fear of Spanish landing constrained Essex to secure his southern provinces first.[80] Also, he captured the 'very important' Cahir castle, which was deemed imperative for operations west of the river Suir.[81]

With regards to the safeguarding of Munster, a Spanish landing had been threatened almost every year since the war began. It is not clear how Essex's progression through part of the province secured the vulnerable southern coasts. While the taking of a castle can be viewed as progress on a small scale, the importance of Cahir castle and its capture was never mentioned as a vital military goal until Essex chose to attack it, and its subsequent loss in May 1600 did little to inhibit Sir George Carew's operations from 1600 onwards. Essex's complaints about shortages were nothing new to Irish viceroys, but his reported lack of carriage horses was puzzling. During his passage through Munster, Essex came within 10 miles of Lord Barry's estate, from which early the next year, Tyrone stole 3,000 garrans and mares.[82] Even if Barry's loss was an overstatement, this still does not suggest a province deficient in horses.

Essex's march to the north requires some further consideration. Was it possible that a negotiated cessation was the only sensible course of action for Essex? A military defeat would leave the Pale open to attack, and a truce provided security for the harvest and newly planted crops.[83] This notion ignored the fact that Tyrone's forces had always benefitted from cessations in the past, using the time to refit and resupply units.[84] The security for the farmers of the northern Pale was illusory. Tyrone needed agricultural production to continue unimpeded as he required a sustainable resource to provide supplies. Less than a month after Essex departed, Tyrone boasted to Sir William Warren that winter 'was the time of his harvest' when he would exact his due from the country.[85] By the beginning of December, Warren reported to Cecil that 'they have all the goods of the kingdom, and do encroach upon us daily'.[86]

Essex's fear of leaving the Pale exposed in the event of a military defeat was another excuse for inaction. Tyrone already had freedom of movement and was effectively taxing the local population. Sir Richard Bingham reported the previous year that the rural population did not fear or run from the Irish anymore and that the rebels were not burning the harvest but turning it to their use.[87] The northern Pale was already effectively under Tyrone's control. Even if Essex was ignorant of the extent of confederate power beyond Ulster, he had the example of the disaster on the Blackwater in 1598 to inform him.

The destruction of the crown's main force in Ireland did not result in a general advance into the Pale, despite the fact that those who escaped the rout were unarmed and unfit for immediate service.[88]

When Essex was faced with defeat on several fronts, rather than address his lack of confidence in his soldiers, he dissipated the strength of the field army. Possibly influenced by his doubts about the army, Essex placed almost three-quarters of his available troops in garrisons or positions of strength, and he advised the lord president of Munster to station men at all the walled towns in the province.[89] Essex was sure that garrisons could achieve victory over the Irish, but he did not appear to have a coherent plan for where to place them or what to do with them once they were there.[90] Many garrisons could not venture far from their defences without danger of attack, but Essex's only remedy was to place ever larger numbers within their walls. He described the inaction of the Philipstown garrison as having 'laid still like drones without doing service'.[91] Rather than attempt to devise an alternative plan, Essex opted to add even more troops to the ward at the end of July. Bereft of any coherent plan, Essex simply made excuses for his lack of success.

Essex was quick to apportion blame to those around him in the event of military failure or limited progress. In situations where he expected criticism of his decisions or on receipt of the news of military defeats for which he, as overall commander, was ultimately responsible, Essex made sure to find fault with others. Before he had even arrived in Dublin after the Munster campaign, Essex wrote how he had been failed by 'a weak and insufficient council'.[92] Sir Warham St Leger and the earl of Ormond were blamed for Essex's decision to start his campaign with an expedition into Munster. Both men had estates that could be secured by the march south, so self-interest was a distinct possibility, but Essex was lord lieutenant, and he could not avoid responsibility for his decision-making. On his return to England, Essex pointed the finger of blame at everyone but himself. Queen Elizabeth recounted to the Irish council how Essex blamed his procrastination with Tyrone on the contestation and dissuasion of his council.[93] Military defeat was ascribed to the cowardice of the troops and incompetence of their officers.[94] According to Essex, the failure of his planted garrisons was due to their inaction and irresolution in dealing with the Irish. He made an ostentatious and dramatic example of troops he regarded as weak or failing in their duty. After the defeat of Sir Henry Harrington's men in Wicklow, Essex decimated an infantry company and had their officer executed. Though punishment in the Elizabethan armies could be severe, a report by one of Cecil's spies, William Udall, considered this to be excessively harsh.[95]

Essex sought to apportion blame for the failure of the campaign to everyone but himself. His unwillingness to accept responsibility may be due to a crippling fear of failure. Five key traits have been ascribed to those with an underlying inferiority which leads to a fear of failure while in positions of leadership.[96] These are: a dependence upon social approval and corresponding hyper-sensitivity to criticism; a tendency to disclaim responsibility for failed actions and a likelihood to seek scapegoats from their subordinates; procrastination and a tendency to avoid failure by not really trying, or engaging in an endeavour under such difficult circumstances or conditions that no disgrace could be attached to that failure; propensity to quickly abandon or distance themselves from a difficult project at the first opportunity.[97] Essex at some point during his tenure as lord lieutenant displayed all of these characteristics.

Essex was deeply troubled by the queen's scathing criticism of his efforts and the disparagement of him in court circles. In response, Essex blamed his council for strategic decisions and his troops for military failure. Essex delayed attacking into the north and then engaged in displacement activity by personally leading the revictualling of the forts in Offaly and Laois. The queen strongly reprimanded Essex for this, noting that more junior officers could have performed the task.[98] When he finally moved towards Ulster, Essex had dispersed so much of his field army to garrison duties that he no longer had an effective force to encounter Tyrone, thereby creating his impossible task.[99] Finally, when Essex agreed to the truce with Tyrone, he promptly abandoned his position and left for England. Under this type of commander, even the massive escalation in troops and resources provided by the crown had little chance of success.

The weakness of English arms in Ireland

It is perhaps unreasonable to heap all the failures of 1599 onto the shoulders of Essex. Armies under Bagenal, Russell, Norreys and Burgh had all proved incapable of successfully engaging with Tyrone's men. This was due mainly to fundamental flaws in their operational plans, field tactics and their soldier's personal equipment. All of this was compounded by many senior officers' failure to realize that the confederates under Tyrone were nothing like any Irish force previously encountered by the crown.

One of the fundamental tactical and operational issues with which English commanders had to contend was the Irish infantry's superior mobility. Tyrone's troops could march faster than English units, and traverse rough terrain. There were some knowledgeable English officers with significant experience fighting the Irish. Sir Henry Duke and Captain John Dowdall fought effective low-intensity campaigns in the southern Ulster borderlands in 1594, and Captain Thomas Lee called for adaptation by the English armies to maximize their effectiveness against the Irish. He recommended surprise attacks primarily at night, shot mounted on horses for superior mobility and the use of Irish clothes, such as mantles and brogues, as they were better suited to war in Ireland than English clothing.[100] Unfortunately for the establishment, men like Lee did not have enough influence to decide how the war was fought. Therefore throughout the conflict lessons from the past had to be painfully re-learned.

With war escalating from 1593, English military expeditions repeatedly demonstrated their inability to march at speed or fight away from roads or trackways. At the Ford of the Biscuits (1594), Crossdall, Clontibret, Mullabrack (1595) and Wicklow (1599), the English army remained anchored to the perceived safety of the roads. In the *Dialogue of Silvynne and Peregrynne*, the author considered that the Irish were well aware of this limitation and commonly fought where bogs or woods provided a safe avenue for their retreat.[101] In 1598, the muster master Sir Ralph Lane was concerned about the poor performance of English troops in Ireland. Principally, he was worried about their lack of martial skill in engagements at bogs and passes.[102]

As armies grew, the impedimenta associated with them increased. The accompanying 'tail', comprising women, children, servants and sutlers, could grow to 50 or 150 per cent of the size of the actual fighting force.[103] This number could be an underestimate for the English foot companies in Ireland. Sir Henry Wallop reported that when Captain Humphrey Willis was sheriff in Fermanagh in 1593, his 100 troops were accompanied by 160 'women and boys'.[104] In 1598, a foot company in the Pale was described. Each soldier had with him 'a boy at least, and for a great p[ar]t their women, and many horses ... to carry them their children and women'.[105] During his campaign in Munster, Essex reported that his forces were unable to pursue the Irish into the Glen of Aherlow as they were 'so pestered with carriages'.[106] The accretion of baggage and hangers-on severely inhibited the army's ability to respond to attacks.[107] This burden of civilian dependants was not uncommon as armies in Europe were similarly encumbered, but against Tyrone's lighter forces it could prove fatal.

English mobility was further reduced if the officer in command had the poor sense to bring artillery. Transport infrastructure in Ireland was primitive; roads were little more than dirt tracks. The passage of troops and the decidedly inclement weather meant that these tracks could quickly transform into quagmires where heavy guns became more of a hindrance than a help. Bagenal's ill-fated advance to the Blackwater in 1598 featured three light guns (falcons) and a saker, which weighed upwards of 2,500–3,000 pounds and was drawn by six oxen. It repeatedly got stuck in the soft ground. Bagenal was forced to stop his advance to extract the gun, causing a gap to develop between Bagenal and the lead regiment. Tyrone took advantage of this, isolating and overthrowing the first regiment. If the composition of the armies on the march greatly weakened their ability to operate, then changes had to be made if they were to succeed against the Irish. Additionally, the equipment of the English forces severely limited their mobility.

Essex opined that his men were too slow to engage the Irish effectively. He noted that 'we shall be able to do little upon them with our heavy footmen, unless we had as light knaves as themselves to follow them'.[108] Some of Essex's men were continental veterans and trained in the most modern military techniques developed by Maurice of Nassau, but new firing methods could not help the English soldier win against the Irish if he was too slow to catch them or was exhausted by burdensome equipment if he did.[109] The personal equipment issued to the English forces was just too heavy, disabling them against the more nimble Irish. Though powerful, muskets were heavy and slow to fire and reload. These were significant disadvantages in warfare where close-range firepower and ease of handling was more important than range and the ability to penetrate armour. Contemporary writers reported that muskets were better for disrupting horsemen and infantry, whereas lighter weapons were more suitable for skirmishing.[110] This problem soon became apparent to officers serving in Ireland. Sir Thomas Norreys complained that reinforcements sent from England were 'overburdened' by heavy muskets.[111] Captain Dowdall considered muskets only fit to defend towns and were not suitable 'to answer so light services … besides the charge of powder and lead, together with the weight of the musket, doth clog and weary the bearer'.[112] Nonetheless, muskets were supplied, and the crown troops were obliged to fight with the arms they were given. Pikemen fared no better than the musketeers as they too were burdened with superfluous equipment. Their weapon weighed up to twelve pounds; to this was added twenty-five to thirty pounds of armour, which did not get much use.[113] The Irish rarely, if ever, came to hand blows unless their enemies were starting to rout, in which case the carrying of heavy armour could become a lethal encumbrance. When contrasted with their Irish opponents, who at most wore a helmet for protection, it is unsurprising that from 1593–1600 English troops rarely held the tactical initiative in combat.

Though it is evident their arms and equipment handicapped the soldiers deployed by the crown, they were catastrophically failed by the arrogance and short-sightedness of those in command. At the strategic and operational level, the queen (and ultimately the foot-soldiers as they paid the price with their blood) was failed by many of her senior officers during the early and mid-phases of the war. Experience from previous conflicts in Ireland had demonstrated that the best way to counter the swiftness of the Irish infantry was firepower, mobility and well-placed garrisons.[114] Every time a new viceroy was appointed these lessons appeared to be forgotten. Modernized Irish forces had been first encountered in Ireland in 1589 and a pike and shot-equipped force had routed Sir Henry Duke's supply column at the battle of the Ford of the Biscuits in August 1594. Therefore would it not be expected that the same Irish adversaries would use the same successful tactics against the crown forces the next time they met? Apparently not. After the battle of Clontibret in May 1595, Lord Deputy William Russell expressed surprise at the modernized equipment and training of the Irish.[115] As late as 1599, English officers were still astonished at the sophistication of their Irish enemies. Robert Osborne, who was part of the reinforcements sent with the earl of Essex in 1599, wrote that 'in England they say they be but naked rogues, but we find them as good men as those which are sent us, and better'.[116]

For much of the war, the English efforts to suppress Tyrone and his allies were debilitated by their inability to recognize that Tyrone's soldiers were not the axe-wielding gallowglass of the type deployed by Shane O'Neill thirty years previous. Russell's arrogance before the battle of Clontibret in 1595 almost cost Bagenal and his men their lives, as he believed the army would overawe the Irish. Writing after the war, Captain John Pooley believed that repeated English defeats at the hands of the Irish were attributable to the English officers' failure to recognize that their Irish adversaries had modernized their troops and tactics.[117]

English conceit was echoed at strategic and operational levels of the crown war effort, where campaigns tended to be blunt and unsophisticated applications of military power. Before 1600, almost all English plans required troops to be concentrated, followed by a march into Irish territory to force an engagement, revictual/relieve a garrison, or establish a fort. However, the Irish neutralized English expeditions by avoiding contact, skirmishing along the English flanks until the column broke contact, or used dissimulation and false truces until shortages forced the English to retreat. Tyrone also constructed fixed defences. Lord Deputy Burgh's advance into Tyrone in 1597, Essex's foray into the Ulster borderlands and Mountjoy's 1601 campaign were all stopped in their tracks by Irish fortifications.[118]

The crown was also cursed with an unhelpful intransigence when defending or maintaining fixed positions. Tyrone quickly recognized and exploited this stubbornness. He used the predictability of the English reaction to besieged or blockaded English garrisons to lure forces into traps, and more significantly draw troops out of regions where Tyrone sought to raid and/or coerce others into joining him in the war. In 1594, Tyrone fixated English attention on his blockade of the Enniskillen garrison in east Ulster; meanwhile, he extended his political domination over the crown's Irish allies in west Ulster. The following year English attention was focused on relieving and resupplying the forts in Monaghan and Armagh. Meanwhile, troops under Tyrone's ally, Hugh Roe O'Donnell, rampaged through Connacht unopposed.[119] The ultimate expression of the dogmatic approach to fixed positions was the disaster at the battle of the Yellow Ford in August 1598. Sir Henry Bagenal disregarded the threat from Tyrone's forces, and marched his regiments into terrain that had been pre-prepared by Tyrone with spiked pits and barricades to canalize and restrict movement; unsurprisingly, disaster for the crown (and Bagenal) was the result.

Tyrone's confederation: command, control and coercion

To be fair to the crown and the English military, the defeats inflicted upon them, and the near-loss of all of Ireland, cannot be attributed solely to their failings. Tyrone's reforms and sophisticated strategy had a profound effect, but his military power needed direction and control. Therefore Tyrone created a network of political and military alliances across Ireland. This was not easily done, as Ireland's native polity was a patchwork of lordships riven with rivalry, faction and self-interest. To bring about a confederation of disparate Irish lords that were responsive to his will, Tyrone used a combination of persuasion, bribery, threats and punitive action. The result was an unprecedented alliance of Irish, Scots and some Old English lords that stretched from the north coast of Antrim to the rocky inlets of Cork and Kerry.

Even in Ulster where Tyrone was strongest, many Irish lords sided with the crown in the early stages of the war. Consequently, the crown's allies in Ulster were repeatedly spoiled or bonnaghts placed in their lands until they agreed to side with Tyrone. Failure to submit could result in ejection from their territory or assassination, as happened to Phelim MacTurlough O'Neill and Ever MacRory Magennis.[120] While many Irish lords joined Tyrone's confederacy, there were others who refused to abandon the crown regardless of enticement or intimidation. Where repeated raiding and attacks made some Irish nobles resign themselves to the realities of the earl's primacy, such as Connor Roe Maguire and Niall MacBrian Fertagh O'Neill (who later defected at the first opportunity), others steadfastly refused to betray the crown. Perhaps the best examples of this were two of the most important lords in Connacht, Ulick Burke, third earl of Clanricard, and Donough O'Brien, fourth earl of Thomond. Both had accrued substantial financial benefits from the composition agreements in Connacht in 1585. Therefore maintaining the status quo of English rule was very much in their interests.[121] O'Donnell assailed Clanricard's territory in January 1597, but despite sustaining significant losses Clanricard stayed loyal to the crown.[122] His son Richard Burke, Lord Dunkellin, also remained loyal and commanded an infantry regiment at the battle of the Curlew Pass in August 1599.[123] Thomond led companies of English foot and horse throughout the war and held a colonelcy in Essex's army in 1599. His lands in Co. Clare were raided in 1599 and 1600 but there is nothing to suggest Thomond's loyalty to the crown ever wavered. Having been raised a Protestant in the English court, he may have found himself isolated from Irish society in Connacht.[124] In O'Sullivan Beare's account of Irish chiefs who remained loyal to the queen, Thomond is not even listed, suggesting he may not have been viewed as Irish by some of his Gaelic contemporaries.[125]

Military strength was used to underpin leadership bids of Tyrone's new allies, such as Philip O'Reilly in Cavan and Glasney MacAgholy Magennis in Iveagh.[126] During O'Donnell's raids in 1595, he raised to power Tadhg O'Dowd, O'Hara Reagh, the 'MacDonagh' of Tirrerrill and the 'MacDermott' of Moylurg.[127] Undecided lords could be influenced by threats to support alternative claimants to their titles. In 1596, O'Donnell sent a letter to Donough O'Connor Sligo, promising both great rewards and dire consequences, including proclaiming another to be the 'O'Connor Sligo' if he did not accept his proposals.[128] The momentum generated by military success precipitated numerous unsolicited alliances, especially in Munster, where many seceded from government rule to secure their patrimony with Tyrone's help. Sponsorship by the confederate leaders was not without its price. In addition to entering into rebellion, many of Tyrone's allies were obliged to provide hostages as a guarantee of their loyalty. Though James MacSorley MacDonnell received troops from Tyrone and had arranged to marry one of his daughters, he was still required to present pledges as a surety for his good behaviour.[129]

Defection to the crown could bring dire consequences for pledges in Irish hands. After O'Connor Don and Connor Óg MacDermot sided with Sir Conyers Clifford, O'Donnell executed O'Connor's and MacDermot's pledges, one of whom was MacDermot's only son.[130] Where direct action was not preferred, acts of dynastic dirty work could be used to bring errant followers back into the fold. For example, to win back Brian O'Rourke from Clifford, O'Donnell captured his rival to the chieftaincy, Tadhg O'Rourke, and offered to hand him over to Brian in return for his renewed loyalty.[131]

Switching sides did not preclude the possibility of reconciliation. When Turlough MacHenry O'Neill of the Fews deserted to the English during May

1597, he was warmly welcomed by the Dublin authorities. After being given command of a foot company and some horse, he proved invaluable during Burgh's summer expedition to the Blackwater, both as a guide and in providing men for a daring commando-style raid on Dungannon.[132] Five months later he was back under Tyrone's command, but his loyalty remained in question, and Tyrone imprisoned him from April to November 1598. After his release, Turlough MacHenry returned to his prominent role fighting for Tyrone along the northern borders of the Pale.[133]

Disloyalty did not always incur retaliatory action. Some of Tyrone's regional allies were important enough for a negotiated reconciliation. As noted above, Brian O'Rourke had defected to Sir Conyers Clifford at the start of 1598.[134] The reason suggested for this was an offence caused to O'Rourke, brought about by O'Donnell's spoiling O'Connor Roe against O'Rourke's wishes.[135] O'Donnell was disinclined to attack O'Rourke (despite O'Rourke affiliating himself with Clifford) because O'Rourke was a relative. He tried persuasion, then threats to get O'Rourke to return to the fold. Ultimately, O'Donnell was satisfied with submission and mutual vows of fidelity rather than punitive attacks and plundering.[136] A softer more diplomatic approach with O'Rourke paid dividends; he re-joined Tyrone's confederation within six months.[137]

Once the allegiance of a regional chief was secured, the northern leaders enhanced the military strength of their new allies. It was vital that they were powerful enough to be capable of successful military engagement with the English, but an act of rebellion did not transform their local kerne and gallowglass into the modern formations deployed by Tyrone. Therefore most, if not all, Tyrone's southern allies received military aid from the north. Maguire was able to make his first open acts of rebellion only after being reinforced by shot and pike from Tyrone in 1593. As the war spread, Feagh MacHugh O'Byrne received military advisors to re-train his men in modern fighting methods, and later received reinforcements of shot.[138] Tyrone provided Philip O'Reilly 300 shot in 1597, and James MacSorley MacDonnell was reinforced with 'borrowed shot' from Tyrone in November 1597, just before he routed Sir John Chichester's companies outside Carrickfergus.[139]

The troops sent by Tyrone were accompanied by experienced and trusted officers, whose presence ensured that the Ulster troops would be used in accordance with Tyrone's wishes. Captain Tyrrell was sent south several times to work with the O'Mores and O'Byrnes, then into Munster to train the *sugán* earl of Desmond's new recruits after the success of the rebellion there. Tyrrell, however, took his orders from Tyrone, not the Munster lords. In *Dialogue of Silvynne and Peregrynne*, Collier noted that Tyrrell obeyed his master's [Tyrone] orders, a quality many English officers should learn.[140] This arrangement appears to have allowed Tyrone to direct widely dispersed forces. This discipline was alluded to by Phelim MacHugh O'Byrne when he stated that 'without Tyrone's consent he could not grow to any peace, because he had his forces from him, and was sworn to follow his advice'.[141] Willingness to adhere to Tyrone's orders contrasted starkly with the actions of rebel officers during the second Desmond rebellion (1579–83), when Irish leaders made their own decisions and joined or left the Desmond confederacy as and when it suited them.[142]

At the start of the revolt in Munster, calls for a peremptory attack on Ormond and Norreys' army were rejected. On 11 November 1598, the main body of the Irish forces in Munster, which included the *sugán* earl of Desmond, Owny O'More and Captain Tyrrell, numbering almost 1,200 men, were near the army of the lord general and lord president.[143] As the English force approached, there were some in the Irish camp eager to fight. They were overruled and reminded of Tyrone's standing orders not to fight unless it was 'to skirmish in straits and fastnesses'.[144] Consequently, the Irish retired to the safety of a nearby wood. The *sugán* earl of Desmond may have had authority in Munster, but probably due to the presence of Tyrrell and Morgan Kavanagh, it was Tyrone's tactical decrees that prevailed.

A significant event in the Munster revolt was the conferring of the earldom of Desmond on James Fitzthomas by Tyrone. In a letter to Ormond, Desmond claimed that he was forced into rebellion due to poor treatment by the crown concerning his inheritance. Furthermore, Fitzthomas alleged that while he had been denied a hearing to settle his title to the house of Desmond, undertakers from England were actively pursuing plans to disinherit or even have him killed 'under colour of law'. Sir Thomas Norreys believed that it was initially pure ambition that drove Fitzthomas to join Tyrone.[145] This becomes more plausible when we see that Fitzthomas hesitated to side with the Irish confederates, but quickly opted to join Tyrone when his brother John was suggested as an alternative successor to the title.[146] Norreys noted that as time passed, the religious aspect of the Munster revolt became more apparent with the entry of priests into the province citing the authority of the pope to rouse rebellion.[147] The *sugán* earl of Desmond's letter to Philip III of Spain was laden with religious analogy, but Philip O'Sullivan Beare stated that the foremost issues that caused the Munster lords to rebel was the insecurity of their patrimonies and a lack of confidence in the Dublin authorities' impartiality. Religion was mentioned as a factor but only as part of general grounds for the revolt, which also included personal grievances.[148]

Religion may have played a small part in motivating the native Irish lords to fight for Tyrone. Religious overtones were absent when attempts were made to win over Irish lords in Connacht and Ulster. When O'Donnell tried to convince O'Connor Sligo to turn against the crown, he offered to cancel O'Connor's debts and provide him with 400 troops.[149] O'Donnell followed this with threats to support another claimant as the 'O'Connor Sligo' but at no point did he cite religion as a reason to change sides. Tyrone only began to reference religious motivations in his demands of the crown at the start of 1596.[150] After rejecting the crown's peace offers, the Ulster leaders sent letters and messengers into Munster during the summer of 1596 to incite dissent based on religious grounds.[151] An unsigned letter, allegedly to or from Desmond, called for soldiers who will fight for 'his faith, his church, his altars, his sacrament and his true religion'.[152] Tyrone began utilizing a 'faith and fatherland' ideology as his forces threatened the Pale.[153] The fatherland element promoted a love of country or native land over cultural or racial identity, and was used by Tyrone to substitute narrow concerns of lordships with patriotism.[154] Moreover, it was hoped that this would bridge the ethnic divide between the native Irish and the Old English Catholics.[155]

Tyrone's relationship with the Old English was complex and proved crucial in the conduct and outcome of the war. For several decades, fractures had appeared between the Old English and the New English-born servitors and government officials. The New English distrusted the other's retention of their Catholicism, linking political dissidence to recusancy. Though continuing to claim loyalty to the queen, many viewed their devotion to the unreformed religion as proof of their unfitness for office.[156] Tyrone used a combination of incentives and threats in an attempt to persuade Catholic Palesmen to join his confederacy. The earl's twenty-two articles passed to the crown in 1599 held many temporal advantages for the Old English, but in the same month Tyrone released a proclamation rebuking Old English Catholics for their inaction against the alleged heresy of the queen.[157] This was probably explained by the increasing prominence of freedom of conscience in the Old English political agenda from the 1580s onwards.[158] Tyrone attempted to exploit their insecurities over religion, and political exclusion by New English Protestant interlopers, by way of nationalist rhetoric.[159]

In and around the Pale, the Old English were active for both the confederate and government causes. Some members of the marcher families, such as the Plunketts and Nugents, joined Tyrone and most famously Captain Richard Tyrrell. Throughout the war, Tyrrell consistently proved himself one of Tyrone's best officers. He had been arrested and imprisoned on 12 September 1596 on the grounds of treason, but after being released on bond he absconded into Ulster and was soon in the pay of Tyrone.[160] When Tyrone wrote to Sir James Fitzpiers, the sheriff of Kildare, he used a range of arguments to convince him to switch sides. Religious references were made throughout his letter, but Tyrone did not depend upon them to alter Fitzpiers' allegiance. Tyrone attempted to pique some level of national sentiment and raised the crown's extra-legal threats against Old English estates. Furthermore, the earl did not forget to deploy the usual threats of despoilment and destruction of Fitzpiers' goods if he did not make his decision in Tyrone's favour.[161] He did eventually join the Irish confederates, but it is not clear if it was Tyrone's letter or Fitzpiers' ill-favour in Dublin that finally caused him to rebel.[162]

There were many in the Pale and its outlying districts that were actively loyal to the crown and prosecuted the war to the best of their ability. Despite misgivings about the loyalty of the Old English Catholics, the crown was forced to rely on them to defend the Pale when the government's field army was conducting operations against Tyrone and his confederates.[163] Palesmen were used for border defence during Russell's foray into Wicklow in February 1595. Lords such as Baron Delvin and Lord Gormanstown were active in the assembling of local forces.[164] However, the effectiveness of the rising out in securing the borderlands is questionable in light of the widespread spoiling perpetrated by Tyrone and his allies.[165] Regardless of their worth as a military force, the rising out represented the only practical way to defend the Pale while crown forces were otherwise engaged and for much of the war they were the mainstay of its defence.[166]

For the most part, the prevailing attitude of the Old English appeared to be one of accommodating impartiality. Their passivity or unwillingness to enthusiastically support the efforts of the crown appeared early in the war. A report claimed the Palesmen's failure to provide sufficient garrans for the carriage of army supplies critically undermined operations in Ulster during 1595.[167] Fenton advertised this weakness to Burghley, when he wrote of the Pale that 'the heart and inward parts [are] weary of their heavy burdens, men's minds are stirred, and the whole state of the realm disquieted'.[168] Hugh Collier gave some idea of the response to raiding in the midlands when he recorded that many of those who would have been expected to serve in the rising out failed to appear. Terming them 'dissembling hypocrites', Collier later noted that raiding parties could pass unhindered as no-one would help neighbours in need or feel obliged to act, despite being 'bound by their tenures'.[169] Collier blamed the intermingling of the native Irish and the Old English, whereby alliances created by marriage, fosterage and gossiprid contradicted their service to the state and led to their complicity in the rebellion.[170]

Fears over loyalties compromised by marriage would have been reinforced by the loss of the abbey at Athy. The constable and fourteen warders, all of whom were English, defected to the Irish in November 1598. Sir Richard

Bingham suggested it was because the constable was married into the O'Mores and it was by this that he was 'drawn to be a villain'.[171] Doubts over the loyalty of the Catholic Palesmen persisted through 1598. Wallop suggested these were due to the underlying question of religion, repeated spoiling by the rebels and the crushing burden of maintaining ever-increasing numbers of crown troops.[172] In 1598, Sir Richard Bingham remarked that in Kildare and its surrounding districts, most people stood by waiting to see which side would become dominant before choosing whom to support.[173] This observation echoed reports from the previous year where it was noted that the Old English were unlikely to join Tyrone but preferred to remain neutral.[174] Ultimately, the majority of the Palesmen could not be won over by Tyrone's appeals to them on ideological and religious terms. The Old English did not believe that Tyrone and his adherents could be trusted as leaders in the new Catholic Ireland which they purported to seek.[175]

The Irish economy and military supplies

The Irish dependence upon cattle farming is an issue that recurs throughout descriptions of the Irish economy at the end of the sixteenth century. Characteristic of this are the nomadic creaghts, herds of cattle that embodied the material wealth of individual Irish chiefs. Contemporary English commentators recounted how Irish agriculture relied upon cattle and had not developed arable farming, but in Ulster and elsewhere, the foundation of the economy was crops as well as livestock.[176] Tyrone relied on corn as much as cattle to maintain the war. Mountjoy noted that the abundance of crops in Armagh in 1602 could have enabled Tyrone to hire more bonnaghts and even to feed the troops of a Spanish landing.[177] Fynes Moryson observed that the corn crop was the only means by which the rebels in Laois paid their bonnaghts, and Mountjoy claimed to have destroyed £10,000 worth in one expedition into the midlands.[178]

The importance of crops to the Irish confederates can be gauged by their efforts to ensure the harvest was successfully gathered. Tyrone gave leave to some of his men in 1599 to return home to bring in their crops, and O'Donnell concentrated his forces around the English garrison in Lifford during 1600 to safeguard the harvest.[179] When Tyrone and O'Donnell's allies were threatened by Docwra's forces operating out of Derry and Dunnalong in 1601, Tyrone advised feigning submission if it could save crops from destruction.[180] During his assault into Ulster in 1601, Mountjoy identified the corn harvest as the primary means for the Irish to continue the war. He opined that if they had not destroyed the corn found in Ulster, Tyrone would have been able to pay for a much greater number of soldiers and make good his losses caused by Mountjoy's campaigns.[181]

The cultivation of crops was widespread in Ireland at the end of the sixteenth century.[182] Tyrone had spent the years before the war developing a system of demesne agriculture, which greatly increased the profitability of the territory under his control.[183] Peter Lombard referred to this when he wrote that agricultural output had increased in Ulster, and that after the war had started Tyrone fortified Ulster's southern borders to enable even greater improvements in productivity.[184] Pictorial evidence of the level of cultivation can be found in the illustration of the battle of the Yellow Ford in 1598. While the attention of the observer is drawn to the dramatic events of the battle, large tracts of land in the centre of the action and on the periphery were shown as enclosed fields and annotated with a 'H' and recorded as cornfields in the legend.[185] English commentators were often surprised at the extent and productiveness of native arable agriculture. While destroying crops in Laois, Mountjoy was amazed at the enclosed fields and beaten roads, while Docwra was astonished at the high crop yields near Coleraine.[186] The collapse of crown control in most parts of Ireland seemed to have no detrimental impact on the productivity of the countryside. By September 1599, the war had been ongoing for six years, and government authority was now limited to fortified towns, garrisons and the immediate locales. Despite this, it was reported that corn was so abundant that troops of the garrisons wanted to be paid in coin rather than food from the government stores, due to the low price of locally sourced commodities.[187]

Agricultural production was the main source of the wealth that financed the Irish war effort. The staple exports were bulk foodstuffs, cloth and raw materials such as hides and tallow, while manufactured and finished goods were imported in return.[188] This may have been true for much of Ireland, but evidence of an embryonic manufacturing capability appeared in Ulster at the start of the war. The two items concerned were firearms and gunpowder. In August 1596, firearms, specifically calivers and pistols, were reportedly made in Dungannon.[189] James Nott expanded upon this the following year when he added that the earl had three gunsmiths sent by Alexander Stewart of Glasgow.[190] This represented a considerable outlay in money for Tyrone, as he would have had to provide suitable facilities for forging metal, crafting wooden stocks, and the proofing and finishing of barrels and locks. There is evidence of Tyrone's efforts to make arms in a letter of advice written for the *sugán* earl of Desmond. It recommended that Desmond set up a centre for making arms 'as O'Neill does at Dungannon'.[191] While the manufacture of firearms in Dungannon could never hope to meet Tyrone's need for thousands of weapons, it does suggest that the Irish leadership were keen to establish centres for manufacturing finished goods; one product was gunpowder.

The Irish capability to produce gunpowder should not be mistaken for the simple mixing processes that were used to create serpentine or meal powder in the early years of gunpowder production in Europe. Late sixteenth-century firearms used gunpowder that had been ground, formed into cakes and then forced through sieves of a specific fineness to produce corned powder.[192] Gunpowder was composed of three constituent parts: potassium nitrate (75%), carbon (15%) and sulphur (10%). The carbon could easily be supplied in the form of charcoal, and the relatively small amount of sulphur needed must have been imported. The potassium nitrate, or saltpetre as it was known, could be found in old dung heaps, stable floors and privies, and is a product of the action of urine on soil.[193] Writing in the early seventeenth century, Lombard wrote that the Irish had learned to make gunpowder.[194] During the opening stages of the war, there were references to Tyrone developing a nascent powder industry.[195] Tyrone would have been unlikely to attempt gunpowder production lightly, as such a move would demand a serious commitment of resources to gather the ingredients and incorporate them into the finished powder.

The cost would have been substantial as the equipment required for grinding, stamping and corning would have had to been fabricated or imported. The quantity of saltpetre required a significant allocation of time and manpower to gather and transport to Dungannon for processing. Saltpetre could have been generated using petre farms, or using a process which involved boiling and condensing a mixture of nitre laden earth and water to produce saltpetre crystals.[196] While there is no direct evidence to substantiate if either method was used by the Irish, there are clear historical references to their collection of nitre rich earth for the purpose of extracting saltpetre. On two occasions in the *Dialogue of Silvynne and Peregrynne*, Collier referred to the Irish digging for saltpetre and once to the existence of privy miners.[197] Privy miners dug the earth out of the bottom of cess pits to recover the nitre rich soil for processing into saltpetre. The quantity of powder generated could only supplement the far larger amounts purchased locally, or brought in from abroad. Despite this limited impact, the willingness of the Irish confederates to develop a local system of manufacture attests to their inclination to move beyond primary economy activities to maintain the war. Regardless of this innovation, Tyrone required trade and external military aid to keep his armies supplied.

The supremacy of mercantile spirit over patriotism provided daily sustenance for Tyrone's war effort and substantial profits were made by merchants residing in towns notionally still under crown control. Sir John Dowdall referred to this when he reported that 'the [loyal] towns had become storehouses for the Irish confederates, where the merchants sold arms and ammunition to the rebels'.[198] Though the crown placed prohibitions on the unauthorized sale of munitions, the potential profits were too great to be ignored. Weapons and ammunition carried from England and the Continent could treble a merchant's investment, and multiply it by a factor of six if sold to the Irish confederates.[199] Factors living in the towns (occasionally priests) acted as middlemen, shipping goods and payments between the merchants and the Irish.[200]

The issue of merchants trading with Tyrone and his allies was a problem throughout the war. There were attempts to curb or cease the commerce between towns and the confederate-dominated countryside, but corporations actively sought to evade proscriptions by citing their independence from martial law granted them by their corporate charters.[201] Russell called for merchants to be ordered to stop selling munitions to the rebels in early 1595.[202] There were demands in 1596 for the trade in arms to the rebels to be declared an act of treason, but four years later similar calls for harsher action were still being made.[203] The following year it was reported that arms were being smuggled out of the towns.[204] Many years after the war, Peter Lombard cited the avidity of the merchants in Ireland as a great help to Tyrone.[205] Their behaviour raised doubts about their loyalty and may explain why Sir John Norreys expressed concern in 1596. He advised that citadels be built in the port towns to assure their loyalty, as he described the towns' inhabitants as having a more 'Spanish heart than the country people'.[206] This was not the last time that the corporate towns' loyalties were questioned. Later in the year, it was suggested that the towns in Munster had refused to give the assistance requested of them by Sir Thomas Norreys.[207]

The mercantile community's stocks of war materials were gathered from a number of sources. Easiest to access were the munitions intended for the crown army in Ireland. Powder and arms were embezzled from the crown stores, and captains were accused of stockpiling munitions to sell on for significant personal profit.[208] Deserting government troops sold their arms, as did cashiered infantry companies. Necessity or want sometimes compelled troops to sell their equipment to merchants who were able to make profits of 600–800 per cent.[209] Stores were bought in English cities such as London and Bristol for transportation to Ireland, and efforts were made to inhibit this traffic. Licensing for selling military stores, the revocation of charters of towns complicit in the trade, and death penalties for merchants found guilty of illegal trafficking in arms were all suggested.[210] Active measures were taken to avoid the prohibitions and to ensure that the lucrative trade continued. Goods were frequently smuggled from England directly to the Irish. The privy council of

England complained that shipments were transported without a licence from along the coast to sundry places in Ireland 'oftentimes ... to the enemy'.[211] The cargoes included not just arms and ammunition, but also commodities and provisions, which were noted to aid the Irish during times of food shortage.[212] Munitions were smuggled through ports in special split casks, with the legal drink in one half and ammunition, arms or armour in the other.[213] Care was taken with deliveries to the confederate customers. Merchants contrived the 'thefts' of supply convoys to get consignments to their Irish clients, with 'stolen' goods paid for by the alleged thieves.[214]

As England was at war with Spain, English merchants were forbidden to trade with Spain and its dominions by both English and Spanish law. Irish traders were subject to the English embargo, but the law was weakly enforced. However, merchants from Ireland were viewed quite differently by the Spanish authorities, who considered them favourably compared to their English counterparts.[215] Irish merchant ships were differentiated as distinctly Irish and were not subject to the same prohibitions that restricted trade between Spain and England. While frowned upon, the trade was tolerated by the crown, but it did cause disquiet as it was believed that the ships carried intelligence between Spain and the confederates.[216] Trade prospered between Ireland and the Iberian Peninsula. This traffic attracted the attentions of the O'Malleys and O'Flaherteys, who raided the merchant shipping along the west coast of Ireland in 1599 and 1600.[217] English naval patrols limited the impact of coastal piracy during 1600 and 1601, but by then Tyrone had extended his personal influence to the southern coast by marching to Kinsale in February 1600. Two months later the Spanish court received and later agreed to a request from Tyrone and O'Donnell that no Spanish-controlled ports should admit Irish ships unless they carried a licence signed by them.[218] Tyrone may have been attempting to force merchants in Ireland to seek authorization from him every time that they wished to transport cargoes to Spanish ports. This policy would have been more efficient than trying to accost merchant shipping in the coastal waters around Ireland. While there was no mention of a duties or tithes placed upon the passports, the imposition would have given the confederate leadership the opportunity to levy a charge instituting *de facto* taxation upon many exports from the towns.

The position of the corporate towns during the war was ambiguous. Rather than resisting the incursions of the Irish, they appear to have served as important logistical hubs in the Irish war effort. One of the failings ascribed to the confederate armies was their inability to take the fortified towns. This was frequently attributed to their lack of heavy artillery with which to breach masonry walls and earthen ramparts. However, considering the significant role the towns played in providing Tyrone and his allies with imported goods, they begin to look more like open cities rather than bastions of crown control. Throughout the war, Tyrone was loath to present fixed targets on which the English could concentrate.[219] The superior logistical ability of the English establishment meant that they had the capacity to maintain large concentrations of forces for sustained periods. If Tyrone had taken any of the corporate towns, he would have presented his enemies with a target for which the English forces were ideally suited. Therefore rather than hazard a defeat for no solid gain, preservation of the status quo of the corporate towns and the services they provided benefitted the Irish confederates. Even if the English army could not retake a corporate town that fell to the Irish, the power of the English navy could have been legitimately used against merchant shipping using the port. When reassessed in this context, Tyrone had little to gain and much to lose by taking towns such as Galway, Limerick or Cork.

Besides utilizing the corporate towns, Tyrone took advantage of the trading links between Ulster and Scotland. He imported much of his war materials from Scotland, which was unsurprising given the proximity of a sovereign nation and its established trade networks with continental Europe and to Ulster. Arms were imported into the province from Glasgow throughout the 1570s and 1580s.[220] Therefore it was no surprise to find this practice escalated during the war. At the outbreak of war, Tyrone landed substantial quantities of powder and munitions from Scotland on the north coast.[221] As the conflict spread and the demands for munitions grew, the traffic from Scotland correspondingly increased, and by 1600 it was noted that shipments were regularly dispatched.[222] Munitions were likely re-exported by merchants who were bringing them in from Baltic ports such as Danzig and Hamburg.[223] Large quantities of war material flowing from Scotland to Ulster prompted Sir James MacDonnell to suggest that if the supply of powder out of Scotland could be stopped, the war in Ireland would be over in six months.[224] Four years later, Queen Elizabeth suggested to James VI that Tyrone had received more arms and ammunition out of Scotland than he had from Spain.[225]

The English crown made substantial efforts to stifle the transport of munitions into Ulster. James VI was entreated to halt the flow of goods into Ulster from Scottish ports in 1597, to which he reportedly acquiesced.[226] The queen's agents in Scotland made strenuous diplomatic efforts to stop trade between Scotland and Ulster, and George Nicholson went as far as to lobby the king to personally instruct the provost of Glasgow on his obligations to enforce the prohibition of trade.[227] The Scottish king made repeated proclamations to bar the traffic in munitions, but the trade continued, and his enforcement of restrictions appeared half-hearted at best.[228] Indeed, there were many accusations that James approved of Tyrone's actions and letters between the two suggested there was a degree of amity between them.[229] The queen withheld a gratuity of £3,000–4,000 from King James for openly allowing supplies to be sent to Tyrone in 1598, as reports out of Scotland claimed that despite her demands, James did not prevent the traffic between Ulster and western Scottish ports.[230] A blind eye appeared to be turned to the ongoing shipments to Ireland.[231] English ships were stationed in the Irish Sea to interdict the traffic between Ulster and Scotland, but had difficulty engaging as the Scottish galleys were more manoeuvrable than the wind-bound English craft.[232] After his defeat at Kinsale and damaging retreat into Ulster, Tyrone turned to his Scottish contacts to make good his losses in arms and munitions.[233] It was only after the secret approaches by Cecil to James regarding his succession to the crown of England, did James appear to take more effective action to cut off aid into Ulster.[234]

The Scottish king's willingness to allow military supplies to flow into Ireland appeared more to do with underpinning his future claim to the English throne than with any affection he held for the Irish cause. James was one of two potential claimants to the crown as Elizabeth had no heir; the Infanta Isabella of Spain was the other. James feared that a peace treaty with Spain, which was actively sought by Sir Robert Cecil, would promote the claim by Isabella. After moving to Brussels, she was well positioned to make her claim to the throne on Elizabeth's death.[235] James believed that 'such as wished peace would also wish the Infanta'.[236] This was not the case. When Cecil was informed of James' misgivings about the peace negotiations, he described them as absurd, further noting that 'no good Christian would wish to have England subject to a Spaniard'.[237] It seems incongruous for James to maintain a war in a kingdom that was likely to be his. Therefore the possibility arises that he allowed arms to be shipped to sustain the Spanish proxy-war in Ireland. The longer this war raged, consuming English treasure and lives, the less likely there would be peace between England and Spain.

The Spanish crown played a crucial role in providing military aid to Tyrone and his allies throughout the war. Over the course of the war, Philip II and later Philip III provided the Irish with ten to twelve shipments of military aid. Examination of the cargoes carried by the ships highlighted what Tyrone needed most to continue the war: money, arms and munitions. Despite Tyrone's access to Scottish trade and the profiteering of the merchants in the towns, the Irish need for powder and arms was insatiable. Demands for munitions were characteristic of the Irish lords' letters to the Spanish crown.[238] The deliveries of firearms, pikes, gunpowder and money demonstrated that their needs could not be sufficiently met by local supplies. Spanish aid provided more than just physical stores to continue the war; it also generated a boost to the morale and confidence of the Irish confederates.[239] Aid from Spain was a physical embodiment of the link between Ireland and Europe's premier power. The Spanish were conscious of this and hoped that the arrival of military aid late in the war would retrench the flagging morale of the confederates.[240]

Irish logistics

Military strategy is hugely influenced by logistics. Unfortunately, while being one of the most important factors in warfare, it is also the most mundane and the least likely to capture the imaginations of historian and reader alike.[241] In recent years the abundance of English documentation regarding the provision of arms, ammunition and victuals for the crown's army in Ireland has enabled detailed explorations of this subject.[242] In comparison, the Irish system of logistics and supply has remained unexamined, due to the relative paucity of contemporary Irish documentation. Though Tyrone's efforts to furnish his armies has left few traces in the historical record, the earl successfully managed to keep his armies supplied.

The flow of war material to the Irish confederates could be best described as sufficient rather than ample, but the acquisition of supplies alone was not enough for Tyrone and his confederates. They had to establish a logistical infrastructure that could provide their troops with appropriate equipment when and where they needed it. Tyrone's logistics in Ulster were supported by a series of supply depots across the province. This should come as no surprise, as throughout the war Tyrone and O'Donnell retained control of critical supplies such as gunpowder, which they then fed southwards. Jeremy Black noted that the monopolization of the provision of arms or munitions was an aspect of early modern state-building, allowing central authorities to dominate other centres of power.[243] Therefore the Ulster lords' monopoly of the movement and storage of arms and munitions suggests they may have intended this as a means to secure their control and direction of the war. However, this ensured that supplies vital to the overall Irish war effort were located at the northern extremity of Ireland.

During the war, the Ulster leadership kept several key supply bases. In the west, O'Donnell maintained a site at Lough Eske, which was described as O'Donnell's powder store.[244] There was a storehouse at Donegal town, which was probably used due to its proximity to Killybegs, the Ulster chiefs' main port for receiving military aid from Spain.[245] In the east, Tyrone established stores on Clea lakes in Dufferin, which were within a few miles of Ringhaddy

(Co. Down). Brian MacArt had used Ringhaddy as a major port to disembark supplies from Scotland, and at one point 20 Scottish ships rode at anchor.[246] Possibly the most substantial base for supporting Irish operations in southern Ulster were those at Moyrourkan and Marlacoo loughs.[247] Both had crannogs built on them, and Tyrone spent much of 1595–6 at Marlacoo. When Tyrone's son Conn intercepted the Armagh garrison's supply convoy in February 1596, he deposited the captured victuals and powder on the crannog at Marlacoo.[248] Mountjoy identified them as Tyrone's strongholds, where 'it is well known he [Tyrone] keepeth his munition'.[249] When Mountjoy destroyed the site the following year, the base was reported as having a 'great house' on the shore and houses surrounding the lough and on the island. The Irish lost in flames a 'great store of butter, corn, meal, and powder, [which] was burnt and spoiled in the island, which all the rebels of the country made their magazine'.[250]

The foodstuffs yielded by the agricultural economy under the control of the Irish confederates found its way into Tyrone's stockpiles in Ulster. Substantial amounts of corn were also amassed at Marlacoo and Clea lakes. Docwra destroyed a site containing thirty large storehouses full of corn in O'Cahan's country near Coleraine in 1602.[251] These depots were used to furnish troops with their necessities before departure, but forces in the field were also supported by itinerant supply convoys, which were reported to be able to travel as much as 100 miles.[252] In preparation for campaigns in Leinster, supplies were stored in advance of the arrival of Tyrone's forces.[253] Stores were also distributed into woods and fastnesses. According to Nicholas Dawtrey, the Irish found means to preserve butter and oatmeal that allowed them to be kept for up to seven years.[254] He also noted how the Irish had amassed vast quantities of victuals and distributed them so widely that Irish troops could march to almost any place and still have stores hidden nearby.[255] Goods such as gunpowder and cattle were kept with clandestine allies who avowed loyalty to the crown in public.[256] Tyrone had effectively created a secret network of supporters (willing or unwilling), whose facade of loyalty meant confederate stores could be kept in open sight.

Postscript to Essex

After Essex's departure, the situation in Ireland steadily deteriorated. Though in general there were few open breaches of the terms of the ceasefire, the towns and garrisons came under increasing pressure. Just as in other cessations, Tyrone was scrupulous in maintaining order in Ulster, but as before his allies in other parts of Ireland continued to isolate crown garrisons. The garrisons of the strategic forts at Philipstown and Maryborough were prevented from gathering firewood and denied supplies by the Irish.[257] Both were eventually resupplied, but Fenton complained that Tyrone's allies were continuing to exact money and goods from the rural population. He noted that Tyrone 'suffereth it [the cessation] to be broken abroad by his confederates, as greatly to the impoverishing of the subjects, as if it were open hostility'.[258] In Munster, the *sugán* earl of Desmond made a public proclamation barring the garrison of Kilmallock from gathering firewood and refused to allow the revictualling of Castlemaine.[259]

The burden of so many English troops in garrisons across the Island became ever more intolerable for the towns and communities in which they were stationed. These tensions flared into violence when civilians attacked a party of English troops in Co. Kildare. While marching from Carbury to Johnstown Bridge, the inhabitants assaulted the column on the march, killing over fifty of them and scattering the rest. So sick were they of the abuses by the soldiers quartered near them, the locals 'determined not to suffer soldiers to be among them, or to pass through them'.[260] In Limerick, Kilmallock and Cork the citizens refused to feed or lodge troops and in Cork refused Captain Edward Digge's foot company entry into the town.[261] By mid-November, Sir Robert Napper reported that Drogheda, Galway, Waterford, Cork and Limerick (among others) 'did refuse to give relief to our soldiers'.[262]

After all the expense in lives and treasure the crown was no further forward than it had been a year earlier. With Essex gone there was no unity of leadership to command and coordinate English strategy. The army was hamstrung, apparently unable or unwilling to leave the perceived safety of their defences. Key allies such as Baron Delvin were neutralized by Tyrone after his lands were overrun, and in Munster Castlemaine was lost to the Irish. Possibly with this in mind Cecil made peace overtures in a remarkable letter to Sir William Warren. Cecil wished that Warren would let Tyrone know that, while they may be the bitterest enemies, what measures could be taken to return Tyrone's allegiance to the queen?[263] As long as the terms were not dishonourable, Cecil was happy that Tyrone could 'spend the remnant of his [Tyrone's] days in quietness'. Tyrone would not have to submit personally, and Cecil hoped that when Tyrone felt safe in returning to court, he would 'see the day to shake him [Tyrone] by the hand in England'.[264] Tyrone's response came at the end of November, and it was not to Cecil's liking. Included in a list of twenty-two conditions for peace, Tyrone demanded toleration of the Catholic religion in Ireland, the restitution of Irish lands, freedom of travel, commerce and conscience for all Irish men. Cecil endorsed the document with the word 'utopia'.[265] Clearly, in Cecil's mind the land envisioned by Tyrone was a fantasy; a fictional place that the queen would never agree to. There would be no peace.

CHAPTER 5

English milk for Irish blood: Mountjoy and English resurgence, 1600–1

TYRONE AND HIS ALLIES WERE at the height of their power. The Irish confederates ranged the length of Ireland and no one in Dublin appeared to have any idea how to halt Tyrone's advance, never mind begin to roll back Irish gains. The arrival of Lord Mountjoy did not portend any radical change in the situation. He did not have Essex's reputation nor the experience of Sir John Norreys. Nevertheless, the new lord deputy rapidly concluded that the army as it stood was not fit for purpose. Furthermore, Mountjoy did not compound failure by repeating the ineffectual strategies of the other viceroys. He rebuilt the army, providing reinforcements, supplies and training – improving his soldiers' skills and inspiring new confidence in his men. Moreover, English strategy moved beyond simply targeting Irish forces to begin a broad assault on the Irish ability to wage war, by attacking economic resources and assailing the alliances that thus far had held Tyrone's confederation together. Currency too became a weapon, as the debasement of the Irish coinage denied the Irish access to money accepted in foreign markets. Without imports, Irish guns would soon fall silent.

Mountjoy's arrival also brought individuals of talent and ability perfectly suited to the Irish war. Sir George Carew took over the pacification of Munster. His prescient observations at the start of the war showed that he was acutely aware of the complexities of fighting a war in which native loyalty was fickle and fluid. Carew's campaign in Munster, with limited manpower and meagre resources, demonstrated that success in Ireland was not soley predicated on the combat power of soldiers, but also on the manipulation of local politics and alliances; at this Carew was a master, returning Munster to the crown without fighting a single battle. Sir Henry Docwra landed in Derry and undermined the loyalties that held together the Irish lords' power base in Ulster. For others, like Sir Arthur Chichester, no act of terror or bloodshed was too extreme if it brought the crown closer to victory.

15 Charles Blount, Lord Mountjoy, *c.*1594

Mountjoy takes the sword

After Essex's departure, the control of the government in Ireland was left in the hands of the Irish council, but a new viceroy was needed. This duty was given to Charles Blount, eighth Baron Mountjoy, in November 1599, though he did not arrive in Ireland until 26 February 1600.[1] The new lord deputy had some practical military experience before his appointment, but he had little practice in the handling of large bodies of soldiers in combat. Mountjoy's first taste of campaigning came in 1585 when he accompanied Sir John Norreys to the Low Countries. There he would have become familiar with the small-unit actions and raiding, which made up the majority of military engagements in the Low Countries. Mountjoy was with Sir John Norreys at the battle at

Zutphen in 1586, and was knighted by the earl of Leicester the following year. In 1588, Mountjoy saw naval action against the Spanish Armada. In defiance of the queen's wishes, Mountjoy left the court in 1593 to re-join his foot company in Brittany, where he was again under the command of Sir John Norreys. However, he was ordered by the queen to return to court and resume his study of military literature.[2]

It was Mountjoy's propensity for learning that led Essex to suggest his experience was limited to the rank of captain and that he was 'given too much to studies'.[3] Mountjoy was the governor of Portsmouth from 1594 to 1600 and commanded the land forces allocated to the Azores cruise of 1597, but the army played a minimal part in the campaign.[4] Mountjoy had not spent time in Ireland, and therefore could not have been expected to have personal experience of the wars there. He was, however, tutored in warfare by Sir John Norreys, who was regarded by contemporary and modern writers to have been one of the greatest English field commanders of the period.[5] Norreys' service in Ireland during 1573–5, which included campaigning in Ulster, would have taught him much that could have been passed on. There are no records of what Mountjoy learned about the wars in Ireland from Norreys, but tellingly the first fort he built in Ulster was named Mountnorris in honour of his old master.[6] Mountjoy may also have been influenced by the classical and contemporary military texts. He was known to have had a keen interest in reading military theory and carried a copy of Julius Caesar's *Gallic wars* during his campaigns in Ireland.[7] A significant feature of classical works was the use of spoliation and devastation to subdue an enemy. Caesar advocated spoliation and crop destruction, noting that after an area had been devastated, those who had managed to evade his troops would 'perish for want of everything when the army was withdrawn'.[8] These methods became central to Mountjoy's strategy to defeat Tyrone.

Before Mountjoy ever set foot in Ireland, detailed instructions were drafted advising the new lord deputy on the course to take. There was to be a reinstatement of religious observance in the English forces and loyal subjects. Corruption and embezzlement severely compromised the strength of the army. Therefore abuses of troop musters and the commissary had to be addressed, and the provision of supplies and money to the troops improved. Garrisons needed to be established in the heart of rebel territory. Most of all, Tyrone had to be engaged directly. Mountjoy was to ignore all attempts to delay or divert his prosecution of the war and to 'use all means possible to cut him [Tyrone] off as a reprobate to God, and leave him to the force of our sword'.[9] All this had to be achieved with a much smaller army than that under Essex; just 14,000 foot and 1,200 horse. Mountjoy had some recommendations of his own, which included regularization of the pay for captains. Furthermore, Mountjoy was cognisant of the suffering of the common soldier; therefore he suggested that hospitals be built in Cork, Dublin and Drogheda. Each was to be staffed by two overseers, a surgeon or physician, a servant and four women, all paid at the crown's expense.[10] These were all logical and coherent proposals for the reformation of the English war effort.

Tyrone threatened to dissolve the ceasefire, but negotiations had managed to maintain it.[11] Ormond met with Tyrone at Blackstone ford between Louth and Farney on 31 November 1599, where the truce was extended to the start of January 1600.[12] Ormond was well aware that the cessation would only last as long as it suited Tyrone. Therefore he ensured that the garrisons and border towns were resupplied. Also, vulnerable passes and fords were fortified and bridges 'ensconced'.[13] Meanwhile in England, 5,000 new troops were levied to shore up the weakened English army in Ireland.[14] As in all previous cessations, there were minor breaches of the truce, but in general, the peace held. Nevertheless, by the start of 1600, there were claims that Tyrone planned to invade southwards.[15] These proved correct when the earl struck south in mid-January. Tyrone was careful to leave many of his trusted adherents behind to contain the garrisons of Carrickfergus and Newry.[16]

Tyrone's army moved south through the midlands and into Co. Tipperary, where he met the *sugán* earl of Desmond. The council in Dublin was appalled that Tyrone could march so far without any attempt made to impeach his progress. Moreover, they were distressed to find that Tyrone passed 'in open daylight, without any encounter, yea not so much as an alarm given', leading the council to question the loyalty of the lords of those regions through which Tyrone passed.[17] Ormond shadowed the Irish army's march south, but made no effort to engage. Tyrone arrived within ten miles of Cork on 16 February 1600. The earl demanded the allegiance of the Munster lords, which he claimed was supported by a papal bull of excommunication for those Catholics who would not join him against the queen.[18] David Barry, fifth Viscount Buttevant (himself a rebel in 1581), refused and his land like others were devastated and his goods taken. Furthermore, the papal bull invoked by Dermot McCraghe, bishop of Cork and Cloyne, reminded Lord Barry of his predicament that refusal would not only lead to material loss but also the destruction of Barry's soul.[19] This was all bluster as no papal bull of excommunication was ever issued in support of Tyrone's cause.

Tyrone lost one of his most capable and loyal allies during his stay in Munster. In a chance encounter the chief commissioner of Munster, Sir Henry Power, stumbled upon Hugh Maguire in command of a troop of horse and some shot near Carrigrohane, approximately three miles west of Cork city. Sir

Warham St Leger spurred his horse into action and charged the Irish, with Maguire responding in kind.[20] As they closed St Leger shot Maguire with his petronel (a long-barrelled pistol), which was double-bulleted.[21] However, the wound was not immediately fatal and Maguire thrust his horseman's staff into St Leger's head. The steel tip of Maguire's lance broke off, embedded in the Englishman's skull.[22] St Leger was taken back to Cork where he soon died. Maguire escaped into the growing darkness of the evening, but after a mile he fell from his horse where according to the bishop of Cork, he died 'under a bush'.[23] Maguire's death caused dismay in Irish ranks, 'a giddiness of spirits, and depression of mind, in O'Neill [Tyrone] and the Irish chiefs in general; and this was no wonder for he was the bulwark of valour and prowess'.[24] Not only had Tyrone lost one of his ablest commanders, but there was now the vexatious question of succession in the lordship of Fermanagh.

The pressure on Tyrone to return north mounted. There were two strong claimants to the lordship of Fermanagh, Cuconnaght and Connor Roe Maguire. Without Tyrone's arbitration, this could flare into a localized private war, as the two fought for supremacy. Furthermore, Sir Samuel Bagenal was proving difficult to contain in Newry. He had carried out some raids at the end of 1599, but on the 18 February, Bagenal launched an audacious attack on a Magennis camp, killing one of Tyrone's captain of shot, six horsemen and taking a prey of cattle and horses, before Brian MacArt O'Hanlon forced him back to Newry.[25] Of more concern to Tyrone were Mountjoy's intentions after his arrival in Ireland at the end of February. Intelligence had reached Tyrone that the English determined to move into Ulster from the south and make a landing of a strong amphibious force on the Foyle, on the north coast of Ulster.[26] Tyrone's presence in Munster was inciting Irish lords previously loyal to the crown to defect, but the earl had little choice, he had to fall back to defend Ulster.

Tyrone marched north through the midlands and was reported to have crossed the Inny river in Westmeath on 13 or 14 March. Little information reached Dublin about Tyrone's movements, and no attempt was made to block his passage north. Mountjoy was appalled that the Irish could march unimpeded the length of the island, noting that 'in his [Tyrone's] returning back altogether untouched, has insinuated a great reputation of himself with the Irish'.[27] The Irish had marched at speeds at which the English could only marvel, perhaps twenty-seven miles in a day.[28] Fenton reported that Tyrone left his baggage in O'Molloy's country in Co. Offaly, under the protection of Tyrrell, enabling him to make even better progress.[29] Tyrone was in Ulster by 17 March, passing through Monaghan and then on to Dungannon, where he prepared to oppose the landings on the Foyle. While Mountjoy was unhappy about Tyrone's return north unhindered, it did teach him several lessons about the conflict.

Mountjoy saw that the rising out could not be counted on to encounter the Irish confederates aggressively.[30] Most importantly Mountjoy had forced Tyrone to tip his hand slightly. By threatening Ulster, Mountjoy precipitated an impressive feat of speed marching by the Irish, but the rush northwards had shown that Ulster was the principal concern of Tyrone; all else could be abandoned to ensure its protection. Mountjoy realized that 'this prosecution of the north has stricken the rebels with a fearful apprehension; which if it be well followed ... clean alter the face of this kingdom'.[31] This insight may have determined most of Mountjoy's strategy for 1600. Ulster was critical to Tyrone. It was the source of his military strength, known in military terms as his centre of gravity. Recognizing this enabled Mountjoy to wrest the strategic and operational initiative from the Tyrone and keep it for the rest of the war. However, that was in the future; if Mountjoy could see the means of gaining victory over Tyrone he needed the tools to realize it.

Mountjoy's reforms: an army reforged

After his arrival in February 1600, Mountjoy took steps to improve and revitalize the army. He restored confidence to his officers and men, making them more willing to venture out of their garrisons and challenge the rebels for supremacy in the field. Several measures achieved this. Mountjoy countermanded an order to cashier 2,000 troops, which would have broken up their foot companies and used the men to reinforce other units. By doing so, he aimed to preserve what little morale remained in the army, as cashiering so many companies would, in Mountjoy's view, have precipitated further discouragement to the officers, and would have risked the wholesale desertion of disbanded units.[32] Mountjoy undid one of Essex's major mistakes by reinstating many of the experienced officers who had been dismissed the previous year. Correspondingly, he also purged the army of many poor captains, whom he described as 'idle drones'.[33] Steps were taken to tackle the abuses of the officers, by outlawing the sale of captaincies, limiting the number of officers absent from their troops at any one time, and employing commissioners to curtail the falsification of musters.[34] Mountjoy encouraged personal physical bravery on the part of his officers, for which his behaviour provided the template. Testimony for this were the substantial numbers of Mountjoy's retinue that were killed or wounded in action at his side.[35]

As much as Mountjoy wished to encourage and give new spirit to his officers and men, he made sure to take severe action against those soldiers who attempted to flee their duties in Ireland. Desertion continually drained the army of manpower. Therefore Mountjoy instituted harsher punishments and demanded their enforcement. In April 1600, he had hanged sixteen deserters and urged Sir Robert Cecil to expedite the same penalty for those found on the other side of the Irish Sea.[36] Though draconian, the measures appeared to have had the desired effect. The mayor of Chester advised the privy council that the threat of execution for desertion 'struck such a terror into their [the soldiers] hearts … it has prevented the running away of whole hundreds'.[37] Mountjoy removed the authority from captains to provide passports to England and proclaimed that ships and goods would be confiscated if found conveying men without valid passes.[38]

Central to the crown's inability to take the initiative in the field was the sluggishness of the English army. Independence from slow-moving supply trains was critical if English troops were to have any hope of catching or outmanoeuvring Tyrone's men. Correspondingly, changes were ordered to enable English troops to march without the burden of carriages. Early in Mountjoy's tenure as deputy, he issued an order barring soldiers from bringing women, children or servants on campaigns.[39] Sir George Carew ordered supplies limited to 'biscuit, cheese and butter, which … is more portable for service'.[40] Mountjoy requested that larger amounts of cheese be sent from England as it was the one provision that could be easily carried by his soldiers. The purpose of this was to enable Mountjoy to abandon the use of carriages, and give greater mobility to his marching columns.[41]

Another means for increasing the mobility of his infantry was the construction of large numbers of fortifications in enemy territory. A vital part of Mountjoy's pacification policy for Ulster was the establishing of a series of fortifications abutting enemy territory. He intended to build forts around Tyrone's lands and those of his allies to keep 'the rebels at home, so as they could not second one another'.[42] Bridling Ulster with forts was not a new idea for neutralizing Tyrone, but it was Mountjoy who made it happen. He ensured that they were close enough to provide mutual support should one position come under attack or need to concentrate a larger force for an expedition.[43] While the construction of fortifications was meant to interdict Irish movement and dominate the landscape, they also influenced the tactical mobility of Mountjoy's infantry. Within a network of supporting forts, garrisons could march without recourse to restrictive baggage. It was noted that garrison troops could operate for short times, perhaps forty-eight hours, independent of the stores.[44] Freed from their carriages they would be able to operate with the kind of mobility demanded by Mountjoy.[45] Addressing the method with which crown units marched was not the only way to increase their speed; amendments had to be made to their equipment. One means to do this was to reduce the weight of the arms and equipment of the English troops.

Burdensome equipment had been an issue of concern for commanders earlier in the war, in particular the use of muskets. Weighing almost twenty pounds, they were considered by several senior commanders to be too heavy for use in Ireland; the much lighter caliver was deemed more appropriate.[46] Correspondingly, a greater proportion of the English shot were equipped with calivers.[47] Furthermore, troops began to abandon the use of heavy armour. For the soldiers landed on the Foyle in May 1600, armour had become unnecessary and in Munster units of light foot were deployed.[48] By August 1602, Sir George Carew considered the army to have evolved to a state where they were substantially lighter and more mobile than the heavy infantry of the Spanish *tercios*.[49] In addition to realizing lighter infantry, crown operations began to demonstrate greater tactical flexibility.

As has been noted earlier, for much of the war, English soldiers were limited to marching along roads and route-ways. In most of the major engagements before 1600, the government forces remained fixed to the roads they were on until they broke contact, or lost cohesion and began to flee. During 1600, government troops started to demonstrate tactical finesse and self-assurance that was not evident before. When Sir Oliver Lambert faced ten 'half-moons' blocking the road to Philipstown, he ordered his men to launch a flanking attack through the bog, forcing the Irish to retreat.[50] On 24 August 1600, in the pass of Cashel, English troops counterattacked into bogs that should have been a safe line of retreat for the Irish.[51] Mountjoy's men demonstrated their growing confidence by moving onto ground normally dominated by the Irish. This fluidity was also accompanied by their adoption of targeteers, which had been an effective element of Tyrone's army for some time.

The catalogue of military setbacks from 1594 to 1599 demonstrated that the basic pike and shot infantry of the crown forces could not cope with the Irish terrain, nor with the Irish forces ranged against them. From 1599, swordsmen, specifically targeteers, appeared in the ranks of the government armies. They could force passages and support the loose shot, which was how Tyrone had deployed them, and was consistent with the practice on the Continent.[52] Some of the earliest of these appeared at the start of Essex's Munster campaign. During his engagement in the pass of Cashel, Essex deployed soldiers armed with short weapons.[53] Essex had requested that 300–400 be sent over in May 1599, but they were not sent due to the expense.[54] However, by late 1600, targeteers were well represented in

Mountjoy's regiments at the Moyry Pass.[55] While the English benefitted from their often-painful experience of engaging with the Irish, they also gained from their continued involvement in the Low Countries.

Queen Elizabeth became embroiled in the wars of the Low Countries in 1572 to aid her co-religionists against the Spanish. This involvement allowed English commanders to profit by the advances in infantry tactics developed by the Dutch.[56] Throughout the 1590s, the Dutch had been reforming and retraining their pike-and-shot infantry to operate in smaller battalia of 580 men, using repetitive drill to enable them to fire, manoeuvre, reload and use counter-marching to maximize their firepower.[57] The Low Country veterans substituted dense pike battalia for broad, shallow formations that were more efficient, and a counter-march firing system that maximized firepower. Captain John Chamberlain referred to these advances in 1598, when he described how his veterans were better at handling their muskets than the garrison troops replacing them, as the latter were 'not acquainted with the new discipline we exercise'.[58] A substantial number of these soldiers, including Chamberlain, were sent to Ireland during 1598–9.[59] This did not impress their Dutch allies, as Prince Maurice complained to the earl of Essex about the loss of 2,000 troops for Ireland, who were 'trained to our methods of service'.[60]

The English infantry were not the only part of the army to benefit from advances in continental methods; the English cavalry also evolved. The cavalry deployed by the English were considered light horse by continental standards, but experience throughout the war demonstrated that they were more than a match for the Irish cavalry and rightly feared by the Irish infantry. They were armoured with a corselet or cuirass over their torso and a steel helmet and were armed with a lance, sword and pistols. The English horse could also carry a petronel, which was a type of large pistol that was effective at a greater range than the short-barrelled pistol. These were quite different from the mailed cavalry depicted in Derricke's woodcut in *Image of Ireland* almost twenty years earlier.[61] Mountjoy called for at least one-third of the English horse be equipped as mounted shot in 1600.[62] By April the following year, all the horse sent to reinforce the garrison in Derry were equipped with petronels.[63] The description of the horse sent to Derry in 1601 recorded their elaborate equipment, which included: a cuirass, a morion, a horseman's stave (a light lance), 'turkey' sword with basket hilt, a long pistol (petronel) and a horseman's coat, which was a buff jerkin of thick leather.

The light horse were an improvement on the heavy horse known as 'demi-lances', whose heavy armour limited their mobility and therefore their usefulness. They could scout, forage and raid convoys as well as charge in battle. When armed with petronels the light horse could operate as *hargulatiers*, which were essentially mounted shot. Sir Roger Williams considered *hargulatiers* to be the most serviceable type of cavalry as they had greater flexibility in combat.[64] In addition to fighting on horseback, they could dismount and fight as infantry.[65] The reinforcements sent to Docwra in 1601 were equipped as both light horse and *hargulatiers*, which was anomalous as the latter did not normally wear armour.[66] They appear to be similar to mounted shot deployed by Spain in the Low Countries. Whereas English *hargulatiers* were unarmoured and only armed with a firearm and sword, the Spanish horsemen were also equipped with armour and a lance, combining the duties of light horse and *hargulatiers*.[67] It is speculative to suggest that the English horse were copying Spanish practices encountered in the Low Countries, as the English cavalry could have been evolving to suit the prevailing conditions in Ireland, but it is clear that the English cavalry developed like most other arms along continental lines.

Mountjoy placed a new emphasis on the quality of the training given to troops. Instructions for the army sent to Lough Foyle included a requirement that officers train their men in martial discipline and the use of their weapons 'for their better experience and health'.[68] The proportion of gunpowder issued to new soldiers was doubled for their first month in Ireland, to allow for sufficient firearms training.[69] He ordered that the cost of powder would not be taken from the soldiers weekly lending, thereby enabling the average soldier enough money to live.[70] Later Mountjoy managed to have his troops spared the cost of their powder if it was spent 'in a days service'.[71] Mountjoy also tried to save his troops any expense in their use of powder in training and while on sentry duty, but this was rejected in no uncertain terms by Cecil. He cautioned Mountjoy that if the money was not deducted from the soldiers' wages, it would be 'defalked out of his Lordship's [Mountjoy's] entertainment'.[72] Despite Mountjoy's efforts to reinvigorate his forces, he did not casually deploy them. Initially, the lord deputy used them warily, taking care not to expose the soldiers to setbacks or defeat, thereby preserving their, as yet unconsolidated and possibly brittle morale.[73] Above all else, Mountjoy knew that their new found strength was predicated on sufficient and timely shipments of supplies.

To renovate the crown's battered army, Mountjoy ordered the provision of ample food and supplies. By 1 April 1600, he reported the army 'better fashioned to follow the service with cheerfulness and resolution'.[74] Just over two weeks later the army was reported to 'desire nothing more than to fight'.[75] Linked to both these statements was the availability of sufficient supplies. Sir Geoffrey Fenton noted that provisions were the means to keep the men's morale up as 'money and victuals ... keep them in love with the service'.[76]

Mountjoy's letter to Cecil on 9 April placed a caveat on the reforms in the army, noting that all their efforts would be undone if supplies from England failed them.[77] However, any amount of provisions would be useless if they could not be carried to the appropriate place promptly.

Thirteen new commissaries were appointed at the start of April 1600 to improve the crown's logistical abilities, adding to the five already in post. They were to oversee the order and distribution of troops and supplies. Fenton reported the arrival of four supply ships in Dublin in one week in May 1600.[78] He added that increased resources had given new vigour to the soldiers, by which they would make good previous defeats that had 'blemished the whole nation'.[79] The newly restored army was ready by the middle of June, as Mountjoy advised Cecil that the soldiers were now in health and strength and that they were willing to repay 'the milk we have received from the estate with the blood of our enemies or our own'.[80] However, even with a newly armed, trained and equipped army, Mountjoy needed to force Tyrone onto the defensive, thereby letting the English dictate the tempo of the war and secure the operational initiative. This plan started in May with the long-awaited arrival of the English on the river Foyle.

Docwra's landing and the bridling of Ulster

An amphibious landing on the Foyle had been advised almost from the start of the war, even before the crown realized that it was dealing with more than just a localized revolt by Hugh Maguire. Among a list of measures to contain the growing power of the northern lords, Captain William Piers advocated the establishing of a garrison at Derry with boats to dominate the river Foyle.[81] Lord Burgh had planned to rendezvous with Sir Conyers Clifford at the Foyle in 1597, and Sir Samuel Bagenal was meant to land 2,000 troops there in 1598, but the destruction of Bagenal's army at the Yellow Ford caused his mission to be redirected to the defence of Dublin. Essex had planned to land troops in 1599, but it took a new lord deputy for the scheme to become a reality in May 1600.

Sir Henry Docwra commanded the amphibious expedition. He was an officer with considerable military experience. Yet despite Docwra's proficiency, Mountjoy was careful to provide him with clear instructions. For the good conduct of the garrison Docwra was to appoint a preacher and such vices as swearing, adultery, fornication, gaming at dice and cards were prohibited in the camp. Exact musters of men and equipment were to be kept and a commissary placed in charge of the stores. A master of the ordinance would take charge of the munitions, maintaining an account of the issue of powder for training and

16 Owny O'More captures the earl of Ormond, Apr. 1600. Note the modern pike and shot deployed by O'More and the absence of old style gallowglass and kerne (Trinity College Dublin, MS 1209/13)

operations. A hospital was to be built for the sick and naval assets used to clear the estuary of enemy boats, but Docwra was warned not to do anything that may antagonize the king of Scotland. It was hoped that a garrison could be established at Ballyshannon, but most importantly Docwra was given authority to 'prosecute by fire and sword all rebels and malefactors' but also encouraged to draw in Irish defectors who could sow dissent and elicit further submissions from the Irish.[82] The effect of a garrison so far in the north would paralyse Irish operations. Fenton wrote that Tyrone had kept himself safe in Ulster by fighting the war elsewhere. However, a large army on the Foyle 'shall be as an iron hook in his [Tyrone's] nostrils, to hold him hard and entangle him at home, while Her Majesty with better commodity may apply [herself to] the recovering of Leinster and Munster'.[83]

Docwra arrived at the Foyle on 14 May with 4,000 infantry and 200 horse. Rather inauspiciously, the fleet almost immediately ran aground, but the following day the tide refloated Docwra's ships, and he landed men on Culmore Point meeting negligible resistance. Over the next six days, a fort was built around the tower house at Culmore, and a garrison was placed at the nearby Elagh castle, which the O'Dohertys had abandoned.[84] After leaving 600 men at Culmore, Docwra marched the army to the old ecclesiastic site of Derry on 22 May, which Docwra decided was 'a fit place to make our main plantation'.[85] That the landing met little opposition was in no small part to Mountjoy's operations in southern Ulster.

Though the lord deputy was keen to have a garrison on the Foyle, he was not prepared to trust its success to the military strength of the landing force. If Tyrone could gather sufficient forces to oppose Docwra, the entire enterprise could founder. Tyrone had been fortifying parts of the coast during 1599 and defences specifically tailored to defeat amphibious landings were built along the Foyle, which Tyrone had further reinforced with earthwork sconces.[86] Consequently, Mountjoy withdrew troops from garrisons in the Pale and Leinster to build a field force capable of marching north to Ulster. The primary goal of this move was to 'make diversion of Tyrone's forces, the better to give way to the landing of those garrisons' that required troops to be sent into southern Ulster 'for the more entangling of the traitors'.[87] While preparations were being made, news arrived of the capture of the earl of Ormond by Owny O'More.[88] While Ormond was one of the pre-eminent lords in Ireland, Mountjoy was ambivalent with his capture. The lord deputy was unimpressed by Ormond's failure to engage Tyrone on his march north, and caustically remarked of Ormond's plight that 'I know not whether this be good or evil news'.[89]

While the English field army gathered for the push north, Sir Samuel Bagenal continued his newfound aggressive spirit in Newry. Aided by intelligence provided by Irish scouts, he raided Tyrone's supply base at 'Loughlackin' (likely Moyrourkan Lough, north of modern-day Markethill, Co. Armagh). During the raid, he burnt storehouses and carried away hundreds of cows, horses and other animals.[90] The lord deputy entered Ulster through the Moyry Pass with 2,400 men on 11 May. The arrival of Mountjoy in Ulster forced Tyrone to march from Newtown (modern-day Newtownstewart, Co.

Tyrone) to Dungannon, then on to the Blackwater where he destroyed the old Blackwater fort on 14 May. Tyrone then burned Armagh and encamped his men at Moyrourkan. The Irish raised trenches just to the south, blocking Mountjoy's route to Armagh. Mountjoy moved to within three miles of Tyrone's defences but did not attempt to assault his positions and later pulled back to Newry to await reinforcement. When the fresh troops under Henry Wriothesley, the third earl of Southampton, marched through the Moyry Pass, Tyrone ambushed the column at the ford of the Four Mile Water. However, when two regiments sent to link up with Southampton arrived, the Irish withdrew with few casualties on either side.[91]

The bulk of Tyrone's men remained in their defensive works, but after several days of waiting, Tyrone led his army out of their fortifications towards the English camp, causing the lord deputy to gather two-thirds of his army to answer the Irish challenge. As the English approached, Tyrone retired his men to the protection of their defences. Mountjoy, however, could not be induced to attack at such a disadvantage and returned his men to camp. Neither side was prepared to abdicate their advantage, but the primary goal of Mountjoy's expedition had been achieved. Docwra had successfully landed on the Foyle; therefore there was no need to assault Tyrone's position. Mountjoy's feint had worked, so he retreated to Carlingford on 28 May.

The Foyle garrison was securely lodged, but military success was initially difficult to achieve; indeed, Mountjoy was critical of the slow progress.[92] The landing force made little headway and Docwra was almost killed at the end of July, but the decisive blow was political. Docwra's force was a catalyst for the defection of disaffected Irish lords. Arthur O'Neill, son of Turlough Luineach, the former chief of the O'Neills, submitted on 1 June 1600.[93] However, the key defection came in November when Niall Garbh O'Donnell defected to the crown. He had lost out to Hugh Roe O'Donnell in the succession to the O'Donnell title in 1592. Moreover, Niall Garbh feared O'Donnell's retribution for killing his uncle.[94] Therefore with English support, Niall Garbh could achieve his ambition of overthrowing Hugh Roe O'Donnell and attaining regional dominance. Niall Garbh aggressively attacked his former allies and enabled punishing raids into Tirconnell and Tyrone. Docwra viewed Niall Garbh and Sir Arthur O'Neill's defections as crucial. Writing after the war, Docwra admitted 'I must confess a truth, all by the help and advice of Neal Garbh and his followers, and the other Irish that came in with Sir Arthur O'Neale, without whose intelligence and guidance little or nothing could have been done of ourselves'.[95] Just as Mountjoy had envisioned, the Foyle garrison curtailed Irish operations in the south. Tyrone was forced to withdraw troops from his allies in the Irish midlands to protect the formerly secure hinterlands.

Sir George Carew and the pacification of Munster

While Mountjoy had a keen strategic insight and a clear idea of how to rehabilitate and re-task his army, he was also fortunate to be accompanied by outstanding officers, possibly the finest of whom was Sir George Carew. Carew joined the army in Ireland in 1575 and the following year was appointed the governor of Carlow and constable of Leighlinbridge, which he successfully defended from an assault by the O'Mores in 1577. He saw action in the Desmond and Baltinglass revolts (1579–83) where he participated in raiding and successfully held Adare against rebel forces in 1579. Carew was present at the defeat of Lord Grey's army at Glenmalure in 1580 in which his brother Peter was killed.[96] Carew was unlikely to forget the dangers of applying brute military force against the Irish on their chosen ground. He was appointed the master of the ordinance in Ireland in 1588, a post he held for four years until resigning to accept a promotion to lieutenant-general of the ordinance in England. Carew held command positions on both the raid on Cadiz in 1596 and the Azores cruise the following year.[97]

Carew had fought in both small- and large-scale operations and had seen the success and failure of English military endeavours in Ireland. He had also lived for many years in Ireland and was familiar with the political and social landscape of the country. This experience may explain Carew's ability to pen the almost prophetic treatise in April 1594.[98] The work was written to advise Sir Robert Cecil on how to deal with the rebellion in Ulster, which was at that stage still limited to Fermanagh and northern Connacht. Carew correctly identified many aspects of the coming war long before they were apparent to many in Ireland. In one document he identified: the involvement of Tyrone behind the trouble brewing in Ulster and the likelihood of his imminent rebellion; the support for the Irish from Spain and Scotland; the modernization of Tyrone's troops in Ulster; the potential of Ulster to raise troops (Carew estimated 6–7000 foot and 1,000 horse which was uncannily accurate); the use of the northern channel between Ulster and Scotland as a principal supply route. Moreover, Carew's recommendation for fighting the war using a dual approach of large and small forces played a significant part in the conflict. Carew advised that the crown should deploy large armies to fix Tyrone's main force, while minor English expeditions ravaged Irish territory in Ulster. This was precisely the tactic Tyrone used against the crown. Carew also predicted that economic warfare, predicated upon spoiling attacks on the civilian food supply, would be the crucial instrument for suppressing the Irish.[99]

Carew's campaign in Munster can be viewed in the context of his army's relative military weakness when compared to the numbers deployed by

Tyrone's Munster allies. Carew had 2,400 men, considerably less than the estimated 7,000 opposing him.[100] Rather than attempt an unequal trial of military strength, Carew took a much more indirect approach in attacking the Irish war effort in Munster. He was aided by the weakened state of the province, both in political and economic terms, which had resulted from the second Desmond rebellion (1579–83). A lasting side effect of this revolt was the question of claims to the defunct earldom of Desmond.

Tyrone chose to support James Fitzthomas' assumption of the Desmond earldom. The title had been vacant since the death of Garret Fitzjames, the fifteenth earl of Desmond, in 1583. James' father, Thomas, was Garret's half-brother from a marriage that the fourteenth earl had repudiated. Thomas Fitzgerald and his son James sided with the crown during the second Desmond rebellion (1579–83), no doubt with the goal of securing the vacant title. Their hopes were misplaced, as after the war the crown dissolved the earldom and established the Munster plantation, relegating Thomas Fitzgerald and his sons to relative political obscurity.[101] Thomas died in 1595 leaving James as claimant to the vacant title.[102] During the overthrow of the Munster plantation in October 1598, Tyrone established James as the new earl of Desmond, though many of his detractors called him the *sugán* or straw-rope earl. His relatively minor social position before Tyrone's intervention suited the earl, as it made Fitzthomas dependent upon him, but chafed with many of the Munster lords who were obliged to show deference to someone whom they believed to be their social inferior.[103] Carew took pains to exacerbate and exploit this friction.

Carew provoked discord among Tyrone's allies. By breaking up any semblance of unity, Irish strength was dissipated in petty squabbles and dynastic disputes.[104] Competitors to Irish titles were raised into positions to compete for the loyalties of Irish lordships.[105] The most ambitious of these plans was the transportation of James Fitzgerald to Munster from England in 1600. James Fitzgerald was the son of the rebel fifteenth earl of Desmond and had been held a prisoner for much of his life. At the time of the Munster rebellion he was incarcerated in the Tower of London. Fitzgerald was released to Carew's custody in 1599 in the hope that, as the queen's 'tower earl', he would draw support away from Tyrone's *sugán* earl. Carew's plans faltered due to Fitzgerald's affection for Protestantism, which soon alienated his potential supporters in Munster.[106]

Carew initiated programmes to undermine the Munster leadership's confidence in their local allies. This involved propagating a sense of mistrust and uncertainty between senior figures in Munster and raising divisions and doubts between local troops and the bonnaghts from Connacht. In April 1600,

he announced a system of rewards or head money for those who would kill the
enemies of the state.[107] During June, Carew's agents attempted to assassinate
John Fitzthomas, Desmond's brother.[108] Though the plot failed in its primary
goal, it did result in an increased wariness, almost paranoia, among the
Fitzthomas brothers.[109]

Opposed by superior numbers, Carew could not confront all his enemies
at once. As a result, he embarked on a programme of divide-and-conquer that
enabled him to focus his limited resources on individual Irish leaders.
Redmond Burke was neutralized with offers of future rewards and Carew
temporized with Florence MacCarthy and Edmund Fitzgibbon.[110] Sir Robert
Cecil suggested that Carew could proffer MacCarthy an earldom to secure his
defection.[111] Dallying with the enemy was a useful expedient that Carew had
used after the capture of the earl of Ormond, when he used temporizing
agreements to check any further collapse in order.[112] Dire threats of financial
and material penalties precipitated the submissions of the White Knight (Sir
Edmund Fitzgibbon) and several other minor lords during May and June
1600.[113] Carew had little faith in the loyalty of the Irish lords' acquiescence,
but their neutrality was sufficient to allow him to restore English authority
with the limited means available to him.

As well as targeting the first tier of the Munster leadership, Carew attacked
the will of the Munster lords' supporters without resorting to military force.
Carew believed that most of the Irish opposing him were not die-hard
politically motivated rebels, but remained in rebellion for fear of prosecution
for their past deeds. To strip away rebels *en masse*, Carew secured a general
pardon in Munster. This amnesty allowed disaffected Irish to gain crown
protection and enabled them to inform on those still in rebellion without fear
of damning testimony from anyone who may be captured.[114] With one stroke
Carew eroded confederate manpower and opened up new avenues for the flow
of intelligence on Irish movements and intentions.[115] Guile worked well in
dealing with the Irish leaders, but it also proved useful in military operations.
Carew used deception to multiply the effect of his forces and to degrade those
of his enemies. His calculated applications of misinformation caused Irish
lords to desert, or to squander their field units' limited resources. At the start
of May 1600, Carew made known his plans to march, causing a concentration
of Irish forces to oppose him, but he had no intention of setting out until
much later in the month. The Irish were obliged to disperse their army after
ten days due to supply shortages. When Carew finally moved north, he met
little resistance.[116]

The lord president made substantial efforts to promote the perception of
resurgent English strength in Munster. In the context of a native society where

allegiances were predicated on power and influence, the more Carew could make government control visible, the more he could expect supporters of the confederates to defect. Carew held court sessions at Limerick, Cashel and Clonmel to demonstrate that civil government was returning to Munster.[117] He paid considerable attention to the clearing of route ways and passes, leading to the re-establishment of land communications between the towns and cities.[118] It was noted that the opening of the road between Limerick and Kilmallock had resulted in the return of trade between the two towns.[119] Submissions were accepted to secure control over disputed roads.[120] The success of Carew's endeavours to open his lines of communication was trumpeted by the lord president and his council in a letter to the privy council. The Irish had previously impeded commerce between the towns by making the roads too hazardous to travel upon, but due to Carew's efforts he reported that six horsemen could go in safety, with the only danger coming from 'straggling persons'.[121]

Carew enacted a series of regulations that restricted freedom of movement, trade, and access to resources, aimed at reasserting crown control and dominance in Munster. Memoranda during April 1600 spelt out what was effectively a counterinsurgency plan to be applied to the population of Munster.[122] Within its prescriptions, Carew demanded that all freeholders would live under the protection of a garrison. Travel was limited outside of towns and castles, with valid passports required for anyone to leave their confines. This particular regulation was aimed at restricting the confederates' access to merchants. Licences were needed to purchase gunpowder, and the selling of munitions or war material to anyone outside the government was made a capital offence.[123]

During his summer campaign in Limerick, Carew attacked the lands supplying Desmond and his allies. By cutting off the Munster confederates' resources, he intended to starve his enemies out of their fastness.[124] At that time Carew (among many others) believed famine was the best device 'by which means only the wars of Ireland must be determined'.[125] Despite this, the Munster campaign in 1600 saw limited use of tactics that were later employed by Mountjoy on a much larger scale in Ulster. Carew later concluded that using localized famine was inefficient for pacification. In his letter to Cecil on 6 August, Carew noted the limitations of spoiling and starvation as a tool of war. He believed its effects primarily impacted the peasants and not the troops who opposed him. If total peace was the goal, then Carew would have to follow a policy that would lead to the 'utter extirpation of that [Irish] nation'.[126] Carew judged that this was not what the queen wanted, as the war would last much longer; conciliation could achieve more. Carew reasoned that to conquer Munster solely by the sword would be his '*opus laboris* [life's work] and almost impossible'.[127] He considered the total reduction of Munster feasible but prohibitively expensive; mercy could bring the peace but not good subjects, and to Carew that was an acceptable compromise.[128] While Carew was not averse to ordering brutal punitive attacks, he tended to use burning and spoiling only as a last resort or as a calculated act to intimidate.[129] Carew destroyed cereal crops to undermine the Irish lords' ability to pay their mercenaries, not to kill those who tended them.[130]

By the final stages of the war, spoiling in Kerry had the stated aim of forcing the population into government-controlled regions of northern Cork and Limerick, thereby separating the Irish confederate lords from their primary source of support and revenue.[131] Though destructive, these attacks were still tempered by Carew's caution, fearing that an overly aggressive campaign could reignite rebellion.[132] Carew's use of devastation was not solely to erode the Irish ability to maintain the war, but also to strengthen the English capacity to defend the region. His destruction of the coastal area between Bantry and Kinsale at the close of 1602 was in response to the threat of a second Spanish landing. Carew planned that if the Spanish returned they would find a country unable to sustain them.[133]

Perhaps one of the most comprehensive displays of Carew's use of deception and cunning was his attempt to capture the *sugán* earl in June 1600. Carew had secured the defection of Dermot O'Connor, who was one of Tyrone's most trusted captains in Munster. O'Connor's wife, Margaret, was the sister of James Fitzgerald, whom Carew planned to have released from the Tower of London, and reinstated as the queen's earl of Desmond. Margaret had persuaded O'Connor to betray James Fitzthomas to secure the release of her brother from the Tower.[134] O'Connor's defection may also have been encouraged by Carew's offer of £1,000.[135] The Irish annals record that O'Connor was turned by the temptation of wealth and land.[136] Carew planned for O'Connor to apprehend the *sugán* earl and hand him over, alive or dead. O'Connor was no simple dupe. He did not trust Carew and demanded pledges to be placed in his custody until Carew made good on his side of the bargain. These were delivered to him via a fake ambush so as not to raise suspicions.[137] There were also practical issues to be resolved before O'Connor could act.

O'Connor had two main preconditions for the plot to succeed. He required an excuse for arresting Desmond as his bonnaghts were still loyal to Tyrone. O'Connor also needed Desmond to be isolated from his troops, as he had too many men nearby for O'Connor to move against him.[138] Accordingly, Carew had a letter fabricated in May 1600 that feigned to be a response by Carew to Desmond's overtures of submission.[139] O'Connor showed this to his Connacht mercenaries to convince them of Desmond's duplicity. To separate Desmond from the bulk of his forces, Carew scattered his army to disparate garrisons, compelling Desmond to match the dispersal to mask and inhibit the potential for small-scale actions by the government troops. Superficially it appeared that Carew was squandering the summer campaigning season, but the dispersal gave O'Connor a localized superiority in troop numbers to enact the plot.

O'Connor planned to trick his men into capturing Desmond in Tyrone's name, then hand him over to the lord president. Using a meeting to discuss the war as a pretence, O'Connor captured Desmond and imprisoned him in Castlelishen (Co. Cork). O'Connor demanded payment before delivering the earl, as he was still unsure of Carew.[140] This delay allowed Desmond's followers to gather and lay siege to the castle which quickly fell, freeing the earl.[141] Desmond had evaded Carew, but the episode poisoned the relationship between the local Munster soldiers and the mercenaries from Connacht, whom O'Connor had commanded. Though they were not privy to O'Connor's machinations with Carew, the plot threw suspicion upon all men from Connacht. On his release, Desmond ordered all of O'Connor's Connacht men out of Munster.[142] Carew considered the failure to capture Desmond offset by the distrust fostered between the local troops and the Connacht mercenaries.[143] By the end of August, large numbers of Connacht bonnaghts were leaving Munster.[144] This was a crippling blow to the Irish war effort in the region, as the mercenaries were considered superior in training and equipment to the locally raised troops.[145]

The episode demonstrated Carew's attitude to fighting the war in Munster. His primary concern was not engaging his enemies in combat but winning the war. With limited resources, Carew subdued a numerically superior enemy without initiating any major military engagements. The Dermot O'Connor plot showed that he was prepared to disperse his military power to enable risky but potentially rewarding conspiracies. Schemes, plots and underhand dealing were the crucial tools for Carew, as he did not have the military strength for anything else. Twenty-one years later, Philip O'Sullivan Beare concurred, writing that the Irish in Munster were too well equipped to be overcome by English military force, but were defeated by subterfuge and trickery.[146]

In contrast with previous campaigns, Carew's pacification of Munster was a spectacular success given his limited resources. Florence MacCarthy was effectively neutralized, and the *sugán* earl was reduced to a fugitive after his forces were attacked and defeated in the Glen of Aherlow in September 1600.[147] Though Fitzthomas' power had been broken, Carew could not induce anyone in Munster to betray him, despite his offer of £400 for the earl's capture. Fitzthomas remained at large until May 1601, when he was captured by Edmund Fitzgibbon, the White Knight.[148] With Desmond imprisoned, Carew turned his attention to Florence MacCarthy whom he had arrested the following month. It seemed that for now, the war in Munster was finished.

Mountjoy on the offensive

It was clear by the summer of 1600 that the crown's strategic position in Ireland was improving. Docwra's arrival on the Foyle had drawn Tyrone's best forces north, and Carew's chicanery in Munster was sowing confusion in the confederate ranks in the far south. O'Donnell raided deep into Connacht, but used troops from Connacht, as he was obliged to leave his Tirconnell men behind to cover Docwra.[149] The garrisons at Newry and Carrickfergus were confident enough to spoil the surrounding districts, where they 'laid all waste about them for 20 miles, taken great preys, and done very good service'.[150] However, Mountjoy's focus was on the now vulnerable Irish midlands. He intended to use the army to burn and spoil Irish crops in Co. Offaly, but was delayed when intelligence suggested Tyrone was massing troops on the south Ulster border, forcing Mountjoy to respond in kind.[151] From Ardbraccan (near Navan, Co. Meath), the army pushed south into Offaly on 25 July and proceeded to burn and spoil to the north and south of the fort at Philipstown. The Irish skirmished with Mountjoy's men every day, but there was nothing to stop the lord deputy's destructive progress through the county.

Mountjoy returned to Dublin on 3 August, but struck south-west into Kildare and Laois on 11 August, destroying crops where he found them. The army reached Ferns abbey (Co. Wicklow) by 17 August, devastating the countryside and taking submissions as it went. A company of Mountjoy's foot fell into a skirmish with troops led by Owny O'More, during which O'More was fatally wounded.[152] His loss was a severe blow to Tyrone, as O'More's death broke the morale of the confederate leaders in Leinster. O'Sullivan Beare wrote that 'On his death almost all the Leinstermen lost heart and very soon afterwards the Viceroy Blount received into favour Daniel, the Spaniard, Felim O'Byrne, the O'Tooles and others, and almost the whole of Leinster wasted and weary of war was pacified'.[153]

Only on Mountjoy's return northwards did he face a substantial Irish force at the pass of Cashel, four miles south of Maryborough (Portlaoise, Co. Laois). The road was blocked by entrenchments held by 2,500 Irish among whom was Captain Richard Tyrrell. However, the right wing of the Irish position was assigned to Domhnall Spaniagh Kavanagh, who had secretly requested safe conduct to the lord deputy – likely as a precursor to his submission.[154] As Mountjoy's force approached Kavanagh met with the lord deputy and begged to be received in Dublin, to which Mountjoy agreed. Kavanagh then withdrew his men from the Irish line allowing the English to attack the Irish on their undefended flank, routing them completely though with few recorded losses on either side.[155]

Mountjoy's campaigns to that point had not resulted in main force engagements with Tyrone or his allies. However, Tyrone's network of allies was significantly reduced. O'More had been killed, but of more concern were the defections of Irish lords to the crown. Conor Roe Maguire defected in July and Kavanagh in August, but they were only the first of many, resulting in the disintegration of Tyrone's confederacy. Nevertheless, the fracturing of Irish loyalties was not enough for some in England. Consequently, the lord deputy came under mounting pressure to produce discernible results. In a stinging rebuke, the privy council accused Mountjoy and his officers of failing in their obligations, noting that 'few or none of you have done your own particular duties'.[156] The queen followed suit suggesting that 'things are not so well ordered as they might be'.[157] During August the privy council again sought to 'advise' Mountjoy, leading him to draft a remarkably frank letter to Cecil, insisting that unrealistic expectations were undermining his ability to prosecute the war.[158] The pressure on Mountjoy certainly goes some way to explaining his belligerent attitude when he marched north and met Tyrone in the Moyry Pass at the end of September. The result was a bloody slogging match in the rain.

Erecting a new garrison at Armagh was the stated aim of the expedition. Mountjoy had (by list) 3,450 foot and 375 horse, but Tyrone had blocked the only way north with strong fortifications at the southern end of the Moyry Pass.[159] The army moved north from Dundalk on 20 September, but the English were beset by poor weather and pestered by Irish skirmishers as they made camp at Faughart Hill. Using the cover of heavy fog, a reconnaissance-in-force on 25 September discovered the Irish occupied three lines of earthwork fortifications, reinforced with sconces and crested with palisades and wattling; all of which was supported by trenches on the high ground on both flanks.[160] This discovery cost Mountjoy twelve killed and thirty wounded.

The rain poured until 2 October, causing atrocious conditions in the English camp, where hundreds fell sick and many more deserted, but on 2 October the rain stopped and Mountjoy moved to clear the pass. Five infantry regiments assaulted the Irish defences. After four hours of fierce fighting, the English had taken two of the Irish barricades, but the third held. The English soldiers were exposed in open ground and taking fire from strong Irish defences on both flanks; Mountjoy had little option but to withdraw from the pass.[161] A second attack was made on 5 October when two regiments were sent to take the heights to the left of Tyrone's positions, but Irish counter-attacks stopped the assault, and again the English were compelled to pull back.[162] The army was now in a sorry condition, and Sir Robert Lovell described the camp as 'lying in the mire'.[163] Mountjoy stubbornly remained at Faughart and ordered up reinforcements, but by 9 October he had enough and pulled the army back to Dundalk. The lord deputy claimed a great victory, but Mountjoy had beaten his army to rags on Tyrone's defences, and only pushed through the pass on 17 October after Tyrone withdrew north.

After resupplying at Newry, Mountjoy marched north into Armagh. The lord deputy established a new campaign fort on 4 November, which he named Mountnorris, roughly half way between Newry and Armagh and just south of the defences Mountjoy encountered during his first journey north back in May. There was regular skirmishing during its construction, but work continued until the fort was completed on 7 November. A garrison was left, and the bulk of the army withdrew to Newry on 11 November. Mountjoy was forced to return to Carlingford via a circuitous route and hazardous river crossing at Narrow Water castle. Sir Ralph Lane claimed this was because Tyrone had re-edified the Moyry Pass.[164] Nevertheless, Tyrone was not yet finished with Mountjoy. On the 13 November, the Irish assailed the flanks the column from fortified positions as the English marched south to Carlingford; 90 more men were killed before the English broke through.[165]

Mountjoy had made his point; Tyrone had been engaged and a new base established at Mountnorris. Munster was in good hands, and Docwra was making progress on the Foyle now that he had secured the defection of local allies. Regardless of these achievements, the lord deputy was wary of how this was reported in England. He need not have worried. Mountjoy's critics in England had been silenced by the successes in Munster and Ulster. The queen's tone changed dramatically. Her scorn was replaced with effusive praise and confidence, writing 'comfort yourself therefore in this, that neither your careful endeavours, nor dangerous travails, nor heedful regards to our service … could ever have been bestowed upon a prince that more esteems them'.[166] Mountjoy's standing had been secured, at least for the time being by the fighting in Ulster, but it was bought with the lives of his men. The army was now worn, depleted and in urgent need of resupply, but Mountjoy was not ready to retire to winter quarters just yet. Just before Christmas Mountjoy rode out of Dublin and attacked the O'Byrnes main residence at Ballinacor. He captured Phelim MacFeagh O'Byrne's son, ate the food set aside for Christmas then burnt the house the following day. Rather than pull back

17 Narrow Water castle

Mountjoy kept his men in the snow-covered fields destroying houses and forcing the Irish to stay within their fastness.

Before Mountjoy's appointment as lord deputy, military expeditions by the English field army tended to be spasmodic or reactive. They were usually limited to a campaigning season between April and October and ended with the dispersal of troops to garrisons. There were also long phases of negotiated cessations or truces, which both sides used to reinforce and refit troops. Mountjoy abandoned this style of stop-start warfare and implemented a policy of all-year-round campaigning. The lord deputy's unremitting persistence was bringing the Irish to breaking point. This strategic shift can be demonstrated by comparing the number of government operations for 1600 to those of previous years. In 1597, Lord Burgh marched to Armagh during July and again in October. The earl of Essex marched out three times in 1599. Mountjoy's first expedition was to Armagh in May; the Ulster borderlands in July; Offaly, Laois and Kildare during August; the Moyry Pass and Armagh from September to November and Wicklow in December, when he took Ballinacor on Christmas Eve. This high tempo of operations became characteristic of Mountjoy's approach throughout the subsequent years of the war.[167] The intensification of English operations stupefied the Irish. Captain Humphrey Willis reported how the Irish spoke among themselves of the lord deputy's incessant action and how no other deputy had done so before.[168] By March 1601, Sir Theobald Dillon reported the Irish 'greatly daunted ... wrought by the lord deputy his continual prosecution and sudden incursions'.[169] Regular shipments of food and munitions from England underpinned Mountjoy's ability to extend his operations into winter. Mountjoy had identified and started to exploit one of the crown's major advantages over the Irish – English economic might.

The English economy greatly overmatched that of Tyrone and his allies. With this in mind, Mountjoy made the war a trial of resources in which the crown had a substantial advantage. By keeping his forces in the field, Mountjoy compelled the Irish to do likewise, forcing Tyrone to expend money and supplies. Sir George Carey recognized this in May 1601, noting how Mountjoy's march to the Ulster borders had forced Tyrone to keep his army together 'which will spend and weaken him [Tyrone] very much'.[170] As well as forcing Tyrone to retain his men in pay, Mountjoy directly attacked the agricultural foundations of the confederate economy.

The majority of Tyrone's men were mercenaries. If he wanted them to fight they had to be paid. The wealth of the northern lords was founded on crop yields and herds of cattle. Sir Henry Docwra wrote in May 1600 that the confederate's ability to maintain the war rested in their cattle and corn.[171] Essex was correct in 1599 when he regarded hunting cattle in Ulster as not worth the effort, as they could be quickly withdrawn to the safety of nearby woods.[172] Rather than pursue the mobile wealth of the creaghts, Mountjoy targeted crops. His reasoning for campaigning in Laois during the summer of 1600, was to deprive the O'Mores of their ability to pay their bonnaghts.[173] The effect of this assault on the Irish economy was magnified by Mountjoy's reversal of the usual campaigning seasons.

Traditionally war was fought during periods of mild weather when abundant supplies and forage were available. This was normally between late spring and early autumn when troops could stay in the field in relative health, fodder could be found for horses and ground conditions were favourable for overland travel. Mountjoy reversed this pattern by attacking during winter and at times of planting and harvest.[174] The Irish were always difficult to intercept due to their superior mobility, and the cover provided by woodland. Operations during winter allowed Mountjoy to pursue his enemy, now deprived of the concealment provided by summer foliage. Expeditions during early spring prevented the sowing of crops, and autumn raids destroyed the harvest wherever it could be found.[175] During the summer Mountjoy's men occupied the plains and pastures on which Tyrone's cattle relied for sustenance. Rather than hazard the woods in search of the Irish creaghts, Mountjoy chose to contain them, thereby isolating the cattle from their food source.[176] Separation of their cattle from pasture forced the Irish to feed them on their reserves of stored corn, further undermining the Irish confederates' ability to pay their troops.[177] As Tyrone's capacity to maintain the war decayed, the political bonds which held his confederation together were assailed.

Before Mountjoy arrived in Ireland, the limitations of the native system of obligation and allegiance were becoming apparent. Tyrone created a confederation of Irish lordships that was able to engage in a coordinated multi-regional war effort. This network functioned for the early years of the war, but in 1599 Sir William Warren noted that the main weakness of the Irish was the many factions that remained within Tyrone's allies.[178] He opined that the application of strong government would soon see many of them fall away. Mountjoy utilized all means at his disposal to break the bonds that tied the confederates to Tyrone. He planned to raise junior Irish lords into positions of military strength where they could compete as claimants to titles of Irish lordships.[179] Of more significance was Docwra's winning over of Niall Garbh O'Donnell and Sir John O'Doherty, which greatly strengthened the crown's position in north-west Ulster. The crown exploited long-standing disputes concerning Tyrone's overlordhip of the O'Cahans and the Magennis, and O'Donnell's position as chief and his claims in north Connacht. O'Donnell overawed Niall Garbh O'Donnell and used force against Sir John O'Doherty to secure his election as chief in 1592.[180] It was unsurprising that those primarily disadvantaged by the prevailing dynastic situation were often the first to defect to the crown. Continuing succession disputes fractured the loyalties of the chiefs in Tirconnell, such as Owen Óg MacSweeny and the MacDaids in 1601.[181]

During July 1600, Mountjoy caused Lord Dunsany 'to blow fire' between the rival O'Rourkes and Maguires in their respective succession disputes in Leitrim and Fermanagh.[182] Mountjoy may also have authorized targeted assassinations to provoke further discord. George Darcy and George Gernon were paid £100 for 'cutting off the head' of Conn MacUladh MacMahon in April 1600.[183] This act was reported to have generated dissension in Monaghan similar to that enveloping Fermanagh due to the loss of Hugh Maguire.[184] Defections from the Irish were encouraged using selective spoiling of Tyrone's allies, and purchased with offers of financial reward. In both cases, these tested Tyrone's promises of protection to his client chiefs. The first involved the devastation of lands belonging to Tyrone's allies. Their allegiance to the earl was conditional on his obligation to protect them militarily.

Therefore Mountjoy challenged this by forcing a choice on Tyrone. He could honour his agreements to protect client chiefs by engaging Mountjoy, or demur, thereby undermining the earl's authority. Ultimately, Tyrone refused to be drawn into a battle of Mountjoy's choosing.[185] As a result, the earl's authority over his allied chiefs was compromised and the likelihood of defections to the crown increased. Mountjoy also used promises of financial gain to secure Irish support and encourage damaging raids on confederate territory.[186] An example was Shane MacBrian O'Neill of Clandeboye. In June 1600, Mountjoy authorized Sir Arthur Chichester to offer land and crown subsidies, but MacBrian was also given terms for spoiling enemy lands. He was promised one-third the value of spoils brought back from raiding in which MacBrian had English help and three-quarters for spoil that was recovered unassisted.[187] Shane MacBrian financially benefitted if he staged attacks without government troops, thereby saving the crown expense and effort.

In addition to the unequal contest between English and Irish resources, Mountjoy was quick to make use of naval power. At his disposal was the royal fleet and merchant ships, which were hired to transport men and material. Though Tyrone used coastal vessels as transport and for small-scale piracy, he had nothing that could realistically interfere with English maritime activity. During the early stages of the war, shipping was used to a limited extent against the Irish.[188] The benefits of using ships to project a ground force into the Foyle estuary were well appreciated, but previous missions had been cancelled or proved impossible to implement; it was under Mountjoy's tenure that English maritime muscle was brought to bear in the Irish war.

If material wealth and abundant supplies underpinned Mountjoy's strategy of constant campaigning, it was English shipping that enabled his plans to become a reality.[189] Captain Humphrey Willis reported that Tyrone's war effort was hindered by problems with shipments of supplies. He noted how the Irish were disheartened fighting an enemy who had received seventy ships from England at one time and two to three ships weekly after that, whereas they had only received two ships from Spain.[190] Sir George Carew recognized that ships had been crucial to the success of his operations in Limerick and Kerry in 1600.[191] The ability to rapidly supply and reinforce by sea was most evident at the siege of Kinsale in 1601, when Mountjoy's precipitous position was maintained by massive shipments of munitions and men.[192]

Ships were used for large- and small-scale troop movements and to avoid areas thought too dangerous to march through. Boats allowed Mountjoy to move men with greater speed than before, and in total safety from Irish attack. In 1602, Carew used ships to bypass an Irish blocking force near Bantry to besiege and then take Dunboy castle.[193] O'Donnell considered the use of naval force a significant advantage for the English. In a letter to Florence MacCarthy, O'Donnell noted how he had not been able to journey into Munster because of the landings on the Foyle. He added that English naval strength allowed them to 'conquer what they may' of districts lying upon the coast.[194]

With vastly superior naval forces, Mountjoy moved to dominate the coastal traffic around Ireland. Much of the confederate war material came via Spanish aid shipments and Scottish trade. From the early stages of the war, Scottish merchantmen had landed consignments along the north coast of Ulster and Strangford Lough. Spanish ships tended to land primarily at the north-west coastal port of Killybegs. Attempts had been made by the English to challenge this interchange in the past, but captains had reported difficulties in engaging the small and manoeuvrable galleys with weather dependant pinnaces and barques.[195] Mountjoy ordered small boats, similar to the galleys, into the North Channel between Scotland and Ulster to interdict the flow of war supplies, and stationed ships off the south-west coast of Ireland to interfere with Spanish shipping.[196] Merchantmen and cromsters were used to clear the mouth of the river Shannon of Irish galleys that had been plaguing English commercial traffic.[197] A standing patrol stationed at the mouth of the Shannon prevented the O'Malleys and O'Flahertys from carrying Irish reinforcements into Kerry during March 1601.

As useful as the coastal patrol ships were, it was the small craft on the inland waterways and loughs that brought the war into Tyrone's heartlands. In May 1601, Sir Arthur Chichester requested money to construct small vessels to add to his flotilla of craft on Lough Neagh.[198] Though his forces were initially restricted to around sixty men, Chichester embarked on a series of amphibious raids along the shores of the lough. The attacks must have been limited in scope due to the relatively few men he was able to land. Nevertheless, Chichester reported how his soldiers killed and destroyed everyone and everything they found during the raid, which came within four miles of Dungannon.[199] Mountjoy was impressed with the results and later demanded that Sir George Carey provide Chichester with whatever resources he required.[200] Tyrone was so concerned about Chichester's raids that he had fortifications built along the western shore of Lough Neagh to oppose the English attacks.[201]

Tyrone and his allies had become adept at neutralizing the impact of the crown's field armies. Troops could be attacked while on the move, or evaded until they exhausted their provisions. English amphibious operations were spared the difficulties of overland marches, as soldiers were relatively safe while being conveyed to their destinations, and could carry much more supplies. This

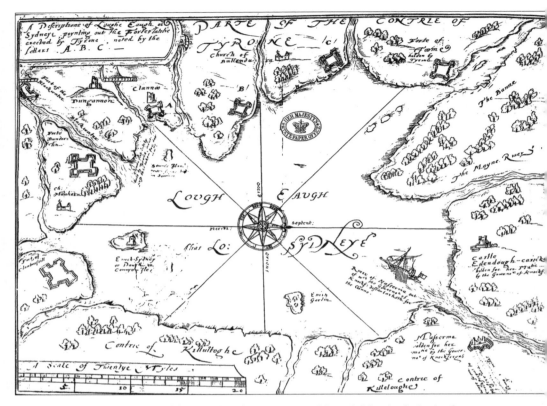

18 Map showing Tyrone's fortifications around Lough Neagh. Only the fort at
Masserine in the lower right corner was built by the English
(The National Archive, Kew, MPF 1/133)

granted them greater endurance in the field plus the possibility of naval
resupply. Of more importance were the restrictions placed on Tyrone's strategic
thinking by the threat of enemy action in his Ulster heartlands. Before
Mountjoy's deputyship, Tyrone could focus his efforts south of the physical
barrier of the Ulster drumlin belt. The garrisons in Carrickfergus and Newry
were too small and distant from Tyrone to pose any real threat. With English
bases established at Masserine priory (Co. Antrim) and Lough Foyle in 1600,
Tyrone's effort to support the war in the south was constantly trammelled by
the danger to his client lords and tenants at home.

Besides amending their tactical and operational methods, the authorities
in Dublin resorted to the use of widespread spoliation and raiding. During the
first half of the war, the crown proved unable or unwilling to launch a
concerted attack on the confederate economy using raids. Whereas the years

from 1593 to 1598 saw the focus of Irish spoiling start in Ulster and migrate southwards, the crown's recourse to raiding was limited. It was not until the arrival of Mountjoy in 1600 that spoliation by the government forces began to rival, and then exceed that of the Irish.

While Mountjoy replicated the Irish use of raids, his approach also displayed similarities with the Irish use of operational deception and diversion. The armies under Tyrone had used deception and duplicity from the very outset of their war against Elizabeth, whereas the crown's campaigns tended to be direct applications of military power. This changed with the arrival of Mountjoy. One of his first forays into the field was to effect a strategic diversion of Tyrone's strength in Ulster, fixing Tyrone in Armagh while Docwra made his landings on the Foyle in May 1600.[202] The following year, Mountjoy ordered the Foyle and Carrickfergus garrison to divert Irish preparations to assist the Spanish landings in Munster.[203] Mountjoy demonstrated that he could use elaborate deceptions to give him a tactical advantage in the field. The persistent threat to the suburbs of Dublin from the Irish based in the Wicklow Mountains caused Mountjoy to take action at the end of 1600, and he surprised Phelim MacFeagh O'Byrne's house at Ballinacor.[204] Rapid marches, facilitated by the English troops' new mobility, became a mainstay of crown operations, whereby they would use swift advances, secrecy of movement, false intelligence and deception.[205]

The subterfuge of Mountjoy and others showed that crown officers were now cognisant of the capabilities of their Irish adversaries, and were not willing to allow arrogance to blind them to native Irish military skill and sophistication.[206] Until the arrival of Mountjoy, English military commanders had relied on the power of their heavy infantry and cavalry to achieve success. Officers such as Russell and Norreys recognized the advances made by Tyrone and the qualities of his new infantry, but took no steps to change English strategy or tactics to counter them. Willingness to use deception as a force-multiplier demonstrated that the English military establishment in Ireland had matured beyond their earlier conceit. They appear to have come to the conclusion that the weight of English military power was not as strong as had been previously believed. More importantly, they recognized that the Irish arrayed against them were not so weak that they could be suppressed or overawed by brute force.

Irish operational and tactical failure

As the English improved, the combat power, cohesion and tempo of Irish confederate operations began to decline. The first seven years of the war from

1593 to 1599 witnessed a series of almost unbroken success for Tyrone and his allies. Yet within a year, Munster had been pacified, the boundaries of Tyrone's power forced back to Ulster and Connacht, and a beachhead established on the Foyle. Changes in English strategy, tactics and equipment go some way to explaining their success, but there were corresponding alterations in the Irish forces that suggest that while the armies and officers of the crown improved, the Irish weakened and correspondingly lost the key advantages that had led to success in the past.

The paucity of Irish records detailing the structure of Tyrone's forces means that evidence for changes in Irish units during the war must be gleaned from analysis of events from 1600 onwards. Tyrone's pikemen were primarily defensive. The principal offensive weapon of Tyrone and his allies was the caliver, but close examination of the characteristics of engagements show that changes were occurring from 1600. In contrast to how the Irish had fought before, the Irish in the south of Ireland started to engage in melee combat with unbroken English units. This occurred when Florence MacCarthy attempted to ambush an English force marching to Cork in April 1600. His troops charged into close combat where they were disordered by close-range gunfire and a charge by the English horse.[207] In September 1600, Irish troops charged into close combat in the Glen of Aherlow (Co. Tipperary), but without recourse to their shot they were quickly routed.[208] Sir Henry Folliot scattered the O'Tooles in a push of pike at the start of 1601. During this engagement, there was no preliminary or protracted fire-fight and all the reported injuries to the English were caused by pikes.[209] In the north, Irish infantry could still depend on firepower. However, Tyrone's allies in the south had started to engage in melee combat with pikes, but the light Irish pikemen were not trained for, and therefore unsuited to this type of combat. All the major Irish victories of the war were battles in which firepower was dominant. Why then would Tyrone's southern allies choose to fight melee actions when they resulted in defeat?

An answer might be found in Pádraig Lenihan's work on the Confederate wars of the 1640s. Lenihan contended that the Irish only resorted to charges into close combat due to local political fragmentation and a chronic shortage of gunpowder.[210] The Irish assaults during the opening phase of the wars of the 1640s were the only options open to disorganized forces who could not match the superior firepower of their opponents. When Irish infantry became better organized and modern arms, equipment and most importantly gunpowder was made available, the Irish forces developed along conventional lines.[211] Application of this model to the military situation in southern Ireland after 1599 suggests that Irish firepower may have been neutralized by a shortage of gunpowder. Consequently, the southern confederates' only option was to attempt shock actions with their pike units, which proved ultimately unsuccessful.

Shortages of gunpowder would not have been damaging to traditional Irish troops, such as the gallowglass and kerne, as their primary weapons did not require it. When Irish soldiers in Munster were transformed into pike and shot formations as in Connacht and Ulster, then a lack of gunpowder would have greatly inhibited their effectiveness.[212] As noted by Robert Barret, pike and shot formations were critically weakened if their shot were ineffective or neutralized.[213] In the case of the new-style Irish, with their dependence on firepower, the neutralization of their shot due to a lack of gunpowder was catastrophic. Without powder to maintain extended skirmishes that had been so effective in the past, they were forced to utilize their pike in offensive shock action. If the Irish pike units were not trained for fighting in close order formations, as an account of training from Dungannon suggested, then their use offensively would result in predictable defeat. Sir John Smythe observed that the close order pike will 'overthrow, disorder and break them [loose order pike] with as great facility, as if they were but a flock of geese'.[214]

Throughout the war, Irish operations had been limited by a shortage of gunpowder. It had to be purchased (both in Ireland and abroad), transported, safely stored, and then conveyed to where it was needed at the appropriate time. This was difficult in a country with a particularly damp climate and few roads. Many of Tyrone's engagements, including his greatest victory at the battle of the Yellow Ford, were curtailed by insufficient supplies of gunpowder.[215] If this were true for battles in Ulster, where the two major ports for landing imports were located (Killybegs and Ringhaddy), then Irish forces in the south would find access to munitions even more challenging. The precarious situation of the Munster confederates was already recognized in 1599. In an unsigned note to Sir George Carew, the author pointed out that should a campaign be launched against the confederates in Munster, Irish ammunition in the province would last two days at the most.[216]

Tyrone's Munster allies repeatedly turned to Ulster when they required reinforcement and resupply. Captain Francis Kingsmill reported in August 1599 that the Munster rebels were having difficulty maintaining their bonnaghts out of Connacht and Ulster.[217] During the same year supplies of men and munitions were shipped by the O'Malleys from Ulster to Munster.[218] John Fitzthomas and Piers Lacy travelled to Ulster in August 1600 to secure aid from Tyrone.[219] As the situation in Munster became critical, Tyrone made a determined effort to reinforce his Muster allies in March 1601, but all his convoys were intercepted on route or forced back.[220]

It was evident to Mountjoy that the key to choking off supplies to Munster was cutting the north–south supply lines, and that these lines were vital to the Irish cause. Therefore much of Mountjoy's campaigns of 1600 focused on Westmeath, Offaly and Laois, interdicting the normal land routes from Ulster to Munster and causing many of Tyrone's erstwhile allies to defect to the crown. Mountjoy focused on the midland septs such as the MacCoghlans and O'Carrolls, securing the territory between the rivers Barrow and Shannon.[221] The submission of the O'Melaghlins effectively blocked north–south communications through Westmeath.[222] The lord deputy maintained this blockade into the next year when he stationed forces along the Inny river to prevent traffic passing from Ulster into the south.[223] Mountjoy astutely observed that Tyrone's allies in the south could not maintain their resistance if they were isolated from reinforcements from Ulster.

A crucial element to the success of the Irish forces was their tactical and operational mobility. During the early stages of the war, the Irish could march at speed as they did not have restrictive baggage trains. Supply trains consisted of pack animals and waggons, carrying the stores and munitions which the troops needed to subsist and fight in the field. Correspondingly, armies could only move as fast as the slow moving carriages. O'Donnell's men carried their supplies in packs, and Captain Nicholas Dawtrey wrote in 1597 that the Irish were not hindered by baggage as they carried what they needed for daily use.[224] However, during 1599 Irish baggage trains begin to appear.

The first reference to an Irish unit accompanied by baggage came in April 1599 when Sir Thomas Norreys followed a body of 300 Irish foot marching to Mallow. Norreys' horsemen charged the Irish, who were lucky to be saved by the proximity of their pike.[225] Increasingly this was repeated as Irish units with attendant carriage were tracked down and engaged. The *sugán* earl of Desmond was caught with a baggage train in September 1600 in the Glen of Aherlow.[226] However, it was not just the provincial units of Tyrone's army that were accruing baggage, as the earl's main force also resorted to them.[227] By late 1601, Tyrone was dependent on baggage trains for maintaining his troops, thereby greatly reducing their mobility.[228]

Time and again the Irish were being caught by English units that earlier in the war could have been easily outmanoeuvred or outpaced. It appears that the Irish had abdicated the tactical and operational mobility that had underpinned their previous success, and so frustrated previous English commanders. What factor caused them to adopt something that put them to such a clear disadvantage? Irish troops on the march gathered much of their supplies from the surrounding area. As explained earlier, the Irish armies were provided for by spoliation, aid from the local inhabitants, itinerant supply columns and pre-sited stores.[229] Ó Clérigh referred to Irish supply columns in his account of O'Donnell's siege of Collooney castle in 1599. They were composed of pack horses and led by ploughmen and 'persons unfit for war'.[230] Moreover, he noted they were unguarded, as no one dared interfere with a supply convoy to O'Donnell. This suggested that fear or local deference ensured the free transport of goods to the confederate armies from secure areas to their rear. In the context of Irish success from 1593 to 1599, this system worked; fast-moving troops carrying their provisions moved independently of their slower supply columns. This method could be used where the convoys could travel in safety, but not when their security was compromised from 1600 onwards by the activities of Mountjoy and his subordinates. Extensive campaigning, increased use of raiding and the subsequent cascade of defections to the government meant that the itinerant supply convoys used by the Irish in earlier phases of the war would no longer be viable. This explains why baggage became a feature of Irish field armies from this point onwards. Uncertain that support elements would catch up with their armies, the Irish were forced to carry everything that they required with them, despite the attendant loss of mobility.

Mountjoy presses his advantage

The revitalized English campaigns had caused a tectonic shift in the course of the war. English troops were operating with a level of direction and operational freedom that had not been a feature of most of the crown's efforts during the war to that point. Defections of large numbers of Irish lords demonstrated that the resurgent power of the crown was keenly felt by Tyrone and those allied to him. Key Irish figures across Ireland were deserting to the crown. Niall Garbh O'Donnell, Arthur O'Neill and Sir John O'Doherty joined Docwra in the north-west, Randall MacDonnell, Shane MacBrian O'Neill and Niall MacBrian O'Neill now fought for the crown in east Ulster. Of critical importance were the midland septs. The submission of the O'Carrolls, MacCoghlans and O'Melaghlins during August and September effectively cut Tyrone's confederacy in half. Barnewall reported that Tyrone had grown wary of some of his closest allies and had taken great pains to ensure the loyalty of his adherents, especially those in Ulster.[231]

Mountjoy entered Wicklow again at the start of February to continue the programme of spoiling he started in January. Mountjoy even opined that the resistance of the Irish lords was broken. He glibly noted that after the bloodletting of the Moyry, Tyrone would have at most 1,200 men and that if he could put together 4,000 men in the field, Mountjoy would 'be content to yield myself their prisoner'.[232] Success in Leinster was matched in the far north. Docwra, now aided by Niall Garbh, made inroads to Tyrone's heartlands. Newtown in Tyrone had been spoiled in November when men, women and children were killed, and 500 cows taken back to the garrison at Lifford. Preys were taken in Donegal, and during March Tirconnell and O'Cahan's country east of Derry were raided.

Tyrone was not prepared to sit idly by while his network of alliances collapsed. Carew received letters suggesting that Tyrone was sending troops south to reignite the war in Munster.[233] Just as Mountjoy knew that a garrison on the Foyle could force the northern lords to draw back into Ulster, it is highly likely Tyrone hoped that reinforcement of his Muster allies would lead to an intensification of the conflict in the south, forcing Mountjoy to divert resources out of Ulster. Tyrone ordered three major supply missions south during March. A naval expedition was attempted along the west coast. O'Malley and O'Flaherty galleys carried 600 troops south, but English naval patrols operating out of the Shannon forced them to turn back.[234] Redmond Burke and Teig O'Rourke led a column through Connacht, but their progress was checked by Captain George Flower in Thomond. Burke and O'Rourke returned north when support from O'Donnell was not forthcoming.[235] Tyrone's third effort was made through the midlands. John Fitzthomas, Piers Lacy and Captain Tyrrell were sent south with 1,500 troops.[236] However, Mountjoy had taken positions on the fords along the Inny, blocking the route south. Tyrrell's men made it past the blockade but were later engaged by Mountjoy and then again by Captain Christopher St Laurence.[237] Tyrrell was wounded in the skirmish with St Laurence and by 12 April had returned to Dungannon.[238] Just as in Thomond, the Irish attempt to reinforce Munster was thwarted.

Extreme measures: monetary debasement

Mountjoy's new strategy was taking effect, but the renewed offensive was hugely expensive. The crown's finances were in a parlous state by 1601. Years of warfare in Ireland and on the Continent had cost far more than the revenue raised by government taxation.[239] To redress this shortfall, the crown debased the coin in Ireland. The old money in use in Ireland was decried and a new standard minted. The new coin had much less intrinsic value than its face value, but it was hoped that all coins moving into and out of Ireland could be channelled through government-controlled exchanges.[240] Besides minting new coins to pay for the war, the debasement was a direct attack on Tyrone's ability to purchase goods in foreign markets.[241] The government hoped to deny the

Irish access to cash by drawing out of circulation coins that were acceptable to foreign merchants. When this was replaced with base money that could only be changed for sterling at the crown exchanges, Tyrone would be unable to pay for imported arms and munitions.[242]

The Irish confederates' capacity to generate wealth and translate that into money to pay for foreign goods proved a serious problem for the English. Tyrone and his allies dominated most of the countryside by 1599, and much of the commodities produced there. Consequently, towns and merchants were obliged buy agricultural commodities from the rebels. As a result much of the coinage in Ireland ended up in the hands of the confederates.[243] Enriched with English sterling, the Irish could pay in cash for imported arms, munitions, wine and salt.[244] The traffic in foreign goods for English sterling led to the loss of money to overseas markets, which was intolerable to the crown. The monetization of the native Irish economy was dangerous in itself, but the loss of coin was detrimental to the English economy as a whole.[245] In 1601, it was hoped that coin debasement would solve this problem.

In a document written late in 1600, unsigned but with amendments to it in Cecil's hand, three reasons in favour of the proposed debasement were clearly articulated: a saving on the cost of the war, the drawing of silver and gold out of Ireland and 'as a consequence of that, that the rebel robbed of his fine moneys, shall have no means to use commerce with other nations … and so of necessity grow weak'.[246] The case for damaging the enemy war effort was evident in the queen's proclamation, which stated that denial of coin to their Irish enemies was the main reason for decrying currency.[247] Despite the apparent advantages of debasement many were opposed to the proposals. Some felt that it would severely damage the economy by causing inflation and suppressing overseas trade. Carew was worried that the move would bolster Irish morale, as their enemies may interpret the move as a sign of English weakness.[248] Despite the inherent dangers of debasement, the political will of Cecil and Lord Treasurer Buckhurst ensured that the measures were enacted on 20 May 1601.[249]

The changes were quick to take effect, but not in the way that the crown hoped, as both Docwra and Chichester soon found it impossible to purchase goods from merchants, who refused to accept the new coins.[250] As the government pressed ahead with the scheme, it became clear that the new currency was failing to gain acceptance in either the domestic or foreign markets. Overseas trade had effectively stopped and commodity prices rose by fifty per cent.[251] Problems with the crown-controlled exchanges meant that even domestic trade between England and Ireland was adversely affected.[252] There were abuses of the exchange system by merchants who profited by inflating prices and buying up the new coins at much less than their face value, then changing them for sterling at the exchange for substantial gains.[253] Orders were issued to force acceptance of the new coin, but merchants continued to hold on to the decried money as its intrinsic worth made it more valuable.[254] By the start of 1603, Mountjoy was driven to advise the privy council of the possibility of mutiny in the army and a new rebellion if they were forced to continue with the base coins.[255] Carew reported the collapse of trade in the towns, and it was later noted how shortages brought about by years of war, were exacerbated by the merchants' inability to pay for imported goods.[256]

Economically, the debasement of the coinage was a catastrophic failure. Regarding money saved to the crown, analysis has shown that there was little if no net profit to the exchequer.[257] The concomitant loss of trade and associated customs and duties further added to the financial cost of the exercise. The only other way in which the project could have succeeded was in causing damage to Tyrone and his allies. This is hard to quantify given the lack of Irish records, but Tyrone's revenue would have been protected to a degree due to his control of substantial reserves of basic commodities, and infusions of Spanish gold and silver. Of more consequence was the extreme sanctions the crown authorities were willing to take to damage the economy of their adversaries. While they may have hoped that the new coin would be accepted, the crown was content to stifle the economic life of loyal subjects if, at the same time, it damaged the Irish ability to pay for foreign goods. It highlighted the degree to which the Irish economy had been monetized by the end of the sixteenth century. Throughout the discourse on the pros and cons of the debasement, the government officers consistently mentioned the substantial quantities of cash with which Tyrone imported arms. This was a far cry from the earlier trade in raw materials and hides for the expensive imports. Writing long after the war, O'Sullivan Beare considered the debasement of the coin to be one of the main reasons why the crown defeated Tyrone, adding that 'the Protestants held the Irish war would never have been finished while the Irish had victuals or gold or silver to procure them'.[258]

Mountjoy's return to Ulster

Mountjoy was becoming confident that the war in Ireland might soon be over. In a report at the start of May, he opined that he was almost in a position where he could 'very shortly banish, the two vipers of this kingdom, Tyrone and O'Donnell'.[259] The lord deputy gathered his forces in the south-Ulster borderlands with the intention of driving for the river Blackwater in June. In east Ulster, Chichester launched the first of his amphibious raids. Chichester's

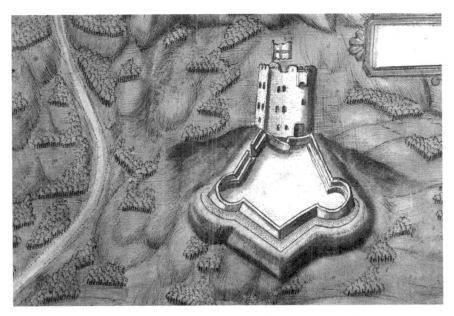

19 Moyry castle, raised by Mountjoy in 1601 to hold the Moyry Pass
(The National Library of Ireland, MS 2656, i)

account of the attacks certainly set the tone for his dealings with the Irish. Of the landings in Tyrone, Chichester wrote 'we spare none of what quality or sex [what] soever, and it hath bred much terror in the people'.[260]

The lord deputy gathered his army at Dundalk then pushed north on 8 June, but stopped at Faughart at the southern entrance to the Moyry Pass. Mountjoy had been vexed by this route more than once, therefore to secure the pass the lord deputy ordered the construction of a small fort to hold the road north. The army remained for six days, but on 14 June Mountjoy ordered his men to march to Newry, leaving a garrison in the fort and some workmen to finish the small masonry tower.[261] The force was resupplied and continued north to Mountnorris on 22 June and then on to Armagh where a garrison was placed under the command of Sir Henry Davers, all without major incident. Troops were sent to reinforce Chichester and columns marched east into Lecale, but a shortage of supply forced Mountjoy to fall back to Newry.

The overall plan for the summer campaign in Ulster called for a coordinated attack into Tyrone by Docwra in the north-west, Chichester from the east and Mountjoy from the south.[262] However, while Mountjoy made every effort to cross the Blackwater, Chichester busied himself raiding Clanbrassil on the southern shore of Lough Neagh. Docwra took Newtown, but baulked at moving towards the Blackwater citing a lack of munitions, specifically match.[263] The menace of a Spanish landing to the south limited the goals of the English summer campaign.[264] Nonetheless, Mountjoy was determined to attack Tyrone directly. Mountjoy returned to Armagh on 12 July and the following morning he was on the south bank of the river Blackwater. Mountjoy discovered that the Irish had not been idle.

Tyrone fortified all the fords along the river making them 'so guardable as we could not have believed unless we had seen the same for ourselves'.[265] As the lord deputy viewed the defences, volleys of Irish fire forced some of his staff to withdraw to a safer distance. While going for what appeared to be a constitutional stroll, Fynes Moryson was obliged to beat a hasty retreat under fire from the Irish on the far bank as he 'found an enemy's soil no place for recreation'.[266] The Irish positions were too strong to be attempted during daylight, therefore a covered approach was cut to enable the English assault force to safely approach the riverbank.[267] In the early hours of 14 July Captain Thomas Williams, the former governor of Burgh's Blackwater fort, led nine infantry companies to assault the defences.[268] There was initially stiff resistance, but English cannon fire helped suppress the Irish defence, and by first light the Irish had been forced to withdraw.[269] Mountjoy had his bridgehead on the Tyrone side of the river, and he set about building a fort on a small hill 600 metres upstream to secure the lodgement. This position became known as the Mullin fort and was recorded by the cartographer Richard Bartlett.[270] Nevertheless, Tyrone was not ready to surrender his control of the river so easily.

Two days later, Mountjoy sent a regiment of foot commanded by Sir Christopher St Laurence west to Benburb to view the passes leading to Dungannon. This was where Lord Burgh's campaign had stalled in 1597, and just as then the passes were heavily fortified with plashing, trenches and sconces, but this time the Irish did not wait behind their ramparts. Tyrone's men emerged to skirmish with the lead regiment for two to three hours. As Tyrone committed more men to the fight, Mountjoy sent forward regiments of foot to second St Laurence. The battle ebbed and flowed, favouring the Irish at one moment, the English the next, but the engagement ended inconclusively with neither side getting the upper hand.[271] Though Mountjoy was bullish in his reporting of the battle, he had not managed to break Tyrone's resistance, nor had he penetrated the strong defences protecting Dungannon. Tyrone withdrew to the fastness at Tobermesson, but Mountjoy did not attempt to follow him. Instead he proclaimed a reward of £2,000 for Tyrone's capture; alternatively, Mountjoy would pay £1,000 for the earl's head.[272]

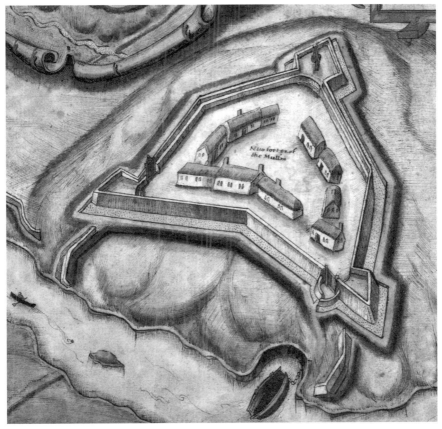

20 The Mullin fort, by Richard Bartlett, 1602–3
(The National Library of Ireland, MS 2656, iii)

The lord deputy was clearly not prepared to attempt to force his way through to Dungannon. Mountjoy considered the reward was not worth risking the army, especially as Docwra was now not able to make the journey south.[273] The focus turned to strengthening the garrisons south of the Blackwater and destroying Irish crops. There were regular small actions and *camisadoes* (night attacks) on the English camp, but Tyrone did not attempt to push south in any significant numbers.[274] Progress was made elsewhere as Docwra extended his control of the north-west. Donegal town fell to Niall Garbh during August, and English garrisons were established in Newtown and Omagh (Co. Tyrone). There were some setbacks though, as Captain Esmond's company was mauled by the MacMahons in Monaghan, losing forty men.[275] Nevertheless, Mountjoy was concerned about the threat of

Spanish landings in the south and the activities of Tyrrell provoking rebellion in Leinster. Therefore the garrisons in Ulster were ordered to hold Tyrone in the north while the army pulled back to Trim at the start of September.[276] The lord deputy called troops out of Munster, thereby unifying his forces to counter the Spanish wherever and whenever they arrived. Reinforcements out of England arrived in Munster, but Mountjoy noted 'As long as we are in suspense as to the coming of the Spaniards we have no policy to engage ourselves any further in the north'.[277] On the afternoon of 21 September 1601, the sails of the Spanish fleet appeared off the old Head of Kinsale.[278] The long-awaited/feared Spanish landings had begun.

CHAPTER 6

The catastrophe of war and the road to Mellifont, 1601–3

K INSALE WAS THE CRISIS MOMENT for Tyrone and Mountjoy and its effect on the war proved decisive and irreversible. The collapse of Irish resistance was as spectacular as it was conclusive. One could almost claim that Irish success from 1593 to 1600 was atypical. Were seven years of success a blip in the narrative that ended with the return of the familiar Gaelic warrior – fierce in battle but easily routed by modern English forces? This idea is a fiction that leans on comfortable stereotypes to explain the breakdown of Tyrone's complex network of alliances, with a corresponding failure of the confederate army's command and control. Within the historiography of the war, this is virgin territory to explore. However, the debate concerning the crown's scorched earth strategy and civilian victimization is well known and contentious.

Without a doubt, the closing stages of the war have provoked the most fractious debates about the conflict. The nature of violence against the Irish has been a source of debate in Irish academia.[1] Moreover, Irish historians have been criticized for failing to address the issue.[2] The case for exceptional levels of violence and barbarism in the conduct of the war against the Irish in the sixteenth century was recently articulated in *Age of atrocity*.[3] Others have gone further to suggest that the war descended to the level of genocide against the natives.[4] Explicit accounts of death and starvation have drawn the narrative into one of brutal excesses by the English, but was the English state capable of manufacturing such a disaster? Direct attacks on civilians were shocking and accounts of atrocities against men, women and children conjure distressing images, but their impact on the Irish population was minor, though the social and political effects could be catastrophic in a society based on lineage.[5] It took the combined effect of agricultural collapse brought on by years of economic strain, English depredation, currency debasement and a naturally occurring harvest failure to produce the rapid onset of famine in Ulster during 1602.

The history of warfare in Ireland is replete with examples of the mistreatment or direct victimization of civilians.[6] While it is undeniable that many of the protagonists in the Nine Years War were fierce and uncompromising, a focus on the harshest elements in the historiography, or avoidance of the issue by the reform-minded historians, has resulted in subtleties and paradoxical behaviour being ignored. The last years of the conflict were savagely violent, but the reasons for attacks on civilians were more varied and nuanced than the simplistic narrative of ethnic/religious antagonism. Strategic frustration, the nature of the war, individual human psychology, revenge and social tensions between the military/civilian populations could all generate brutality and atrocity.

The winter crucible: Kinsale 1601

The arrival of the Spanish had not been propitious. Thirty-three ships had set sail from Lisbon at the end of August with 4,500 troops on board, but a storm scattered the armada off the Irish coast, causing some ships to return to Spain. Don Juan del Águila, the expedition's commander, landed 1,700 men and took Kinsale with little resistance on 21 September.[7] Stragglers from the Spanish fleet arrived by the start of October, bringing the strength of the army to 3,400.[8] The town was protected by medieval walls, but the advent of cannon made defending Kinsale an appalling proposition. The surrounding hills overlooked Kinsale to the extent that Águila described it as a '*hoyo*', a pit or a hole.[9]

Águila consolidated his hold on the town by occupying Rincurran castle and Castle Park which commanded the approaches to the harbour. However, the Spanish force was not strong enough to break out against the gathering English, nor did they have cavalry to scout the surrounding countryside. The Irish were expected to provide suitable mounts, but by September 1601 Irish allies were few and far-between in Munster. Carew's pacification of the province was thorough, with the principal leaders of the Munster confederates now safely imprisoned. Almost immediately after arriving Águila entreated the northern lords to march for Kinsale.[10]

Mountjoy moved quickly to gather the forces needed to counter the Spanish threat. Troops were stripped from the Pale and the garrisons in southern Ulster, with only a skeleton force left to maintain the forts. Mountjoy demanded shipments of supplies, munitions and arms, including heavy artillery out of England.[11] The lord deputy ordered his army to Kinsale on 14 October. It was not at full strength and lacked the requisite cannon, but any delay risked the Spaniards joining with their Irish allies. Light shot skirmished with the Spanish around the walls of Kinsale, while the English horse ranged about the surrounding hills, destroying anything which may have been of use to Águila.[12]

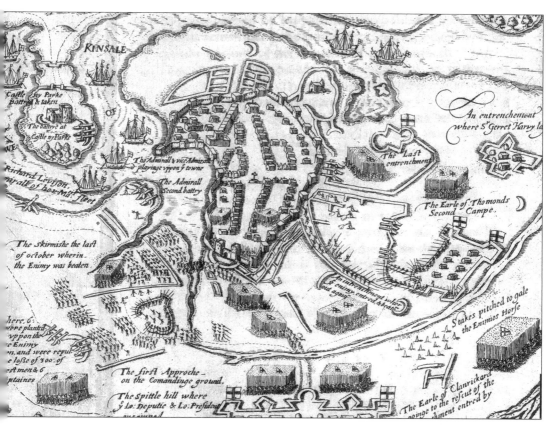

21 The siege of Kinsale, Sept. 1601–Jan. 1602 (*Pacata Hibernia*, i)

Mountjoy's first camp was on Knockrobin Hill, one-and-a-half miles north of the town. On 25 October, Sir John Barkley with 300 men launched a night assault on the Spanish outworks on Spittle Hill, beating them back into Kinsale. Barkley's action cleared the way for Mountjoy to erect his main fortified camp overlooking the town. The numbers of English soldiers around Kinsale rose (in theory) to 6,900 foot and 611 horse, but Carew reported that this was more like 4,300.[13] However, large shipments of men, munitions and much-needed artillery were en route. The arrival of heavy guns on 27 October allowed Mountjoy to turn his attention to the forts outlying Kinsale – Rincurran and Castle Park. Two culverins battered Rincurran, and despite several determined attempts to reinforce the position from Kinsale, the Spanish defenders yielded the castle on 1 November. There were regular skirmishes around the town as Mountjoy pushed his trenches closer to the walls, but a winter siege can be deadlier than any battle, and the miserable conditions took a terrible toll on his troops. Mountjoy wrote that 'the trenches we made were continually filled with water, and the decay of our men was so great, by continual labour, sickness, sword and bullet'.[14]

Mountjoy's tactical situation improved during November when an English fleet under Sir Richard Leveson arrived, taking station within the outer harbour and cutting Águila off from naval resupply or support. Furthermore, the Spanish fortifications at Castle Park fell after a brief bombardment on 20 November. English ships could now fire directly on Kinsale. Under cover of darkness Leveson's ships warped into the harbour and pounded the town, forcing the Spanish to take shelter in cellars. Houses were destroyed and stores damaged, but the ships withdrew before daybreak. The English had total command of the harbour and reinforcements arriving from England meant Mountjoy could maintain the siege despite his losses in men. Though Mountjoy did not consider a direct assault on the town feasible, his numerical advantage and strong defences meant Águila would not be able to break out. If the Spanish were to prevail, they needed Tyrone to engage the English outside Kinsale.

Initially, the Spanish landing at Kinsale provided a respite for Tyrone and his allies in Ulster.[15] The Irish confederates were reeling from the assaults by Mountjoy, Docwra and Chichester, but Águila's arrival forced Mountjoy to withdraw the bulk of his forces from south Ulster to counter the Spanish, though Docwra and Chichester remained to menace Tyrone from the north-west and east. Tyrone quickly took advantage of the vacuum left by the departing English by marching south into Cos. Armagh and Down to reclaim former allies and errant Irish lords who had recently submitted to Mountjoy. The earl then pressed into Leinster where he burned and spoiled as far as Drogheda. Tyrrell raided to Athlone and the O'Reillys and Cuconnaght Maguire spoiled Meath. Mountjoy resisted pleas from the Pale for troops to counter Tyrone's depredations. The spoiling and broad-fronted attack on so many counties at once was a ploy to force the lord deputy to draw troops away from Kinsale. Tyrone used this stratagem in previous campaigns, most effectively against Burgh in 1597, but Mountjoy remained focused on the Spanish. Kinsale was the place where the war would be decided, as Mountjoy noted 'If we win here the rest will all be ours, and if we lose here the rest will all be his [Tyrone's]'.[16] Mountjoy ordered two-thirds of the army in Leinster to march for Kinsale – 2,000 foot and 200 horse. Only 1,250 foot remained to hold Dublin and the Pale against Tyrone.[17] Mountjoy was clearly willing to bet it all to prevail in Munster.

Tyrone returned to Dungannon to make plans for the relief of the beleaguered Spanish. He was not blind to the threat posed by Docwra and

Chichester, and a sizable contingent of his army, possibly one-third, remained in Ulster to counter the garrisons on the Foyle, Carrickfergus and the Blackwater. Tyrone finally left Dungannon on 9 November and concentrated his forces near Lough Ramor, Co. Cavan, but did not display the same alacrity demonstrated on his previous expedition to Munster at the start of 1600. O'Donnell, who marched south despite the devastating advances made by Docwra in Tirconnell, found the earl's progress irritatingly slow. Niall Garbh was stubbornly ensconced in Donegal abbey and O'Donnell's departure endangered Ballyshannon, which was the western gateway into Ulster.[18]

O'Donnell's army marched through Roscommon and Galway, reaching Cashel by 18 November. Mountjoy ordered Carew north to counter the Irish advance, but on 21 November O'Donnell sidestepped Carew's blocking force. Described as 'the greatest march that hath been heard of at this time of year', O'Donnell stole a night march on the lord president, crossing over the frozen Slieve Phelim Mountains.[19] With O'Donnell now to his rear, Carew fell back to the camp at Kinsale. O'Donnell began garnering support from the Irish lords in Munster, while Tyrone made his way south. Confederate strength was significantly improved with the coming of six Spanish ships to Castlehaven on 1 December. Sir Richard Leveson attacked the new arrivals with a small fleet on 6 December, forcing most of the ships to run aground and caused the Spanish flagship to founder on rocks, but the 650 troops under the command of Don Pedro de Zubiaur were safely disembarked.

After his drawn-out progress south, Tyrone joined O'Donnell near Bandon, and on 7 December Mountjoy reported that Tyrone's men were preventing English foraging parties from gathering supplies and fodder.[20] Mountjoy was in a precarious position. He had contained Águila in Kinsale, but Tyrone had linked up with O'Donnell and Zubiaur. Many of the Irish in west Cork joined Tyrone, such as the O'Driscolls, MacCarthys and more significantly Donal Cam O'Sullivan Beare. However, Carew's pacification of Munster was thorough, and the insurrection of 1598 was not repeated. Furthermore, Zubiaur appeared more determined to secure Castlehaven, Baltimore and Bearehaven than reinforce Tyrone. He dispatched 200 Spanish troops to Tyrone but retained the rest to guard the harbours. Tyrone had all the men he was ever going to get to break the siege and defeat Mountjoy; 1,000 Munstermen, 200 Spanish; 2,500 foot and 500 horse he had brought, 400 troops with Tyrrell and 1,500 foot and 300 horse under O'Donnell and O'Rourke; 5,600 foot and 800 horse in total.[21]

The Ulster lords held back as Mountjoy's troops died in their droves within the siege lines. The English army may have received 6,000 new levies since the start of the siege, but by 23 December Mountjoy had no more than when he started. Moryson referred to 'the new men dying by the dozens each night, through the hardness of the winter siege, whereunto they were not inured'.[22] Within the town, the Spanish were also enduring hardship and privation. Águila pressed Tyrone to take decisive action.[23] It was reported that Tyrone was not keen to engage the English in the open nor their trenches, but encouragement from Spanish officers assuaged these fears.[24] Águila's plan called for Tyrone's army to approach the English lines and fortify on a nearby hill; the Spanish would then break out of Kinsale with 2,000 men to link up with the Irish.[25] Even with their Spanish advisors advocating the plan, the Irish were not happy but eventually they agreed to move; Tyrrell led a squadron *volant* composed of Irish and Spanish, Tyrone led the van and O'Donnell the rear.

The Irish set out at midnight on the 24 December to cover the two miles to Ardmartin Hill, one mile north-west of Kinsale. Tyrone arrived in good order, but around daybreak Sir Richard Greame's cavalry scouts spotted Tyrone's men as they lit their matchcords for their firearms.[26] The alarm was sounded in the English camps, and Mountjoy moved to engage the Irish with 1,200 foot and 300–400 horse. As the English troops approached, Tyrone pulled back off the hill and retreated to a ford two miles to the west where he made his infantry stand with a stream and bog covering his front. A brisk skirmish was maintained during which the Irish stood firm, but the English discovered another ford on the Irish right. Sir Richard Wingfield pushed his cavalry across, who along with the earl of Clanricard charged the nearest Irish foot but were repulsed. With reinforcements of foot and horse the Irish left was assailed again, but this time Tyrone's cavalry broke and fled. English, Spanish and Irish sources claimed the Irish cavalry broke through Tyrone's battalia of foot, causing confusion and disrupting the formation.[27] Realizing their opportunity, the English cavalry and three bodies of infantry attacked the rear of Tyrone's formation that 'presently brake and fell into disorder and began to fly'.[28] O'Donnell's infantry were not engaged but few things are as contagious as panic on the battlefield and they too fled, discarding arms and equipment to hasten their escape. Only Tyrrell and his Spanish made any attempt to stand, fighting off a flank attack by Captain Roe's infantry, but with no support they too were forced to retire.

The pursuit was limited to around two miles, as the half-starved English horses were in no condition for a prolonged chase. Initially, Águila did not attack out of Kinsale as he believed the gunfire was an English ruse to draw him into a trap.[29] When the Spanish eventually sallied out of the town, the battle was already lost, and they were driven back into Kinsale. The English casualties were slight. Mountjoy accounted for 1 horseman and 5 or 6 foot killed, others reported only 1 Englishman killed, though this may have ignored Irish killed fighting for Mountjoy.[30] Either way, it was evident that Mountjoy lost very few men. In contrast, the losses inflicted on the Irish were crushing; 800–1,000 were killed, and huge quantities of arms, stores and munitions were abandoned. Moreover, Tyrone's aura of invincibility, which had buoyed his allies and cowed his enemies, was shattered forever.

Tyrrell and the Spanish officers advised Tyrone to stay in Munster and renew his attack on the English lines, but the Ulster lords had no desire to remain. On 26 December the Irish broke camp and started their long march north. Absent from this was O'Donnell. Docwra and Niall Garbh had already driven O'Donnell out of Tirconnell before the journey to Kinsale; he had little to return to. O'Donnell hoped that he could elicit further assistance from Philip III. Therefore he travelled to Castlehaven where he boarded a ship for Spain on 27 December. The Spanish attacked the English trenches twice on Christmas day and again on the 26 December, but Águila's men were repulsed each time.[31] On 31 December 1601, Águila sued for terms, and after some negotiation articles were signed on 2 January 1602, allowing the Spanish to leave for Spain with their arms, munitions, money and all the Irish in their company. Also, Águila surrendered the positions at Castlehaven, Baltimore and Dunboy.[32]

The retreat north for the Irish was harrowing. Men died fording the river Blackwater at Mallow (Co. Cork), and more were lost crossing the river Maigue in Connello (Co. Limerick). Soldiers deserted to shift for themselves, but many were killed by the inhabitants of districts who, daunted by the Irish army's progress south, took their opportunity to exact revenge and at the same time prove their loyalty to the crown. There were few regular English forces to block the route north, but many local Irish lords turned on the retreating army. Shane Sheale, Tyrone's trumpeter, reported that 'they that would kiss them in their going forward did both strip them and shoot bullets at them in their return; and, for their arms, they did drown them and tread them down in every bog'.[33] Despite the perils Tyrone arrived in Dungannon on 10 January, but his army was a spent force. An estimate put the Irish losses in battle and the retreat at 3,000 men, 500 pack horses and all the army's baggage.[34] Tyrone's army was devastated, yet the earl proclaimed that a new force of 20,000 men was expected from Spain. O'Donnell met Philip III at Zamora in February 1602, and a new more powerful force was proposed, but O'Donnell died of a fever on 10 August 1602, and the Spanish promises came to nothing. Fenton claimed that Tyrone tried to downplay the defeat by raising new troops in Ulster, but the loss of experienced officers and soldiers could not be ignored.[35]

The collapse of Irish command and control

The destruction of Tyrone's army at Kinsale was the hammer blow that shattered the Irish confederacy, but steady progress by Mountjoy and his officers during 1600–1 had already eaten away at Tyrone's power structure. Tyrone created a military alliance that moved beyond the bounds of traditional frameworks of Gaelic loyalty, enabling orders drafted in Dungannon to be acted upon in Munster. Instructions were issued to regional septs who previously had no traditions of loyalty to the O'Neills, but the bonds holding his alliance together were new and brittle. Tyrone did not have time to create formal institutions of power; to create a modern state.

As the growing strength of the royal armies eroded Tyrone's authority in the south, attrition of Irish commanders exposed a major weakness of the Irish command structure. The Gaelic political system meant that military strength was in many respects intrinsically linked to political power. The dual role of military leadership coinciding with political leadership meant the loss of a commander in action could have a far greater impact on the Irish war effort than a similar loss to the crown. Moreover, it was not for Tyrone to decide who would emerge as the new leader. The victor in any succession could be less effective, or worse still, less loyal to Tyrone and the cause he championed. It would be overstating the case to suggest that the English were immune to adverse effects posed by the loss of a commander such as Essex or Mountjoy. Nevertheless, the death of high- or middle-ranking officers did not have any profound impact on the crown's ability to continue the war and had little, if any, political fallout.

The killing or capture of an Irish confederate commander went beyond the obvious loss of their martial skill. Bitter succession disputes erupted, denying the confederate leadership the use of troops and economic resources from within the contested lordship. It also created an unstable political situation that the crown could exploit, normally by supporting rival claimants to those proposed by Tyrone. The loss of Hugh Maguire in a minor skirmish in Munster at the start of 1600 was a prime example of this.[36] His death sparked a succession dispute in Fermanagh that degenerated to the point of open hostilities between the rival claimants.[37] A similar confrontation was initiated by the assassination of Conn MacUladh MacMahon.[38] Even where the death of an Irish leader did not spark dissension, their loss could lead to confusion and vulnerability. After Brian Riabhach O'More had been killed, Captain Thomas Lee believed that the crown could have smashed the Leinster rebellion if prosecuted promptly, due to the anxiety brought about by O'Mores death.[39]

Given the nature of the Gaelic political systems, it is perhaps predictable that without substantial change or revision, the structures that served a factionalized and disparate polity could not be harnessed to support a coordinated and homogeneous war effort over a sustained period. Tyrone attempted to replace insular concerns of lordship with patriotism or 'faith and fatherland' ideology, but ultimately this was a failure. Despite his best efforts, the underlying dynamics of loyalty between an Irish lord and their adherents remained stubbornly traditional. The political prestige of an Irish chief was measured in the number of clients or vassals under them.[40] The capability of an overlord to use force, either punitively against a recalcitrant chief or in support of a threatened client, underpinned the relationship between overlord and *uirríthe*. In return for military support and tribute in the form of money or goods, the vassal could expect protection by his overlord from encroachment by other lords or sub-lords. An attack on a sub-lord was considered an attack on the overlord, obliging them to take action in defence of their client.[41] Where this was undermined, or the protection demonstrated to be unreliable, it was not unreasonable to expect the vassal to seek out a more reliable protector. Therefore perceived or actual erosion of the overlord's influence, power and reputation could precipitate defection. This appears to be what Tyrone and O'Donnell experienced in the latter stages of the war. The northern leadership found that when the power they had to coax or compel those to serve diminished, their erstwhile associates soon fell away or ignored their demands. Even those lords who were not enthusiastic about siding with the crown were not keen to ally themselves to what was becoming a lost cause. Fenton articulated this after Kinsale when he noted that many Irish lords would be disinclined to join Tyrone as 'he cannot help them, when he is puzzled how to defend himself'.[42]

In many cases, Tyrone secured loyalty and obedience using a combination of incentives and threats. When the tide of success swung against the Irish in 1600, those lords allied to Tyrone by compulsion were less inclined to be overawed by the Ulster chief's diminishing power. For intimidation to work, the victim must believe that non-compliance will result in retribution. It was unsurprising that those coerced into service under Tyrone defected as soon as the power of the crown could offset Tyrone's, or at least assure them that they could seek effective crown protection. This was seen in the speedy defections to the crown of Connor Roe Maguire and Niall MacBrian Fertagh O'Neill. As the crown's fortunes improved in 1600, both men appeared on the government payroll despite the fact there were few if any government forces threatening their lands.[43]

Tyrone's ability to give orders to his southern allies was substantially underpinned by his capacity to provide regular reinforcements of troops and equipment.[44] Correspondingly, Tyrone's authority outside Ulster diminished after he was forced to recall soldiers back to Ulster, and the quantity of supplies passing from north to south decreased. Sir Francis Shane noticed that Tyrone's withdrawal had caused concern in Leinster, leading the local Irish to 'conceiveth a distrust in themselves, Tyrone having left them to their own fortune'.[45] Without the presence of Tyrone's captains and troops among the Irish armies of Leinster and Munster, local leaders were less inclined to observe orders from Ulster. This appeared evident in two major breakdowns in Tyrone's command – the taking of Ormond, and the relationship between the *sugán* earl of Desmond and Florence MacCarthy. When Owny MacRory O'More captured the earl of Ormond in April 1600, he ignored Tyrone's instructions to send Ormond north.[46] O'More opted to release him in exchange for a large surety.[47] Further south, Tyrone had difficulty controlling the Irish lords in Munster. The O'Sullivans had refused to take orders from Florence MacCarthy, and MacCarthy proved unwilling to co-operate with the *sugán* earl of Desmond.[48] Tyrone ordered MacCarthy to take more decisive action against the enemy, but with little effect; MacCarthy never took to the field to aid Desmond.[49] As the military fortunes of the Irish confederates worsened from 1600, the ties that held them together started to dissolve.

Setbacks and failure compounded the predicament of the Irish. Tyrone's inability to counter Mountjoy was perceived as weakness by those who had previously been allies.[50] From 1600, the progress of the crown's armies was matched by Irish submissions and defection. Mountjoy's thrust into the midlands during 1600 and south-east Ulster in 1601 can be plotted using the names and lordships of those who submitted.[51] More significantly, these defections endured, as even after the landing of the Spanish in 1601, most remained loyal to the crown. The defeat at Kinsale delivered a catastrophic blow to Tyrone's reputation.[52] Fenton believed that the purpose behind Tyrone's preparations for an invasion of the Pale in 1602 was to present a façade of strength.[53] The transient nature of deference to Tyrone was exhibited by the attacks on his army by former allies as he retreated to Ulster after Kinsale.[54] It should come as no surprise that Irish defections to the crown accelerated as the tide of the war went against Tyrone and his allies. Many former confederates acknowledged the *realpolitik* of the situation; no one wanted to end the war on the losing side.

After Kinsale

The disaster at Kinsale had delivered a fatal blow to the Irish confederacy. An envoy from Tyrone to Mountjoy claimed that Tyrone wished to be received into the queen's mercy. The lord deputy was unmoved by Tyrone's new-found humility and returned the messenger with demands that Tyrone submit in writing.[55] Tyrone was undoubtedly playing for time. When he returned north, the earl attempted to buy new stores of gunpowder and lead from 'diverse places, especially out of Scotland'.[56] In the immediate aftermath of the battle of Kinsale, Mountjoy was more concerned with getting the Spanish rounded up and transported back to Spain. His men were still dying by the score in the fields around Kinsale. Though the Munster lords remained loyal (for the most part), their behaviour and that of the townspeople during the siege instilled little confidence in their fidelity. Carew rounded on the supposedly faithful subjects in Munster for withholding their aid, who 'looked on, ready to join the strongest sword'.[57]

The Spanish had capitulated, but their presence sustained embers of hope in Muster. Therefore Mountjoy focused on getting Águila's men out of Ireland.[58] The Spaniards were shipped to Spain on 16 March 1602, but the generous terms and assistance provided by Mountjoy drew criticism, with some suggesting that the lord deputy and his officers had 'avoided' the Spanish out of Ireland.[59] It was clear that even the astonishing victory could not silence the sceptics at court. A minute from the privy council opened with a veiled criticism of the lord deputy for concentrating on transporting the Spanish out of Ireland instead of pursuing Tyrone north. They drew attention to 'the great opportunities which one lost by your being detained in that province [Munster]'.[60] This was a petty slight. The army was in no condition to march into Ulster after enduring the horrors of a winter siege, neither was the lord deputy. Mountjoy fell dangerously ill at the end of March and took almost a month to fully recover.

Though Kinsale was the desperate and bloody fulcrum of the war, the English garrisons in the north took ample advantage to improve their position in Ulster. Chichester assailed north Antrim during November, burning and spoiling almost to the gates of Dunluce castle; there was little resistance as the MacDonnells were with Tyrone.[61] Around the same time, Docwra raided east across the river Bann into Donal O'Cahan's country near Coleraine and the following month Captain Willis raided the Derg valley in Tyrone, burning houses and taking a prey of 300 cows.[62] O'Cahan attempted to negotiate his submission during March, but he altered this to a three-month cessation and a large bribe for Docwra. Docwra rebuffed O'Cahan's offer and sent his men on punitive raids, burning houses, destroying stores and killing anyone they found.[63] The suggestion that Tyrone may have been stirring to attack south prompted Chichester to raid Killetra.[64] Tyrone's freedom of movement became ever more restricted, but Mountjoy had to come north if he wanted to finish Tyrone once and for all.

While Mountjoy focused on repatriating the Spanish, Carew moved against the Irish in west Cork and Kerry. Carew despised the Irish that had sided with Tyrone after the arrival of the Spanish. He believed their faithless defection deserved a punishment that would deter future rebellion, but Carew was also a pragmatist. The war had cost the crown dearly in lives and money, therefore accepting their submission would not transform the Irish into dutiful subjects, but it could bring peace. When the O'Driscolls, O'Donovans and some of the MacCarthys capitulated, Carew recommended 'all kind of mild usage' to ensure their surrender was permanent.[65] Cecil was not pleased and directed a forthright letter to Carew demanding that the queen's mercy should not be applied so liberally.[66] Carew protested that he would not do anything to compromise the honour of the service, but at the same time he was a realist who wanted to end the war in Munster as soon as possible, especially with rumours of a second Spanish invasion during 1602.[67]

Troops were sent to take charge of the Spanish positions at Castlehaven, Baltimore and Bearehaven, but when O'Sullivan Beare received news that Castlehaven had been surrendered, he marched on and occupied Dunboy castle at the end of February. The earl of Thomond spoiled Carbery and Beara, and Sir Charles Wilmott became the governor of Kerry at the head of 1,700 soldiers. Carew hoped that their campaigns would serve to isolate the Irish forces in Dunboy castle. Wilmott made short work of the Irish in Kerry. A series of sharp engagements put paid to Irish opposition.[68] After the earl of Thomond had planted garrisons in Carbery, the only major Irish forces remaining in Munster were those under O'Sullivan Beare, Tyrrell and William Burke. Carew believed the last vestiges of Irish resistance in Munster could be crushed if he could trap the Irish on the Beara peninsula, where the only remaining Irish stronghold was Dunboy castle.[69] Unfortunately for Carew, the Irish position at Dunboy had been significantly strengthened. The masonry walls had been lowered and faced with earth flankers in the modern continental style, making them resistant to cannon fire. Ten cannons served by Spanish gunners provided heavy defensive firepower; taking Dunboy by assault would be no easy task.

Carew concentrated his forces at Bantry during May 1602, but a landward approach was out of the question as Tyrrell and William Burke held strong positions at Glengarriff with 1,200 troops supported by 400 Munstermen.[70]

The Rebells entrenchment in the Sandye Bay, and there grosse to receaue vs at our Landinge there as they Expected.

The Small Iland

Castle Dermond

Here the 6: of June the Army Landed, in the Mayne, fought w' the Rebells, put them to flight and that night encamped nere vnto Castle Dermond.

22 Captain Richard Tyrrell's defences at Castletown, June 1602 (*Pacata Hibernia*, ii)

Carew's advisors warned that 100 Irish could stall the entire army on the narrow coastal route.[71] However, Carew was sure that when Dunboy fell Tyrrell and Burke would soon leave the province. The lord president started shipping his troops to Beare Island on 1 June, the last arrived the following day. The army decamped to the smaller Dinnish Island on 6 June. Tyrrell constructed defences on the sandy bay north of Dunboy to oppose the impending amphibious assault, but Carew landed his regiments north of Castle Dermond (modern Castletownbere, previously known as Castletown). By the time Tyrrell had marched his men to counter the landing, Carew had sufficient troops to hold the beachhead.[72] The Irish attacked but English cannon fire stalled their advance, and after a skirmishing with Carew's force, Tyrrell's men retreated. The next day the English began to entrench around Dunboy castle.

Carew's guns began battering the fortifications on 16 June, and within twenty-four hours the English artillery had demolished much of the central keep. Four cannons pounded a breach in the western flank of the outer walls, which was followed up by an assault by infantry under Captain Edward Dorrington.[73] They secured a lodgement on the defences, and though the Irish put up stiff resistance, the defender's heavy guns were soon in enemy hands, forcing them to retreat within ruins of the castle vaults. Some Irish attempted to escape by sea, but they were quickly cut down by English gunfire. The constable of Dunboy sought to destroy the position by detonating the garrison's gunpowder store, but he was prevented by his men, who preferred to take their chances surrendering to Carew; they should have let him, as Carew hanged them all.

Tyrone's army was shattered and Águila's men repatriated, but the threat of another Spanish landing significantly influenced English strategy throughout 1602. Defeat at Kinsale had scattered and disorganized the Irish, but Mountjoy could not concentrate his military assets against Ulster due to the danger of a second invasion. During June, Cecil received intelligence that a new landing was planned, which appeared to be corroborated the following month by John Burleigh, a former prisoner of the Spanish.[74] The arrival of a Spanish ship in Kilmakillogue Bay (Co. Kerry) at the start of June did little to alleviate English fears. It carried money, munitions and the bishop of Ross, Owen MacEgan, who brought assurances of a new army from Spain.[75] Sir Richard Leveson was dispatched with twelve ships to patrol Spanish waters and an ambitious (and hugely expensive) programme of fortifications was started to protect the southern coast and port towns from Spanish attack.[76] Furthermore, Mountjoy kept forces in Munster to counter any Spanish landing, thereby limiting the troops and resources available to crush the intractable Irish in Ulster. Mountjoy was concerned that reinforcing the south would prolong the war in Ulster, noting that 'upon bruits as we hear of a new invasion out of Spain ... we are much distracted what next to do, for if we should draw that way to provide to entertain them, we should lose the advantage of this prosecution [in Ulster]'.[77]

The menace from Spain also defined how Carew framed his 1602 campaign in Munster. Coastal strongholds with harbours were targeted to prevent their use as safe anchorages. Carew then burnt the castles to save on the expense of placing garrisons to hold them.[78] The programme of destruction was extended to ravaging the coastal zone later in the year. Mountjoy ordered Carew to focus on devastating the countryside, as a new Spanish force would be starved of local supplies.[79] Houses and crops were destroyed and whatever could not be carried was burned as the territory between Kinsale and Bantry was wasted.[80] Sir Charles Wilmott evicted the Irish inhabitants of Kerry to nearer Limerick so that the Spanish 'might make no use of them'; all to create a sterile zone in which Spanish troops would find it impossible to operate.[81]

Endgame in Ulster

Commitments in Munster sapped Mountjoy's military strength, but he still had sufficient assets in the north to push the Irish back on all fronts. Sir Oliver Lambert brushed aside light resistance at the Moy river to make Sligo town his base of operations on 6 June.[82] In the north-east, Chichester threatened the Irish fort at Toome, whereas Docwra continued making inroads into Tyrone, where he fortified Omagh by 26 June. However, Mountjoy's army marching from the south was the hammer to smash Tyrone. He brought 3,000 men into Armagh and by 20 June held the southern bank of the river Blackwater. Mountjoy was determined not to repeat the attritional slogging match of the previous summer. Rather than attempt to force the formidable defences between the river and Dungannon, the lord deputy by-passed them by building a new fort and bridge two miles downriver – what would become known as Charlemont Fort. Troops secured a foothold on the Tyrone side of the river while the bridge and fortifications were built. Only five miles of 'plain and open' ground separated Mountjoy from Dungannon.[83]

Tyrone had nothing left to stop the English. Therefore he retreated into the forests of Glenconkeyne, leaving Dungannon a blazing ruin. Mountjoy led just 100 horse and 500 foot into Dungannon on 23 June, meeting no resistance. In a letter to Carey in Dublin, Mountjoy wrote 'We have drunk your health at Dungannon, Tyrone is turned wood kern'.[84] Chichester took the Irish fort at Toome on 20 June, and by 28 June Docwra had linked up with Mountjoy in Dungannon. After Chichester had arrived on the western shore of Lough Neagh, the lord deputy established a massive *trace italienne* fortification on the lough shore, later naming it Mountjoy Fort. With Tyrone a fugitive, Mountjoy expanded upon the scorched earth strategy of the previous year. The lord deputy withdrew south to Monaghan where he raised another fort, then proceeded to devastate the country surrounding it.[85] Docwra and Chichester were given twenty days to rest and refit their troops, but throughout the summer both embarked on a systematic programme of burning and crop destruction.

Mountjoy described the English operations in the north where 'we do continually hunt all their woods, spoil their corn, burn their houses, and kill so many churls'.[86] Chichester reported that famine was already taking effect

23 Mountjoy Fort, drawn by Richard Bartlett, 1602–3
(The National Library of Ireland, MS 2656, vii)

during March, noting that 'no course … will cut the throat of the grand traitor … and bring the country into quiet but famine, which is well begun and will daily enlarge'.[87] The renewed English assault exacerbated the shortages; moreover, the attacks forced Irish leaders to submit or face annihilation. The dramatic improvement in English fortunes was so rapid that some were wary of the collapse of Irish resistance. Fenton was anxious that the swift reversals were a ploy by the Irish to play for time for renewed Spanish assistance or to find a means to secure their escape.[88] In reality, the agricultural economy in Ulster was disintegrating under the pressures of nine years of war, compounded by the devastating attacks of Mountjoy and his subordinates. Sir Garret Moore reported people dying of want in Tyrone at the end of June.[89] The lord deputy related how none were left to oppose the English in O'Cahan's country; the only Irish seen were 'dead carcases, merely starved for want of meat'.[90]

Mountjoy returned north at the start of August, confident that by stationing large numbers of troops in the garrisons he would be able to corner Tyrone and dominate the countryside. Docwra secured the submission of the O'Cahans and held Termonmagurk to prevent Tyrone from escaping, but as the lord deputy moved across the Blackwater to Dungannon, Tyrone broke south-west down the Clogher valley to Fermanagh.[91] With striking symmetry, the war had now come full circle as the remnants of Tyrone's forces were again concentrated in the county where the war had burst forth over nine years earlier. The Irish stronghold at Inishloughan, south of Lough Neagh, fell to Sir Arthur Chichester on 16 August, eradicating the last vestiges of organized resistance in east Ulster. With the earl in Fermanagh, nothing stood in the way of English depredations. Mountjoy placed a garrison in Dungannon on 29 August and then marched to Tullaghogue. This was the traditional inauguration site of the O'Neills and held the stone chair on which The O'Neill was proclaimed.[92] The chair was smashed, and the surrounding districts spoiled. Chichester was sent to clear Tyrone of its remaining inhabitants and destroy whatever supplies could not be used by the garrisons.[93]

Food shortages were not limited to Ulster as there were reports of poor harvests in the Pale and Munster. The unseasonal weather had destroyed crops; deaths due to famine were expected.[94] However, nine years of war in Ulster had imposed a crippling burden on the agricultural economy. Coupled with Mountjoy's systematic spoliation, the effects were immediate and catastrophic. Reports out of the north painted a picture of a famine of horrific proportions: 1,000 dead lying unburied between Tullaghogue and Toome, and 3,000 who had died since Mountjoy had arrived at the Blackwater.[95] The famine grew worse as shortages became acute. Mountjoy's secretary, Fynes Moryson, wrote the most graphic accounts. He related cases of cannibalism. Children were described 'eating and gnawing with their teeth the entrails of their dead mother, upon whose flesh they had fed twenty days past, and having eaten all from the feet upward to the bare bones, roasting it continually by a slow fire, were now come to eating her said entrails in like sort roasted, yet not divided from the body being as yet raw'.[96] Moryson elaborated, noting that 'no spectacle was more frequent in the ditches and towns, and especially in wasted countries, than to see multitudes of these poor people dead with their mouths all coloured green by eating nettles, docks, and all things they could rend up above ground'.[97] The famine became so widespread that Mountjoy was concerned his army would starve in their garrisons.[98] Despite the horrors visited upon the unfortunate population in 1602, the war would inexorably drag on into the following year.

A war of extermination?

The horrors of starvation and the ensuing outbreak of disease undoubtedly visited Ulster, but was this evidence for a policy of extermination of the native Irish? The final campaigns to defeat Tyrone have been decried as more brutal than the contemporary norms of warfare.[99] Vincent Carey believed the scorched earth campaign in Ulster was exceptional in scale and violence.[100] Some have suggested that famine became a potent tool of war in Ireland, but famine had long been a part of warfare. Throughout contemporary Europe, it was the preferred means to secure victory by Europe's most enlightened military thinkers. Cautious professional competence replaced the outmoded notions of the chivalric desire for glory.[101] Authors of military books and their readership advocated the validity of classical texts despite the introduction of gunpowder weapons.[102] The most copied classical text on warfare in the Middle Ages was *De re militari* by Vegetius.[103] One of Vegetius' general rules of war was to subdue an enemy by famine, raids and terror rather than battle, which he believed depended more on fortune than the bravery of troops.[104] As a scholar of military texts, it is unlikely that Lord Deputy Mountjoy would be unfamiliar with Vegetius.[105] Though Mountjoy had available Edmund Spenser's *View of the present state of Ireland*, which espoused starvation as the best way to end the war, Mountjoy was a practical and erudite commander.[106] It is speculative to suggest that Mountjoy based his decision to conduct a scorched earth campaign because of the military literature he had read, but it is worth noting that many texts espoused the style of warfare that Mountjoy used to defeat Tyrone.

Mountjoy clearly believed that destroying crops was the best and fastest way to succeed in Ulster. By limiting Tyrone's access to corn, Mountjoy could degrade the earl's capacity to pay his bonnaghts.[107] Mountjoy also hoped that wasting and crop destruction would force Tyrone to live off others, thereby leaving him vulnerable to betrayal.[108] Whereas it has been suggested that Mountjoy intended to make a 'blank slate' of Ulster, he was clear that this was not the intention of the crown.[109] Mountjoy noted that if the queen had wished to maintain the army in such numbers, he could have either totally cleared Ulster or occupied it long enough to impose a robust infrastructure of government.[110] At no point did Mountjoy declare that he preferred extirpation as a means to secure the north. The killing of civilians troubled Mountjoy, who noted how 'it grieveth me to think that it is necessary to do it'.[111] In an attempt to provide some relief from the miseries inflicted upon the civilians in Tyrone, Mountjoy allowed refugees to cross south over the river Blackwater, where it was hoped Henry and Conn MacShane O'Neill would re-establish some level of agriculture.[112] In the same letter, he displayed a degree of compassion for civilians when he commiserated with them for knowing no master other than Tyrone.[113] This pity was mirrored by Captain Nicholas Dawtrey who railed against the general slaughter of the Irish. While he viewed the primary agitators as rebels, deserving of nothing but death by execution, Dawtrey believed that it was better to reform than kill rebellious subjects. Therefore a more lenient approach should be taken with the general masses. Possibly with a view to post-war reconstruction, he perceived the reformed peasantry as a means to generate new wealth.[114]

The actions of Mountjoy and his officers in Ulster have been interpreted as an attempt by the crown to depopulate Ulster of its recalcitrant natives. However, the culpability for the famine and the actual impact of the English military campaign on the population have seldom if ever been questioned. While the lurid descriptions of the massacre of civilians by Sir Arthur Chichester and the horrifying scenes related by Moryson make for disturbing reading and have become iconic representations of the excesses and brutality of the Ulster campaign, their relation of civilian deaths may have been overstated.[115] Chichester was aware of the limited impact of direct victimization on civilians. In November 1601, he was frustrated that his attacks did not have the desired effect, when 'our swords ... work not that speedy effect which is expected, for our overthrows are safeties to the speedy runners, upon which we kill no multitudes.'[116] Chichester was clearly stating that civilian casualties were not as high as he wished. This may have been due to the greater mobility of civilians compared to heavily laden infantry forces. A study of civilian victimization in fourteenth-century France noted how villagers could escape spoils by troops if given sufficient warning.[117] This was especially pertinent in Irish society, where transhumance farming was practised, possibly conferring a greater degree of mobility to the Irish peasantry than that enjoyed by the more sedentary population of late-medieval France. An analysis of mortality during the Thirty Years War concluded that death inflicted upon civilians by direct attacks were quantitatively insignificant, with little effect on a region's demography.[118] This would explain Chichester's frustration when he declared that 'little can be done with violence'.[119]

If troops (specifically infantry) were not as effective at killing civilians as supposed, were they efficient at destroying crops? Mountjoy's ability to spoil crops has never been questioned. His quantification of the damage suggested soldiers effected widespread destruction, but were Mountjoy's assessments of crop destruction accurate or even plausible? During his attack into Laois and Offaly from July to August in 1600 Mountjoy calculated the value of the destroyed crops as upwards of £10,000 of wheat.[120] This would appear to be a massive swathe of devastation, but it may also be a gross overstatement to inflate his success. With wheat prices running at approximately 50 shillings per quarter, destroying £10,000 equated to 32,000 bushels of crops.[121] Using a conservative estimate of wheat yields at 9 bushels per acre, this suggested that Mountjoy's 500–700 men destroyed 3,555 acres of crops in nine days, which was 395 acres per day.[122] It is hard to determine just how much standing crops an individual can cut using non-specialist tools, or swords for that matter. Mountjoy specifically mentioned that crops were cut down and not burnt. Furthermore, his officers had great difficulty getting their men to cut with their swords as it was 'extremely painful'.[123] Standing crops can be burned in dry conditions, but it was not possible in this case. Difficulties destroying standing crops could explain why Mountjoy changed his focus of depredations between the summer of 1600 and 1601. The limited impact of cutting standing corn in 1600 may have convinced Mountjoy to modify his methods, preferring instead to focus his efforts in spring and autumn to prevent sowing and harvesting of crops.[124]

It would be wrong to suggest that the destruction of food supplies and property did not exacerbate the hardships of the local population, but it is likewise difficult to claim that English military operations were the sole, or even primary causative factor. There had been no systemized crop destruction in Connacht in 1597, but the famine still broke out. Maurice Kyffin described seeing 'hunger starved carcases … spread up and down the fields'.[125] William Farmer reported that in 1602 famine visited both the Irish and English in the north. The English had some relief from imports from England, whereas the Irish were driven to extremes of want.[126] By January 1603, the entire country was facing famine, leading Mountjoy to request food shipments to supply the army. He noted that while all would the feel effects of famine, the Irish rebels and former rebels would feel it worse.[127]

The rapid onset of famine in Ulster did not reflect commonly held expectations for the time required for ravaging to have an impact on the civilian population's food supply. When describing his depredations in the north, Docwra expected his efforts to precipitate a famine the following year, indicating that spoiling would not produce immediate results.[128] This was also true of Munster in 1601, where crop destruction was not expected to take effect until 1602.[129] When Mountjoy finally entered Dungannon in June 1602, he described the area as 'so eaten I think we can hardly live there'.[130] The earl of Tyrone's lands to the north of the Blackwater were already subject to a subsistence crisis before Mountjoy arrived. The onset of famine in Tyrone was faster than expected. Given that Mountjoy found Tyrone in a poor state when he arrived and the short time taken for horror stories to emerge, it was entirely possible that Mountjoy's campaign coincided with an emerging disaster. He certainly made it worse but did not cause the crisis. The demands of the Irish war effort seriously denuded the resources of Tyrone. Furthermore, Tyrone moved his forces into Fermanagh in August 1602, prompting Mountjoy to observe that concentrations of Irish forces did as much damage to the country as his spoiling operations.[131]

Concurrent with the campaign in the north, the harvest in the Pale was poor, raising fears of famine there.[132] In October 1602, Carew reported that bad weather had damaged much of the crop in Munster, which he expected would cause much hardship as there was not enough to spare for seed the following year.[133] The crown's debasement of the Irish coinage aggravated the shortages. Base currency and rapid inflation meant that merchants found it impossible to pay for imported goods and commodities.[134] Shortages continued into 1603, with famine and pestilence reported in Dublin in November 1603, and the Irish annals recorded starvation throughout Ireland.[135]

Depopulation of the countryside, as described in Ulster and elsewhere, did not necessarily mean that the people had been killed or died from famine or disease. It is possible that many inhabitants migrated out of the area of military activity, either to less troubled regions or to refuges in woods or upland areas. To avoid crown depredations in the midlands in 1600, the inhabitants fled to Ulster and did not return until the end of the year.[136] In direct response to crop devastation, many of the rural inhabitants of Tyrone and Kerry relocated to Armagh and Limerick respectively.[137] Civilians abandoned the country entirely to escape the ravages of the war. Sir Arthur Chichester referred to refugees to France and Spain in 1605, stating that they had fled Ulster, Munster and Connacht during the famine at the end of the war.[138] Moryson corroborated this, noting that many Irish had travelled to England and France, 'where great multitudes of them lived for some years after the peace was made'.[139]

Extermination of the native population was never a matter of policy for the crown during the conflict. In 1595, Norreys rejected Irish claims that the queen wanted a war of conquest, noting that malicious rumours were circulated to encourage others to revolt.[140] When referring to a policy of extirpation, Sir George Carew opined that 'on utter extirpation ... I am sure was never harboured in her majesty's heart nor yet advised by any of her council'.[141] Martial law (and the brutality which resulted) was used to spread terror in the native population, but at no stage did Elizabeth or her government's policy aim to eradicate the Irish.[142] As the war dragged on, there was an increasing mood for peace among the highest ranks of the English political and military establishment. In Ireland, the most prominent of these was Lord Deputy Mountjoy. Possibly appalled by the human cost of the war, but certainly aware of the financial cost, he noted in April 1602 that the state could not afford to win the war solely by military means.[143]

Expressions of war weariness and a desire for peace were found at the highest levels of state. The queen recommended leniency for those wishing to submit 'where he [Mountjoy] could not ruin them'.[144] For the queen, vengeance was becoming too expensive. In 1602, Francis Bacon suggested Cecil take a more conciliatory line.[145] Cecil was keen that the war came to a rapid conclusion. Though the queen refused Tyrone any possibility of pardon, Cecil encouraged Mountjoy to conclude the war as 'the sword cannot end the war [quickly]', whereas England 'cannot well endure it'.[146] Desires for peace aside, as the war dragged on civilians continued to burden the greatest measure of suffering and death.

Civilian victimization and the limits of violence

English attitudes towards the native Irish, and their bearing on the crown's use of violence in Ireland, have been hotly debated by Irish historians. Edmund Spenser's harsh polemic, *View of the present state of Ireland*, which advocated the eradication of the native Irish, was considered unrepresentative of a new English ideology.[147] However, many others have strongly disagreed, claiming that the ideological basis of radical reform and thereby the drastic measures enacted to win the war could be found in the works of Spenser, and Richard Beacon's *Solon his follie; or, A politique discourse touching the reformation of the common-weales conquered, declined or corrupted.*[148] More recently, Spenser's *View* and Beacon's *Solon* have been presented as expressions of the ideology of violence and conquest towards the Irish that found its climax at the end of the Nine Years War.[149] Morgan succinctly described this as a case of 'was Spenser a bastard or were they all (the New English colonists, that is) bastards?'[150]

David Edwards argued that government-sanctioned violence escalated throughout the sixteenth century, climaxing with an unprecedented scorched earth campaign in Ulster from 1600 to the end of the war.[151] It is possible to infer that the destruction wrought on Ulster was a natural progression from the brutal repression of Sir Humphrey Gilbert during the first Desmond rebellion (1569–73).[152] The brutality and methodology seemed comparable, but there was a break in continuity. War raged in Ireland for seven years before the crown adopted a systematic scorched earth policy. This begs the question, what was happening to civilians in the years 1593–9?

The behaviour of the Irish confederate forces towards civilians varied from relatively benign, if sometimes firm overlordship, to brutally violent. The Irish disposition towards civilians was most clearly seen during raids. For much of the war, spoiling and raiding by the Irish in Ulster, the midlands and the Pale was rarely accompanied by the killing of civilians, though isolated instances may have been committed due to local tensions. One such atrocity was the massacre of the Floods at Kilclonfert (Co. Offaly).[153] However, while the Irish confederates made extensive use of raiding and preying from 1593 to 1599, there were relatively few cases of murder or unrestrained brutality in Ulster, Connacht and Leinster. Murders were written about in general terms as accompanying spoiling, but named victims were rare.[154] While there were cases of violence and widespread intimidation, killings were not a common feature of Irish raids. The levels of violence attendant on raids could vary depending on who was carrying out the attack and the motivating factors behind it.

Spoils could be gathered with little or no violence, with goods handed over without resistance or attempts by the rural population to escape. When Tyrone spoiled Bagenal's tenants in 1596–7, some farmers lost only horses or cattle, whereas others had their houses burnt.[155] This inconsistency may be explained by different individual raiders or the influence of personal animosity or grudges. Though there may have been isolated cases of murder or killing of people who attempted to resist the exactions, this was not a feature of most attacks. During a raid on the Pale in 1600, the Irish took preys and burned houses, but nobody was killed, and any prisoners taken were later released.[156] While Tyrone's confederates dominated most of the countryside by the end of 1598, Bingham observed how the country people 'neither fear nor flee the rebels'.[157] However, this does not mean that no one was ever killed during raids.

Fatalities normally ensued whenever there was an attempt to resist or recover a prey from confederate spoiling parties. There appears to have been accepted conventions when it came to the behaviour of both the victims and perpetrators of the attacks. As long as no resistance was met, violence tended to be minimal or absent. Increased opposition to a raid could dramatically magnify reciprocal aggression. In 1596, a farmer following those who had just taken some of his livestock was threatened with the loss of this head.[158] An attempt to recover preys by a small force of cavalry in Ards led to the deaths of all eight of the pursuers.[159] Where a preying party was caught and killed by the locals, retribution from the confederates could be brutal. The defeat of one of Edmond Burke's raids by Dermot O'Dwyer precipitated a furious reaction by Burke. His troops returned to kill men, women and children, burn all the houses and drove off all the cattle in O'Dwyer's country.[160] O'Donnell's attack into Connacht in 1598 was described as having massacred both low and high-born, but this may be a stylized description by Ó Clérigh as mass-killings in Connacht were not reported in the government papers.[161] Despite the suggestion of widespread and indiscriminate slaughter, there was no resulting flood of refugees from Connacht and no outcry from the government in Dublin that would have followed such an event.

The relative lack of civilian bloodshed of the confederate campaigns in Ulster, Connacht and Leinster stood in stark contrast to what unfolded in Munster at the end of 1598. The unprecedented levels of violence directed towards the English in the province was atypical of the Irish soldiers' conduct to that point. Undertakers abandoned their charges, and their tenants were subjected to brutality that had not been experienced by the English in the rest of the country. Regions with significant populations of Old English or English farmers, such as Laois and Offaly, and territories in east Ulster such as Lecale and Ards, while heavily taxed by Irish spoiling, were not visited by the kind of gratuitous violence articulated by Moryson, or in the unsigned *The supplication of the blood of the English*.[162] It could be suggested that both these are anti-Irish diatribes and the reports were subject to embellishment by the authors, but the accounts of mass killing and brutality were corroborated by other Irish and English sources.[163]

O'Sullivan Beare described how the Irish expelled the English from their holdings, but refugee columns seeking safety within the walled towns were generally unique to Munster.[164] The confederate troops led by O'More and Tyrrell had returned to Leinster by 19 October and took no part in the killings. The Irish peasantry perpetrated the surge of violence. William Saxey observed that murders and mutilations were committed by the tenants and servants of the English.[165] An anonymous author claimed that it was the churls, tenants and country people who spoiled their landlords and ran to the rebels.[166] Nevertheless, the displacement of the English settlers was not universally violent. When insurgents forced Anthony Randall and his family from their castle at Carknavill, 'John McHuillick' promised under oath that he would keep the lands for Randall and return them to him after the war.[167] Whether McHullick would have returned Randall to his holdings is debatable, but the account is relatively benign compared to what was experienced elsewhere.

The rapid escalation of inter-personal violence and resort to brutalization of civilians suggest that this phase of the war has more in common with the bloodier episodes of the 1641 rising than the Nine Years War.[168] The attacks spread throughout the province faster than O'More or his men could march. Therefore it is clear that civilians carried out the attacks, not troops under any form of direction from Tyrone's officers. The disorganized forces that rapidly coalesced in Munster had little in common with the kind of soldiers fielded in Ulster. Many were unarmed, and the anonymous author's description to Loftus suggested the Munster insurgents were essentially a mob.[169]

Tyrone had tapped into a vein of animosity that may have been rooted in the destruction associated with the crown's suppression of the Desmond revolt fifteen years earlier.[170] The speed of the revolt shocked observers. Henry Power wrote that the overthrow took just three days.[171] The scale of the revolt amazed O'Sullivan Beare, as there had previously been little support for Tyrone, apart from those with 'little power or resources'.[172] Correspondingly, he recorded a degree of surprise at the number of Irish nobles that came out against the crown; 'more Munstermen than was at all expected'.[173] The descriptions of the Munster rebels as an unarmed and disorganized rabble and the unanticipated actions of the Munster nobility suggests that popular discontent from the common labourers and husbandmen animated the revolt in Munster, fomenting a surge of violence directed towards the English settlers. The sudden enthusiasm of the Munster lords for rebellion may have been guided by a sense of self-preservation, when surrounded by a popular insurrection in which they had little (if any) control.

Civilian victimization by the confederates became more common in the latter stages of the war. When Tyrone assaulted O'Carroll lands in Ely (Co. Offaly) during February 1600, the attack was in response to Calvagh O'Carroll's murder of 100 MacMahon soldiers billeted upon them by Tyrone the previous year.[174] Crown documents state that Tyrone killed all men able to bear arms, but the Irish annals go further, claiming he killed men, women and children.[175] Revenge or retribution was the primary motivator for Irish attacks on civilian targets. Redmond Burke assailed the O'Dwyers in May 1600, killing civilians in retaliation for their attack on one of his raiding parties.[176] Captain Richard Tyrrell, who has been portrayed as the epitome of martial ability in the confederate army, attacked civilians in Muskerry in October 1602.[177] He believed Cormac MacDermond [MacCarthy] had betrayed the whereabouts of his camp to the crown, and in retaliation 'killed and hanged divers poor men, women and children appertaining to Cormocke'.[178]

While crown troops had attacked civilians before 1600, it was after Mountjoy's appointment that victimization of non-combatants intensified.

Superficially this looked like a policy of extirpation, but the reality was more complex. Though it is true that civilian brutalization increased, attitudes among the crown's senior leaders were not uniformly hostile or committed to slaughtering civilians. As noted earlier, Sir Arthur Chichester openly called for unfettered aggression and a policy of eradication against the native Irish.[179] Notwithstanding Chichester's approach, not all crown officials were unrestrained in their attacks on Irish civilians. Sir George Carew was more pragmatic in his approach when it came to pacification. His use of civilian victimization was directed to achieve tangible military goals and not as a broad assault on the Irish population of Munster.

The irregular characteristic of much of the warfare waged by Tyrone and his confederates may in itself have precipitated much of the barbarity and atrocities against civilians. There have been several studies addressing English cruelty to civilians during the war, and reasons such as military necessity, the personal animosity of officers and xenophobic attitudes towards the Irish have all been cited.[180] Decisions to engage in civilian victimization were taken at two distinct levels; localized persecution by troops in the field, and as an act of policy created by their political and military leaders. Localized attacks could transpire regardless of the plans or policies of government or army officers. Dangerous frustrations and tensions can grow within military units when they are unable to counter or effectively respond to enemy attacks.[181] This has been particularly true for irregular wars in which troops, denied any chance to elicit limited psychological solace from enacting a bloody revenge on a real enemy, are likely to lash out at a perceived hostile civil population.

Damaged morale or a sense of ineffectiveness due to soldiers' inability to close with an opposing military force can be allayed by a sense of empowerment that comes with mass-murder or executions.[182] Moreover, once soldiers commit an atrocity, the individuals involved must justify their actions by viewing their victims as moral, social or racial inferiors. Once established, this affirmation of superiority further enables greater acts of killing and atrocity.[183] When considered in the context of what was happening in Ireland, it becomes apparent that isolated units such as Sir Arthur Chichester's garrison in Carrickfergus, or the small garrisons in Munster, were capable of civilian victimization irrespective of crown policy. As confederate forces were unlikely to engage these troops in large actions without good reason, they were subject to small-scale or desultory engagements that would have sapped morale, and led to rising frustration and resentment.[184]

It should be no surprise that some of the first instances of gratuitous attacks by the crown forces occurred near Carrickfergus in June 1599, and in Munster during January 1600.[185] Add revenge into the equation and brutality becomes almost inevitable. Vengeance on a personal level can be a strong motivating factor in cases of brutality. Troops can react differently to the loss of friends or comrades in violent circumstances, but feelings of anger and a desire for revenge are common.[186] The death of Sir John Chichester in 1597 was considered a key factor in Sir Arthur Chichester's belligerence towards the Irish.[187] Docwra's mutilation of Turlough Magnylson O'Neill's followers can be understood in the context of the Irish officer's betrayal and killing of the fifty-man garrison at Newtown in 1602.[188] He was a trusted ally of the English in the region. Therefore Magnylson's treachery incensed Docwra, and he spared no details describing the pursuit and punishment of those responsible for the massacre; Docwra ordered his men to hew Irish captives 'in pieces with their swords'.[189]

The nature of the war had a grievous effect on how the queen's officers conducted it. This was again due to Tyrone's preference for engaging only on his terms and when the odds were most favourable. Casualties caused by battle were substantially lower than the natural wastage of the crown's armies due to disease and desertion. Therefore Tyrone was content to refuse contact and allow the English to wither, at little cost to him in either men or munitions. In modern studies, this tactic has been identified as a precursor to officially sanctioned victimization against civilian populations.[190] Seen in the context of European colonial wars in later centuries, the treatment of non-combatants had more to do with the type of resistance offered than racial or social differences.[191] Typically, most cases of civilian victimization in war have occurred after a counter-force military policy has failed to deliver victory.[192] The conduct of the war by the English appears to conform to this pattern.

From 1593 to 1599, the main goal of the crown's army was to close with and defeat the military power of the Irish confederates. The hostings by Bagenal, Russell, Burgh and Essex were primarily aimed at engaging with or provoking a military response from the Irish. In May 1597, Burgh noted that force was the only way to defeat Tyrone, and two years later Essex clearly voiced his desire for a general battle to end the war.[193] Essex's 1599 campaign was the greatest concentration of Tudor military power since the Armada of 1588, and its failure marks the transition from the defective hosting strategy to the policies of Mountjoy that coupled sustained and aggressive military action with attacks targeting the population and economy of the Irish. Consequently, brutalization was more likely to occur in long wars where rising costs and lack of success led to desperation.[194] Armies that normally gained victory by direct attacks, such as the crown attempted between 1593 and 1599, were likely to turn on the civilian population in these circumstances.

As noted earlier, the role of ethnic hatred has spawned a torrid debate on the issue, but looking at this question in purely military terms, did it matter? Analysis of military behaviour suggests that civilian victimization does not require deep ideological motivation. Aggression against civilians could be produced by the logic of military conflict itself. The conduct of warfare in differing political, geographic and ethnic contexts did not (and does not) require ideological input to produce atrocities and civilian persecution, only the frustration of the direct application of military power. This of itself does not invalidate either side of the argument. It merely shows that in war, the demands of necessity, expediency and the need to avoid defeat will drive people to extreme actions regardless of their pre-war values. This does not excuse the brutality, but it does help explain how military forces decide to attack civilian populations. The brutality experienced in the 1600–3 period may have been as a result of how the war was fought and not the ideological preconceptions of the belligerents.

The attacks on civilians did not require hatred of the Irish as a prerequisite. Highly vocal proponents of extirpation according to ethnicity or religion, such as Sir Arthur Chichester or Edmund Spenser, illustrate the undeniable bigotry of elements within the English society towards the native Irish. Junior officers may have also held these sentiments, but these attitudes in themselves do not explain civilian victimization; bigoted or racist intolerance of enemies are not always causative issues in attacks on civilians.[195] It becomes difficult to sustain an argument for ethnic intolerance for localized attacks, such as those of Captain Flower in Munster in 1600, when the typical ethnic composition of the English infantry companies is considered.[196] Throughout the war, the crown supplemented manpower shortages with Irish troops.[197] A return of soldiers stationed near Newry in 1597 showed that Captain Flower's company was one of several who were entirely composed of Irish soldiers.[198] Sir George Carew noted in January 1600 that many of his infantry companies in Munster were all Irish and some had Irish captains.[199] Furthermore, one of the crown's most enthusiastic exponents for attacking civilians was Niall Garbh O'Donnell.[200] If ethnic hostility or intolerance are not key enabling factors for attacks on non-combatants, there was another issue shared by both Irish and English troops: animosity towards civilians.

Throughout the history of early modern warfare (and most other periods for that matter), except when troops were in their home countries or depended upon civilian aid, the needs of civilians were always secondary to military decisions. Almost as soon as a soldier enrolled in the ranks, he began to regard civilians' needs as secondary to military necessity.[201] Elsewhere in Europe, military service could bring status to peasants that they would protect by treating others with extreme harshness.[202] Once enrolled into the ranks, soldiers were unlikely to return to civilian life on demobilization at the end of a conflict. Many resorted to crime or sought alternative military employment.[203] Both Tyrone and the crown had swollen the ranks of their armies with men drawn from the peasantry. In the latter stages of the war, crown officials were concerned that large numbers of unemployed soldiers would prove hazardous to the stability of a newly pacified Ireland.[204] This suggested that on demobilization, Irish soldiers shared their continental counterparts' reluctance to return to a life of agricultural drudgery. Mountjoy noted in April 1603 the desirability to transport idle troops to the Continent as 'petty eruptions and stealths' would only end when they were gone.[205] Therefore it is possible that animosity between troops and civilians, which was assumed to be racial or religious, was related to social tensions between soldiers and civilians.

A difficult question with regards to the violence during the war was the role of religion and ethnicity; in this context Catholic–Protestant and Irish–Old English–New English. Examination of interpersonal violence and aggression against the civil population suggest that ethnicity was not a decisive factor in deciding who was targeted during the war. Some of Tyrone's closest confidants were English or of English descent, such as Henry Hovenden and Captain Richard Tyrrell. According to Carew, an Englishman called Thomas Taylor, who was a son-in-law to Tyrrell, was with Ulick Burke when he murdered George Bingham at Sligo in 1594.[206] English troops served in Tyrone's army, and English and Welsh officers travelled from Europe to find employment with the confederates.[207] They may have been few when compared to the number of native Irish soldiers in Tyrone's pay, but there was no proscriptions on recruiting non-Irish or non-Catholic troops.

Though the Irish controlled most of Ireland by 1599, there was no organized effort to remove the English from Irish territory. English tenants in Ulster and the midlands, while required to provide goods to the confederate troops, were not forced off the land. Even in Munster where religious tension was greatest and Irish aggression against settlers could be extreme, English labourers and artisans could remain if they were willing to conform to Catholicism.[208] Religious differences could clearly rouse passions and divisions. In 1600, the queen's earl of Desmond was well received by the inhabitants of Kilmallock until he attended a Protestant service, after which the townspeople jeered and spat on him.[209] Carew believed that religious bonds were stronger than those of ethnicity. In 1594, he feared that there was connivance with Tyrone in the Pale, the west coast of England and in Wales solely on the grounds of religious affiliation.[210] However, these fears were unfounded, as sharing a faith was not a strong enough pretext for most Old English to join with Tyrone against their sovereign.

The embers extinguished

Despite the widespread devastation and scattering of Irish forces, there were still a few pockets of resistance defying Carew in Munster. O'Sullivan Beare remained in Glengarriff forest on the southern shore of the Beara peninsula, Tyrrell was still at large, as was Cormac MacDermond MacCarthy, lord of Muskerry, but on 22 October MacDermond submitted to Carew.[211] Tyrrell had expected MacDermond to send money to pay his troops. Instead, Owen MacTeig, a MacCarthy sub-chief, led Sir Samuel Bagenal with a force of infantry and cavalry to Tyrrell.[212] Bagenal's infantry crept up on the Irish camp, but with just 200 yards to go, a raw recruit tripped and discharged his weapon, alerting the Irish.[213] The Irish rushed to arms, but the English were almost upon them; Tyrrell and his wife fled into the night. Many of Tyrrell's men also made good their escape, but at the expense of the baggage train holding the army's money, arms and equipment.

Carew reported 50–60 horses captured, along with 400 garrans, cattle, and the surprisingly rich contents of the baggage which included 'hollands [fine linen], velvet, gold and silver lace, English apparel of satin and velvet'.[214] A portmanteau full of Spanish gold was discovered, but Carew never got his hands on it. The soldiers who took it 'had more wit than to proclaim it in the market place', and filled their own pockets instead of Carew's.[215] Not without cause, Tyrrell believed the MacCarthys had betrayed him to Carew, and vented his fury with punitive attacks on the civilians of Muskerry, burning corn and hanging 'diverse poor people of the country'.[216] It was Tyrrell's last offensive action of the war. He made several efforts to submit, but Carew rebuffed his overtures. O'Sullivan Beare offered Tyrrell cash and goods as incentives to stay in the province, but Tyrrell was done with Munster. He struck north for Ely O'Carroll in December, leaving his sick, wounded and anyone or anything else that could slow his pace.[217]

The small army led by John Fitzwilliam Fitzgerald, the knight of Kerry, suffered a similar fate to Tyrrell's during November. His location was betrayed to Sir Charles Wilmott, who attacked during the night. As with Tyrrell, Fitzgerald escaped with most of his men, but the English took his cattle, arms and baggage train holding two months of provisions. However, spoils did not satiate Wilmott's men, whose attention turned to the Irish remaining in the camp. Without protection the civilians stood no chance as the English 'in the fury of their advance … spared neither sex nor age'.[218] Fitzgerald was out of options, as there were no strongholds to retreat to and nothing to feed his men; Fitzgerald had to submit.

With little prospect of help from outside, Irish resistance in Munster crumbled. Nevertheless, O'Sullivan Beare still defied Carew from his strong position in Glengarriff forest. Carew had complained about the difficult terrain presented by the Beara peninsula, but his troops gathered to seize the fastness in December. Recent experience had shown that Irish resolve was waning. Therefore a close assault by English foot should have been enough to evict O'Sullivan's men. However, the Irish had received munitions from Spain during the summer, which may have tipped the scales, ever-so-briefly, in O'Sullivan's favour. Firepower had been the crucial ingredient in Irish victories from 1593 to 1599. The Munstermen gave the English an unsettling reminder of the lethal qualities of well-supplied Irish shot.

Sir Charles Wilmott's troops made their camp near Glengarriff on 30 December, where he proclaimed the queen's mercy for any who would desert O'Sullivan.[219] The Irish responded with an hour-long skirmish while the English camp was established, then sporadic fire throughout the night. The following day Wilmot ordered 200 foot under Lieutenant Selby and 400 rising out led by Captain John Barry into the glen.[220] They captured the Irish baggage, but a ferocious firefight erupted lasting six hours, forcing the English to retreat. O'Sullivan's troops pursued them back to their camp, causing Wilmott to deploy two regiments of foot to cover the withdrawal. Barry and Selby were in trouble as the Irish engaged the rear-guard with sword and pike. Wilmott sent 120 men to reinforce the hard-pressed English rear, and the fighting continued until darkness separated the two sides.[221] The English claimed a victory, but it was clear that Wilmott's soldiers had been roughly handled. Even Carew admitted the English had taken serious losses, though as usual he reported that the Irish suffered more.[222] Philip O'Sullivan Beare claimed the Irish kept their hold on Glengarriff for another three days, driving off successive attacks, but the defenders' will to resist was fading. Furthermore, desertion weakened the army more than battle casualties.[223] The final blow came when William Burke, leader of O'Sullivan's bonnaghts, decided to quit Munster. According to Stafford, Burke had lost enough men and no amount of Spanish gold could convince him to stay.[224] Without Burke's men O'Sullivan's army was finished. Therefore on 4 January 1603, he joined Burke and started the long march north.

The loss of Munster was emphatically confirmed the next day when the last remaining Irish army, with little over 400 men of the MacCarthys, was engaged by English troops in Carbery. The Irish initially prevailed against Captain Taffe's infantry, killing forty and routing the rest, but a charge by the English horse forced the Irish to retire.[225] Seeing the Irish falter, the bishop of Ross, Owen MacEgan, led a renewed attack 'with one hundred men … came boldly up to the sword and maintained a hot skirmish until he was slain with a shot'.[226] Dismayed, the Irish broke and fled, but the Bandon river blocked their way, and many were cut down or drowned as they tried to cross.

The fugitives from Munster now embarked upon one of the greatest feats of fortitude seen during the Nine Years War – O'Sullivan's march to Leitrim.[227] Munster was lost to the confederates. Therefore the remnants of O'Sullivan's army, 400 infantry and a few cavalry, accompanied by their families, made their way north through hostile territory, in bad weather and pursued all the way by the crown's Irish allies.[228] Time and again attacks on the flanks and rear of the column were beaten off, but casualties eroded the small army. Their numbers were reduced as each new attack claimed more lives and sapped morale. Hunger and exhaustion weakened O'Sullivan's small band further, but they pressed on to the river Shannon. They built boats from timber and horse hides to cross the river north of Portumna (Co. Galway), but an attack by the Donough MacEgan during the operation caused mayhem in the baggage train before being driven off.[229]

Though diminished, the last stalwarts of the Irish confederacy could still prove deadly to their enemies. Captain Henry Malby should have kept this in mind when he attempted to intercept O'Sullivan's desperate band at Aughrim (Co. Galway). Malby had survived the bloody rout at the battle of the Yellow Ford in 1598, and endured the collective privations in the frozen siege lines around Kinsale in 1601. However, Malby's mixed force of English infantry, horse and local Irish outnumbered O'Sullivan and were confident of victory. Moreover, the cacophony of their approach with trumpets, pipes and beating drums unnerved the Irish, causing eighty men in the baggage train to lose their nerve.[230] O'Sullivan rallied his men, reminding them that there was nowhere to hide if they were defeated. The Irish moved onto boggy ground to protect themselves from the menace of the English cavalry, who could ride them down over firm ground. The English shot pestered the rear of the Irish column, but a sudden *volte face* by the Munstermen checked Malby's advance. Confusion crept into the English ranks as the infantry wheeled about. A volley of Irish shot raked through the English before the two sides came to blows. Malby was killed in the vicious melee, and as the tide of battle swung against them, the English and their allies ran, falling back 'not slowly, but pell-mell', for the safety of a nearby fort.[231]

The ordeal of O'Sullivan's ever-shrinking party continued as they made their way north, but at last, they crossed the Curlew Mountains and entered Leitrim, where they met Sir Brian O'Rourke who provided aid and shelter to the survivors. Only 35 remained of the 1,000 who had marched out of Glengarriff.[232] O'Sullivan was still willing to continue the war despite his losses. Therefore O'Sullivan travelled into Fermanagh with Tyrrell and Cuconnaght Maguire to meet with Tyrone. Captain Laurence Esmond, with Conor Roe Maguire, tried but failed to stop the small force of roughly

300 men, crossing the Erne. This error by the English set the stage for the final actions of the war.

While Esmond's men vainly searched for the Irish near Belturbet, O'Sullivan and Cuconnaght Maguire fell on the English camp, capturing the baggage and executing fifty of the 'defenders'.[233] Maguire took most of the remaining Irish troops to spoil the surrounding districts, leaving O'Sullivan with just one hundred men to face Esmond. However, O'Sullivan deployed an elaborate ruse, using women and children masquerading as pikemen to deter an attack until Cuconnaght returned. Esmond chose to withdraw to the safety of the islands until he could be reinforced. As darkness closed in, the English took refuge within the Maguire inauguration site at Cornashee (a large earthwork enclosure near Lisnaskea, Co. Fermanagh), described as 'a deserted old fortress built of small stones, and surrounded by a trench and lofty trees planted on the sides'.[234] With daylight the English push to the Erne resumed, and in four hours Esmond's force had reached their boats on the shoreline, but the Irish had followed them.

O'Sullivan and Maguire attacked just as Esmond started to ferry his people to the nearby islands. The sudden onslaught sparked panic, as 'some jumped into the boats in such haste and confusion that some were sunk; others loaded the nearest ships with such a crowd that they went down with them; others, throwing themselves into the lough, were drawn down by the weight of their armour; others were killed by the Irish'.[235] Desperate to escape, soldiers and civilians packed the largest boat, but with no one to cast off it remained just yards from the bank. The Irish blasted the hapless passengers with point-blank fire until a shot or blade severed the line, allowing the boat to carry away the bloodied survivors. After the slaughter on the shore, the Irish attacked and captured seven small garrisons on the lough, hanging all who fell into their hands.[236] The English records are silent on the details of the operations at the end of the war, making it difficult to get a contrasting view. Nevertheless, any number of local successes in Fermanagh could not alter strategic reality; the defiance of O'Sullivan, Maguire and O'Rourke was futile. Tyrone was a spent force. Small victories in Fermanagh could achieve nothing but take lives and delay the inevitable. After defeating Esmond, O'Sullivan and Maguire made for the wooded fastness of Glenconkeyne in search of Tyrone, but the earl had left. He had gone to submit to Mountjoy.

Mountjoy's pursuit of Tyrone continued unabated throughout autumn 1602. When the earl entered Fermanagh, Mountjoy tried but failed to contain him south of the Erne with garrisons along the lough. A fort was raised at Augher, Co. Tyrone, to block the important route through the Clogher valley but to no avail; Tyrone was back in Glenconkeyne by December. Despite

Chichester's best efforts, Tyrone could not be run to ground.[237] Tyrone could rely on the loyalty of Irish lords who had already submitted to the crown, who provided him with supplies and intelligence on English movements. In January 1603, Mountjoy admitted that it would be a matter of luck to capture Tyrone.[238] Writing to Cecil, he noted that 'he [Tyrone] hath a shrewd head … and except it be by good fortune I think it will be hard to come by it'.[239] Try as he might, Mountjoy could not induce anyone to betray Tyrone.[240]

The earl had already proffered his submission on terms, but the queen was adamant that no mercy was due to the 'author of so much effusion of blood, and the most ungrateful viper'.[241] However, the cost of maintaining the war was taking its toll in England.[242] Regardless, the queen insisted that Tyrone be stripped of his title, becoming the baron of Dungannon, his lands reduced and passes cut through Tyrone's lordship.[243] Even with the queen's intractability, Cecil advised Mountjoy to do whatever he could to secure Tyrone's surrender. Mountjoy should be flexible when dealing with Tyrone, as 'all honest servants must strain a little when they will serve princes'.[244] Furthermore, while Tyrone's offer of submission on 22 December 1602 appeared penitent, it contained an implicit threat that if the crown did not accept his submission, Tyrone would be 'forced wither to fly or seek to any other prince'.[245] The last thing the crown needed was the earl becoming a figure to rally support for another Spanish invasion. Indeed, this appears precisely what Tyrone intended. Several days after writing to Mountjoy, Tyrone dispatched a letter to Philip III requesting that the delivery of aid be expedited; if not a ship should be sent to evacuate him and his remaining allies by 1 May 1603.[246]

Unfortunately for Tyrone, the letter took three months to reach Brussels, during which time the unrelenting pressure from Mountjoy's depredations and the devastating famine in Ulster forced many of Tyrone's closest allies to submit. Even his most unwavering adherent and gifted field commander, his brother Cormac MacBaron, conceded defeat in February 1603. Tyrone finally submitted to Mountjoy at Mellifont abbey on 30 March 1603, where he received decidedly generous terms.[247] Tyrone renounced the title of The O'Neill, but remained the earl of Tyrone (which the queen had repeatedly insisted was not to happen) and retained much of the territory he controlled before the war. The conflict had one final twist. On presenting his formal surrender in Dublin, Mountjoy told Tyrone that the queen had died on 24 March, six days before his capitulation at Mellifont.[248] The likelihood of the queen's death possibly proved decisive in Mountjoy agreeing to such lenient terms, as Tyrone could claim that he had never been in rebellion against the new king, James I and VI.[249] Moreover, Moryson's fanciful tableau of Tyrone's craven submission 'kneeling … before the lord deputy and council' obfuscated the hard bargaining and negotiations that brought Tyrone to this point.[250] Nonetheless, Tyrone had submitted, and soon after most of the last remaining Irish confederates followed suit; the war was finally over.[251]

Tyrone's war: an epilogue

After all the years of destruction and bloodshed, Tyrone and his allies received remarkably generous terms for their surrender. The earl received a royal pardon but was forced to renounce his position as The O'Neill. Despite this, Tyrone retained most of his lands and estates. The earl swore to renounce 'all foreign power whatever and all kind of dependency upon any other potentate but his majesty [James I and VI] … and do now to serve him faithfully against any foreign power invading his kingdoms, and to disclose truly any practices that I do or shall know against his royal person or crowns'.[252] Tyrone specifically repudiated his contact with the Spanish state, Philip III and his 'forces or confederates'.[253] Tyrone journeyed to England with Mountjoy during the summer to meet with King James and even went hunting with the new king. However, defeat had not changed Tyrone's nature or blunted his ambitions. While in England the earl dispatched a letter to Philip III offering to take up arms for Spain if the peace negotiations between the English and Spanish failed.[254] Many in England and Ireland were unhappy with the mild treatment of Tyrone, reflected by Sir John Harrington who wrote

> I have lived to see that damnable rebel Tyrone brought to England, courteously favoured, honoured and well liked. Oh! My lord, what is there which does not prove the inconstancy of worldly matters! How did I labour after that knave's destruction! I was called from my home by her majesty's command, adventured perils by sea and land, endured toil, was near starving, ate horse-flesh in Munster; and all to quell that man, who now smileth in peace at those who did hazard their lives to destroy him.[255]

Mountjoy was made earl of Devonshire and Tyrone returned to rebuild his estates. The lacklustre government of Sir George Carey, Mountjoy's replacement as lord deputy, was no impediment to the earl's efforts.[256] Yet the completion of the conquest of Ireland had profound effects for native society as traditional Irish laws and lordships were swept away. The appointment of Sir Arthur Chichester as lord deputy saw a new, more aggressive approach to reform. Tanistry, the system of law used to inherit the land and property of an Irish lordship was abolished and Irish lords were obliged to follow primogeniture and English common law.[257] Chichester worked with Sir John

Davies, the solicitor-general in Ireland, to undermine the power of the Irish lords. Gaelic exactions on lesser lords were banned. Furthermore, junior Irish nobles were freed from their obligations as *uirríthe* to Tyrone and Rory O'Donnell, earl of Tirconnell, and made freeholders with obligations to pay fixed yearly rent. Chichester went further during October 1605 when he issued a proclamation banning Catholic clergy from Ireland and forcing the laity to attend Protestant church services.[258]

Tyrone was protected to some extent by the earl of Devonshire (Mountjoy), who's influence still trammelled the activities of Chichester and Davies, but this disappeared at the start of April 1606 when Devonshire died. Chichester and Davies did their utmost to accuse Tyrone of treason, but no solid evidence could be found. Catherine, countess of Tyrone, was even approached to inform on her husband, but she rejected this out of hand. Matters reached a head in September 1607, when feeling their position untenable and their arrest inevitable, Tyrone, Tirconnell and many of their adherents sailed for the Continent from Rathmullan, Co. Donegal, never to return. Their lands were escheated by the crown and became the foundation of the plantation of Ulster two years later.

CHAPTER 7

Tyrone's military revolution

TYRONE WAS THE DRIVING FORCE behind the modernization of Irish troops, first in Ulster, then as the power of the Irish confederates spread, throughout Ireland. However, within the historiography of the war, there is disagreement on the extent of Tyrone's influence. Ó Báille dismissed the influence Tyrone had on the progressive and modernizing trend in the late sixteenth-century Irish armies. He asserted that it was a new politico-religious idealism imported from counter-reformation Europe coupled with Tudor aggression that stimulated the transformation of the Gaelic military.[1] O Báille relegated Tyrone's role to that of an opportunist who exploited a favourable situation. Falls disagreed, according 'Tyrone's genius' a factor in the creation of the modern soldiers in Ireland.[2] He added that Irish methods were transformed by their experience of fighting against English pike and shot formations, by the influence of officers such as Captain Richard Tyrrell, Spanish military advisors, and expertise gained serving in the crown and continental armies.[3] Nevertheless, Falls believed that these advances represented the minority in an otherwise traditional Gaelic military.[4] Hayes-McCoy claimed that Tyrone deliberately and systematically built a modern army, armed with the latest weaponry and utilizing contemporary methods of pike and shot warfare prevalent on the Continent.[5] Regularly paid with a supporting infrastructure of munitions and food depots, Hayes-McCoy described Tyrone's new formations as a 'native militia'.[6] Morgan rejected the idea of a native militia, noting that Tyrone's hired soldiers had no political rights within the lands for which they fought, but he did agree that the modern forces emanating from Ulster were quantitatively and qualitatively superior to what had gone before.[7] Canny referred to Tyrone's overhaul of the Irish military as evidence of his progressive leanings; he considered Tyrone an innovator, free of the constricting ligatures of tradition and custom.[8]

It is not an overstatement to claim that Tyrone's reforms revolutionized the means and manner in which the Irish under his command fought. When Tyrone engaged the crown in open warfare, it was not with the outdated kerne and gallowglass, but with disciplined and well-equipped troops trained in modern pike and shot tactics. Firearms were deployed on a scale never before seen in Ireland. It is simplistic, however, to presume that the injection of

195

technology caused this transformation, as firearms had been available long before 1593; it was Tyrone's reforms that changed native soldiers into a force unprecedented in Irish history. Melee combat was replaced with firepower and an ability to deploy and manoeuvre on the battlefield that shocked contemporary observers.

The new Irish tactics did not merely imitate continental or English methods, as Falls and Hayes-McCoy believed, but were a hybrid that emphasized the power of modern firearms while maintaining operational and tactical mobility. Hayes-McCoy wrote that Tyrone created a force composed of pike and shot that fought 'in the accepted manner of the age'.[9] This idea has been reiterated in many subsequent publications.[10] There was an alternative interpretation that stressed the Irish preference for close combat. This view proposed that despite the changes made by Tyrone, his forces still used the 'Irish charge', an antiquated tactic of their primitive antecedents.[11] This premise has proliferated in other texts dealing with warfare of the period.[12] Neither positions were correct. Tyrone's reforms did not slavishly copy pike and shot tactics. The revolutionary changes in infantry combat seen in continental Europe were modified to accept the realities of fighting within the Irish landscape.

The battle of Clontibret in 1595 sent shudders through the English authorities in Dublin. Letters to the court in England suggested a real sense of shock at Irish military skill and their ability to successfully confront the English army with modernized weaponry and sophisticated tactics. However, this was either the disquiet of officials unused to war in Ireland or short-sightedness caused by unwarranted presumptions that the Irish could not field substantial armies or deploy infantry equipped with modern arms. This misconception is puzzling, as the native Irish had already demonstrated throughout the sixteenth century that they could raise large armies. Furthermore, as the century wore on, the size and logistical endurance of the forces fielded against the crown in Ireland steadily increased to extraordinary levels.

Before Tyrone and the roots of reform

The potential for raising sizable bodies of native troops in Ireland was limited due to a relatively low population and available resources, yet the scale of Irish armies still rose dramatically by the end of the sixteenth century. At the start of the century, Irish armies had been relatively small, although alliances, as seen at the battle of Knockdoe (1504), could create larger concentrations of forces for limited periods.[13] However, there was a marked rise in the quantity of troops mobilized in the second half of the sixteenth century. Shane O'Neill broke with tradition by training and arming churls and husbandmen, enabling him to field an army estimated to comprise approximately 4,000 foot and 700 horse.[14] The marriage of Turlough Luineach O'Neill to Lady Agnes Campbell in 1569 gave him access to 3,000 Scots mercenaries. While Turlough was not as overtly bellicose as Shane, the addition of the Scots to his locally raised forces granted him an army larger than any in the country.[15]

The English concern at the skilful use of firearms by the Irish is also perplexing as native soldiers had been using firearms long before 1595. Despite its position on the periphery of Europe, Ireland was not immune to the proliferation of firearms technology across Europe throughout the fifteenth and sixteenth centuries. Indeed, Henry VIII made good use of Irish shot on the Scottish borders.[16] Although the deliberately archaized writings of Ó Clérigh suggested that firearms were in some way alien to the native Irish, there were enough in Ireland by the mid-sixteenth century to cause the authorities in Dublin grave concern.[17] While the Irish were familiar with modern weapons, technology on its own did not inevitably lead to a change in combat methods of the traditional Irish host. Gallowglass and kerne were present in Ulster at the start of the war. In the illustration of the battle of the Erne Ford near Belleek in October 1593, the Irish to the north of the river can be clearly seen to carry gallowglass axes and bows.[18] Darts were thrown at Sir Henry Duke's men at the battle of the Ford of the Biscuits in August 1594, but traditional Irish weaponry was rarely mentioned later in the war.[19]

One of the major advantages of gunpowder weapons was that raw troops could be rapidly trained to use them.[20] Shane O'Neill enthusiastically adopted firearms, but there is no evidence to suggest he used them in the modern fashion. The two major battles fought by Shane, Glentaisie (1565) and Farsetmore (1567), were decided by a clash of heavy infantry, with no critical role attributed to firearms.[21] He subsumed shot into the traditional Gaelic army, but Shane did not depend on firepower like Tyrone. The technology was present, but knowledge of how to maximize the effect of firearms, or the will to train Irish forces in the new techniques of warfare were absent.

This did not mean that the Irish could not use firearms to good effect even when used as a supplement or replacement for traditional missile weapons. In certain circumstances, the Irish could deploy shot in positions of such tactical advantage that massed firepower alone was enough to succeed. This was seen during Feagh MacHugh's stunning victory over Lord Grey de Wilton at Glenmalure in August 1580. Lord Grey entered the valley with just over 2,000 men, with the intention of putting down a rebellion by James Eustace, third Viscount Baltinglass, and Feagh MacHugh O'Byrne. The glen was steep-sided, rocky, and provided ample cover for the Irish shot positioned on its northern slopes. Grey's army was drawn to attack uphill by a volley of fire from concealed Irish positions, but in their haste to close with the Irish shot they failed to secure their flanks. The English foot started taking fire from three sides and the ferocity of the sudden onslaught caused a precipitate retreat. When Baltinglass and O'Byrne committed their reserves to pursue the English, the retreat became a rout. Firearms had been a valuable element in the success at Glenmalure, but the tactical situation and topography was so advantageous to the Irish, and the English tactics so inept, that the victory could likely have been achieved with the bows, darts, swords and axes of the traditional Irish soldiery.

A key element associated with the military revolution was the transformation of tactics.[22] More specifically, the use of firepower as the primary means to dominate the battlefield. When the word 'modern' is used regarding infantry of this period, the emphasis is on combined arms teams of pikemen and shot (armed with muskets or calivers), in which pike were primarily used to defend the slow-firing shot from attack by cavalry. Pikemen normally formed a central core with the shot on either flank and sometimes to the front and rear.[23] Even as war raged in Ireland, the incessant fighting on the Continent produced more advanced ways of deploying pike and shot, but in Ireland, 'modern' forces were primarily a tactical combination of pike and shot, though Tyrone made modifications to suit his tactical needs.

Many Irish officers fought alongside English pike and shot units or commanded them on continental service, but familiarity with modern infantry tactics did not guarantee that new techniques would be applied to the native Irish military. There were Irish officers with continental experience who apparently felt no compunction or desire to retrain their household forces on their return home. Examples of this could be found in Munster where several Irish lords, including Florence MacCarthy, who would later become embroiled in the war, had served with English forces in Ireland and with Sir William Stanley on the Continent.[24] It is without question that they would have been familiar with modern tactics and formations, but when the war engulfed Munster in 1598 Captain Richard Tyrrell remained in the province to instruct the local forces.[25] This suggested that at the end of 1598, the Munster soldiers had not been trained like the modernized troops raised by Tyrone and his allies in Ulster and Connacht. Certainly the previous war in Munster, the Desmond revolt (1579–83), was fought in the traditional manner of the Irish chiefs. Large battles and prolonged sieges were rarely seen; guerrilla tactics and small-scale raids were the norms.[26]

Nonetheless, the English establishment's main concern was the training of the Irish in the proper and efficient use of firearms and not the proliferation of the technology per se.[27] Despite the risks in training native Irish troops, the practicalities of maintaining the crown's military strength meant that using Irish manpower was unavoidable. There was also the impact of the crown policy to anglicize the native Irish. It was hoped that raising the children of the Irish nobility in English households in the Pale would help achieve the aim of encouraging the adoption of English customs and manners among the native Irish. Collier railed against this, noting that many of the rebels had grown up in English households as horseboys or scullions, and then enrolled in the foot bands where they learned to 'skilfully handle their weapons, at her majesty's no small charge'.[28] Wallop referred to the practice of training the Irish in modern military practices starting during the deputyship of Sir John Perrot, and accelerating under Fitzwilliam, describing it as a 'high oversight'.[29] A substantial proportion of the modern troops deployed by the Irish at the start of the war had been taught and had gained experience in the foot companies raised or supplied by the Dublin government.[30] The most famous recipient of crown aid was Tyrone, who trained and equipped his household troops as pike and shot.[31]

Though many of the forces ranged against the crown at the start of the war were trained in crown service, the Armada of 1588 introduced a new source of military expertise to the native Irish lords that was beyond government control. After 1588, there is evidence for the appearance of non-state sponsored pike and shot units as part of native Irish retinues. Throughout September 1588, ships of the defeated Spanish Armada had taken shelter or had been wrecked along the western coast of Ireland. Thousands of men from the fleet were stranded, many of whom were soldiers trained in modern continental warfare. Of approximately 6,000 men caught up in the disaster, over half drowned or died of disease, and 1,500 were killed or executed by the English and Irish, but around 750 survived.[32] Most were transported to Scotland, but others were retained by the Irish chiefs in Connacht and Ulster. Some of those who remained in Irish hands were employed training the forces of the local lords. This was most evident when survivors landed in regions where crown control was at its weakest.

Teige O'Flaherty was the eldest son of Sir Morrough ne doe O'Flaherty and was involved in handing over Spanish prisoners in Connemara during September 1588.[33] The next year he broke out into rebellion against the crown. It quickly became evident that both had kept Spanish soldiers to train their household troops. When Captain Edward Bermingham engaged Teige in March 1589, the forces deployed by the Irish were not the gallowglass, kerne and horsemen as would be expected, but a formation of pike and shot.[34] There was an initial trading of volleys of shot, before both English and Irish advanced to push of pike during which Teig was killed, throwing the Irish into disorder. Bermingham exploited this and charged horsemen and infantry into a breach in the Irish ranks routing them and leaving over eighty dead on the field. A Spanish officer discovered among the dead was described as 'of reckoning and was their marshal'.[35] By the time the O'Flahertys had joined with the Burkes in rebellion, the council in Dublin reported that in addition to 20 Spaniards, the Irish rebels' combined forces had 2,000 men armed and equipped with weapons and ordinance recovered from the Armada wrecks.[36]

The O'Flahertys were not the only Irish to take advantage of the windfall of modern equipment and expertise. The Burkes of Mayo were reported to have an indeterminate number of Spaniards.[37] When Sir Richard Bingham engaged the O'Rourkes in April 1589, he noted that they were accompanied by fourteen Spaniards and had a large store of equipment from the wrecks.[38] Sir Brian O'Rourke used twenty-four Spaniards to train his kerne and equipped them with Spanish arms and armour.[39] At the time, there were no accusations that Tyrone had harboured any Spaniards, but Spanish papers show that by October 1596 at the latest, Tyrone maintained Spanish officers; after the war, the earl admitted as much to Mountjoy.[40]

While it was fortuitous that trained personnel had been deposited on Irish shores, others came willingly from the Continent to serve in the Irish armies. After the outbreak of open hostilities in 1595, Irish officers and soldiers returned to Ireland from the Low Countries and Spain. William Waad reported in September 1595 that Irish soldiers of Sir William Stanley's regiment were returning to Ireland via Denmark and Scotland.[41] In addition to Irish, there were Welsh or English names noted such as Edward Tobay and Bartholomew Owen.[42] The passage of soldiers to Ireland continued during the war, as in 1598 there were several reports of troops travelling to Ireland from the Continent.[43] Throughout the war, Tyrone tried to get Irish soldiers in Spanish service sent back to Ireland.[44]

Sir Ralph Lane reported the arrival of four 'Spanish captains' in Wicklow during 1594, after which Feagh MacHugh O'Byrne began retraining and re-equipping his men with modern weapons.[45] The intelligencer [spy], John Danyell, advised Cecil that Spanish captains had been sent into Ulster from Brittany during 1596. He considered that this was likely to encourage more to travel from the Low Countries.[46] There are no detailed records of the ethnic makeup of the Irish forces, but the report of a Walloon officer serving the *sugán* earl of Desmond suggests that the officers under the Irish lords were not just native soldiers with European experience, but may have included a cosmopolitan contingent taking advantage of the opportunities for work in

Ireland.[47] The impact of experienced officers on native infantry, both as advisors and field commanders, was soon to be felt by the crown in Ulster.

Irish pike and shot were encountered by the English during Hugh Maguire's raid into northern Connacht in May 1593. When Bingham's horse engaged Maguire outside Tulsk, he found his cavalry checked by an Irish 'battalia of footmen'.[48] Maguire's men stood their ground against a force of English horse, a feat not normally ascribed to native Irish infantry. The year following Maguire's raids into Connacht, the relief force on its way to Enniskillen was attacked and routed by forces under Maguire and Cormac MacBaron O'Neill at a ford on the Arney river. However, it was at Clontibret in 1595, that the Irish first successfully deployed a coordinated attack that used combined arms teams of pike, shot and cavalry.[49]

Russell noted that the Ulstermen at Clontibret had exceeded what had been expected of them in arms, leadership and the deployment of pike and shot.[50] This displayed apparent ignorance of the earlier rebellions of the O'Flahertys and Burkes in Connacht, which had spawned pike and shot units. Russell had only been lord deputy in Ireland since August 1594, so he may have been unaware of previous appearances of modernized Irish infantry. The same cannot be said of his military advisors, who would have seen the changes now becoming ever more evident in the military power of the northern lords. However, the discovery of modernized Irish forces in Connacht, while noteworthy, did not cause much concern in Dublin.

The development of pike and shot units in 1589–90 came at a time of economic crisis and shortages in north-west Connacht.[51] The O'Flahertys and Burkes did not have the money to sustain modern troops. Modernized infantry formations required regular supplies of match, powder and lead to remain effective, most of which had to be imported. With access restricted to what could be sourced locally and stores recovered from the stricken Armada ships, any large-scale increase in the number of modern troops would have been difficult to maintain. The references to combat with the O'Flahertys and Burkes show that they fought in a manner consistent with continental tactics.[52] There appeared to be no real sense of alarm as the English commander knew how to defeat a battalia of pike and shot; Bermingham charged the Irish with a loose wing of horse and infantry that he had set aside to exploit any breach in the Irish formation.[53] Why then did Tyrone's army cause so much anxiety in 1595, when Bermingham was undaunted six years earlier? The differences between the battles in Connacht and at Clontibret were the size of forces engaged, the discipline of the Irish infantry and the tactics they deployed. They were not analogues of the English; Tyrone had created something new.

Shot instead of steel: Irish warfare remade

Tyrone's reformation of the troops under his control has been well recognized by historians addressing the period.[54] Before the outbreak of war, Tyrone had been permitted to retain a force of horse and infantry, paid for by the crown and drilled by English captains. These were the so-called 'butter captains' who trained the earl's troops to counter the power of Turlough Luineach O'Neill. In 1597, an anonymous author, possibly Nicholas Dawtrey, wrote that Tyrone had been allowed 50 horse and 100 foot, but under cover of this arrangement Tyrone had trained 'all the lusty bodied men of the province … in a soldier like manner of service'.[55] Fynes Moryson later repeated this, claiming that Tyrone processed recruits through the ranks, to establish a large reserve of trained men without raising suspicion from Dublin.[56] Throughout the war, Tyrone benefitted from the crown's need to reinforce its army using native Irish recruits. Desertion meant many of these ended up serving under Tyrone. Significant numbers of soldiers defected to the confederates after the English defeats at the Yellow Ford (1598) and the Curlew Mountains (1599).[57] There were also allegations that the Irish frequently joined the English army solely to receive training only to desert to Tyrone when the opportunity arose.[58]

The basic structure of the infantry units raised by Tyrone was the company, commanded by a captain and a number of junior officers.[59] A report from 1594 suggested that Irish companies had substantially more officers than English units. An estimate of Tyrone's forces in November 1594 claimed that leaders were appointed 'to 40, to 20, and to 10 of their foot, for the fitness of their service of the passes'.[60] With anything up to eight officers per company, the Irish foot would have possessed greater tactical flexibility than English units, who were normally staffed with only a captain, a lieutenant, an ensign and two sergeants.[61] The companies of bonnaghts were nominally composed of one hundred men, but in reality, there were eighty-four as Tyrone continued the English custom of 'dead pays' for his captains.[62] Dead pays allowed a captain to be paid for more troops than he had. The first reference to the English use of dead pays was in France in 1562 to generate extra money for deserving officers, but the avarice of many officers led to abuse of the system.[63] In Ireland, English officers were authorized to have six dead pays per hundred men, but they later lobbied for this to be increased to ten.[64]

While it was apparent that Tyrone was developing pike and shot formations, he was not creating an analogue of his English adversaries. English infantry were based upon a combination of pike and shot, with the shot armed with a mixture of muskets and lighter calivers. The ratio of shot to pike varied between one-to-one and one-to-two.[65] Tyrone's formations had a much more pronounced dependence upon firepower, with a ratio of one pike to every four or five shot.[66] The Irish shot also primarily used the caliver, which weighed half as much as the more cumbersome musket. It had a shorter range and less penetrating power than a musket, but calivermen were correspondingly more mobile than the English. The preponderance of light shot in Tyrone's infantry was reflected in their tactics, where skirmishing was the primary means to weaken and disorder enemy units in battle.

A feature of many of the reports coming from English officers was their admiration of the Irish shot and their talent for skirmishing. Captain Francis Croft described the Irish shot as fighting 'with as good discretion as ever I saw for loose skirmishers'.[67] Skirmishing was a regular part of combat during the Nine Years War and in many ways epitomized the Irish way of war during the early modern period. However, the term has often been used to suggest that this was something other than or inferior to 'regular' war. Skirmishing, however, was not loose, irregular or something that was done with poor quality troops; quite the reverse, it required a greater degree of training and motivation than soldiers in tight formation. Troops deployed in close-order battles needed to display coordination and discipline under fire, but little personal initiative. Officers kept close personal supervision over their men, which dissuaded less-than-enthusiastic recruits from slipping away before battle was joined. In contrast, skirmishing was more taxing on the individual soldier, who was also required to have greater flexibility, independence and superior individual weapon skills. Furthermore, skirmishers had to be able to operate effectively while beyond the control or sight of their officers. Fernando Alvarez de Toledo, duke of Alba, one of Philip II's most trusted and skilled officers, had no doubt about the nature of skirmishing. He believed that any troops could be used in a battle whereas skirmishing required veterans to prevail.[68] This being the case, what was happening in Ireland?

There are many detailed descriptions of skirmishing throughout the war. The engagements at Crossdall and Clontibret in 1595 were described as skirmishes lasting four and eight hours respectively.[69] The bloody stalemate at the Moyry Pass during September–October 1600 witnessed skirmishing that drew in hundreds if not thousands of troops. Lord Deputy Mountjoy described the fighting in the Moyry Pass on 2 October 1600 as 'one of the greatest skirmishes and best maintained in all places, that hath been in this kingdom, and continued for three hours'.[70] What was actually occurring? The image that springs to mind (and the author is guilty of this himself) is of dispersed infantrymen taking pot-shots at each other from behind cover. However, this notion is illusory, concocted from too many Hollywood movies; the conduct of disciplined skirmishing was more complex.

The English soldier Sir John Smythe provided a detailed explanation of skirmishing techniques.[71] Loose shot separated themselves into groups of three and four where one advances to fire while the others make their weapons ready. After firing his weapon, the first shooter withdrew behind his companions to reload, and his place was taken by another from his group. This pattern continued throughout the course of the engagement by 'many societies of three dispersed in the field'. Smythe opined that four was preferable to three as there would always be at least two loaded weapons to respond to the unexpected, and their firearms were less likely to overheat. Smythe described a second skirmishing method that required alternate 'societies' of three or four advancing and firing volleys, then retiring while those on their flanks advanced to fire. These were skilful and orderly methods for skirmishing, but Smythe also described inexperienced shot. He explained how badly trained soldiers would move in crowds, discharge their weapons whenever they chose, overheat their firearms, and fail to provide mutual support to their comrades. This appears to reflect the erroneous mental picture of skirmishing noted earlier, but it is clear that the shot deployed by Tyrone did not fall into the last category.

Nevertheless, descriptions of Irish firing techniques suggested that Tyrone's shot could be wasteful or ill-disciplined. At most stages of the war, there were reports of the Irish opening long-range fire on English units. Sir John Norreys found this in Armagh in 1595. It was an experience repeated by the earl of Essex in 1599 and several times by Lord Deputy Mountjoy after 1600. The caliver, which was the predominant firearm of the Irish, was a short-range weapon, therefore why did this happen when the Irish were regarded as better trained and more proficient with their firearms?[72] Simply ascribing this to poor fire discipline is incongruous with the Irish infantry's tightly controlled actions at Crossdall or Clontibret. However, when we take into account who was instructing the Irish troops, it is less of a mystery.

Spanish officers had been retained at Dungannon by Tyrone since the Armada of 1588, and there is an unambiguous description of a Spanish officer training troops there in 1601. Also, many of the Irish officers returning from the Continent were in Spanish service; therefore Spanish military methods would have predominated, but how does this explain the profligate use of firearms? The answer was given by Sir John Smythe in his treatise *Certain discourses military*. He wrote that experienced soldiers were well aware of the limited effective range of muskets and calivers. Therefore they were careful not to skirmish or give volley fire beyond forty metres; that is except veteran Spanish shot. They would open long range fire at their enemies 'with no other intent but to procure them to give their volleys with all fury, that thereby they may spend their powder and bullets, heat their pieces, and work no effect, whereby they still keeping the force of their shot, may after give their whole volleys at their enemies, approaching within ten, fifteen or twenty paces, and for that effect the Spaniards do use this phrase '*disparese de lejos, para atraher, y engañar bobos*', translated by Smythe as 'discharged afar off to draw on and deceive the fools'.[73]

Tyrone's shot were not the only part of his infantry to adopt Spanish methods. His army used a wider variety of soldiers, one of which was the targeteer, who was armed with a short sword and a shield called a target. By the outbreak of the war in 1593, their use in the Elizabethan armies had practically ceased.[74] This was not true of Spanish units, who continued to deploy them. Sir Roger Williams wrote of their utility in breaches, trenches and, most importantly with regards to their use by the Irish, 'to cover shot that skirmishes in straights'.[75] While it is unclear if targeteers were a natural progression from Irish swordsmen, or if they were specifically trained by the Spanish captains to conform to continental practice, they were used to great effect. This was most evident at the battle of the Yellow Ford in 1598, where they destroyed the lead English regiment. They were also shown protecting the Irish skirmishers in the best illustration of the battle.[76]

While shot made up the majority of Tyrone's forces, it was crucial to protect them from the English cavalry. Therefore they were supported by units of pikemen.[77] At first glance, the deployment of Tyrone's pike may have differed from that of the English only in respect to numbers and armour. As noted above Tyrone had fewer in proportion to his shot, and apart from a helmet they were unarmoured.[78] This was in contrast to the English pike who wore steel corselets or breatplates. The conduct of the Irish pike in battle and accounts of their training illustrated that their dissimilarity to English pike was more than sartorial. The serried lines of couched pikes could deter a determined cavalry charge, but at no point in the war did Tyrone's pikemen ever assault into *melee* on an unbroken enemy. The Irish pike acted as a mobile defensive screen to protect the Irish shot from attack by cavalry, but not an offensive shock arm, as was the case with the crown's army.

English pike could be used offensively, as at Clontibret where they charged to push back the Irish skirmishers.[79] In contrast, the Irish pike provided defensive support but did not attack. Indeed, Sir Robert Salesbury suggested that it would have been a much bloodier affair if Tyrone's pike had advanced like his shot.[80] Irish pike were present at Clifford's retreat from Ballyshannon (1597) and the battle of the Yellow Ford (1598), but throughout these engagements they never closed with unbroken English infantry. When rain extinguished the match for both the English and Irish shot at Ballyshannon, Clifford's unbroken pike deterred any further attacks.[81] The clearest reference

to the Irish pikemen's reluctance to engage in hand-to-hand fighting came
from Captain Richard Cuney after the disaster at the Yellow Ford, who wrote
that his men would have been totally routed if the Irish had charged at the
closing stages of the battle.[82] In arms and equipment, the Irish pike were
similar to the Spanish *pica seca* who supported the armoured pike but were not
expected to bear the brunt of the *melee* fighting.[83]

The only description of Irish pike training came from a Scottish merchant
named Thomas Douglas out of Dungannon in 1601. He observed Spanish
captains training Irish pike, but noted that despite their long experience in war,
the soldiers were trained only to 'discharge their pikes and run up and down'.[84]
Douglas was amazed that they did not drill in close order as continental
pikemen, but the Spanish captain answered that the terrain prevalent in
Ireland made the use of close order irrelevant.[85] In 1598, Robert Barret wrote
of pike and shot that 'the armed pike is the strength; the shot the fury, one
without the other is weakened'.[86] Despite their necessity, the rugged terrain of
Ireland was not entirely suitable for their use. In 1593, Matthew Sutcliffe
wrote in *The practice, proceedings and laws of armes* that pikes were unwieldy in
woods, shrubby ground and straights 'where they could not be managed'.[87]
They were also vulnerable to shot or targeteers if not backed by their own
calivermen or musketeers.

The limited role of the Irish pike may be discerned from Tyrone's
reluctance to deploy them when other options could be used to gain the same
effect. Mountjoy recognized that the Irish tended to initiate actions where the
topography precluded any use of cavalry.[88] This was a characteristic of most of
Tyrone's major victories. His primary option to neutralize the English cavalry
tended to be the clever use of topography or modification of the battlefield
using trenches and barricades.[89] Where this was impossible, the defensive
qualities of the pikes allowed them to oppose English units on open ground.
An examination of the accounts of battles fought by the Irish confederates
suggests that the Irish were not entirely confident in their pikemen's ability to
perform this role, but it was better to have them as a tactical option than to
have nothing at all.[90] Given that Irish pike were expected to keep pace with
the shot over difficult terrain, they would have rarely been able to maintain the
tight cohesion required for a resolute defence; therefore it was unreasonable to
expect it. The availability of pike meant that the Irish retained the ability to
fight in the open when needed.

Tyrone's reforms found less fertile soil with regards to the Irish cavalry.
Contemporary accounts were dismissive of the Irish horse; Sir John Norreys
thought they were only fit for rounding up cattle.[91] Later historians, such as
Cyril Falls, tended to agree.[92] The failure of Irish cavalry to modernize has

24 English and Irish cavalry, 1581 (John Derricke, *Image of Irelande*, 1581)

been interpreted as a sign of military backwardness, but there was some attempt at reorganization, primarily through the introduction of new technology.[93] Pistols were made at Dungannon in 1596, and in 1597 Irish horsemen were described as armed with a 'chasing stafe' or lance as was normal, but also with one or two pistols.[94] However, despite having access to firearms, the Irish cavalry continued to fight as it had been accustomed: screening, reconnaissance and pursuits. New weaponry did not transform the way they fought. This may reflect a cultural conservatism of the Gaelic nobility, who formed the bulk of the confederate cavalry, as much of the more potent English cavalry was composed of Irish troopers, demonstrating that reform was possible at an individual level.[95]

Reference should also be made to the role of the mercenaries from the west of Scotland in the Irish armies. Known as redshanks, they were lightly equipped Highlanders armed with bows, axes, swords and shields. They were hired on seasonal contracts and could provide thousands of troops at short notice. Despite the growing predominance of firepower on European battlefields, Highland soldiers remained potent into the eighteenth century.[96] They proved a formidable force during the Wars of the Three Kingdoms (1641–53) but had little impact during the Nine Years War. Scots mercenaries were present in the early stages of the war and were never truly absent, but they did not arrive in the numbers that could have tipped the strategic balance. Tyrone had requested supplies of Scots in 1594, but he did not like using them due to their indiscipline.[97] Regardless of this, the option to recruit redshanks was taken out of Tyrone's hands by the ongoing dispute within the Clan Ian Mor (Clan Donald South). The resulting instability in Scotland meant that access was cut off, just when Tyrone could have made the best use of them.[98] Occasionally the crown considered using Scots mercenaries in Ulster, but there were questions over their willingness to fight Tyrone, and fears that once introduced into the north it would be difficult to remove them.[99]

While Irish warfare echoed many aspects of the military modernization process in other parts of Europe, the adoption by the Irish of military reforms and the accompanying change in equipment, arms and methodology was exceptionally rapid. Before 1588, Irish infantry were composed of gallowglass and kerne. Following the Spanish Armada in 1588, native pike and shot infantry started to appear. The transformation of the Irish infantry was swift, whereby pike, shot and supporting swordsmen became the primary infantry force deployed by the Irish confederates under Tyrone. The speed of this change was noted by contemporary English commentators. Alarm was evident in the *Dialogue of Silvynne and Peregrynne*, where it was noted of the Irish in Ulster that 'within these few years, knew not what the due order of fighting was and now it is a professed art amongst the cowherds of Ulster, God send some good man to unarm these rogues and put them to cow-keeping again'.[100] This rapidity was made more remarkable as it was done despite the vested interests of traditional hereditary institutions such as the gallowglass. The melee-orientated and shock-based combat exemplified by the gallowglass, which took years for an individual to master and had served as the core of Irish armies for three-and-a-half centuries, was swept away in less than a decade without any apparent resistance.

With regard to the degree of progressiveness in Irish society, in military terms the evidence suggests that during the conflict the Irish military community was highly flexible and adaptive. The speed of their adoption of modern military methods reinforces this view. The Irish adaptability was also recognized by contemporaries. In his memorandum on the state of Ireland, Captain Francis Stafford condemned the Irish for their perfidy, ungratefulness and inclination to rebellion, but also noted that they were 'ever disposed to innovation'.[101] This opinion was repeated by Sir George Carew four years later. He pointed out that the Irish were 'naturally inclined to desire change and innovation'.[102] Given that neither man was overly fond of the Irish, this gives some indication of contemporary assessments of the Irish ability and willingness to effect change.

The Irish guerrilla war?

Tyrone's destruction of Bagenal's army at the battle of the Yellow Ford demonstrated that Irish field tactics could defeat the largest and best-equipped English force deployed to Ireland. The English army was not overwhelmed with numbers or critically hobbled with poor leadership (though some officers were decidedly mediocre). Bagenal's men were out-fought and routed by the disciplined firepower and coordinated battlefield manoeuvre of Tyrone's infantry and cavalry. This victory was not a one-off, nor should it have come as any surprise. Over the previous five years of war, the queen's armies had experienced repeated battlefield reverses. As noted earlier, it was only a fortuitous rainstorm that prevented the destruction of Clifford's command at Ballyshannon. However, the view that guerrilla, or hit-and-run warfare predominated during the Nine Years War has managed to endure into modern literature.[103]

The defeat at Kinsale overshadows other occasions when confederate forces successfully engaged English troops in the open, as at Mullabrack (Co. Armagh) in 1595, the Togher (Co. Offaly) in 1600, and Benburb (Co. Tyrone) in 1601.[104] At Mullabrack, Tyrone's willingness to fight on rising ground disconcerted Sir Geffrey Fenton, who noted that the Irish had engaged Norreys on ground where there was 'neither bog nor bush'.[105] Mountjoy's encounter with the Irish fighting in the open at nearby Benburb in 1601 was possibly the most strategically important. Tyrone's deployment in the open stymied the English push towards Dungannon. Despite Fynes Moryson's insistence that the action was a success, Mountjoy's advance had stalled.[106] The Irish may have lost the largest set-piece battle of the war at Kinsale, but these examples demonstrate that it is a mistake to assume that they could not fight effectively away from defiles or advantageous ground.

A frequent misconception about the Irish was their ability to capture fortified positions. It has often been claimed that though Tyrone's troops could dominate the countryside and even defeat large English armies, they were unable to take the well-defended towns and forts. That Tyrone and his allies did not attempt to storm any of the major towns suggests such an undertaking was beyond the abilities or resources of the Irish confederates. Furthermore, many of the more well-known fortifications taken by the Irish fell without need of an assault. Enniskillen castle was lost after a prolonged siege forced the ward to capitulate; the first Blackwater fort fell to a ruse by Art MacBaron; Belfast castle was betrayed by one of the ward and Burgh's Blackwater fort fell after Tyrone defeated the relief army at the Yellow Ford. Taking a fort by assault appears to confirm the martial ability of troops, but an assault was the least preferable option for all concerned, as it took a heavy toll on both attackers and defenders.

Nevertheless, there were occasions when direct assaults by the Irish succeeded in capturing English fortifications. In 1596, Irish troops equipped with scaling ladders captured the fort at Ballinacor (Co. Wicklow).[107] O'Donnell's soldiers stormed Longford castle in May 1596.[108] Even late in the war when the tide of fortune was with the English, the Irish could mount a vigorous assault if needed. At the siege of Carriganass castle (Co. Cork) in 1602, the Irish captured the castle by 'raising a rampart, partly by towers, mantlets, sows and gabions, and partly by battering it with brass cannon'.[109] Donal Cam O'Sullivan Beare also took the imposing edifice at Carrigaphooca (Co. Cork). Irish shot suppressed the defensive fire from within the castle, while pikemen assaulted over the walls, precipitating the occupants' surrender.[110]

Contrary to the accepted narrative on the hit-and-run style of warfare practised during the war, the Irish made substantial use of fixed defences.[111] These structures were constructed throughout Ireland for reasons ranging from localized tactical expediency to long-term strategic advantage. The largest and most durable of the defences built by the Irish were forts composed of elaborate systems of ditches, palisades and earth ramparts. The best-illustrated example was Inishloughan (Co. Antrim), which was one of at least nine in Ulster.[112] Moryson noted 'It had about it two deep ditches, both compassed with strong pallisadoes, a very high and thick rampier of earth and timber, and well flanked with bulwarks'.[113] Outside Ulster the Irish erected strong forts in Co. Offaly, on the river Shannon and in Co. Cork at Dunboy castle and on Dursey Island.[114] However, hindering or blocking routeways or lines of advance was often the sole purpose of most Irish field fortifications. These could take the form of plashing, trenches or sconces.

Plashing was one of the most common features of Irish fieldworks. Trees or bushes were cut at their base then bent over, and their branches intertwined, forming a formidable breastwork barrier of interlaced wood and foliage. This method was extensively used to block passes and roads, as seen in the Curlew Mountains in 1596, Dungannon in 1597 and Mogeely (Co. Cork) in 1599.[115] Where nature did not provide sufficient advantage, the Irish built formidable earthwork defences. Sconces and fire trenches provided stout cover for Irish shot. Ormond's efforts to clear Camagh Woods to the west of Maryborough encountered plashing and entrenchments.[116] The Irish raised sconces in the passage from Athlone to Roscommon, and ten 'half-moons' blocked the road to Philipstown at the Togher.[117]

As well as defending passes, the Irish erected defences along rivers and shorelines. Defended fords appeared early in the war at Lisgoole abbey in 1593 and along the Avonmore river in 1599.[118] Perhaps the largest system was along the river Blackwater, where extensive defences had been raised by 1597.[119]

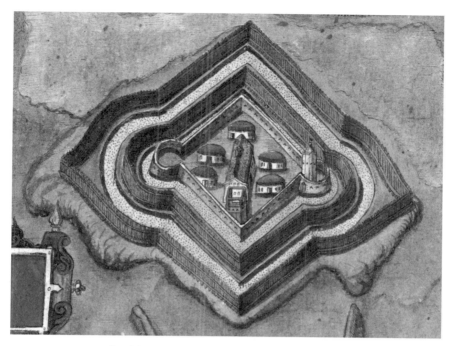

25 Inishloughan fort, Aug. 1602, by Richard Bartlett
(The National Library of Ireland, MS 2656, vi)

Moreover, Mountjoy found the fortifications on the river significantly stronger by 1601. The Irish entrenchments were so formidable that Mountjoy would not countenance a daylight assault on the works.[120] Tyrrell raised coastal defences opposing Carew's landings at Dunboy, and there were reports that Tyrone erected a sophisticated defensive scheme to repel Docwra's expedition to the Foyle.[121]

Fixed defences and engagements in the open were not characteristics associated with guerrilla or hit-and-run warfare. These types of war have often been defined as fought between fundamentally unequal opponents, or methods used by the weak to resist the powerful.[122] A closer look at military activity during the war reveals many elements that are incompatible with guerilla warfare; fixed supply bases with a functional system of logistics, and large, well-equipped mercenary forces with little, if any, ideological motivation. The conduct of the confederate armies had more in common with the concept of mobile warfare. This strategy utilized guerrillas or irregular forces operating in concert with highly mobile, regular formations.[123] Indeed, the use of the term guerrilla is not wholly accurate, as Tyrone's detached troops had more in common with the professional soldiers seen in partisan units of the eighteenth century.[124] Orthodox units could be split up to perform small irregular operations and concentrated for major actions. Where numbers permitted it, Tyrone deployed large bodies of troops and raiding detachments at the same time, presenting the crown with the dilemma of which force to counter. If the English armies concentrated to confront Tyrone or O'Donnell's main force, the countryside was left open to spoliation. If the English dispersed their companies to resist the raids, there was nothing to check the Ulster armies. Fenton noted at the end of 1598 how the concentration of crown troops at Naas meant they had no 'itinerant army' with which to oppose Irish raids.[125]

The parallel use of small-scale attacks led some to use the term hit-and-run to describe this effective Irish tactic. Examination of the major engagements from the first half of the war, however, showed that rather than retreating, it was usually Tyrone's men who held the field. For the first six years of the war, the Irish retained the ground or it was the crown forces that broke contact in most major engagements. Even when Tyrone's power was waning, engagements at the Moyry Pass (1600) and Benburb (1601) demonstrated that confederate soldiers could still hold positions in defiance of English efforts.[126] While there were many small actions and raiding throughout the war with all the characteristics of guerrilla warfare, these operations supported a broader strategy, which in many cases depended on the deployment of major regular units for decisive results.

The versatility of spoiling: foraging, destruction, deception and intimidation

A defining feature of Tyrone's strategy (and later Mountjoy's) was spoiling and raiding. It was by far the most prevalent form of warfare, and judicious, well-timed deployment of raiding forces managed to achieve significant strategic and operational success. The historiography of the war tends to view Irish raids as localized banditry or large-scale foraging by Tyrone and his allies, but the motivation and goals of the attacks were often far more complex than simple thievery. Cattle raiding and spoliation were such persistent features of Irish life that they were embedded in sagas such as the *Táin Bó Cúailnge*.[127] Indeed, Irish warfare for much of the medieval period was characterized as little more than cattle raiding.[128] An Irish chieftain's inauguration could lead to forays into adjoining territories to cement his authority and challenge his neighbours by stealing their cattle.[129] An attack normally took the form of a sudden incursion into enemy territory, rounding up cattle which were driven back to the safety of the attacking chieftain's lands before a sizeable force could be assembled to oppose the raid. The key role of Irish cavalry, composed of the

Irish nobility and their families, was to act as a rear-guard for successful preying parties, highlighting raiding's importance as an expression of power.[130] The significant role of raiding in Irish society has resulted in all instances of preying being accorded similar motivation in the modern historiography, namely wealth accretion by theft and localized assertions of power. In the context of the Nine Years War, simplistic assumptions have led to misinterpretation of the role and impact of raids by both the confederates and the forces of the crown. Indeed, the multiplicity of applications for which raiding proved useful suggests that it was one of the most effective tactics used to influence the outcome of the war.

The Irish methodology for conducting raids followed a similar pattern throughout the war. Raiding forces could range in number from several hundred to over a thousand. Hugh Collier described how a central core of troops supported smaller units, which broke off from the main body and spread out over the countryside.[131] The individual spoiling parties that descended on farms and hamlets could be tiny, and in some instances they consisted of as little as two horsemen and three shot.[132] The dispersal of large numbers of small units ensured that they were hard to intercept, but when crown forces did engage them, normally when the preying parties were burdened with cattle and goods, the Irish abandoned their spoil or faced defeat. While this might have been fatal for the small bands of raiders, the limited availability of crown troops meant that the overall success of the spoiling in any territory proved difficult to counter.[133]

The most elementary explanation for spoiling was the need to maintain forces where their commanders could not provide sufficient supplies from outside the area of operations. The limited logistical abilities of early modern armies meant that the organized plundering of the surrounding countryside met their immediate subsistence needs.[134] This applied to both sides throughout the war. Sir John Chichester used spoiling to sustain the English troops in Carrickfergus during 1597, and depredations on the loyal population in the Pale by the local garrisons were commonplace.[135] In 1595, Tyrone's reinforcements for Feagh MacHugh O'Byrne were to be provided for solely by spoiling.[136] The confederates addressed their longer term supply needs with preying actions, as stockpiles were established in future areas of operations. Collier referred to supplies being gathered in Co. Offaly to support Tyrrell's anticipated advance later in the year.[137] Spoiling and foraging were features of warfare until the advent of modern supply systems in the twentieth century. It was, therefore, unsurprising to find it in Ireland. However, immediate supply needs were not the only reasons for attacks.

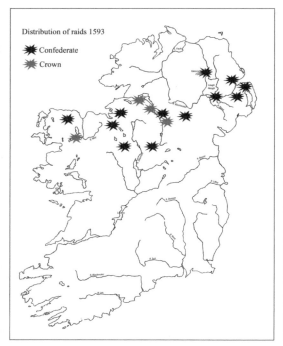

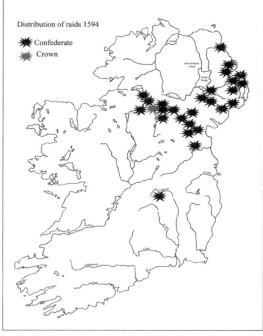

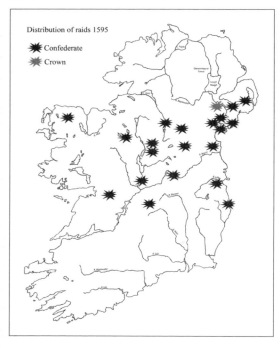

26 The distribution pattern of raids from 1593–1602. From early in the war it was clear that the focus of Tyrone's attention was far beyond the borders of Ulster.

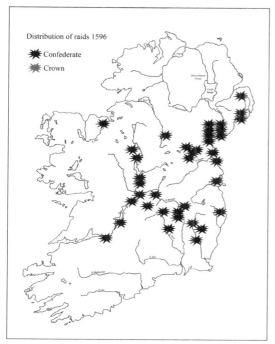

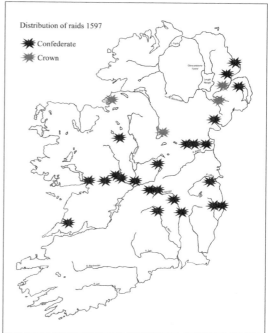

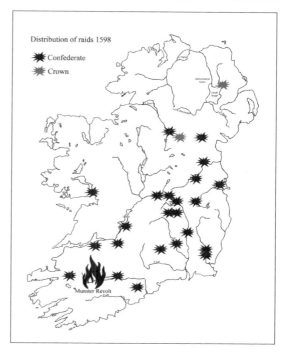

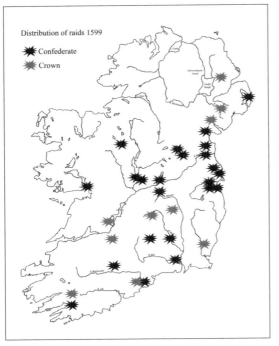

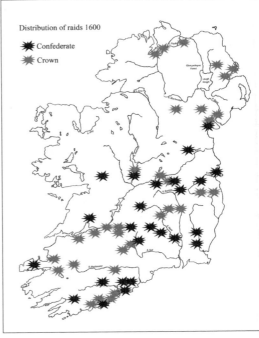

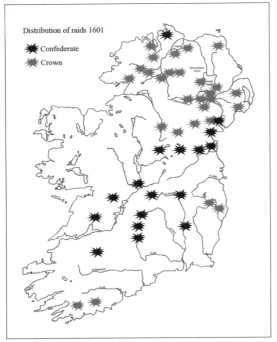

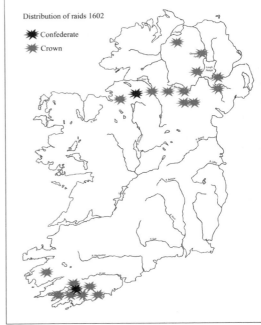

The rationale behind the Irish raids was often more than a simple need to forage for supplies. Raids supported broader military planning, and the timing of some attacks demonstrated that they could influence operations in disparate theatres of the war. Raids could distract and displace enemy regional forces. Carefully timed outbreaks of spoiling obliged the crown to dispatch troops to suppress or chase off raiding parties. This led to a corresponding weakening of English military strength available to counter Irish advances in other theatres. This ploy was primarily employed by Tyrone from the start of the war but was later adopted by English commanders. Tyrone sent raiding forces into Louth in 1595 to relieve the pressure of the government offensive against Feagh MacHugh O'Byrne.[138] In 1597, Tyrrell's attacks induced Lord Burgh to pull out of Ulster.[139] This allowed Irish reinforcements to stream westwards to break Sir Conyers Clifford's siege of Ballyshannon, almost trapping his entire army.[140] In addition to being used at a strategic and operational level, raids were also used for localized tactical advantage.

Spoiling could lure garrisons out of the relative safety of their forts, leaving them vulnerable to attack or ambush. This occurred near Carrickfergus in 1597, when James MacSorley MacDonnell devastated the surrounding districts. The parley with the governor Sir John Chichester to discuss the raids was a trap, which resulted in the death of Chichester and the killing of most of the garrison.[141] O'Donnell attempted to lure the Boyle garrison out beyond their defences by stealing their cattle, but the English saw through the ruse and did not try to rescue the prey.[142] As the war progressed, the purpose of many raids focused more on destruction and resource denial.

Raids and spoiling were effective tools for depopulating large tracts of land. Removal of rural populations meant that operations within those areas became difficult for troops that did not have access to supply depots, or the logistical means to transport supplies from rear areas. Wasting of an enemy's lands and depopulating it by famine, massacre and relocation of the inhabitants was a feature of war long before the sixteenth century. The Roman military author Vegetius wrote in the fourth century AD that it was preferable to subdue an enemy by famine than battle.[143] Though Vegetius' writings may have been ancient history even in the sixteenth century, a resurgence in the study of classical texts during the European Renaissance meant that the writings of military scholars were the foundations of modern military theory.[144] While devastation tactics have frequently been associated with English operations from 1600 onwards, both English and Irish used crop destruction and devastation tactics much earlier than this. It was believed prudent to destroy anything that could not be protected in a troubled region. The privy council recommended Sir Conyers Clifford destroy whatever victuals could not be kept from the Irish, and O'Sullivan Beare noted that the English would raze their own subjects' goods to prevent their use by the Irish confederate troops.[145] Tyrone ordered repeated attacks on Lecale to destroy supplies that may have been of use to nearby garrisons.[146] During 1596, Tyrone devastated Louth and Meath to the extent that by April the following year, two English companies sent to Ardee were withdrawn after only one week due to shortages.[147]

Raids were also used to impose authority. In many cases, demonstrations of military strength were enough to precipitate defection to the confederate cause and ignite the rebellion in previously quiescent districts.[148] Tyrone employed raiding to compel acquiescence from Sir Henry Bagenal's Irish clients in the east of Ulster during 1593–4. Subordination to Tyrone could also be accompanied by the requirement to maintain troops or provide cash or goods in the form of a payment known as a buying.[149] Where simple coercion was ineffective, punitive raids were sent to penalize those not willing to support or join the confederate war effort or to chastise wayward allies.[150] Tyrone assailed Niall MacBrian Fertagh O'Neill and Connor Roe Maguire until they finally (though with little enthusiasm) submitted to his authority, but the antipathy between Tyrone and Bagenal ensured that Bagenal's lands and tenants attracted special attention. On 2 March 1594, Bagenal's stud was stolen and removed across the river Bann by Brian MacArt's son.[151] Just over two weeks later, forces led by Art MacBaron's sons (probably Brian and Conn) spoiled Bagenal's lands around Newry and on the Cooley peninsula. The MacBarons carried off cattle and goods into Armagh, leaving seven towns in flames.[152] Bagenal claimed that Tyrone's troops killed men, women and children by burning them in their houses but this does not tally with accounts of raids elsewhere. These details were most likely added by Bagenal to defame Tyrone in Dublin. Russell wrote to the privy council in July 1595 describing the damaging attacks by Tyrone on Bagenal's property. The Irish had spoiled to the gates of Newry and burned Bagenal's mills, causing his tenants to flee and depriving Bagenal of revenue.[153] Russell estimated that the loss of income to Bagenal was £1,200 annually.[154] Cessations provided little respite for Bagenal, as the attacks continued unabated from 1595 to 1597.[155] Financially, Bagenal was ruined, and it was only with support from the crown that he could maintain his position at Newry.

Raiding for revenue

Tyrone had reorganized the Irish military. He had a clear idea how to use them and built an island-wide network of alliances to ensure that his orders were carried out, but this was not a war of national liberation fuelled by sentiment and patriotism; this was a war where troops were paid to fight. This needed money and lots of it. Tyrone may have been one of the richest and most powerful lords on the island, but war was expensive, therefore resources, be it goods or money, had to be exacted from the civilian population. Before the war, there were a number of measures and customs used by the crown and the Irish chiefs to exact taxes. Since the time of Sir Anthony St Leger, the tradition of purveyance and the hosting duties of the local population had been commuted to a cash payment, essentially a tax, which was called the cess.[156] This was extended under the earl of Sussex whereby the country and towns within the Pale were obliged to pay for the feeding and billeting of the crown's entire military establishment.[157] A general cess raised commodities from the country at set prices that were normally much lower than market rates, but it was the billeting of soldiers that caused the most discontent. When shortages meant the government could not adequately pay for the army, the burden fell onto the rural population.[158] There was also coyne and livery, which were exactions by Irish lords over those whom they claimed overlordship. It allowed for the free quartering of an Irish chief's dependants on the rural population.[159] Farmers living adjacent to powerful Irish lords were forced to pay 'black-rent' as protection from raiding by their Irish neighbours.[160] Protections could be acquired from powerful Irish nobles, through the custom of *ceannuigh-eacht* or a 'buying', which would entitle the buyer to assistance as well as protection from depredation by the Irish lord.[161] *Buannacht* was a form of free quartering of troops on civilians but could also be imposed on areas without physically stationing troops within affected regions.

While the confederate demands were burdensome for the rural communities, in general the cost of the exactions could be absorbed by the landholders and their tenants. Individuals and districts made agreed payments to confederate forces in order to safeguard their property. *The supplication of the blood of the English* claimed that loyal subjects could afford to pay £60 per month to the rebels, despite the fact they begrudged paying £60 per year to the queen.[162] It was reported at the start of 1600 that all of Westmeath had concluded private contracts for the security of their property with the confederate forces.[163] Fynes Moryson observed how some regions agreed contributions to be made to the confederates, and arranged for cattle to be taken on the pretence of theft so their loyalty could not be questioned by government officers.[164] After the war it was suggested that many reports of raids and preying were peaceful transactions, utilizing subterfuge to deflect accusations of aiding the crown's enemies.[165]

Although preying by confederate forces was reported to the government as episodes of wholesale burning and destruction, in many cases rules were laid down about what could be appropriated. There were inevitable excesses due to local animosities or greed, but there is evidence that there was, to some degree, a level of regularization of the exactions taken from the rural population.[166] According to Collier, Captain Tyrrell defined fixed rates for his men for what could be taken from the local inhabitants of Co. Offaly.[167] Accounts of the spoiling of Sir Henry Bagenal's tenants in late 1596 suggest that there were limitations on how much could be taken in raids. One of his tenants bought back a horse and another had one of his mares returned without charge.[168] This suggests that, for the most part, the attacks did not intend to leave their victims destitute, and that Irish predation could be measured and controlled.

Tyrone and his officers recognized that sustainability was crucial to maintaining supplies in the southern theatres. Agriculture needed to continue to enable exactions to be repeatedly made. Districts were given time to recover and generate new wealth, which would be collected by the Irish at a later date. Connacht was subjected to attacks in 1593, then again in 1595, but remained quiet in 1596 and only O'Connor's and Clanricard's lands were assailed in 1597. Collier noted that Leinster was targeted to allow Connacht to recuperate.[169] It was to the benefit of the confederate war effort that agriculture flourished. This would explain why farmers were forced back onto their land holdings near Philipstown in 1597, as empty farms generate no wealth.[170] An indication of Tyrone's attitude came in a report from O'Connor Sligo in 1599. It suggested that O'Donnell had wanted to burn the entire Pale to Dublin, but Tyrone had refused to countenance such a move, as the English would 'devour our country by begging and otherwise'.[171] It was clear that Tyrone did not intend to destroy productivity or impoverish landholders. In 1598, Bingham reported that the rebels did not spoil or burn in Kildare as they intended to obtain the harvest 'being in hope to have it for themselves'.[172] The success of Tyrone's attempt to maintain agricultural output in regions formerly under crown control can be inferred from Lord Deputy Mountjoy's report of his raid into Co. Offaly in 1600. The lord deputy observed that despite the area being beyond government control for five years, he was amazed how 'the ground was manured, how orderly their fields were, their towns inhabited, and every highway and path so well beaten'.[173]

To achieve the desired sustainability, spoliation by the Irish had to be conducted within the boundaries of accepted behaviour. In other wars, unrestrained foraging by troops led to localized resistance, as seen in Ireland during the wars of the 1640s.[174] As noted above, there were limits to how much could be taken to ensure continued agricultural productivity. There also appeared to be political lines that were not to be transgressed, whether the victim sided with the crown or not. This was demonstrated in 1598 when

Brian Riabhach O'More ordered that goods taken from the earl of Ormond be returned, and in 1599 Conn O'Neill was forced to release the bishop of Cashel and restore his property.[175] There was also restraint on the levels of violence associated with the raids. While there was intimidation and occasions when people were assaulted or murdered, in general violence was not a common feature of raiding for much of the war.

Analysis of what was taken and what happened to confiscated property sheds light on the needs of Tyrone and his allies. In some cases, stolen livestock were used to improve agricultural output of land worked by the Irish lords' tenants. In one case, a horse taken near Newry was later spotted by its former owner working a plough.[176] Most reports of spoiling throughout the war wrote in general terms about losses, but some accounts gave details of stolen livestock and household goods. Preying parties carried off movable commodities, but on several occasions, the thefts were not to satisfy the perpetrator's needs for cattle or provisions, but for cash. Some of Bagenal's tenants were allowed to buy back a proportion of their property, and when O'Donnell had ravaged Clanricard's lands, he attempted to sell the spoils to the merchants in Galway.[177]

Often the Irish needed money, not the goods being stolen, but coins were much easier to hide. Therefore it may have been simpler to force farmers to part with their money by threatening what could not be hidden. Sir John Dowdall referred to this in 1600 when he considered the Irish to have 'all the money of the Kingdom'.[178] He noted how the Irish could steal and sell back the same cow four times in the space of six months. Of particular importance was his claim that the Irish sold the cattle back for cash. This was a problem highlighted by Mountjoy in 1602 when he referred to his Irish enemies having large quantities of sterling money which they used to 'furnish themselves with powder, arms and munitions'.[179] At this stage in the war, it is apparent that the Irish required money far more than they needed livestock or basic commodities.

The pattern of Irish raids after 1594 shows that the horizon of attacks moved steadily south. Reports of spoiling dropped sharply during 1599, but this may be due to the success of Tyrone and his allies in dominating the country. Bingham pessimistically described how the crown had few holds left at the end of 1598, and a report from 1599 claimed the 'rebels do swarm in all parts of the realm, commanding all except the towns and a few castles'.[180] The extension of raids southwards represented the expansion of Tyrone's authority into Connacht, Leinster and later Munster, which added to the territories from which revenue could be generated.

The dispersed agrarian population prevalent in Ireland meant that the Irish confederates were faced with the problem of how to maximize their control of the countryside. During the early modern period, the increasing size of armies and corresponding logistical burden meant that a premium was put on territorial control. On the Continent, this was normally achieved through the dispersal of troops and the imposition of static garrisons.[181] This was not a viable option for Tyrone as any overt fixed point of defence was liable to attract English attention. John Landers observed that elsewhere in Europe, a policy of raiding enabled a commander to forgo a strategy of sustained domination.[182] As Tyrone expanded the territories over which his armies held sway, he sequestered resources that would have been otherwise available to the crown.[183] Revenue could be raised across the regions under confederate rule; the greater the area controlled, the larger the return. After the war, Hugh Collier wrote how one of the principal means of raising cash in the south was the imposition of black rent. It was noted that the Irish dispersed men into 'civil' counties where pacts were made with the local landholders to pay an agreed proportion of their income. In return, their tenants were free from attack by the Irish.[184]

This interpretation of the use of spoiling and raiding suggests an entirely different complexion to the war. As noted earlier, Irish strategy was significantly more aggressive than has been previously believed. On the economic aspects of the war, the broad expansion of confederate political and resultant economic domination over the majority of the population in Ireland, suggests that Tyrone and his allies maintained a southerly directed offensive from mid-1595, which culminated with Tyrone's march to Munster in February 1600. This was Tyrone's 1593–5 misdirection plan for Ulster writ large. As crown military forces were directed against Irish troop concentrations and perceived military threats in Ulster, the real danger came from the ascendancy of confederate political and economic control over the rest of the island. Confederate authority replaced that of the crown enabling Tyrone and his allies to tax the country instead of the government.

Tyrone was not the first Irish lord to bring modern weapons into Ireland as gunpowder weapons had been in Ireland since before he was born. Nor was he the first Irish lord to have experience fighting and commanding troops trained in modern pike and shot techniques. However, perhaps due to Tyrone's dual role as both Gaelic lord and English ally, the earl was in a unique position to see the strengths of modern combat methods and technology, and the traditional tactics of the native Irish. The addition of continental experience from his Spanish and Spanish-trained officers enabled his development of a hybrid force capable of outmanoeuvring and bringing superior firepower to bear on English forces that appeared flat-footed in comparison.

Tyrone had created a force that utilized the fundamental precepts of the military revolution by building pike and shot based infantry formations that relied on firepower as the mainstay of their combat power. This makes them more in keeping with continental practice than English, as the crown forces' willingness to enter *melee* with pikemen was inconsistent with accepted practice in Europe, which viewed firepower as superior to the pike.[185] Tyrone did not slavishly copy European practice, rather he created a hybrid force that combined the advantages of modern firepower-oriented infantry with the flexible and highly mobile nature of Irish warfare. Furthermore, Tyrone's military tactics recognized that the landscape of Ireland placed limitations on how and where troops could march and fight. Much of the Irish landscape was covered in scrub woods and bogland, with roads or tracks traversing defiles, passes and rivers. Vegetation and woods inhibited the use of close order pike. Therefore rather than attempt to impose the new system of infantry onto a landscape unsuited to it, Tyrone adapted the reforms to minimize the restrictive effects of the Irish terrain. This was a feat which the English were unable to match for most of the war.

Often described as a guerrilla war, Tyrone's campaigns had elements of irregular or mixed war. However, this was only part of a war in which the Irish made extensive use of fixed fortifications, could storm fortifications (when required) and fought in the open when tactical necessity demanded it. Raiding, which has frequently been interpreted as mere pillaging operations, was harnessed to Tyrone's overall strategy and used not just to gather supplies, but also to intimidate, punish, deceive, delay the earl's enemies, and expand the political and economic power of the Irish confederates. The expansion of Tyrone's influence across the island allowed him to levy payments from those within territories under Irish control; this was taxation in practice if not in name. Tyrone's war was far more sophisticated than previously thought; it was certainly no backwater rebellion, but was it a European war?

CHAPTER 8

Tyrone's rebellion: a European war?

'BUT METHINKS, it cannot be called a war ... I cannot do them so much credit, to say they maintain wars, but that they stir up tumults, dissentions, uproars, commotions, insurrections'.[1] Barnabe Rich was one of the first post-war writers to begin the reimagining of Tyrone's rebellion. The war was portrayed as a conflict between the modern English and the uncouth and brutish natives, who stubbornly rejected attempts to nurture English civility, and nothing like the more ordered war between states and sovereigns on the Continent. This narrative found fertile ground and still flourishes in popular and academic imagination. In his influential book *Elizabeth's army*, Charles Cruickshank chose to ignore the Irish wars almost entirely, preferring to cover campaigns in Scotland, France and Spain.[2]

It is no understatement to claim that the war in Ireland was a calamitous disaster for those living on the island, and Tyrone's defeat signalled the death-knell of native political structures. Nevertheless, was the war in Ireland any different from contemporary warfare in Western Europe? The old notion of a singularly primitive, dirty or lesser guerrilla war is a myth, as the conflict reflected many of the changes associated with the European 'military revolution'. Parker defined the fundamental features of the military revolution of land warfare in Europe as: growth in army size; a profound change in military tactics, notably the adoption of firearms and use of firepower as the decisive factor in land warfare; increasing levels of destruction during war.[3] All were exhibited in Ireland during the ten years of war from 1593 to 1603.

The nature of the conflict in Ireland paralleled much of those in Europe. Apart from sieges, which were not a major factor in the Nine Years War (Kinsale excepted), the conduct of military operations was comparable to the wars in France and the Low Countries. Both in Ireland and the Continent, set-piece battles were a rarity, indeed avoided by most prudent commanders. Instead, skirmishing and small-scale actions predominated. The adoption of technology and military methodology was an important factor during this period, but the acceptance of new technology and methods was considerably faster in Ireland. For the most part, the Irish infantry embraced revolutionary change, though the native cavalry proved less malleable.

The need to pay, feed, arm and quarter soldiers is common to armies throughout history. Therefore it is useful to contrast how these requirements were met in Ireland and on the Continent. Unsurprisingly, the limited logistical infrastructure in Europe quickly broke down resulting in crushing burdens on the civil populations. As a result, foraging, depredation and fractious relations between soldiers and non-combatants were found in continental warfare as in Ireland. However, the violence against civilians, while frequent, did not follow the same pattern. There was no replication of the confessional or gender specific aggression frequently found in France and the Low Countries. Attitudes to enemy prisoners in Ireland could be inhumane, and the ferocious campaigns during the closing stages of the war in Ulster could match anything found in Europe, but atrocities were infrequent during the first seven years of the conflict.

The military revolution and Ireland

A characteristic of the early modern military revolution was an increase in the size of armies. In Ireland, the numbers of troops deployed by the Irish, and correspondingly by the English, rapidly increased during the second half of the sixteenth century. Moreover, the quantity of troops raised by Tyrone and his allies exceeded anything previously seen in Ireland. Though the maximum size of a single army deployed by the Irish confederates appeared to be 6–8,000, as at the Yellow Ford (1598) and Kinsale (1601), the numbers mobilized throughout Ireland as a whole were significantly higher. At the beginning of the war Tyrone was estimated to have 6,000 men, but this increased rapidly as the war escalated. Estimates of the Irish forces compiled in 1599 claimed the Irish had over 20,000 men under arms.[4] The following year Sir George Carew believed the Irish could field 7,000 men in Munster alone, and a report of the same year quantified the Irish armies as totalling 23,000 foot and 1,550 horse.[5] These were not just large armies assembled for hosting or for a single battle but were maintained in pay for prolonged periods to oppose the corresponding increase in English forces. The threat from the increasingly large numbers of Irish soldiers was reflected in the reciprocal growth in the crown's army. In 1600, the Tudor army peaked at over 19,000 horse and foot.[6] By the end of the century, the scale of forces deployed by both sides in Ireland exceeded anything that could have been expected at its beginning.

The growth in army size in Ireland mirrored the situation in Europe, where similar expansions in military manpower occurred. While accurate calculations of troop mobilization are difficult to arrive at due to fraudulent recording by army officers, the inefficiency of the musters and fluctuations between peace and wartime armies, a pattern of growth can still be discerned. During the French involvement in the Italian wars (1494–1559), the number of French soldiers peaked at around 70,000 men.[7] Throughout the 1620s, the French army's nominal strength varied between 135,000 and 211,000 and by the end of the seventeenth-century Louis XIV had between 250,000 and 340,000 men under arms.

Other major European powers replicated this expansion in army size, such as the Dutch Republic and Spain, though Spain's army growth had effectively stopped by the end of the seventeenth century as Spain's military power waned. This pattern of army growth was an indicator, albeit a rough one, of the spread of the fiscal-military state, by which the resources of a country were harnessed with greater effectiveness to maintain ever-increasing numbers of troops.[8] Larger armies required more sophisticated systems of administration, both for raising capital to pay for soldiers, and distributing supplies to feed and equip them; otherwise, armies would quickly disintegrate under their own weight. Ireland echoed this trend, which raises the question of Gaelic Ireland's potential for development during the seventeenth century. This question cannot be definitively answered, as defeat truncated the growing military and political power of the native Irish. That Ireland shared a similar trajectory with burgeoning fiscal-military states suggests that an untrammelled Gaelic Ireland had the potential to do the same.

A frequent misconception about the conflict is that the prosecution of the war in Ireland was somehow different from the wars in Europe. The Nine Years War is commonly portrayed as one of ambush and skirmishes, with little in the way of conventional warfare usually ascribed to continental Europe.[9] Regular warfare has often been conceived as set-piece battles, where armies faced each other in ordered ranks or battalia. Opposing forces engaged with infantry, cavalry and artillery until one side broke contact or was routed from the field. This remains the epitome of armed action in popular, and in many cases, academic imagination, but an examination of contemporary warfare suggests that the image of massed infantry or serried ranks of pikes and muskets was not an accurate representation of how most Western European warfare was being fought at the end of the sixteenth century.

While it is tempting to define war by the scale and frequency of battles, it was only one aspect of warfare from the medieval through to the early modern period. Wars tended to focus on ravaging and destruction of the countryside, and possessing strong fortifications to dominate territory.[10] Battles were a factor but not the sole, or even primary means to secure victory. During the medieval period, the dominant form of war was the deployment of cavalry and infantry with the aim of devastating the regions through which they marched.

Sieges were frequent but battles were uncommon; they tended to be inconclusive when they did occur.[11] Medieval belligerents often eschewed battle due to its uncertainties and the greater profitability of laying waste to enemy territories.[12] Though some commanders actively sought combat, most believed it too risky and its political impact too uncertain.[13] The decline in the occurrence of battles appeared to reverse in Italy during the fifteenth century, but as the sixteenth century progressed it became apparent that, if possible, wise commanders avoided battle.[14]

The occurrence of set-piece battles in Western Europe continued to decline during the sixteenth century, and was recorded in the growing corpus of published material on the theory and conduct of war. Many contemporary authors recommended avoiding battle and its inherent risks, in favour of waiting out enemies in the field and exhausting them with constant movement and frequent skirmishing. Indeed, avoiding battle was a characteristic of a good and prudent commander. Writing in 1549, Raimond Beccarie de Pavie advised that major engagements should never be entered into unless a general was sure to have the advantage.[15] The Austrian general Lazarus Schwendi believed a commander to be a fool to choose battle if he could defeat an enemy by waiting. Bernardino de Mendoza also cautioned against it, and recommended that battle should be approached with a 'leaden foot'.[16] This tract may have special relevance to Ireland, as Sir Edward Hoby dedicated his 1597 translation of Mendoza to Sir George Carew; three years later Carew was tasked with the pacification of Munster. Carew took just under a year to subdue the revolt in Munster without provoking a single major confrontation.

In contemporary reports and subsequent historical analysis, discussion of the war in Ireland suggested that the Irish conflict was different to war practised on the Continent.[17] An aspect of this was Tyrone's Fabian strategy of refusing to meet the crown's army in a pitched battle. It is true that these were rare during the war and that Tyrone avoided battle in the open, apart from Kinsale (1601), preferring to use conventional troops to suit his prevailing operational or tactical needs.[18] References to Tyrone's avoidance of battle implied that this tactic was different to the European norm, but this inaccurately portrayed battle as central to the conduct of continental warfare. The avoidance of set-piece battles was a trend that continued throughout the seventeenth century and into the eighteenth. Writing in 1732, Maurice du Saxe's attitude to battles was unambiguous, 'I do not favour pitched battles, especially at the beginning of war, and I am convinced that a skilful general could make war all his life without being forced into one'.[19]

Fernando Alvarez de Toledo, the third duke of Alba, was one of Philip II's finest commanders. Alba had fought the Ottomans, the French, and shattered the army of the Schmalkaldic League at the battle of Mühlberg in 1547, and it was to him Philip II turned to bring the Low Countries to heel. Spain could field the most powerful armies in Europe, but despite having a numerical superiority over his opponents, Alba regularly avoided set-piece battles. His use of disciplined and regularly paid troops allowed Alba to shadow enemy forces until shortages caused them to disperse. The duke did this against the army of the prince of Orange in 1568. William's troops were continually harassed by Alba's skirmishers all the way into France, where William's mercenary army broke up, with little cost in Spanish blood.[20] English soldiers had first-hand experience of battle-shy enemies in the Low Countries. Captain John Ogle noted how he had marched to where the enemy was encamped and offered battle but was ignored by the Spanish, who were content to remain within their defences. Ogle reported that there were few encounters during the march, and that the greatest threats to his men were food shortages and the hot weather.[21]

Skirmishing and low-intensity conflict were a regular feature of combat during the war in Ireland. The majority of engagements were minor actions with small numbers of casualties sustained on either side. Instead of interpreting this as a degenerate feature of what Essex described as a 'miserable and beggarly ... war', a direct parallel with contemporary European experience can be identified.[22] Skirmishing and small unit engagements dominated war at the end of the sixteenth century. Aside from sieges, which were the most high-profile military actions in the Low Countries, contemporary commentators noted that their service was marked by persistent skirmishing and petty actions. Most engagements described by Sir Roger Williams were skirmishes and ambushes, not battles of massed infantry or stirring cavalry charges.[23] Reports of fighting associated with sieges tended to involve ambushes or night time *camisadoes* into the enemy camp. This was the type of war against which Sir John Smythe railed in 1590. He wrote how continental warfare had become 'greatly altered' and that the fighting in France and the Low Countries was 'disordered and tumultuary, without formed militia [military system] ... different from the well-ordered wars ... betwixt emperors and kings'.[24]

The impact of irregular and small-scale warfare was not limited to the experience of English captains. In Holland's northern quarter during 1573, the war bore no resemblance to the ideal image of orderly ranks of troops described in military manuals. It was a war of skirmishes, unconnected limited engagements and ambushes, fought around isolated fortifications, villages and houses.[25] Localized irregular warfare played a significant part during the French wars of religion (1562–98). In his account of the conflict in Mayenne and Burgundy during 1587–96, Henri Drouot described how the war had

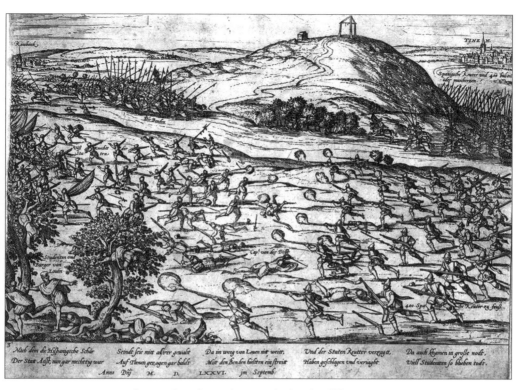

27 Loose shot skirmishing at the battle of Tienen, 1576
(Rijksmuseum Amsterdam, FMH 413–153)

fragmented into a series of local conflicts of small units pitting neighbour against neighbour. Small garrisons of twelve, ten, or even five men fought what was described as '*la guerre aux vaches*' or 'the war on cows'.[26] The opinion that 'small' war was ascendant over large regular battle was articulated by Blaise de Monluc, who summarized war as a series of 'fights, encounters, skirmishes, ambushes, an occasional battle, minor sieges, assaults, escalades, captures and surprises of towns'.[27] The battle of Coutras in 1587 ended an eighteen-year hiatus of pitched battles in France.[28] Into the seventeenth century, small actions were far more common that large encounters. During the English Civil War, which is noted for battles such as Edgehill (1642) and Naseby (1645), only 15 per cent of combat deaths were incurred in the nine major engagements of the war and 24 per cent in sieges, whereas almost half (47 per cent) died in minor actions.[29] The importance of small-scale warfare was first referred to by Parker, when he opined that modern historians had ignored or overlooked the importance of irregular war in favour of the more impressive and better-documented sieges and battles.[30]

As has been stated above, the predominant type of warfare fought in Ireland during the war was one of skirmishes and ambush, but the Irish did also engage in major actions involving strong field armies, with both the crown and confederates deploying thousands of troops. Despite the large numbers involved, modern descriptions of these battles have tended to attach provisos which appear pejorative, such as terms like 'running fights' or 'ambushes' on difficult ground or in passes.[31] However, many contemporary battles in France and the Low Countries were not the stereotypical lines of battle, but were a complex series of ambushes, traps and skirmishes. The battle of Heiligerlee in May 1568, which is seen as the start of military resistance in the Dutch Revolt, was in effect an elaborate ambush. A feigned cavalry withdrawal by the Dutch, drew the Spanish army into an ambush by 300–400 shot hidden in peat holes that flanked the road the Spanish were advancing along. The resulting rout killed almost half the Spanish force with little loss to the Dutch.[32] At Alba's annihilation of the Dutch at Jemmingen the same year, prolonged skirmishing and concealed troop movements drew Louis of Nassau's men out of their trenches before Alba overwhelmed them with attacks from multiple directions.[33] The Battle at Zutphen in 1586, at which the earl of Essex and Sir John Norreys fought, was an ambush and a confused cavalry melee in the fog.[34]

A recurring element of the war in Ireland was the use of defensive sconces and field fortifications by Tyrone and his allies. The Irish shot regularly deployed behind earthwork ramparts. This was bemoaned by Mountjoy who, after the bloodbath in the Moyry Pass in 1600, noted that the Irish had 'barricadoes, piled with stones and sods of earth, so that we had only their heads for our marks, they our whole bodies for their butt'.[35] Raising breastworks and earthen banks can be linked to the use of firepower as an effective means to win field engagements. Gonsalvo de Cordoba built a long bank and ditch for his arquebusiers at Cerignola in 1503, protecting them from direct attack and allowing them to slaughter the French and Swiss with point-blank gunfire.[36] The butchery of the Swiss columns at Bicocca in 1522 showed that the combination of firearms and properly constructed field-works was a powerful tactic that was difficult to overcome. After enduring the murderous fire of Spanish cannons, the Swiss believed they were safe, having occupied a ditch below the maximum depression of the Spanish guns. However, arquebusiers on the ramparts blasted the heaving mass of troops with repeated volleys, devestating the Swiss ranks.[37]

The duke of Alba used earthworks to defend his troops in the field. During his shadowing of William of Orange in 1568, Alba ensured that his army could be rapidly redeployed into entrenchments, and the protection of his shot from attack by cavalry was always a priority.[38] Alba travelled in the vanguard of his army with his pioneers, enabling him to quickly order the construction of entrenchments if William attempted to force a battle. During England's moment of crisis in 1588 when the Spanish Armada threatened invasion, the queen's officers did not rely on elaborate systems of ramparts and bastions found in the Low Countries, but hurriedly erected earthworks. Sir John Smythe referred critically to the simple sconces raised along the threatened coasts of Suffolk, Essex and Kent. Composed of turf banks and trenches, with 'certain points, angles and indents', the defences were basic structures from which firearm-equipped troops could delay an invasion until greater forces could be concentrated.[39] What was clear from the construction of these defences, and what Smythe condemned, was that the crown's military commanders had opted for a land strategy that relied on defensive firepower protected by ad-hoc and temporary field defences. Less than a decade later the same techniques were used by Tyrone to block route-ways and defend threatened coastlines in Ireland.

The manner in which the Irish lords came to adopt firearms and use them effectively had much in common with how technology and expertise were transmitted across Europe and beyond. However, the transfer of technology on its own did not result in a transformation of native Irish fighting methods. Despite the existence of firearms throughout sixteenth-century Ireland, it was only after the arrival of soldiers of the Spanish Armada in 1588, with their specialist knowledge of firearms and the means to use them proficiently, that native Irish leaders exploited military expertise independent of government control. This model of military adaptation was very similar to events elsewhere in Europe. Warfare dominated by firepower spread across Europe during the sixteenth and seventeenth centuries. The introduction of weapons technology and foreign military expertise facilitated military transformation along the Habsburg-Ottoman frontiers in the Balkans. Until the mid-1550s, Hungary had experienced little of what would later be called the military revolution, but the introduction of firearms and their use *en masse* radically altered previous methods of warfare.[40] The use of firearms did not grow at a local or even regional level due to a sudden appearance of technology, but was mainly because of the arrival of Western European troops, such as Walloon, French and Italians, who were the principal carriers of military innovation into the region.[41] The need to import foreign expertise was also seen in Russia at the start of the seventeenth century. Swedish captains trained Russian recruits in the 'Belgian manner' of war, and in the 1630s substantial cash bounties were paid to foreign mercenaries willing to train Russian troops to fight in 'foreign [pike and shot] formations'.[42]

A key aspect of the military revolution was the adoption of firearms and the implementation of associated tactical changes to maximize their potential.

Infantry modernization led to combined-arms formations of pike and shot, but firepower was considered superior and preferable to the *melee* of a push of pike.[43] Spanish units remained defensive and tactically conservative throughout the sixteenth century, with a higher proportion of pike to shot, but as the century progressed they put a greater emphasis on firearms with the ratio of shot and pike reaching parity by 1600.[44] The military reforms of the Dutch, instituted by Maurice of Nassau, were primarily aimed at increasing control and order on the battlefield and maximizing the firepower of infantry units, but the proportion of shot to pike remained roughly equal.[45] The importance of firepower continued to grow during the seventeenth century. The ratio of pikes in infantry units diminished until they were relegated to a purely defensive measure against cavalry. Pikes were finally rendered obsolete by the invention of the bayonet at the end of the seventeenth century.

Tyrone's adoption of firepower for his infantry was nearly total, with a five-to-one ratio of shot to pike by 1595. The Irish preference for the melee weapons of the gallowglass and kerne was replaced by combat predicated on the use of firepower. In little over five years, Tyrone transformed traditional Irish hosts into battalia of modern pike and shot. The gallowglass were a prominent and powerful class of military professionals, whose methods and equipment were medieval in origin.[46] Despite their familial associations, hereditary positions and traditional arms, not to mention the considerable investment in training that went into making a gallowglass, there is no evidence of any resistance to the dramatic change of military methodology. John Dowdall reported that by March 1596, Tyrone had converted all his kerne to shot and his gallowglass to pike.[47]

Tyrone had less success modernizing his cavalry, who were drawn from the Gaelic aristocracy. However, they were still useful for reconnaissance and harassment and were very similar in arms and equipment to the Spanish *jinete*. The Spanish cavalry were lightly armoured with a helmet and mail, and armed with javelins, lance and a light shield. Sir Charles Oman's description of their tactics could speak equally of the Irish horse, where the *jinetes* 'swarm round the enemy, to overwhelm him with darts, to draw off if charged in mass, but to hang upon his flanks and charge him if he grew tired, or fell into disorder'.[48] Gonzalo de Córdoba made use of them fighting his irregular war in Italy at the start of the sixteenth century, but by the time of the Dutch Revolt they had been replaced with light lancers, *hargulatiers* and pistol-armed *reiters*.[49] The Irish noble elite did not or could not replicate these changes, which came to haunt them at Kinsale (1601) when the rout of the Irish cavalry led to the cataclysmic overthrow of Tyrone's army.[50]

In comparison to the native Irish acceptance of Tyrone's reforms, the English military community proved substantially more resistant to change. The introduction of pike and shot infantry as the mainstay of English armies was slow, and met with opposition from professional soldiers.[51] The longbow was rooted in the English imagination as something quintessentially English and was associated with victories such as Crécy (1346) and Agincourt (1415). While reasons for maintaining the bow were not just military, publications such as *Certain discourses military* by Sir John Smythe showed that some military men remained enthusiastic advocates of the longbow.[52] Despite the presence of shot in Henry VIII's armies, it took until 1589 for bows to be declared unfit for use.[53] Moreover, reforms appeared to take even longer for the rising out of the Pale in Ireland. When a hosting was gathered at the Hill of Tara (Co. Meath) in 1593 to confront Maguire in Ulster, the mounted force had a decidedly medieval feel, as a substantial proportion of the horse were mounted archers.[54] A gestation period of over fifty years does not appear so terrible when compared to some polities, for which modernization appeared near impossible.

As technology and innovation spread from Western Europe, through Africa, Eastern Europe and the Near East, the impulse to modernize faced resistance from military professionals and elites, who were unwilling to relinquish their prestige or traditional martial skills, even though they were becoming obsolete.[55] This was the case in Russia, where conservatism restricted military modernization.[56] Russia had made advances in the fifteenth century by creating the firearm equipped *strel'tsy*, but they became a hereditary force that proved unreceptive to later modernization.[57] The gentry obstructed reform by refusing to join foreign [Western European] style units.[58] When an effort was made to enlist 2,000 *deti boyarskie*, or poor noblemen, in 1630 into modern infantry units, the vast majority refused to serve under foreign captains.[59] To field pike and shot units, the Russian crown was forced to raise foreign style troops in parallel with the traditional military institutions. As they proved impervious to reform, *strel'tsy* forces co-existed with new model infantry until they were gradually replaced over time.[60]

For the Ottomans, an adaptation of their infantry to cope with the prevailing modes of warfare proved impossible in the sixteenth and seventeenth centuries. The outbreak of war in Hungary demonstrated that Ottoman field tactics were obsolete when faced with modernized Austrian infantry.[61] Despite the presence of thousands of western veterans in the Muslim armies of the period, there is no evidence to suggest that the new tactics were adopted; weapons technology spread but tactical techniques did not.[62]

Analogous political and military strategy

The war in Ireland has often been placed in the pantheon of colonial wars, but the striking similarities with contemporary European conflicts are hard to ignore.[63] A shared feature was the diverse ethnic composition of the armies engaged. For much if not all the war, crown armies in Ireland were composed primarily of Irish, Old English and New English soldiers. As the war progressed and an increasing number of Irish leaders sided with the crown or defected from Tyrone, the conflict became more of an internecine war. In the Low Countries, the conflict appeared superficially to be a contest between Dutch rebels and the Spanish crown. Despite Alba's army totalling 54,300 in 1573, only 7,900 of them were Spanish. Most were native to the Netherlands, notable among whom were the Walloon noblemen Berleimont and Bossu, who slaughtered civilians in the Waterlant and sacked Rotterdam respectively.[64] Though both wars had the outward appearance of natives resisting an outside power, the reality was more complex.

Common to Ireland and the Netherlands was a necessity for the involvement of outside agencies in maintaining both wars. From the outset of the Irish war, Tyrone and his allies sought to engage the support of Spain (the most powerful nation in Europe at that time). It is beyond question that Spanish aid, especially money, was crucial in allowing Tyrone to continue the war, as troops and supplies were often paid for with Spanish money.[65] The authorities in Dublin were concerned enough by the influx of Spanish coin that they made an effort to undermine Irish confidence in the currency by questioning the Spanish coins' authenticity. Fenton had them checked for purity and started rumours that the Spanish silver was fake.[66]

As well as war materials and money, aid came in the form of political support. The Irish confederates were not aiming to become a self-governing republic, but were attempting to supplant one sovereign for another. Tyrone and his associates requested that Philip II appoint Cardinal Archduke Albert as their prince in 1596.[67] The requirement for outside aid and international political support to reject the authority of a sovereign was also seen in the early stages of the Dutch Revolt. As William of Orange attempted to unite the rebellious Dutch provinces, he realized that the rebels could not defeat Spain on their own. William believed that the war could only be won with the support of an outside power, either France or England.[68] There was never any suggestion that the Dutch could militarily overcome Spanish forces by themselves, and English and French troops were vital in countering the advances of Alexander Farnese, duke of Parma.[69] The Act of Abjuration in 1577 was intended to open the way for the adoption of sovereignty by a new prince. Queen Elizabeth rejected the offer, but it was taken up by Francis of Anjou. This proved a dismal failure, but it demonstrated that the intention of the States General was not for a revolutionary transformation of the structures of government, but a return to the earlier equilibrium of government by the collaboration of sovereign and states.[70]

War and the rural population

The use of plunder and spoliation to provide for the needs of armies was not unique to Ireland, but an ever present feature of war until modern times. Though many states in Western Europe possessed a more developed agricultural and industrial infrastructure than Ireland and were more densely populated, countries such as France, Spain and the rich estates of the Low Countries were unable to provide for troops without recourse to widespread confiscations and extortion. Though there were attempts to implement rudimentary systems of supply, either through provisions furnished by central authorities, or purchased from local markets and travelling sutlers, the huge growth of the armies deployed and the rigours of war eventually caused these efforts to fail. Consequently, troops commandeered whatever they needed from civilians, normally with implicit or explicit threats of violence.[71]

Even in theatres of war where relations between soldiers and civilians were good, supply failures forced troops to take what they needed from the surrounding population. Relations rapidly degenerated as soldiers resorted to wanton theft and the abuse of civilians. Regardless of the designs of commanders, the desires or wants of soldiers led to unsanctioned and uncontrolled depredations. This occurred in France during the wars of religion, where repeated ordinances issued by the king failed to stop the depredations of crown troops, who mistreated civilians along their lines of march and those who lived in proximity to their camps.[72] In some cases, exactions were vital elements for military campaigns to succeed and were incorporated into plans from the outset. The 12,000 soldiers needed for the Spanish invasion of Holland in 1575 were to be paid with whatever plunder they found.[73] Troops could be ordered to disperse throughout the countryside to meet their supply needs. Before the siege of Alkmaar in 1573, the duke of Alba sent his soldiers to lodge in the rich villages of Holland, where his master of camp, Don Francisco de Baldeso, 'caused all the villages to bring him such necessaries as pleased him'.[74] Depredations were not limited to enemy territory as demonstrated by the activities of the armies of the Dutch States General, whose forces terrorized even their home populations. It was reported that Dutch troops were often unhappy with the basic foodstuffs they received.

Therefore they extorted money from peasants, and if they were not satisfied broke into houses and took whatever they pleased.[75]

Systems of contributions were established in Europe in an attempt to regularize and bring some degree of order to the exactions made by armies.[76] They had their root in a lawful tax used by princes to raise money from within their home countries to finance war but were also related to what in German was known as *brandschatzung*. This was money extorted under threat of force, or more precisely a ransom paid to prevent destruction and theft of civilian property.[77] The amount taken was always less than the estimated cost of the damage if villagers or townspeople refused to pay. By the 1620s there were several types of contribution; those levied by troops occupying a territory and those levied on unoccupied lands but vulnerable to raiding.[78] However, this system broke down very quickly when local economies received the attention of more than one belligerent. The protections from spoil purchased from one side did not protect farms and towns from the ravaging of another. Therefore the resources of a district were rapidly exhausted if the inhabitants were compelled to contribute to all sides.

In Ireland, the use of raids to gather supplies followed a very similar pattern. Tyrone and his allies subjected much of Ulster, Connacht and the Pale to spoiling during the early stages of the war, but this evolved into a less chaotic system, where set rates were established with regards to the amount of goods or money Irish troops were entitled to exact from the rural population. Landowners made contracts with the confederates, and regular payments were used to replace unpleasantries associated with an actual raid. While the crown army was primarily supplied by shipments from England, English troops frequently subjected the rural population to spoliation. The inevitable shortages caused by breakdowns in the system of supply resulted in crown garrisons roaming the countryside, robbing and extorting loyal subjects as they went. Livestock and domestic goods were often ransomed or sold back to their previous owners at the local marketplace.[79] This was also seen in Europe, where pillaging soldiers would kidnap people in addition to stealing property, with the goal of exacting a fee for their safe return.[80]

The effects of war on the civilian populations in Ireland resembled much of what was experienced on the Continent. The intensification of the war in Ulster during 1601–3 depopulated much of the rural landscape. While this has been ascribed to the effects of deliberately orchestrated famine and massacres tantamount to genocide, there is evidence to suggest that a substantial number of civilians had migrated out of the active war zone. This behaviour was entirely consistent with that of civilians in other parts of Europe, where victimization by soldiers or their demands for supplies became intolerable to the local communities. The description of empty landscapes in Ireland was comparable with the effects of war on the Low Countries. During the Dutch Revolt, there was a collapse of agriculture due to the abandonment of land that had become too dangerous or unprofitable to cultivate. Parker suggested that only around one per cent of the rural population remained in southern Flanders during the 1580s, and the proportion of land farmed around Ghent fell by 92 per cent.[81] Though the contribution system attempted to control the demands of soldiers from civilians, eventually the insatiable demands of armies led to a breakdown in this relationship. In response, farmers and town dwellers fled in the face of continuing depredations.[82]

It is interesting to note that depopulation was frequently coincident with subsistence crises and a raised civilian mortality rate. Rather than place the responsibility for these deaths directly upon military aggression, studies have suggested that a complex interaction of military exactions, civilian victimization, refugee episodes and a reduction in agricultural productivity led to significant population mortalities. Myron Gutman noted that the seasonal occurrence of excess deaths, notably in autumn (September–November), suggests that military forces could not be solely responsible for the increased mortality.[83] The very presence of armies in regions could bring the onset of epidemic disease. When this was combined with reduced food supply due to confiscation and deliberate destruction of crops, civilians became highly vulnerable to contagious disease.[84] An already bad situation could be exacerbated by movements of refugees, whose interaction with soldiers and other civilians could rapidly increase disease transmission rates.[85] While increased mortality was linked to military activity, it cannot be attributable solely to direct military action. With regard to the disaster unfolding in Ireland during 1602–4, there was an intensification of military activity, deliberate destruction of crops, exhaustion of the agricultural resources and civilian flight as found on the Continent. Therefore the increased deaths in Ulster and the rest of Ireland were a result of the same complex interaction of specific conditions.

Brutality and violence in the conduct of war

Brutality and victimization of the civilian population were characteristics of the wars between the crown and the Irish during the sixteenth century. Vivid descriptions of the excesses of Sir Humphrey Gilbert coupled with the uncompromising attitude of Sir Arthur Chichester have facilitated a vein of bloody narrative in the historiography.[86] Analysis of civilian brutalization and land devastation shows that, in some ways, Ireland replicated the experience of war in continental Europe. However, the events in Ireland and the nature of the violence are both typical and atypical.

Tyrone and the crown had planned, or had already used, crop destruction and burning as a tool for area denial before 1600. Tyrone had preyed and burned in Lecale and the southern borders of Ulster in 1596, specifically to inhibit English military operations. The crown had already shown its readiness to use similarly harsh measures in England during the Armada crisis of 1588. Though the primary defence of England was vested in the navy, a ground force was raised to oppose the Spanish in the event they managed to make landfall. The population along the Spaniards' line of advance was to be evacuated, all animals removed, and the crops spoiled.[87] It was considered acceptable to lose the harvest rather than have it fall into Spanish hands. As the landings never materialized the tactic was never put into practice, but that the plans were in place suggested that Queen Elizabeth was willing to devastate large tracts of fertile English farmland in defence of her realm.[88] Not only were scorched-earth tactics used (or planned) in Britain and Ireland, they were a common feature of warfare on the Continent.

Systematic crop destruction was deployed in Granada in 1483 and during the devastation of Provence in 1536, but scorched-earth tactics were frequently used during the medieval period as the principal method to realize military success.[89] Most medieval military campaigns embarked on widespread spoiling of the countryside and contemporary writings on warfare claimed that success in war depended upon ravaging. Advice on how Scotland should invade England in the late twelfth century suggested that 'first lay waste the land, then destroy one's enemies'.[90] Indeed, sieges and battles became prohibitively expensive. Therefore the *chevauchée*, pillaging and burning of territory, was increasingly used to attack an enemy's vulnerable 'soft targets', such as civilians, villages and food supplies.[91] Written in 1300, Pierre Dubois' *Doctrine of successful expeditions and shortened wars* advised King Philip IV of France to avoid costly sieges by devastating his enemies' agricultural economy.[92] In France, campaigns of fire and devastation became commonplace throughout the fourteenth century. The medieval *chevauchée* quickly devastated entire regions, as troops took what could be carried and put a torch to whatever remained.[93] The use of devastation for military aims was considered equally valid in early modern Europe.

Philip II chose to use a strategy of devastation and terror to suppress the rebellion in the Low Countries. He considered two options: flooding the rebel states by breaching the sea dykes or systematic burning of rebel territories. Philip opted for burning as it was deemed less likely to induce an adverse political response from the rest of Europe.[94] By torching the Dutch

28 Soldiers hanging civilians, from *Les Misères et les Malheurs de la Guerre*,
by Jacques Callot (Paris, 1633)

countryside, agricultural production would be disrupted, thereby starving (both literally and financially) the rebel states into submission. Total wasting was planned to take place in 1575, specifically starting during winter to maximize the effect, as food and livestock would be concentrated in barns and storehouses.[95] Orders were given that all of Holland was to be burned and to kill anyone who fell into Spanish hands. The Spanish commander of the operation, Don Luis de Requesens, was unambiguous with his instructions. The plan called for far more than the usual wartime devastation, but aimed 'to wipe out the memory of such an unfortunate people'.[96] Requesens intended to hold the countryside until June to destroy the hay harvest on which the dairy industry depended, which was a principal source of income for the Dutch.[97] The campaign was a deliberate assault on the ability of the rebels to subsist and the Dutch state's economy. Ultimately, the Spanish proposals did not materialise, as the troops allocated to carry out the destruction mutinied due to a lack of pay, but the objective of the Spanish crown was unmistakeable – to force rebel capitulation due to fear, economic collapse and the threat of starvation. The similarities with the situation in Ireland are evident, but the chronology for implementing the strategies was entirely different.

For the Spanish, terror was deployed as an initial response to the revolt in the Low Countries. The English had been embroiled in the war in Ireland for seven years before resorting to draconian measures. In response to the iconoclast riots of 1566, Philip II sent Alba to restore order at the head of 10,000 men. Alba's methods were severe, but they achieved the desired result –

Dutch military resistance collapsed.[98] After the revolt was suppressed, Alba's extra-judicial proceedings, known as the Council of Troubles/Blood, led to over 1,000 executions and an exodus of rebel leaders and their adherents out of the country.[99] Five years later when rebellion flared again, Alba returned to his tried and trusted methods, embarking on campaigns that saw the destruction of towns such as Mechelen, Zutphen, Naarden and Haarlem, in which thousands of civilians and captured troops were executed.[100] The initial policy of terror and destruction was an attempt to minimize the financial burden of sustaining so many troops in arms and deny the rebels the resources they required to maintain their resistance.[101] Philip II only took a more conciliatory line after the army mutinied, thwarting his plan to devastate Holland.

The approach of Queen Elizabeth and her officers in Ireland to Tyrone and his allies was almost the reverse to Alba's methods in the Low Countries thirty years earlier. The crown's response was relatively low-key when Tyrone used proxies to fight at the start of the war. Lord Deputy Fitzwilliam dispatched small forces with local support to put down what was seen as a local rising. As the war escalated and Tyrone's involvement became apparent, the crown engaged in a series of attempts at securing a negotiated settlement. It was only after the abject failure of Essex's hugely expensive campaigns in 1599 that negotiation became less of an option and more focus was put on a direct military solution to the war. It could be argued that the English could not have supported a devastation policy before 1600, as they had neither a sufficient number of troops in Ireland to achieve the requisite degree of wasting, nor the logistical infrastructure in place to feed that army solely with supplies sent out from England. Given the parsimonious nature of Queen Elizabeth, her desire for a negotiated settlement was probably guided by the same sentiment that drove Philip II to look for a quick victory – minimizing costs.

Brutality and civilian victimization became a significant feature of the literature addressing the war, both in contemporary publications and in the modern historiography. While bloodshed and barbarity plagued Ireland at the end of the sixteenth century (and more so in the seventeenth), continental Europe was no better, as cruel and severe methods were recommended and regularly practised by military commanders in France and the Low Countries. France was wracked by a series of religious wars from 1562 to 1598, from which came the *Commentaires* of Blaise de Monluc. He believed severity and cruelty to be essential in the conduct of war, specifically in the suppression of rebellion.[102] During his passage through Guyenne in 1562, Monluc boasted that his route could be traced by the bodies hanging from trees lining the roads.[103]

The duke of Alba counselled that the Dutch Revolt could only be put down with force, without 'mildness, negotiations or talks, until everything has been flattened. That will be the right time for negotiation'.[104] Alba's terror tactics worked as Dutch resistance was crushed, and only resurfaced five years later after he attempted to impose a new tax.[105] It would be easy to condemn Alba or de Monluc as especially bloodthirsty individuals and unrepresentative of their times, but Alba's methods were approved of by his friends and foes alike. The French ambassador condoned the slaughter of civilians at Mechelen in 1572, as the terror-tactics caused many Dutch troops to abandon their positions.[106] Though Sir Roger Williams fought for the Dutch, he espoused Alba's methods and thought Philip II was wrong to replace him with a more moderate commander, as 'to say truth, fury and resolution well used or executed, had been the only ways to suppress that [Dutch] nation'.[107]

The harsh treatment of Irish prisoners was a feature of the English campaigns to subdue the Irish. The crown had a poor record when it came to taking prisoners of war, with executions and the rejection of quarter commonplace. Many English officers (and the queen) considered the Irish wars acts of rebellion, which put the Irish outside the protection of contemporary customs of war, making summary executions perfectly acceptable. This attitude was entirely consistent with the treatment of captured rebels in France, Spain and the Low Countries. During the suppression of a revolt in the Azores in 1582, all prisoners were executed by Philip II's commander as he viewed it a police action to quell a rebellion and not war.[108] Alba was uncompromisingly harsh with captives in the Low Countries. He gave no quarter at Jemmingen in 1568, where approximately 6,000 troops were killed in the battle or hunted down to a nearby island and slaughtered. He had the entire garrison of Haarlem put to the sword after they surrendered in 1573.[109] Alba's actions appear excessively brutal to modern sensibilities, but William Maltby argued that Alba scrupulously, if bloodily, observed the customs of war in relation to rebellion.[110]

Examples of the summary execution of captives continued throughout Europe contemporarily with the war in Ireland. Though the fear of reprisals allowed a degree of restraint in the wars of the Low Countries to develop, prisoner executions still occurred on a scale that far exceeded those seen in Ireland. Unsurprisingly, both sides on the Continent committed brutal acts, either ignoring the prevailing customs of restraint or as an act of retribution for enemy actions. After the Spanish defeat near Wormer in 1574, the victorious Dutch placed 150 German captives into a boat, then drowned them in the Zuiderzee near Hoorn.[111] In a letter to the earl of Essex, Captain John

Chamberlain recounting the battle of Turnhout in January 1597, noted that 2,000 of the enemy were killed, and 450 prisoners taken, but casually mentioned at the end of his letter that they 'put to the sword the greatest part of those troops'.[112] The following year Sir Henry Docwra described how the Spanish slaughtered captive soldiers.[113] A Spanish fort taken on the Rhine in 1599 had its defenders put to the sword, and a small English garrison of 30 men suffered the same fate in 1604.[114] Clearly, surrendering was no simple matter, even on the Continent where the rules of war were ostensibly applied.

Comparison of the type and extent of interpersonal violence at this time shows that while the Dutch Revolt, the French Wars of Religion and the Nine Years War were confessional to a greater or lesser degree, there was a significant difference in the treatment of the clergy and church property in Ireland. Some eminent officers of the Catholic church were killed in battle or executed after their capture. The archbishop of Armagh, Edmund Magauran, was killed in Connacht in 1593, and Owen MacEgan in Munster in 1603. There were some isolated cases of attacks on clerics and churches, such as Bingham's destruction of Rathmullan abbey (Co. Donegal) in 1595, the order for the destruction of Multyfarnham friary (Co. Westmeath) in 1600 and the murder of Redmond O'Gallagher, bishop of Derry, and twenty of his priests at Derry in March 1601.[115] Nevertheless, there was little orchestration of or policy for violence towards priests or ecclesiastic property.[116] Specific orders were given during the occupation of Donegal abbey in 1600 that the monks were not to be harmed, and priests and friars near Ballyshannon were to be accommodated.[117] At the start of 1603, Mountjoy cautioned against the urge by some to engage in religious repression, not out of any sense of compassion for Catholics, but due to his observation that it was counterproductive, citing how Protestantism had grown in the Dutch republics in spite (or because) of Spanish efforts to suppress it.[118]

In Ireland, church property was more likely to be destroyed by the Catholics under Tyrone for sound military reasons. Churches were regularly converted into fortified garrisons by the crown, therefore in some instances, they were burnt by Tyrone to deny their use.[119] Ecclesiastical vandalism or iconoclasm, which occurred in the Low Countries, was not a facet of the war in Ireland. In Bartlett's map of south-east Ulster of 1602–3, the church at Ardboe, marked 'Dromboe', was a fortified garrison.[120] Despite the presence of English troops, when the war was at its most ferocious, the intricately carved early Christian cross remained free from unwanted attention and remains in good condition.[121] Major structural damage to churches was occasionally accidental. Niall Garbh O'Donnell had garrisoned Donegal abbey during August 1601, but a fire in the store detonated several barrels of gunpowder 'in which blast a great part of the walls were shivered'.[122] Sections of the abbey collapsed and many troops were killed or seriously injured, including Niall Garbh's brother.[123]

During the early stages of the troubles in the Low Countries, religious buildings and images were frequently targeted. The iconoclast riots of 1566 saw churches attacked and religious objects destroyed, but at this stage there was little violence against people.[124] The Dutch Sea Beggars were notoriously harsh with captured priests, churches and religious objects.[125] After the taking of the castle at Gorcum (modern-day Gorinchem), they tortured and murdered twenty monks, and repeatedly disregarded local agreements to safeguard ecclesiastic property and personnel.[126] Clerical buildings were attacked throughout the Dutch Revolt, leading to an absence of religious provision for Catholics in many regions controlled by the Dutch Protestants.[127]

In France, the attacks and atrocities committed along confessional divisions are almost synonymous with cruelty incited by religious discord. The murder of clerics during peacetime was rare, but not during times of conflict. On average three were killed in each diocese every year.[128] For many French Catholics, the Protestant/Huguenot threat was one which had to be purged from society, and many of those who committed acts of brutality against their Protestant neighbours believed themselves to be fulfilling their civil duty by enforcing the will of the king, and by extension the will of God.[129] In many cases, Catholics viewed their violent acts as analogues of religious rites such as baptism (in blood for some victims) or purification by fire.[130]

The cruelties inflicted on the population of Ireland during the war should not be minimized in any way, but one aspect of interpersonal aggression in Europe that was notably missing from Ireland were attacks on women, more specifically sexual violence. This absence can be explained by one of two reasons: either it was not frequent enough to be widely reported, or there was a failure to comment on it by both sides of the conflict. Rape was seldom reported during the next descent into war in Ireland – the Confederate wars of the 1640s. Mary O'Dowd noted that documented cases of rape were rare though this may be due to a reluctance to discuss such matters or a reticence on the part of the victim to report incidents due to a sense of shame.[131] Accounts of rape emerged in the reports of the collapse of the Munster plantation in 1598, but the polemical quality of *The supplication of the blood of the English* may have overstated the atrocities to incite a more vigorous response from the crown.[132] In a draft response to 'Tyrone's libel' in 1600, the unsigned author referred to the brutalities of the war in terms such as 'robberies, murders, extinguishing of families, burning of houses and all kinds of bloody licentiousness and cruelty'.[133] This sentence was later amended by the lord high treasurer, Lord Bruckhurst, to include the word 'rapes'. The alteration of what was already a strong rebuke of Tyrone and confirmation of the Palesmen's loyalties suggested that despite all the savagery and destruction seen in seven years of war, sexual violence was not frequent enough to warrant mention. Where rape has been noted, it was usually in a general sense with little elaboration or description of individual cases.[134] However, the crown was quick to seize the opportunity to accuse Tyrone's men of sexual crimes. In 1598, Ormond claimed the O'Mores and O'Connors had 'abused men's wives, and their daughters in such villainous manner, as it is not to be spoken'.[135] Tyrone denied the accusation, but Thomas Jones claimed that the Leinster Irish had even caused disorders while in Ulster, and annotated in the margins of the manuscript that 'the inhabitants of Tyrone have vowed to cut their throats if they come there'.[136] After bringing the ringleaders into Tyrone's presence, the earl was unable to defend his allies actions causing him to '[grow] into a rage, partly against those rascals themselves and partly because he was so strictly charged for them'.

Gender and violence were recurring issues throughout the sixteenth century. English officials were wary of Irish women, whose influence as wives could persuade otherwise loyal husbands to commit traitorous or seditious actions.[137] However, despite the documented criticism of Irish women, they were not deliberately targeted during the war. Palmer claimed that Irish women were subject to greater hostility than their English counterparts, but if one looks further afield into contemporary European warfare, it is clear that while women were killed along with men and children in Ireland, this was no different from what occurred in France and the Low Countries.[138] Indeed, the brutality inflicted upon women in Ireland during the war was part of the general victimization of civilians and not specifically directed according to gender. In Europe the situation was quite different. In the Low Countries and France, reports of rape, murder and torture of women were frequent and graphic.

Accounts of violence against Huguenot women in France demonstrated a sexual motivation. Lurid descriptions of attacks indicated that for some, the demonstration of sexual dominance was perhaps more of a motivating factor than religion.[139] Gratuitous violence against women was a characteristic of the St Bartholomew's Day Massacre in Paris in 1572.[140] Women fared no better during the Dutch Revolt, where rape was commonplace.[141] This was not just during the large-scale ransacking of towns, such as of Antwerp in 1576, but also at a local level in rural districts. An account of a woman tortured to reveal the whereabouts of her money had an unmistakable sexual element.[142] Though she was not physically raped, the soldiers' behaviour was intended to effect sexual degradation and humiliation. Sexual violence has been seen as an ever-present feature of war and has a long history, which included attacks not only on women but also on men and children.[143] The pattern of sexual abuse of women during warfare was continued through the seventeenth and eighteenth centuries. In his study of violence and atrocity in the eighteenth century, Philip Dwyer claimed that ill-treatment and murder of women was prevalent throughout the Revolutionary and Napoleonic wars.[144] Into modern times rape remains an enduring aspect of war; however, for the Nine Years War in Ireland, there is little evidence to suggest that rape, sexually motivated assault or gender violence was a major issue. As noted earlier, the crown was always ready to seize on any atrocity to paint the Irish as base and brutal. Therefore the frequent occurrence of such acts would have undoubtedly been exploited by the crown to demonize the Irish confederates and smear Tyrone's reputation.

If contemporary Europe had massacres and atrocities that far exceeded those in Ireland, both in duration and the numbers of civilians killed, why have claims of English policies of genocide and the exceptional nature of violence in early modern Ireland become prevalent in the historiography? Possibly because the Irish conflict has been compared to the conduct of wars in England, which has been used as a model for the manner in which contemporary warfare should be fought. However, the conflicts of the English Civil Wars (1642–6, 1648, and 1650–1) were more restrained than those seen in continental Europe. While there were atrocities, execution of prisoners and victimization of civilians, a balance was established that constrained the kind of wanton brutality that had been commonplace during the Thirty Years War (1618–48).[145] When warfare in Ireland and England is contrasted, Ireland emerges as aberrant with regards to the scale of the destruction. However, viewed in the context of the European experience of warfare, it is the civil war in England and not the conflict in Ireland that could be considered abnormal.

When the effects of war in England and Germany are compared, war has been shown to be significantly more violent and destructive in Germany.[146] This may have been due to the retention in England of an 'imagined community' held between civilian and soldier. This created a space for agency and facilitated restraint during military campaigns.[147] In England, there were no large-scale refugee migrations as seen in Europe. Refugees were a symptom of the breakdown of relations between civilians and soldiers. Despite reports of altercations and brawls, plundering troops rarely killed civilians during the English Civil War; there was no reason for any mass exodus from threatened districts.[148] The imagined community allowed Parliamentarian and Royalist troops to expect treatment according to the 'laws of war, nature and

Christians'.[149] The English Civil War was fought largely without mercenaries. Therefore the belligerents shared a similar sense of community. Correspondingly, their political and religious divisions were relatively shallow in comparison to those seen across Europe and in Ireland.[150] Where differing nationalities or cultures clashed, there was often little ground on which restraint or moderation could be founded.

This calls into consideration the nature of society in Ireland during the Nine Years War. The first significant outbreak of civilian victimization did not occur until 1598 with the revolt in Munster. Before this there were few cases of civilian flight from confederate troops. Between 1593 and 1598 Tyrone and his allies came to dominate large tracts of the countryside, which included significant Old and New English populations, as in Lecale and Ards (Co. Down) and Cos. Laois and Offaly. Why was there restraint? An economic imperative may be one reason why Tyrone allowed loyalist farmers to remain on their land. The Irish war effort drew heavily upon the agricultural economy throughout Ireland. Empty lands produced nothing that can be taxed. Therefore it was vital that productivity was not interrupted or suppressed.

There may also have been the same imagined community described by Quentin Outram, between the Old English and the native Irish leadership and their adherents. Certainly, there were bonds of kinship and amity built up between the native Irish and the Old English Catholics over years of association, which fostered a degree of trust.[151] These relationships may have encouraged restraint and curtailed uncontrolled devastation and victimization. The atrocities of the Munster revolt can be explained by the existence of hostility and religious antipathy between the newly arrived (Protestant) English and the native Irish, coupled with bitter memories of the suppression of the Desmond revolt only fifteen years previously. The tension between the two communities in Munster may have hindered the development of any sense of community, thereby enabling the outrages of 1598.

A European war (mostly)

How do the events in Ireland from 1593 to 1603 relate to warfare witnessed across Western Europe during the same period? One of the simplest issues to address is the growth of armies. Just as in Europe, larger numbers of soldiers were mobilized in Ireland. Far more troops were raised in Ireland during the Nine Years War than at any time before. Concerning the development of firepower as the dominant means to affect battlefield victory, it is without question that the new forces raised by Tyrone followed this trend. The use of firepower by soldiers deployed in Ireland was similar to the practice of troops in the Low Countries and France. Where Ireland differed was the rate of transformation of the Irish forces, who offered little resistance to the replacement of traditional fighting methods by the new firepower-dominated style of war.

The Nine Years War shared many characteristics with the Dutch Revolt. Both wars were fought to replace one sovereign authority for another, not establish independent republics. The need for international involvement was common to the Irish and the Dutch causes. The problems attendant with feeding large concentrations of soldiers were the same in Ireland as in continental Europe. Ultimately, soldiers took what they needed from the surrounding population with greater or lesser degrees of intimidation or force. Efforts were made to regularize the demands, but when systems of supply failed, it was inevitably the civilians who suffered. The ravages of war in Europe and Ireland were almost identical, with the attendant collapse of rural agriculture followed by associated subsistence crises. In Ireland as on the Continent, landscapes were depopulated by extended periods of warfare. This was due to food shortages, epidemic disease, migration and to a lesser extent direct brutalization of civilians by soldiers. The efficacy of scorched earth tactics in Ireland had a similar utility in Europe. Its effectiveness had been demonstrated since classical times, through the medieval and into the early modern period. Spain was willing to use it against the Dutch and Queen Elizabeth was prepared to put the English countryside to the torch to impede a Spanish invasion. Therefore it was almost inevitable that a strategy of devastation was used in a protracted struggle like the Nine Years War.

When viewed in the context of suppressing a rebellion, the violence witnessed during the war in Ireland was no different from that of continental Europe. Rebellions were commonly associated with harsh treatment of soldiers and civilians. Indeed, brutal behaviour was often seen as the best way to quash revolts against sovereign authority. Where customs of accepting surrenders existed, such as France and the Low Countries, the threat of summary execution persisted, and survival could depend upon a military commander's interpretation of the customs of war, or his willingness to ignore them. When massacres did occur, their scale could far exceed the worst atrocities of the war in Ireland.

Where the Irish war was different from Europe was the absence of several types of violence that characterized the Dutch and French wars, notably iconoclasm, confessional aggression and sexual abuse. European warfare exhibited a marked increase in violence against those of a different religion. Confessional atrocities proliferated and were sometimes accompanied by rape and sexually motivated aggression. It is wrong to claim that this did not occur in Ireland, but this was more anti-colonial in motivation than sectarian. Reports of this type of violence were relatively few when compared to the wars on the Continent.

Conclusion: Tyrone's rebellion and European warfare

It is easy to assume the advances in military methodology passed Ireland by as the most obvious innovation, the *trace italienne*, had no measurable effect on the war, but this accepted the topographic realities of Ireland and the limits they placed on transporting artillery. The war witnessed the same general trend of increasing army size. As in continental Europe, troop numbers in Ireland increased. Correspondingly, the expanding armies had a devastating impact on the country and its population. The unprecedented cost, levels of destruction and the appalling toll in human suffering in Ireland replicated the experience of war in Europe.

Tyrone's prosecution of the conflict can be defined as mobile war, where large-scale deployments of forces co-operated with smaller partisan or irregular units to effect tactical advantage and operational success. Large Irish units could be as mobile as smaller formations, allowing them to choose when and where to engage crown forces. Moreover, large concentrations of Irish troops could split into smaller units, engaging in irregular operations as needed. Describing this as guerrilla war confuses the dual-use of regular and irregular tactics, as one did not preclude the other. While hit-and-run attacks were an aspect of the war, the Irish fought in the open when required and, for most of the war, Tyrone's soldiers held the field at the end of engagements. Fixed field defences, rarely a feature of classic guerrilla war, were widely used. Coordinated actions using deception and misdirection allowed the confederates to keep the initiative for much of the war. This sophisticated strategy required a high degree of command and control over disparate regional leaders, who had little experience in military collaboration or taking orders from an Irish lord with whom they had no traditional affiliation.

Confederate strategy was defensive during 1594–5, as Tyrone and his allies consolidated their position in Ulster. Even then, raiding into Connacht and Leinster expanded Tyrone's influence and allowed him to solicit support from Irish and Old English lords. A protracted shooting war in southern Ulster drew crown forces north, leaving the Pale, the midlands and Connacht vulnerable to spoiling by those allied with Tyrone. Repeated raiding allowed the confederates to dominate much of the countryside, enabling them to exploit the wealth of the rural economy. The power of the Irish confederates peaked in February 1600 with Tyrone's march into Munster, but after

Mountjoy became lord deputy, constant military pressure and a new strategy by the crown reversed Irish gains.

War in Ireland was more than just combat. Raiding fulfilled diverse military, political and economic objectives: operational deception; foraging; area denial; punishment; intimidation; and extension of political power. In support of the military aspects of the war, both the crown and Tyrone depended to a greater or lesser extent on ceasefires to retrench their military, political and logistic resources for the expected resumption of hostilities; delay and dissimulation were as important as killing and burning. During Tyrone's campaigns, aggressive and offensive warfare could not be exclusively defined by movements of military forces or patterns of battles. War was also a matter of extending power and influence utilizing persuasion and intimidation, which also increased the economic base on which the Irish confederates' war effort depended.

The native Irish economy was moving beyond its focus on timber, hides and tallow. The economy in Ireland was heavily dependent upon arable farming; this is not new, but it was true for Ulster as well as the rest of Ireland. Gaelic Ireland was no longer a preserve of traditional pastoral farming with its attendant practice of transhumance. Arable farming was as important as husbandry, if no more so, for generating income. Furthermore, the Irish were not content to produce primary commodities; there were signs of diversification in Irish manufacturing capability with the production of gunpowder and firearms at Dungannon. Use of ready money by the Irish was significantly greater than previously believed. The crown was so concerned about the supply of cash to Tyrone that the Irish coinage was debased to deny the confederates access to currency acceptable on the international market, even though this meant stifling all international trade into Ireland.

Irish success compelled the crown to pour men and material into Ireland. Elizabethan England sent its most respected military men to suppress the recalcitrant Irish. Essex, as it turned out, was entirely unsuited for warfare in Ireland (and possibly anywhere else), whereas Mountjoy, supported by Carew, led the successful campaigns to recover Ireland. With limited resources, Carew adopted an indirect war that pacified Munster in less than a year. Mountjoy refurbished the battered Tudor field army and directed aggressive military campaigns. The English adopted many of Tyrone's infantry reforms and exploited their Irish enemy's weaknesses: vulnerable supply lines; inability to engage in effective shock action; fragile alliances; a brittle command structure that was severely damaged by the loss of senior commanders. Mountjoy also made better use of Elizabethan naval power to transport and supply land forces.

The effects of the war may have been ruinous and resulted in the deaths of thousands of soldiers and many more civilians, but the conflict was not waged without restraint or toleration. For much of the war, levels of civilian victimization were lower than continental norms. Confessional and sexual violence were not prevalent, unlike the wars in France and the Low Countries. Moreover, ethnic animosity has been overstated as a causative factor in the excesses seen in the closing stages of the war in Ulster. Violence was rarely meaningless or random and could usually be explained. The ferocity of the war was a result of multiple factors: its irregular aspects, the frustration of counter-force' methods and antipathy between soldiers and civilians. Though English writers and officers often denigrated the Irish as barbarous, the irregular nature of the war may have caused more civilian victimization than religious animosity or bigotry. Atrocities were more likely the result of individual commanders' attitudes and the frustrations of their men than deliberate government policy. Also, the thwarted counter-force strategy of the crown and the resulting desperation to win catalysed the devastation campaigns of 1601–2, not xenophobia. Moreover, the mortality crisis seen at the end of the war was not just a result of English scorched earth policies, but a failure of food supplies due to intensified military activity and harvest failure.

The Irish demonstrated a remarkable capacity for transformation during the war. Implementation of new technology and military techniques was rapidly achieved, made more notable as this occurred without perceptible resistance by the Irish military elite, who were compelled to set aside arms, equipment and skills that had served them in battle for generations. Tyrone's adoption of firepower was so rapid and complete that whenever tactical situations arose where shock troops would have been of benefit, none were available to Tyrone's commanders. The Irish openness to innovation was commented upon by even their harshest critics, such as Sir George Carew. However, their proclivity for improvement proved the utter ruin of Tyrone's army at Kinsale. Tyrone attempted to confront Mountjoy using massed infantry formations when proven hybrid methods would have served him better. Yet Tyrone and many of his commanders were not burdened with redundant chivalric and mock-heroic sensibilities like Essex, but were modern leaders who avoided battle and whose primary goal was victory, not glory. This ability to adapt was not total, as Tyrone was unable to dispel the self-interest and localism that dominated the thinking of many of the Irish lords. In the end, this defect enabled the crown to bring the edifice of Irish military power crashing down.

Abbreviations

AFM	*Annals of the kingdom of Ireland by the Four Masters*, ed. and trans. John O'Donovan (3rd ed., 7 vols, Dublin, 1990)
APC	*Acts of the privy council of England*, ed. J.R. Dasent, 32 vols (London, 1890–1907)
Bagwell	Richard Bagwell, *Ireland under the Tudors*, 3 vols (London, 1885–90)
BL	British Library
Cal. S.P. Scot.	*Calendar of the state papers relating to Scotland and Mary, queen of Scots, 1547–1603*, ed. J. Bain, W.K. Boyd, A.I. Cameron, M.S. Giuseppi, H.W. Meikle and J.D. Mackie, 13 vols (Glasgow, 1898–1969)
Cal. S.P. Spain	*Calendar of state papers, Spain*, ed. M.A.S. Hume, 4 vols (London, 1892–9)
Cal. Salisbury MSS	*Calendar of the manuscripts of the marquis of Salisbury: preserved at Hatfield House, Hertfordshire*, ed. R.A. Roberts, E. Salisbury, G. Montague and O. Geraint Dyfnallt, 24 vols (London, 1883–1976)
Carew	*Calendar of the Carew manuscripts preserved in the archiepiscopal library at Lambeth, 1551–1642*, ed. J.S. Brewer and William Bullen, 6 vols (London, 1867–73)
Cecil–Carew Letters	*Letters from Sir Robert Cecil to Sir George Carew*, ed. John Maclean (London, 1864)
Chronicle	Sir James Perrot, *The chronicle of Ireland, 1584–1608*, ed. Herbert Wood (Dublin, 1933)
CSPI	*Calendar of state papers relating to Ireland*, ed. H.C. Hamilton, E.G. Atkinson and R.P. Mahaffy, 24 vols (London, 1860–1912)
DIB	*Dictionary of Irish biography*, ed. James McGuire and James Quinn (Cambridge, 2009) and online edition
DSP	Hugh Collier, *Dialogue of Silvynne and Peregrynne* (TNA, SP 63/203, fos. 283–354), ed. Hiram Morgan, viewed at http://www.ucc.ie/celt/online/E590001–001.html on 16 Sept. 2010
ECO	Exeter College Oxford
HHA, CP	Hatfield House Archives, Cecil papers
HMC	Historic Manuscripts Commission

IHS	*Irish Historical Studies*
Itinerary	Fynes Moryson, *An itinerary: containing his ten years travel through the twelve dominions of Germany, Bohmerland, Switzerland, Netherland, Denmark, Poland, Italy, Turkey, France, England, Scotland and Ireland*, 4 vols (Glasgow, 1907–8)
Life	Lughaidh Ó Clérigh, *The life of Aodh Ruadh O' Domhnaill, Part 1*, ed. and trans. Paul Walsh (London, 1948)
Lombard	Peter Lombard, *The Irish war of defence, 1598–1600: extracts from the De Hibernia Insula Commentarius*, ed. and trans. M.J. Byrne (Cork, 1930)
NIEA	Northern Ireland Environment Agency
NLI	National Library of Ireland
OSB	Philip O'Sullivan Beare, *Ireland under Elizabeth: chapters towards a history of Ireland under Elizabeth*, trans. M.J. Byrne (Dublin, 1903)
Pacata Hibernia	Thomas Stafford, *Pacata Hibernia: Ireland appeased and reduced, or a history of the late wares of Ireland, especially in the province of Munster under the command of Sir George Carew*, ed. Standish O'Grady, 2 vols (London, 1896)
Q&A	Nicholas Dawtrey, 'A booke of questions and answers concerning the wars or rebellions of the kingdome of Irelande', ed. Hiram Morgan, *Analecta Hibernica*, 36 (1995), pp 79, 81–132
TCD	Trinity College, Dublin
TNA	The National Archives, Kew, London
ULC	University Library Cambridge

Notes

INTRODUCTION

1 M.K. Walsh, *Destruction by peace: Hugh O'Neill after Kinsale* (Armagh, 1986, repr. 2015); Hiram Morgan, *Tyrone's rebellion: the outbreak of the Nine Years War in Tudor Ireland* (Dublin, 1993); John McCavitt, *The flight of the earls* (Dublin, 2002).

2 Timothy O'Donnell, *Swords around the cross: the Nine Years War* (Font Royal, 2001), covers the entirety of the war but it is very much a Catholic/nationalist narrative with very limited use of primary sources.

3 Richard Bagwell, *Ireland under the Tudors*, 3 vols (London, 1885–90); Cyril Falls, *Elizabeth's Irish wars* (London, 1950); G.A. Hayes-McCoy had enormous influence on Irish military history and wrote extensively on the Nine Years War. See G.A. Hayes McCoy, 'Strategy and tactics in Irish warfare, 1593–1601', *IHS*, 2:7 (1941), pp 255–79; G.A. Hayes-McCoy, 'The army of Ulster, 1593–1601', *Irish Sword*, 1:2 (1949–53), pp 105–17; G.A. Hayes-McCoy, *Irish battles* (London, 1969) to name a few.

4 John J. Silke, *Kinsale: the Spanish intervention in Ireland and the end of the Elizabethan wars* (Liverpool, 1970); Hiram Morgan (ed.), *The battle of Kinsale* (Bray, 2004).

5 Seán O'Faolain, *The Great O'Neill* (Dublin, 1986); Morgan, *Tyrone's rebellion*.

6 Conor O'Brien (ed.), *Feagh McHugh O'Byrne: the Wicklow firebrand* (Rathdrum, 1998); John McGurk, *Sir Henry Docwra, 1564–1631: Derry's second founder* (Dublin, 2006); John McCavitt, *Sir Arthur Chichester: lord deputy of Ireland, 1605–1616* (Belfast, 1998); F.M. Jones, *Mountjoy, 1563–1606: the last Elizabethan deputy* (Dublin, 1958); Cyril Falls, *Mountjoy: Elizabethan general* (London, 1955); Darren McGettigan, *Red Hugh O'Donnell and the Nine Years War* (Dublin, 2005). Fascination with Essex is matched with an ever-increasing quantity of publications, e.g., Robert Lacey, *Robert, earl of Essex: an Elizabethan Icarus* (London, 1971); Paul E. Hammer, *The polarisation of Elizabethan politics: the political career of Robert Devereux, second earl of Essex, 1585–1597* (Cambridge, 1999); Alexandra Gajda, *The earl of Essex and late Elizabethan political culture* (Oxford, 2012).

7 Eoin Ó Néill, 'Towards a new interpretation of the Nine Years' War', *Irish Sword*, 26:105 (2009), p. 245.

8 Walsh, *Destruction by peace*, p. 193.

9 *OSB*, p. 85; Standish O'Grady, *Red Hugh's captivity: a picture of Ireland, social and political, in the reign of Queen Elizabeth* (London, 1889), p. 16.

10 Hiram Morgan's entry for the Nine Years War in Sean Connolly (ed.), *The Oxford companion to Irish history* (Oxford, 1998), p. 388; Colm Lennon, *Sixteenth-century Ireland: the incomplete conquest* (Dublin, 2005), p. 294; Mary Ann Lyons, 'French reaction to the Nine Years War and the Flight of the Earls, 1594–1608', *Seanchas Ardmhacha*, 19:1 (2002), pp 70–90.

11 'Expenses of the Tyrone rebellion', 24 Mar. 1603, *Cal. Salisbury MSS*, xv, pp 1–2.

12 Ian F.W. Beckett, 'War, identity and memory in Ireland', *Irish Economic and Social History*, 36 (2009), p. 64.

13 Stephen Morillo and Michael Pavkovic, *What is military history?* (Cambridge, 2008), p. 1.

14 Tami Davis Biddle, 'Military history, democracy and the role of the academy', *Journal of American History*, 93:4 (2007), pp 1143–4.

15 John Shy, 'History and the history of war', *Journal of Military History*, 72:4 (2008), p. 1035.

16 Clodagh Tait, David Edwards and Pádraig Lenihan, 'Early modern Ireland: a history of violence' in David Edwards, Pádraig Lenihan and Clodagh Tait (eds), *Age of atrocity: violence and political conflict in early modern Ireland* (Dublin, 2007), p. 15.

17 Brendan Bradshaw, 'Nationalism and historical scholarship in modern Ireland', *IHS*, 26:104 (1989), pp 329–51. He was later seconded in Willy Maley, 'Nationalism and revisionism: ambiviolences and dissensus' in Scott Brewster (ed.), *Ireland in proximity: history, gender, space* (London, 1999), pp 12–27.

18 Nicholas Canny, 'The ideology of English colonialism: from Ireland to America', *William and Mary Quarterly*, 30:4 (1973), pp 575–98.

19 Nicholas Canny, *The Elizabethan conquest of Ireland: a pattern established 1565–1576* (Hassocks, 1976), pp 122–3.

20 Ciaran Brady, 'Court, castle and country: the framework of government in Tudor Ireland' in Ciaran Brady and Raymond Gillespie (eds), *Natives and newcomers: essays on the making of Irish colonial society, 1534–1641* (Dublin, 1986), pp 22–49.

21 Ciaran Brady, 'The captain's games: army and society in Elizabethan Ireland' in Thomas Bartlett and Keith Jeffery (eds), *A military history of Ireland* (Cambridge, 1996), pp 136–59.

22 Ciaran Brady, *The chief governors: the rise and fall of reform government in Ireland, 1536–1588* (Cambridge, 1994), pp 298–300.

23 Steven G. Ellis, *Ireland in the age of the Tudors, 1447–1603: English expansion and the end of Gaelic rule* (London, 1998), p. 302.

24 David Edwards, 'The escalation of violence in sixteenth-century Ireland' in Edwards et al., *Age of atrocity*, pp 34–78.

25 Ibid., p. 72.

26 Vincent Carey, 'Elizabeth I and state terror in sixteenth-century Ireland' in Donald V. Stump, Linda Shenk and Carole Levin (eds), *Elizabeth I and the 'sovereign arts': essays in literature, history and culture* (Temple, 2011), pp 202, 215.

27 Rory Rapple, *Martial power and Elizabethan culture: military men in England and Ireland, 1558–1594* (Cambridge, 2009).

28 Ibid., p. 127; see also Rory Rapple, 'Writing about violence in the Tudor kingdoms', *Historical Journal*, 54:3 (2011), pp 829–54.

29 Ben Kiernan, *Blood and soil: a world history of genocide and extermination from Sparta to Darfur* (New Haven, 2007).

30 A.L. Rowse, *The expansion of Elizabethan England* (London, 1973), pp 18–19.

31 Richard Berleth, *The twilight lords* (London, 1978); Brendan Bradshaw, 'The Elizabethans and the Irish: a muddled model', *Studies: an Irish Quarterly Review*, 50:278–9 (1981), pp 233–44.

32 Brendan Bradshaw, 'Native reaction to the Westward Enterprise: a case study in Gaelic ideology' in K.R. Andrews, N.P. Canny and P.E.H. Hair (eds), *The Westward Enterprise: English activities in Ireland, the Atlantic and America, 1480–1650* (Liverpool, 1978), pp 66–80.

33 Michelle O'Riordan, *The Gaelic mind and the collapse of the Gaelic world* (Cork, 1990).

34 Nerys Patterson, 'Gaelic law and the Tudor conquest of Ireland: the social background of the sixteenth-century recensions of the pseudo-historical prologue the Senchas Már', *IHS*, 27:107 (1991), pp 193–215.

35 Mary O'Dowd, 'Gaelic economy and society' in Brady and Gillespie (eds), *Natives and newcomers*, pp 120–47.

36 Katharine Simms, *From high kings to warlords: the changing political structures of Gaelic Ireland in the later Middle Ages* (Woodbridge, 1987).

37 Michael Roberts, 'The military revolution, 1560–1660' in C.J. Rogers (ed.), *The military revolution debate: readings on the military transformation of early modern Europe* (Oxford,

1995), pp 13–35; Geoffrey Parker, 'The "military revolution" 1955–2005: from Belfast to Barcelona and the Hague', *Journal of Military History*, 69:1 (2005), pp 205–6.

38 Thoroughly summarized by C.J. Rogers, 'The military revolution in history and historiography' in Rogers (ed.), *The military revolution debate*, pp 1–10.

39 Later published in Geoffrey Parker, 'The "military revolution" 1560–1660 – a myth?', *Journal of Modern History*, 48:2 (1976), pp 196–214.

40 Geoffrey Parker, *The military revolution: military innovation and the rise of the West, 1500–1800* (2nd ed., Cambridge, 1996).

41 C.J. Rogers, 'The military revolutions of the Hundred Years War' in Rogers (ed.), *The military revolution debate*, pp 55–94.

42 Jeremy Black, *A military revolution? Military change and European society, 1550–1800* (London, 1991), p. 94.

43 Bert S. Hall, *Weapons and warfare in Renaissance Europe* (Baltimore, 1997), p. 210.

44 Thomas Bartlett, *'The academy of warre': military affairs in Ireland, 1600 to 1800, 30th O'Donnell lecture 2002* (Dublin, 2002), p. 9.

45 Rolf Loeber and Geoffrey Parker, 'The military revolution in seventeenth-century Ireland' in Jane Ohlmeyer (ed.), *Ireland from independence to occupation, 1641–1660* (Cambridge, 1995), p. 71.

46 Ó Néill, 'Towards a new interpretation of the Nine Years War', pp 241–62.

47 Landers placed the population of England in 1600 at 4.11 million whereas Houston estimated the Irish population to be approximately one million. See John Landers, *The field and the forge: population, production and power in the pre-industrial west* (Oxford, 2003), p. 42; R.A. Houston, *The population history of Britain and Ireland, 1500–1750* (Cambridge, 1992), pp 18–19.

48 *Lombard*, pp 31–3, 45.

49 Morgan, *Tyrone's rebellion*, p. 59.

CHAPTER 1

Tyrone's proxy war, 1593–4

1 Nicholas Canny, 'Taking sides in early modern Ireland: the case of Hugh O'Neill, earl of Tyrone' in Vincent Carey and Ute Lotz-Heumann (eds), *Taking sides? Colonial and confessional mentalities in early modern Ireland. Essays in honour of Karl S. Bottigheimer* (Dublin, 2004), p. 104.

2 Morgan, *Tyrone's rebellion*, Chapters 7 and 8.

3 *Itinerary*, ii, pp 188–9.

4 Sir Ralph Lane to Lord Burghley [William Cecil], 8 May 1593, TNA, SP 63/169, fo. 144.

5 *Chronicle*, p. 143.

6 The examination of Moris O'Skanlon, 19 June 1593, *CSPI, 1592–6*, pp 112–13.

7 The O'Hagans occupied high positions within Tyrone's household. They were traditionally the O'Neill lord's high sheriffs and held the O'Neill inauguration site at Tullaghogue. See Éamon Ó Doibhlin, 'Ceart Uí Néill: a discussion and translation of the document', *Seanchas Ardmhacha*, 5:2 (1970), pp 328, 357.

8 The examination of Moris O'Skanlon, 19 June 1593, *CSPI, 1592–6*, pp 112–13.

9 Sir Henry Duke to Sir John Perrot, 24 Aug. 1589, *CSPI, 1588–92*, p. 228.

10 Morgan, *Tyrone's rebellion*, pp 63–4.

11 Sean Connolly, *Contested Island: Ireland 1460–1630* (Oxford, 2007), p. 220.

12 Articles agreed to by the earl of Tyrone before the privy council, 17 June 1590, *Carew, 1589–1600*, pp 37–9.
13 Morgan, *Tyrone's rebellion*, p. 76.
14 Tyrone to the privy council, 31 Oct. 1591, *CSPI, 1588–92*, pp 433–6.
15 Sir Henry Bagenal to Burghley, 20 Feb. 1592, *CSPI, 1588–92*, pp 458–60.
16 Rory Rapple, *Martial power and Elizabethan political culture: military men in England and Ireland, 1558–1594* (Cambridge, 2009), pp 280–1.
17 M.K. Walsh, 'Archbishop Magauran and his return to Ireland, October 1592', *Seanchas Ardmhacha*, 14:1 (1990), p. 70.
18 Ibid., p. 76.
19 Sir Richard Bingham to Burghley, 6 June 1593, TNA, SP 63/170, fo. 6.
20 Sir George Bingham to Sir Richard Bingham, 25 May 1593, TNA, SP 63/170, fo. 13.
21 *AFM*, vi, p. 1937.
22 Sir Richard Bingham to the privy council, 28 June 1593, TNA, SP 63/170, fo. 47.
23 *AFM*, vi, p. 1937; *OSB*, pp 70–2.
24 Bingham to Lord Deputy William Fitzwilliam, 23–4 June 1593, *CSPI, 1592–6*, pp 118–19.
25 Ibid.; *Life*, p. 63; *AFM*, vi, p. 1937.
26 *OSB*, p. 71.
27 Captains Charles Eggarton and John Dalway to Fitzwilliam, 1 June 1593, TNA, SP 63/170, fo. 20; Neale MacBrian Fertagh to Fitzwilliam, 1 June 1593, TNA, SP 63/170, fo. 21.
28 Declaration of Ever O'Neill, 1 June 1593, TNA, SP 63/170, fo. 3; Declaration of Thady Nolan before Fitzwilliam and the council, 17 May 1593, *CSPI, 1592–6*, pp 99–100.
29 Captain Edward Keyes to Fitzwilliam, 8 July 1593, *CSPI, 1592–6*, p. 126.
30 Fitzwilliam and council to the privy council, 15 Sept. 1593, TNA, SP 63/171, fo. 120.
31 Ibid.
32 Bagenal to the Fitzwilliam, 11 Oct. 1593, TNA, SP 63/172, fo. 47.
33 Tyrone to Archbishop Adam Loftus [lord chancellor], 16 Oct. 1593, *CSPI, 1592–6*, pp 167–8. Tyrone noted 4–500 but later revised this to 5–600. See Tyrone to the privy council, 5 Nov. 1593, *CSPI, 1592–6*, pp 170–2.
34 *OSB*, p. 72.
35 An extract from The battle of the Erne Ford, 10 Oct. 1593, by John Thomas, BL, Cotton Augustus I. ii, fo. 38; R. Dunlop, 'Sixteenth-century maps of Ireland by Baptista Boazio', *English Historical Review*, 20:78 (1905), pp 309–37.
36 Sir Philip Holles to Sir Robert Cecil, 18 Oct. 1593, *CSPI, 1592–6*, pp 168–9.
37 Bagenal's journal, 10 Oct. 1593, *CSPI, 1592–6*, p. 179.
38 Holles to Cecil, 18 Oct. 1593, *CSPI, 1592–6*, pp 168–9.
39 Bagenal to the Fitzwilliam, 11 Oct. 1593, TNA, SP 63/172, fo. 47; Bagenal's journal, 10 Oct. 1593, *CSPI, 1592–6*, p. 179; *OSB*, p. 72.
40 Bagenal's journal, 10 Oct. 1593, *CSPI, 1592–6*, p. 179.
41 Fitzwilliam to Burghley, 21 Oct. 1593, TNA, SP 63/172, fo. 66.
42 *OSB*, p. 72.
43 Bagenal to Fitzwilliam, 11 Oct. 1593, TNA, SP 63/172, fo. 47.
44 Fitzwilliam to Burghley, 10 Jan. 1594, TNA, SP 63/173, fo. 3.
45 Nicholas Canny, 'Taking sides in early modern Ireland: the case of Hugh O'Neill, earl of Tyrone' in Carey and Lotz-Heumann (eds), *Taking sides*, p. 104; Morgan, *Tyrone's rebellion*, p. 155.
46 Bagenal's journal, 27 Sept. 1593, *CSPI, 1592–6*, pp 175–81.
47 Ibid.
48 Bagenal's journal, 2 Oct. 1593, *CSPI, 1592–6*, pp 175–81; Bagenal to Fitzwilliam, 11 Oct. 1593, TNA, SP 63/172, fo. 47.

49 Intelligence brought to Sir Richard Bingham, 29 Sept. 1593, *CSPI, 1592–6*, p. 163; *Life*, p. 67.

50 Intelligence brought to Sir Richard Bingham, 29 Sept. 1593, *CSPI, 1592–6*, p. 163.

51 Morgan, *Tyrone's rebellion*, pp 133–4.

52 Declaration by Darby Newman, 19 Feb. 1594, TNA, SP 63/173, fo. 173.

53 Richard McCabe, 'Fighting words: writing the "Nine Years War"' in Thomas Herron and Michael Potterton (eds), *Ireland in the Renaissance, c.1540–1660* (Dublin, 2007), p. 115.

54 *Q&A*, p. 94.

55 Fynes Moryson, *The Irish sections of Fynes Moryson's unpublished Itinerary*, ed. Graham Kew (Dublin, 1998), pp 70–1.

56 Quoted in Ian Heath, *Armies of the sixteenth century: the armies of England, Scotland, Ireland, the United Provinces, and the Spanish Netherlands* (Guernsey, 1997), p. 90.

57 Sir Richard Bingham to the privy council, 28 June 1593, TNA, SP 63/170, fo. 47.

58 Bagenal's journal, intelligence note 2, 23 Sept. 1593, *CSPI, 1592–6*, pp 181–2.

59 Bagenal's journal, 11 Oct. 1593, *CSPI, 1592–6*, pp 175–81.

60 The principal men slain in the defeat of Maguire at the ford of Golune, *CSPI, 1592–6*, pp 169–70.

61 G.A. Hayes-McCoy, *Scots mercenary forces in Ireland (1565–1603)* (Dublin, 1937, repr. Dublin, 1996), p. 216.

62 Lane to Cecil, 4 Dec. 1593, *CSPI, 1592–6*, p. 189.

63 Hayes-McCoy, *Scots mercenary forces*, pp 215–16.

64 Morgan, *Tyrone's rebellion*, p. 156.

65 Tyrone to the privy council, 5 Nov. 1593, *CSPI, 1592–6*, pp 170–2.

66 *Life*, p. 65.

67 Fitzwilliam to Burghley, 10 Jan. 1594, TNA, SP 63/173, fo. 3.

68 G.T. Hammond, *The mind of war* (Washington, 2001), pp 147–8; Jon Latimer, *Deception in war* (London, 2001), p. 3.

69 Tyrone to the privy council, 5 Nov. 1593, *CSPI, 1592–6*, pp 170–2.

70 Captain John Dowdall to the Fitzwilliam, 24 Nov. 1593, *CSPI, 1592–6*, p. 186; Dowdall to Fitzwilliam, 26 Jan. 1594, *CSPI, 1592–6*, pp 203–4.

71 Dowdall to Fitzwilliam, 7 Feb. 1594, TNA, SP 63/173, fo. 104; Declaration by Connor O'Cassidy, Feb. 1594, *CSPI, 1592–6*, pp 208–9; *OSB*, pp 72–3; *Life*, p. 69; *AFM*, vi, p. 1949. For a detailed examination of the siege see James O'Neill, 'Three sieges and two massacres: Enniskillen and the outbreak if the Nine Years War, 1593–5', *Irish Sword*, 30:121 (2016), 241–50.

72 Bagenal to Fitzwilliam, 25 Feb. 1594, TNA, SP 63/173, fo. 185.

73 The examination of William O'Kennedy and Donough O'Shey, 18 Apr. 1594, *CSPI, 1592–6*, p. 236; Duke to Fitzwilliam, 21 Apr. [1594], *CSPI, 1592–6*, pp 232–3.

74 Duke to Fitzwilliam, 1 May [1594], *CSPI, 1592–6*, pp 240–1; Captain Thomas Henshaw to Fitzwilliam, 30 Apr. 1594, TNA, SP 63/174, fo. 100.

75 Captain Robert Bethell to Bagenal, 27 Apr. 1594, TNA, SP 63/174, fo. 103; Bethell to Bagenal, 30 Apr. 1594, TNA, SP 63/174, fo. 109; Randall Bruertone to [Unknown], 28 Apr. 1594, TNA, SP 63/174, fo. 105; Ever MacRory Magennis to Fitzwilliam, 29 Apr. 1594, *CSPI, 1592–6*, p. 239; Tyrone to the earl of Kildare, 5 Apr. 1594, TNA, SP 63/174, fo. 118.

76 Henshaw to [Fitzwilliam], 30 Apr. 1594, TNA, SP 63/174, fo. 100; Bethell to Bagenal, 30 Apr. 1594, TNA, SP 63/174, fo. 109.

77 James Eccarsall, constable of Enniskillen to [Fitzwilliam and council], 22 May 1594, TNA, SP 63/175 fo. 39.

78 Advertisements of Maguire's forces and others, 19 July 1594, TNA, SP 63/175, fo. 168.

79   Eccarsall to [Fitzwilliam and council], 11 July 1594, TNA, SP 63/175, fo. 160.

80   Duke and Herbert to Fitzwilliam, 29 July 1594, TNA, SP 63/175, fo. 181.

81   A summary collection of the estates of the realme of Ireland, 7 Aug. 1594, Somerset Heritage Centre, DD/TB/56/51/8.

82   Duke and Herbert to Fitzwilliam, 10 Aug. 1594, TNA, SP 63/175, fo. 243; *AFM*, vi, p. 1951.

83   *Life*, pp 74–5. For a detailed account see Seamus MacCionnaith, 'Beal Atha ns mBriosgadh. Srath Fer Lurg Loch lamrugan', *Clogher Record*, 1:3 (1955), pp 111–17 and James O'Neill and Paul Logue, 'The battle of the Ford of the Biscuits, 7 August 1594' in Foley and McHugh (eds), *An archaeological survey of County Fermanagh*, vol. 1, pt 2 (2014), pp 913–22.

84   Lord Deputy William Russell to Burghley, 13 Aug. 1594, *CSPI, 1592–6*, p. 261.

85   Russell to Burghley, 17 Aug. 1594, *CSPI, 1592–6*, pp 262–3.

86   Morgan, *Tyrone's rebellion*, pp 170–1.

87   John Price to Burghley, 14 Sept. 1594, TNA, SP 63/176, fo. 61.

88   Russell and council to the privy council, 12 Sept. 1594, *CSPI, 1592–6*, pp 267–9.

89   Tyrone to Russell, 25 Aug. 1594, *CSPI, 1592–6*, p. 270; Hugh Roe O'Donnell to Russell and council, 25 Aug. 1594, *CSPI, 1592–6*, p. 270; Hugh Maguire to Russell and council, 26 Aug. 1594, *CSPI, 1592–6*, p. 270.

90   Russell to Burghley, 12 Sept. 1594, TNA, SP 63/176, fo. 41.

91   Confession of Joan Kelly, 7 Oct. 1594, TNA, SP 63/176, fo. 171; Russell and council to the privy council, 5 Dec. 1594, TNA, SP 63 /177, fo. 91.

92   Lane to Burghley, 26 May 1594, TNA, SP 63/174, fo. 248.

93   Fitzwilliam and council to the privy council, 2 Aug. 1594, TNA, SP 63/175, fo. 158.

94   Russell to the privy council, 23 Jan. 1595, TNA, SP 63/178, fo. 30; Lane to Burghley, 25 Jan. 1595, TNA, SP 63/178, fo. 40.

95   Russell and the council to Burghley, 6 Feb. 1595, TNA, SP 63/178, fo. 73.

96   Confession of James Fitzmorris Fitzgerald, … brother to Walter Reoghe, 13 and 17 Feb. 1595, TNA, SP 63/178, fo. 124. See also James O'Neill, 'The cockpit of Ulster: war on the river Blackwater, 1593–1603', *Ulster Journal of Archaeology*, 74 (2013–14), pp 184–6.

97   Declaration of Thomas Stubbing, 21 Feb. 1595, TNA, SP 63/178, fo. 176.

98   Russell and council to the privy council, 26 Feb. 1595, TNA, SP 63/178, fo. 126.

99   Sir Robert Wilbraham to Burghley, 7 Sept. 1593, *CSPI, 1592–6*, pp 144–5.

100 Hiram Morgan, 'Slán Dé fút go hoíche: Hugh O'Neill's murders' in Edwards et al. (eds), *Age of atrocity*, pp 108–9.

101 Declaration of Thady Nolan to Fitzwilliam and the council, 17 May 1593, *CSPI, 1592–6*, pp 99–100.

102 Ever MacRory Magennis, Captain of Kilwarlin, to Fitzwilliam, 29 Apr. 1594, TNA, SP 63/174, fo. 106; Morgan, 'Slán Dé fút go hoíche', p. 114.

103 Keyes to Fitzwilliam, 8 July 1593, *CSPI, 1592–6*, p. 126.

104 Ibid.

105 Brian Fertagh O'Neill to Fitzwilliam, 4 June 1594, *CSPI, 1592–6*, p. 253.

106 Hiram Morgan, *Tyrone's rebellion* (Woodbridge, 1999), p. 187.

107 Bagenal to Fitzwilliam, 20 March 1594, *CSPI, 1592–6*, p. 229.

108 John McGurk, 'Terrain and conquest 1600–1603' in Pádraig Lenihan (ed.), *Conquest and resistance: war in seventeenth-century Ireland* (Leiden, 2001), p. 94.

109 Declaration of Patrick MacArt Moyle [MacMahon], 21 Apr. 1593, *CSPI, 1592–6*, pp 94–5.

110 Captain Charles Eggarton to Bagenal, 8 July 1593, *CSPI, 1592–6*, pp 126–7.

111 Fitzwilliam and council to the privy council, 15 Sept. 1593, TNA, SP 63/171, fo. 120.

112 Confession of Donnel O'Cahan, messenger to Eoin O'Neill, 18 July 1594, TNA, SP 63/175, fo. 167.

113 Declaration of Sir Edward Herbert and Captain Humphry Willis to Fitzwilliam, 24 June 1594, TNA, SP 63/175, fo. 114.

114 Confession of Joan Kelly, 7 Oct. 1594, TNA, SP 63/176, fo. 171.

115 Walsh, *Destruction by peace*, pp 142–3, 365–6.

116 *Q&A*, p. 93.

117 *Itinerary*, ii, p. 189.

118 John Dalway to Russell, 28 Oct. 1594, TNA, SP 63/177, fo. 18.

119 Edward Brandon and Patrick Stanley, bailiffs of Dundalk, to Russell, 10 Feb. 1595, TNA, SP 63/178, fo. 96.

120 Prices of munitions and habiliments of war for supply of Ireland, 28 Aug. 1594, TNA, SP 63/175, fo. 286.

121 Memorandum by Fenton [Nov.] 1594, TNA, SP 63/177, fo. 88.

122 *Chronicle*, p. 68.

123 Presumptions against the earl of Tyrone's loyalty, Aug. 1594, TNA, SP 63/175, fo. 300.

124 *Lombard*, p. 33.

125 See Chapter 3.

CHAPTER 2
The war for the north, 1595–6

1 Morgan, *Tyrone's rebellion*, p. 24.

2 Walter Devereux, first earl of Essex, to the privy council, 5 July 1575, TNA, SP 63/52, fo. 89.

3 See The Blackwater fort, 1587, TNA, MPF 1/99.

4 Keys to Burghley, 28 Mar. 1588, *CSPI, 1586–8*, p. 506.

5 Declaration of Thomas Stubbing, 21 Feb. 1595, TNA, SP 63/178, fo. 176; Declaration of Edward Cornwall, 19 Feb. 1595, TNA, SP 63/178, fo. 172; Declaration of Henry Marche, 20 Feb. 1595, *CSPI, 1592–6*, p. 298.

6 Russell and council to the privy council, 26 Feb. 1595, TNA, SP 63/178 fo. 126.

7 Advertisements sent to Sir Henry Duke by several espials, 20 Feb. 1595, TNA, SP 63/178, fo. 122.

8 Russell and council to the privy council, 26 Feb. 1595, TNA, SP 63/178, fo. 126; Bagenal to Russell, 6 Jan. 1595, TNA, SP 63/178, fo. 9.

9 Muster of 1,304 men brought out of Brittany, 7 Apr. 1595, TNA, SP 63/179, fo. 43.

10 *Life*, pp 79–85.

11 Sir Richard Bingham to Burghley, 12 Mar. 1595, *CSPI, 1592–6*, p. 303.

12 *Life*, pp 91–2.

13 Fenton to Burghley, 5 May 1595, TNA, SP 63/179, fo. 151.

14 Russell and council to the privy council, 18 May 1595, *CSPI, 1592–6*, p. 317.

15 Russell to Burghley, 12 Mar. 1595, *CSPI, 1592–6*, p. 303.

16 Russell and council to the privy council, 13 Jan. 1595, TNA, SP 63/178, fo. 18.

17 *Chronicle*, p. 94

18 Ibid.

19 Bagenal to Burghley, 29 May 1595, TNA, SP 63/179, fo. 240.

20 *Chronicle*, pp 94–5.

21 Captain Francis Stafford to Fenton, 4 June 1595, TNA, SP 63/180, fo. 66; *Chronicle*, pp 94–6.

22 *AFM*, vi, pp 1967–9; Bingham to Cecil, 7 June 1595, TNA, SP 63/180, fo. 60.

23   Charles G. Cruickshank, *Elizabeth's army* (2nd ed., Oxford, 1966), pp 114–15.

24   Henry J. Webb, *Elizabethan military science: the books and practice* (Madison, 1965), pp 86–9.

25   Falls, *Elizabeth's Irish wars*, p. 39.

26   John X. Evans (ed.), *The works of Sir Roger Williams* (Oxford, 1972), pp 37–8.

27   Robert Barret, *The theorike and practike of moderne warres* (London, 1598), p. 142.

28   Lane to Burghley, 28 June 1595, TNA, SP 63/180, fo. 179.

29   A report of the service done by Sir Henry Bagenal in the relieving of Monaghan by Lieutenant Tucher, 1 June 1595, *Carew, 1589–1600*, pp 109–10.

30   *Chronicle*, p. 96.

31   Lane to Burghley, 28 June 1595, TNA, SP 63/180, fo. 179.

32   For a detailed discussion of the battle of Clontibret see G.A. Hayes-McCoy, 'The tide of victory and defeat: I. The battle of Clontibret, 1595', *Studies: an Irish Quarterly Review*, 38:150 (1949), pp 158–68; Lorcan Ó Mearáin, 'The battle of Clontibret', *Clogher Record*, 1:4 (1956), pp 1–28.

33   Russell and council to the privy council, 4 June 1595, TNA, SP 63/180, fo. 9.

34   Sir John Norreys to Burghley, 4 June 1595, TNA, SP 63/180, fo. 40.

35   Donal O'Carroll, 'Change and continuity in weapons and tactics 1594–1691' in Lenihan (ed.), *Conquest and resistance*, p. 222.

36   John Dymmock, *A treatise of Ireland*, ed. Richard Butler (Dublin, 1842), p. 7.

37   Ibid.

38   Ibid.

39   Morgan, 'The end of Gaelic Ulster', p. 16.

40   Sir Robert Salesbury referred to the presence of gallowglass but there is no account of them taking any part in the battle. See Sir Robert Salesbury to Burghley, 3 June 1595, TNA, SP 63/180, fo. 5.

41   Russell and council to the privy council, 4 June 1595, TNA, SP 63/180, fo. 9.

42   See Chapter 7 for a full discussion of Tyrone's reforms.

43   Sir Richard Bingham to [Cecil], 7 June 1595, *CSPI, 1592–6*, pp 326–7.

44   Emmett O'Byrne, *War, politics and the Irish of Leinster, 1156–1606* (Dublin, 2003), p. 226.

45   A journal of the late journey by the Lord Deputy [Russell], 17 July 1595, *Carew, 1589–1600*, pp 113–18; Russell and council to the privy council, 10 July 1595, TNA, SP 63/181, fo. 48.

46   Russell to Cecil, 14 July 1595, TNA, SP 63/181, fo. 60.

47   A journal of the late journey by the Lord Deputy [Russell], 17 July 1595, *Carew, 1589–1600*, pp 113–18.

48   Russell and council to Sir John Norreys, 24 July 1595, *Carew, 1589–1600*, pp 118–19.

49   Bagenal to [Burghley], 9 Sept. 1595, *CSPI, 1592–6*, pp 384–6.

50   Norreys to Cecil, 26 Aug. 1595, TNA, SP 63/182, fo. 249.

51   *Life*, p. 101.

52   Bingham to Burghley, 20 Aug. 1595, TNA, SP 63/182, fo. 244.

53   Bingham to Russell, 6 Sept. 1595, *CSPI, 1592–6*, pp 375–7.

54   Captain George Thornton to Bagenal [July] 1595, TNA SP 63/182, fo. 196.

55   Morgan, *Tyrone's rebellion*, p. 188.

56   Tyrone and O'Donnell to Philip II, 27 Sept. 1595, *Carew, 1589–1600*, p. 122; Tyrone to Don Carlo, 27 Sept. 1595, *Carew, 1589–1600*, pp 122–3; Tyrone, O'Donnell and Montfort to Don John Del Águila, 27 Sept. 1595, *Carew, 1589–1600*, p. 123.

57   Bagenal to Burghley, 9 Sept. 1595, *CSPI, 1592–6*, pp 384–6.

58   Ibid.; Captain Rice ap Hugh to Russell, 7 Sept. 1595, TNA SP 63/183, fo. 100.

59   Norreys to Burghley, 8 Sept. 1595, TNA, SP 63/183, fo. 51.

60 Lane to Burghley, 15 Dec. 1595, TNA, SP 63/185, fo. 45. For more detailed analysis see C.F. McGleenon, 'The battle of Mullabrack 5 September 1595', *Seanchas Ardmhacha*, 13:2 (1989), pp 90–101.

61 Norreys to the Russell, 16 Sept. 1595, *CSPI, 1592–6*, p. 395.

62 Norreys to Russell and council, 3 Oct. 1595, *CSPI, 1592–6*, pp 414–16.

63 John S. Nolan, *Sir John Norreys and the Elizabethan military world* (Exeter, 1997), pp 223–4; Articles agreed unto the cessation of arms taken the 27 October 1595, *Carew, 1589–1600*, p. 126.

64 Queen Elizabeth to Russell, 28 Sept. 1595, *Carew, 1589–1600*, pp 123–5.

65 Queen Elizabeth to Russell, Norreys, Wallop and Fenton, 8 Jan. 1596, *Carew, 1589–1600*, p. 131.

66 Bingham to Burghley, 10 Oct. 1595, TNA, SP 63/183, fo. 271.

67 *OSB*, p. 83.

68 Bingham to Russell, 7 Oct. 1595, *CSPI, 1592–6*, pp 418–20.

69 Ibid.

70 Lane to Burghley, 23 Dec. 1595, TNA, SP 63/185, fo. 58.

71 Norreys to Cecil, 17 Oct. 1595, *CSPI, 1592–6*, p. 421.

72 Bingham to Russell, 7 Oct. 1595, *CSPI, 1592–6*, pp 418–20.

73 John Bingham to Cecil [1599], HHA, CP 75/59.

74 Lane to Burghley, 28 June 1595, TNA, SP 63/180, fo. 179.

75 Certificate of the arming of the 1,000 sent from Chester to Ireland, 20 Apr. 1595, TNA, SP 63/179, fo. 99.

76 A brief of the foot that were hurt and slain [1595], TNA, SP 63/179, fo. 242.

77 *OSB*, p. 89

78 Ibid., p. 83.

79 Note of the eight companies which encountered the rebels in Mayo [1595], TNA, SP 63/183, fo. 278.

80 Lane to Cecil, 14 Nov. 1600, *CSPI, 1600–1*, pp 22–3.

81 Russell to Burghley, 26 Dec. 1595, TNA, SP 63/185, fo. 143.

82 Russell to Burghley, 19 Oct. 1595, TNA, SP 63/183, fo. 302.

83 Sir Richard Bingham to the queen, 22 Oct. 1595, *CSPI, 1592–6*, pp 423–4.

84 Report by Anthony Brabazon, 11 Dec. 1595, TNA, SP 63/185, fo. 21.

85 Russell and council to the privy council, 26 Dec. 1595, TNA, SP 63/185, fo. 127.

86 Fenton to Burghley, 24 Dec. 1595, TNA, SP 63/185, fo. 124.

87 Russell and council to the privy council, 26 Dec. 1595, TNA, SP 63/185, fo. 127. Six soldiers of the garrison described as 'ringleaders' were later executed.

88 Bingham to Russell, 25 Dec. 1595, TNA, SP 63/186, fo. 10.

89 Russell and council to the privy council, 26 Dec. 1595, TNA, SP 63/185, fo. 127.

90 Bingham to Russell, 3 Jan. 1596, *CSPI, 1592–6*, pp 449–50.

91 Captain Humphrey Willis and George Flower to Russell, 25 Jan. 1596, TNA, SP 63/186, fo. 271; Sir Brian O'Rourke to the Lord of Killeen [Christopher Plunkett, 9th baron of Killeen], 26 Jan. 1596, *CSPI, 1592–6*, p. 478.

92 Thomas Butler, tenth earl of Ormond to Burghley, 11 Feb. 1596, *CSPI, 1592–6*, p. 469; Ulick Burke, earl of Clanricard to Bingham, 18 Feb. 1596, *CSPI, 1592–6*, pp 479–80.

93 Russell to the privy council, 14 Mar. 1596, *CSPI, 1592–6*, pp 489–90.

94 *Chronicle*, p. 115.

95 Russell to the lord high admiral [Charles Howard, first earl of Nottingham], 10 Feb. 1596, *CSPI, 1592–6*, p. 469; Norreys to Cecil, 14 Feb. 1596, *CSPI, 1592–6*, pp 473–4.

96 Norreys to Cecil, 31 Jan. 1596, *CSPI, 1592–6*, pp 464–5; Russell and council to the privy council, 9 Feb. 1596, TNA, SP 63/186, fo. 179.

97   Tyrone to Norreys, 13 Mar. 1596, *CSPI, 1592–6*, pp 495–6.

98   Bingham to Russell, 20 Feb. 1596, TNA, SP 63/186, fo. 277.

99   Lieutenant William Martin to Bingham, 22 Feb. 1596, TNA, SP 63/186, fo. 282.

100 Bingham to Burghley, 20 Mar. 1596, *CSPI, 1592–6*, pp 499–501.

101 Norreys to Cecil, 20 Mar. 1596, *CSPI, 1592–6*, pp 498–9.

102 Russell to Burghley, 12 Feb. 1596, *CSPI, 1592–6*, pp 469–73.

103 Tyrone to Russell, 5 Feb. 1596, *CSPI, 1592–6*, p. 473.

104 Captain John Morgan to Russell, 28 Feb. 1596, TNA, SP 63/187, fo. 10.

105 Fenton to Burghley, 23 Apr. 1596, TNA, SP 63/188, fo. 153.

106 Morgan, *Tyrone's rebellion*, p. 209.

107 Certificate given by Captain Alonso de Cobos to the Irish Catholics, 15 May 1596, *Cal. S.P. Spain, 1589–1603*, p. 619, King Philip II of Spain to Tyrone, 12/22 Jan. 1596, *CSPI, 1592–6*, p. 527; Morgan, *Tyrone's rebellion*, pp 208–10.

108 Tyrone received 20 firkins of gunpowder (approximately 2,000 pounds), O'Donnell 15 firkins and MacWilliam Burke 5 firkins. See Thomas Reynolds to Bingham, 29 May 1596, TNA, SP 63/189, fo. 157.

109 Russell to Burghley, 14 May 1596, TNA, SP 63/189, fo. 60.

110 Tyrone and O'Donnell to Norreys, 6 May 1596, *CSPI, 1592–6*, p. 519.

111 Norreys and Fenton to the privy council, 6 July 1595, *CSPI, 1596–7*, pp 2–8; Note for the disposing of the companies of horse and foot, 5 July 1596, TNA, SP 63/191, fo. 14.

112 *AFM*, vi, p. 2003.

113 Henry Hovenden to Tyrone, 27 June 1596, *Carew, 1589–1600*, pp 178–9.

114 Tyrone to [Sir Edward Moore], 29 May 1596, TNA, SP 63/190, fo. 46; Stafford to Russell, 10 July 1596, TNA, SP 63/191, fo. 96.

115 Tyrone's Rebellion, *Carew, 1589–1600*, p. 179.

CHAPTER 3
The war for Ireland, 1596–8

1   'The translation of a letter in Irish, signed by the earl of Tyrone, O'Donnell, Brian O'Rourke, and MacWilliam, sent by the Clanishies into Munster to stir up rebellion there', 6 July 1596, *Carew, 1589–1600*, p. 179.

2   *AFM*, vi, fn. c, pp 2006–7.

3   Rice ap Hugh to Russell 27 July 1596, TNA, SP 63/191, fo. 261; Russell and council to the privy council, 9 Sept. 1596, *CSPI, 1596–7*, pp 100–1.

4   Tyrone to the commissioners, 20 July 1596, TNA, SP 63/191, fo. 218.

5   Dowdall to Burghley, 7 June 1596, TNA, SP 63/190, fo. 40.

6   Declaration of George Cawill, 24 June 1596, TNA, SP 63/190, fo. 167.

7   Advertisements delivered by Captain James Fitzgarrett, 12 Aug. 1596, *CSPI, 1596–7*, pp 74–6. This was a vast quantity of munitions as just two years previously gunpowder cost 10d. per pound in London. Therefore £2,000 could buy up to 48,000 pounds of gunpowder.

8   García Hernán, 'Philip II's forgotten armada' in Morgan (ed.), *The battle of Kinsale*, p. 55.

9   A brief declaration of the monthly charge growing due to her majesty's forces in Ireland, 6 June 1596, TNA, SP 63/191, fo. 148.

10 Confession of Mahon MacDonagh, 20 Aug. 1596, *CSPI, 1596–7*, pp 83–4.

11 Russell and council to the privy council, 16 July 1596, *CSPI, 1596–7*, pp 34–7. See also David Edwards, 'In Tyrone's shadow: Feagh McHugh O'Byrne, forgotten leader of the Nine Years War' in O'Brien (ed.), *Feagh McHugh O'Byrne*, pp 212–48.

12 Fenton to Burghley, 21 July 1596, *CSPI, 1596–7*, pp 41–2.

13 Parkins to Russell, 13 Aug. 1597, TNA, SP 63/192, fo. 44; Feagh MacHugh to Tyrone, 17 Aug. 1595, *CSPI, 1596–7*, pp 81–2.

14 Report by John Chichester and Captain Thomas Lee, 10 Sept. 1596, TNA, SP 63/193, fo. 158.

15 Russell to the privy council, 14 Oct. 1596, TNA, SP 63/194, fo. 39.

16 The journal of Sir William Russell [18 Sept.–30 Nov. 1596], *Carew, 1589–1600*, pp 248–53.

17 Fenton to Burghley, 25 Nov. 1596, *CSPI, 1596–7*, pp 175–6.

18 Sir Edward Moore to Russell, 31 Aug. 1596, TNA, SP 63/193, fo. 142.

19 Norreys to Cecil, 27 Sept. 1596, *CSPI, 1596–7*, pp 123–4.

20 Rice ap Hugh to Russell, 25 Oct. 1596, TNA, SP 63/195, fo. 19.

21 Tyrone to Bagenal, 12 Nov. 1596, *CSPI, 1596–7*, p. 166.

22 Garrett Moore to Sir Anthony St Leger, 30 Nov. 1596, TNA, SP 63/195, fo. 132.

23 *OSB*, p. 93.

24 Memorial thought convenient to be delivered to Sir Robert Gardiner, 7 Dec. 1596, TNA, SP 63/196, fo. 196.

25 John Morgan to Sir William Clarke, 6 Oct. 1596, TNA, SP 63/194, fo. 82.

26 Advertisements by Patrick Caddell, 16 Oct.–10 Nov. 1596, *CSPI, 1596–7*, p. 166.

27 García Hernán, 'Philip II's forgotten armada', p. 56.

28 Gerrott Comerford, attorney general in Connacht, to Ormond, 17 Jan. 1597, *CSPI, 1596–7*, pp 223–4.

29 *Life*, p. 139, *AFM*, vi, p. 2013.

30 Clifford had some experience serving in Ireland, but most of his soldering was on the Continent, where he served with distinction in France under the earl of Essex and on the expedition to Cadiz in 1596.

31 A note of diverse things wherewith Sir Richard Bingham is charged [Nov. 1595], TNA, SP 63/191, fo. 180; Rapple, *Martial power and Elizabethan political culture*, pp 295–6.

32 Clifford to the privy council, 4 Mar. 1597, *CSPI, 1596–7*, pp 239–40.

33 Norreys to Cecil, 17 Mar. 1597, *CSPI, 1596–7*, p. 243.

34 *AFM*, vi, p. 2015; Clifford to Cecil, 3 June 1597, TNA, SP 63/199, fo. 171.

35 *Life*, pp 143–5; *AFM*, vi, p. 2017; Burgh to Cecil, 22 June 1597, *CSPI, 1596–7*, pp 322–3.

36 Opinion of the privy council, 26 Dec. 1596, *CSPI, 1596–7*, pp 189–90.

37 Russell to Burghley, 17 Feb. 1597, *CSPI, 1596–7*, p. 235; Russell to the privy council, 24 Mar. 1597, *CSPI, 1596–7*, pp 247–8.

38 Loftus to Burghley, 11 May 1597, TNA, SP 63/199, fo. 60.

39 Bagenal to Burgh, 21 May 1597, TNA, SP 63/199, fo. 90.

40 Burgh and council to the privy council, 31 May 1597, TNA, SP 63/199, fo. 129.

41 Ibid.

42 Burgh and council to the privy council, 4 July 1597, *CSPI, 1596–7*, pp 333–5.

43 *Chronicle*, pp 134–8.

44 Ibid., p. 135; Edward Loftus to Adam Loftus, 15 July 1597, TNA, SP 63/200, fo. 102. See also Lord Burgh assaults O'Neill's Blackwater fort, 1597, TCD, MS 1209/34 for an illustration of the fort.

45 Burgh to Cecil, 15 July 1597, TNA, SP 63/200, fo. 95.

46 *OSB*, pp 100–1.

47 *Chronicle*, pp 135, 137; Burgh to Cecil, 3 Aug. 1597, *CSPI, 1596–7*, pp 364–6. Given the risks of such a mission it was possible the mills referred to were Tyrone's facilities for making gunpowder.

48 Plot of the Blackwater fort, 1598, TNA, MPF. 1/311.

49 Burgh and council to the privy council, 4 July 1597, *CSPI, 1596–7*, pp 333–5; Burgh to Cecil, 16 July 1597, TNA, SP 63/200, fo. 95.

50 Burgh to Loftus and the council, 23 July 1597, TNA, SP 63/200, fo. 169; Sir Anthony St Leger to Burghley, 2 Aug. 1597, *CSPI, 1596–7*, pp 363–4; Burgh to Cecil, 3 Aug. 1597, *CSPI, 1596–7*, pp 364–6; *AFM*, vi, pp 2025–7.

51 Sir Thomas Norreys to Burghley, 7 Nov. 1597, *CSPI, 1596–7*, pp 439–40.

52 Fenton to Cecil, 5 Aug. 1597, *CSPI, 1596–7*, p. 370; Burgh to Cecil, 16 Aug. 1597, *CSPI, 1596–7*, pp 383–5.

53 *Life*, pp 153–5.

54 *AFM*, vi, p. 2029. Clifford claimed to have made a lodgement in a cellar, but no useful headway could be made against the stubborn Irish defence. See Clifford to Burgh and the council, 9 Aug. 1597, *CSPI, 1596–7*, pp 373–7.

55 *AFM*, vi, p. 2035.

56 Clifford to Burgh and the council, 9 Aug. 1597, *CSPI, 1596–7*, pp 373–7; *Life*, pp 159–61; *AFM*, vi, pp 2033–7.

57 Clifford to Burghley, 11 Aug. 1597, *CSPI, 1596–7*, pp 379–81.

58 Burgh to [Cecil], 19 Sept. 1597, *CSPI, 1596–7*, pp 399–401.

59 *Chronicle*, p. 140.

60 *DSP*, fo. 399; *OSB*, p. 103.

61 Loftus and the council to the privy council, 16 Oct. 1597, *CSPI, 1596–7*, pp 419–20; *Chronicle*, p. 141

62 Queen Elizabeth to the council of Ireland, 29 Oct. 1597, *CSPI, 1596–7*, p. 430.

63 Philip Williams to Cecil, 31 Oct. 1597, *CSPI, 1596–7*, pp 432–3.

64 Anthony Dering servant of Captain Eggarton, to Mrs Eggarton, 30 June 1597, *CSPI, 1596–7*, pp 326–7; Sir John Chichester to Burghley, 16 Sept. 1597, TNA, SP 63/200, fo. 317.

65 The circumstances of the Scots' entry into parley with Sir John Chichester, 7 Nov. 1597, TNA, SP 63/201, fo. 234.

66 Copy of a letter from Captains Charles Eggerton, Edward North, Charles Mansell, and Nicholas Merriman, 6 Nov. 1597, TNA, SP 63/201, fo. 140.

67 A certificate of the overthrow of Sir John Chichester by Lieutenant Hart, 4 Nov. 1597, *CSPI, 1596–7*, pp 441–3.

68 The manner of the defeat of the governor of Carrickfergus, the 3 [sic] November 1597, 8 Dec. 1597, TNA, SP 63/201, fo. 234.

69 Ibid.

70 Tyrone to Sir Thomas Norreys, 10/20 Nov. 1597, TNA, SP 63/201, fo. 179; Tyrone to Norreys, 27 Nov./7 Dec. 1597, TNA, SP 63/201, fo. 188.

71 Ormond to the privy council, 10 Dec. 1597, *CSPI, 1596–7*, pp 467–9.

72 Ibid.

73 Heads of matters for the earl of Ormond to urge upon Tyrone at the parlay, 5 Dec. 5 1597, *CSPI, 1596–7*, pp 463–4.

74 Ormond to Burghley, 11 Dec. 1597, TNA, SP 63/201, fo. 244.

75 Private instructions for one to be sent into Ireland, 1597, TNA, SP 63/201, fo. 302; *AFM*, vi, p. 2047.

76 Russell to Cecil, 16 July 1596, *CSPI, 1596–7*, p. 38; Adam Loftus, archbishop of Dublin, and Thomas Jones, bishop of Meath, to Burghley, 22 Nov. 1596, *CSPI, 1596–7*, pp 167–71.

77 Stafford on the state of Ireland, May 1598, *CSPI, 1598–9*, pp 165–9.

78 Russell and council to the privy council, 12 Apr. 1597, TNA, SP 63/198, fo. 268.

79 Bingham to Burghley, 14 Feb. 1596, *CSPI, 1592–6*, p. 474; Bingham to Russell, 7 Feb. 1596, *CSPI, 1592–6*, p. 478.

80 An indication of how keen Tyrone was to secure a cessation in Connacht in 1596 was his threat to use force against the Connacht lords if they refused to place the required pledges into Norreys' custody, which was a requirement of the truce. See Tyrone to O'Donnell, 16 June 1596, *CSPI, 1596–7*, p. 9.

81 *Life*, pp 125–7.

82 *AFM*, vi, p. 2003.

83 *Q&A*, 131.

84 *DSP*, fo. 337.

85 Russell to Queen Elizabeth, 16 May 1596, *Cal. Salisbury MSS, vi*, pp 185–6; 'Paper on the causes of the rebellion in Ireland', Dec. 1600, *CSPI, 1600–1*, pp 118–26.

86 'Private instructions for one to be sent into Ireland', 1597, TNA, SP 63/201, fo. 302.

87 Cecil to Russell, 10 July 1596, BL Add. MSS, 4728, fo. 82.

88 Russell and council to the commissioners, 23 Jan. 1596, Lambeth, MS 627, fo. 222v.

89 Russell to Cecil, 16 July 1596, *CSPI, 1596–7*, p. 38.

90 'Paper on the causes of the rebellion in Ireland' [Dec.] 1600, *CSPI, 1600–1*, pp 118–26.

91 Thomas Lee, *The discovery and recovery of Ireland with the author's apology*, BL Add. MSS, 33743, fos. 23–4, John McGurk (transc.) viewed at http://www.ucc.ie/celt/published/E590001–005/index.html on 2 Feb. 2013.

92 The cess had been a divisive tax as it was initially intended to provide supplies for the royal household but was extended in Ireland to cover the costs of the garrison. Coupled with corruption and the appearance of confessional politics and new English colonization, it became a central feature of discontent in the Pale. See Victor Treadwell, 'Sir John Perrot and the Irish parliament of 1585–6', *Proceedings of the Royal Irish Academy*, vol. 85c (1985), 262–3.

93 'Sir Henry Wallops relation of the progress of Tyrone's rebellion' [1600], BL, Cotton Titus C/VII, fo. 153.

94 'Commissioners for the northern causes [Wallop and Gardiner] to Russell and council', 29 Jan. 1596, *CSPI, 1592–6*, pp 461–2.

95 Sir John Norreys to Cecil, 26 Aug. 1595, TNA, SP 63/182, fo. 249.

96 'Advertisements drawn out of a letter written to Sir Geffrey Fenton from the Ranelagh, being Feagh MacHugh's country', 31 Oct. 1599, *CSPI, 1599–1600*, pp 213–14.

97 Eggerton to Loftus and Gardiner, 6 Jan. 1598, TNA, SP 63/202 pt 1, fo. 76.

98 Tyrone to Tyrrell and others [1597], TNA, SP 63/201, fo. 309; *AFM*, vi, p. 2053; Bagenal to Fenton, 12 Jan. 1598, TNA, SP 63/202 pt 1, fo. 61.

99 Clifford to Loftus, Gardiner, Ormond and the council, 24 Feb. 1598, *CSPI, 1598–9*, pp 132–4.

100 Ormond to Burghley, 19 Apr. 1598, *CSPI, 1598–9*, pp 120–2.

101 Ibid.; Fenton to Cecil, 'and in his absence' to Burghley, 20 Apr. 1598, *CSPI, 1598–9*, pp 123–5; [Anon.] to Fenton, 18 Apr. 1598, *CSPI, 1598–9*, p. 125.

102 Fenton to Burghley, 22 Apr. 1598, TNA, SP 63/202 pt 2, fo. 90.

103 William Paule to Captain Henry Skipwith, 24 May 1598, TNA, SP 63/202 pt 2, fo. 156.

104 Brian Reogh [Riabhach] O'More to Teig M'Mortogh and Lysagh Oge and their followers, 20 May 1598, TNA, 63/202 pt 2, fo. 150; Loftus, Gardiner, Ormond, and the rest of the council to the privy council, 17 June 1598, *CSPI, 1598–9*, pp 183–7.

105 Fenton to Cecil, 11 June 1598, *CSPI, 1598–9*, pp 173–4; Loftus, Gardiner, Ormond and the council to the privy council, 17 June 1598, *CSPI, 1598–9*, pp 178–82.

106 James Birt to Fenton, 14 June 1598, TNA, SP 63/202 pt 2, fo. 306.

107 Clifford to [Loftus and Gardiner], 15 June 1598, TNA, SP 63/202 pt 2, fo. 202.

108 Fenton to Cecil, 22 June 1598, TNA, SP 63/202 pt 2, fo. 240; A list of forces upon the northern borders, 12 June 1598, TNA, SP 63/202 pt 2, fo. 213.

109   Loftus, Gardiner, Ormond and the council to the privy council, 17 June 1598, *CSPI, 1598–9*, pp 178–82.
110   Ormond to Cecil, 18 June 1598, *CSPI, 1598–9*, pp 187–8.
111   Fenton to Cecil, 24 July 1598, TNA, SP 63/202 pt 2, fo. 333; Ormond to Burghley, 31 July 1598, *CSPI, 1598–9*, pp 213–14; *AFM*, vi, pp 2057–9; *OSB*, pp 104–5; O'Byrne, *War, politics and the Irish of Leinster*, p. 238.
112   There are a number of different estimates of Bagenal's army. See Ormond to Cecil, 31 July 1598, TNA, SP 63/202 pt 2, fo. 343; Loftus, Gardener Ormond and the council to the privy council, 2 Aug. 1598, *CSPI, 1598–9*, pp 217–19; The ill news out of Ireland, [14 Aug.] 1598, TNA, SP 63/202 pt 3, fo. 28.
113   Defeat of Bagenal at the Blackwater, 14 Aug. 1598, *Carew, 1589–1600*, pp 280–1. The formations are illustrated in 'The description of the army which was defeated by the earl of Tyrone the [14] of August 1598', TCD, MS 120/35.
114   'Texts relating to Lord Essex in Ireland and the battle of the Yellow Ford, by John Pooley', 1638, TCD, MS 10837, p. 45.
115   *AFM*, vi, p. 2061.
116   For a discussion on the number of troops available to Tyrone see Logue and O'Neill, 'The battle of the Yellow Ford', p. 64.
117   Lieutenant William Taffe to H. Shee [Henry Shee, Ormond's secretary], 16 Aug. 1598, *CSPI, 1598–9*, pp 237–8; *OSB*, p. 109.
118   Taffe to Shee, 16 Aug. 1598, *CSPI, 1598–9*, pp 237–8.
119   Declaration of Captains Richard Percy and William Devereux [2 Oct.] 1598, TNA, SP 63/202, pt 3, fo. 177.
120   Portions of some manuscript history of time [Oct.] 1598, TNA, SP 63/202, pt 3, fo. 281.
121   Targeteers were infantry armed with a sword and small shield. See Chapter 7.
122   *OSB*, p. 111.
123   'Texts relating to Lord Essex in Ireland and the battle of the Yellow Ford, by John Pooley', 1638, TCD, MS 10837, p. 46.
124   *AFM*, vi, p. 2073.
125   Captain Richard Cuney to Essex, 28 Oct. 1598, HHA, CP 177/131.
126   Irish sources put the English losses as 2,500. See *AFM*, vi, p. 2075. Years later Fynes Moryson claimed approximately 1,500 were killed. See *Itinerary*, ii, p. 217.
127   *OSB*, p. 112.
128   Wingfield to Cecil, 8 Mar. 1600, HHA, CP 67/77.
129   *Itinerary*, ii, p. 217.
130   Loftus, Gardiner and council to Tyrone, 16 Aug. 1598, TNA, SP 63/202, pt 3, fo. 33.
131   Declaration of Ferdinando and George Kingsmill to certain questions demanded of them touching the late service, 23 Aug. 1598, TNA, SP 63/202, pt 3, fo. 63.
132   Fenton to Cecil, 16 Aug. 1598, *CSPI, 1598–9*, pp 229–30.
133   Clifford to Cecil, 28 Aug. 1598, *CSPI, 1598–9*, pp 246–7; Clifford to Cecil, 30 Oct. 1598, TNA, SP 63/202 pt 3, fo. 258.
134   Clifford to the Gardiner, Loftus, Ormond and the rest of the council, 13 Sept. 1598, *CSPI, 1598–9*, pp 312–16.
135   Ibid.; A true declaration of the state of the province of Connacht, 31 Oct. 1598, *CSPI, 1598–9*, p. 304.
136   Existing interpretations of the war generally conceive it to have been defensive. See John McGurk, 'Terrain and conquest 1600–1603' in Lenihan (ed.), *Conquest and resistance*, p. 87; Donal O'Carroll, 'Change and continuity in weapons and tactics 1594–1691', idem, p. 225.

137 'Certificate given by Captain Alonso Cobos to the Irish Catholics', 15 May 1596, *Cal. S.P. Spain, 1587–1603*, p. 619; 'King Philip of Spain to the earl of Tyrone', 12–22 Jan., *CSPI, 1592–6*, p. 527.

138 Captain Anthony Brabazon to the commissioners, 22 Apr. 1597, TNA, SP 63/198, fo. 347.

139 'The translation of a letter in Irish, signed by the earl of Tyrone, O'Donnell, Brian O'Rourke, and MacWilliam, sent by the Clanishies into Munster to stir up rebellion there', 6 July 1596, *Carew, 1589–1600*, p. 179.

140 Fenton to Burghley, 9 Jan. 1596, TNA, SP 63/186, fo. 23; Norreys to Cecil, 31 Jan. 1596, *CSPI, 1592–6*, pp 464–5.

141 Lieutenant Robert Gosnould to Captain [James] Baker, 7 Dec. 1596, TNA, SP 63/196, fo. 101; *OSB*, pp 94–5; Garrett More to Sir Anthony St Leger, 30 Nov. 1596, *CSPI, 1596–7*, p. 178; Gosnould to Baker, 7 Dec. 1596, TNA, SP 63/196, fo. 101.

142 Bagenal to Russell, 23 Dec. 1597, *CSPI, 1596–7*, p. 192; Russell to Cecil, 18 Jan. 1597, *CSPI, 1596–7*, p. 207.

143 Norreys, Bourchier and Fenton to the privy council, 24 Jan. 1597, *CSPI, 1596–7*, p. 217.

144 Comerford to Ormond, 17 Jan. 1597, *CSPI, 1596–7*, pp 223–4.

145 Russell and council to the privy council, 26 Jan. 1597, *CSPI, 1596–7*, p. 221.

146 William Paule to Captain Henry Skipwith, 24 May 1598, TNA, SP 63/202 pt 2, fo. 156.

147 Fenton to Cecil 11 June 1598, *CSPI, 1598–9*, pp 173–4.

148 Fenton to Cecil, 16 Aug. 1598, *CSPI, 1598–9*, pp 229–30.

149 Hiram Morgan, 'Mission comparable? The Lough Foyle and Kinsale landings of 1600 and 1601' in Morgan (ed.), *The battle of Kinsale*, p. 73. See also Óscar Recio Morales, 'Florence Conroy's memorandum for a military assault on Ulster, 1627', *Archivium Hibernicum*, 56 (2002), p. 71.

150 Russell and council to Burghley, 6 Feb. 1595, *CSPI, 1592–6*, p. 295.

151 Declaration of Thomas Stubbing, 21 Feb. 1595, TNA, SP 63/178, fo. 176; declaration of Edward Cornwall, 19 Feb. 1595, TNA, SP 63/178, fo. 172; declaration of Henry Marche, 20 Feb. 1595, *CSPI, 1592–6*, p. 298.

152 'Advertisements sent to Sir Henry Duke by several espials', 20 Feb. 1595, TNA, SP 63/178, fo. 122.

153 In contrast to this, Anthony McCormack noted how the Irish military strategy during the second Desmond revolt had no discernible strategy. See Anthony McCormack, *The earldom of Desmond, 1463–1583: the decline and crisis of a feudal lordship* (Dublin, 2005), p. 158.

154 Feagh MacHugh O'Byrne to Tyrone, 17 Aug. 1596, *Carew, 1589–1600*, p. 182; report by Sergeant Major John Chichester, 10 Sept. 1596, TNA, SP 63/193, fo. 158.

155 Fenton to Burghley, 25 Nov. 1596, *CSPI, 1596–7*, pp 175–6; Norreys to the council, 28 Nov. 1596, *CSPI, 1596–7*, pp 177–8.

156 Fenton to Cecil, 5 Aug. 1597, *CSPI, 1596–7*, p. 370; Burgh to Cecil, 16 Aug. 1597, *CSPI, 1596–7*, pp 383–5.

157 Clifford to the Burgh and council, 9 Aug. 1597, *CSPI, 1596–7*, pp 373–7.

158 Clifford to the privy council, 31 Oct. 1598, *CSPI, 1598–9*, pp 310–12.

159 A.J. Sheehan, 'The overthrow of the Plantation of Munster in October 1598', *Irish Sword*, 15:58 (1982), p. 13; *OSB*, p. 116.

160 Sheehan, 'The overthrow of the Plantation of Munster', p. 13; William Farmer, 'Chronicles of Ireland from 1594–1613', *English Historical Review*, 22 (1907), p. 110.

161 A discourse delivered by William Weever touching the proceedings of the rebels in Munster, Oct. 1598, TNA, SP 63/202 pt 3, fo. 278.

162 *OSB*, p. 117.

163 Portions of some manuscript history of the time [Oct. 1598], TNA, SP 63/202 pt 3, fo. 281.

164 Sheehan, 'The overthrow of the Plantation of Munster', p. 18; Information of William Saxey, chief justice of Munster [to Cecil] concerning the state of the province, 26 Oct. 1598, *CSPI, 1598–9*, pp 300–2.

165 Anon., 'The supplication of the blood of the English most lamentably murdered in Ireland, crying out of the earth for revenge (1598)', ed. Willy Maley, *Analecta Hibernica*, 36 (1995), pp 3–77; Sheehan, 'The overthrow of the Plantation of Munster', p. 18.

166 *AFM*, vi, pp 2081–3,

167 A discourse delivered by William Weever touching the proceedings of the rebels in Munster, Oct. 1598, TNA, SP 63/202 pt 3, fo. 278; [Anon.] to Loftus and Gardiner, 1 Nov. 1598, *CSPI, 1598–9*, pp 331–2.

168 Loftus and Gardiner and the council to the privy council, 23 Nov. 1598, *CSPI, 1598–9*, pp 354–8.

169 Captain Thomas Reade to [Cecil], 1 Dec. 1598, TNA, SP 63/202 pt 4, fo. 1.

170 Bingham to Cecil, 5 Dec. 1598, *CSPI, 1598–9*, pp 392–3.

CHAPTER 4
A kingdom near lost, 1599

1 Ellis, *Ireland in the age of the Tudors*, p. 328; 'Sir William Russell' in *DIB*, viewed at http://dib.cambridge.org/viewReadPage.do?articleId=a7849&searchClicked=clicked&quick advsearch=yes on 29 June 2011.

2 *Bagwell*, iii, p. 342; Falls, *Elizabeth's Irish wars*, p. 246; G.A. Hayes-McCoy, 'The completion of the Tudor conquest and the advance of the counter-reformation, 1571–1603' in T.W. Moody, F.X. Martin and F.J. Byrne (eds), *A new history of Ireland; iii, early modern Ireland, 1534–1691* (Oxford, 2009), p. 127.

3 L.W. Henry, 'The earl of Essex in Ireland, 1599', *Bulletin of the Institute of Historical Research*, 32:85 (1959), pp 1–23; Bruce Lenman, *England's colonial wars, 1550–1688: conflicts, empire and national identity* (Harlow, 2001), p. 133.

4 Hammer, *The polarisation of Elizabethan politics*, pp 232–3.

5 Queen Elizabeth to Loftus, Gardiner, Ormond and the rest of the council, 12 Sept. 1598, *CSPI, 1598–9*, pp 257–9.

6 Disposition of the forces upon the borders of Ulster, and for Leinster, 3 Oct. 1598, TNA, SP 63/202 pt 3, fo. 169.

7 Ormond to the privy council, 21 Oct. 1598, *CSPI, 1598–9*, pp 290–2.

8 Sheehan, 'The overthrow of the Plantation of Munster', p. 20.

9 Ormond to Cecil, 5 Nov. 1598, TNA, SP 63/202 pt 3, fo. 315.

10 Hammer, *The polarisation of Elizabethan politics*, pp 47, 51.

11 Falls, *Mountjoy: Elizabethan general*, p. 31.

12 Paul E. Hammer, *Elizabeth's wars: war, government and society in Tudor England, 1544–1604* (Houndmills, 2003), pp 158–9.

13 Hammer, *The polarisation of Elizabethan politics*, pp 104–6.

14 Lacey, *Robert, earl of Essex*, pp 154–6.

15 L.W. Henry, 'The earl of Essex as a strategist and military organizer (1596–7)', *English Historical Review*, 68:268 (1953), pp 363–93. During the Armada emergency of 1588, Essex raised the largest contingent of cavalry of any nobleman, despite being unpaid. See Hammer, *The polarisation of Elizabethan politics*, pp 72–3.

16 Robert Devereux, *An apology of the earl of Essex. Against those which falsely and maliciously tax him to be the only hinderer of the peace and quiet of his country* (London, 1603), E1ᵛ.

17 Hammer, *The polarisation of Elizabethan politics*, p. 137.

18 Hammer, *Elizabeth's wars*, p. 212.

19 *Itinerary*, ii, pp 240–2.

20 Essex and council to the privy council, 15 July 1599, *CSPI, 1599–1600*, pp 91–5.

21 'Officers and bands of horse and foot, appointed for a new army in the realm of Ireland', 25 Feb. 1599, *CSPI, 1598–9*, pp 482–3.

22 Privy council to Essex, 16 May 1599, *CSPI, 1599–1600*, p. 35; Richard W. Stewart, 'The "Irish road": military supply and arms for Elizabeth's army during the O'Neill rebellion in Ireland, 1598–1601' in Mark C. Fissel (ed.), *War and government in Britain, 1598–1650* (Manchester, 1991), p. 28.

23 *Bagwell*, iii, p. 217.

24 *AFM*, vi, p. 2117.

25 Proceedings of the earl of Essex, 22 June 1599, *Carew, 1589–1600*, pp 301–8; *OSB*, pp 125–6.

26 Sir John Brooke to Cecil, 5 July 1599, *CSPI, 1599–1600*, pp 78–9; William Udall to Queen Elizabeth, *c.*Oct. 1599, HHA, CP 186/159.

27 Sir John Brooke to Cecil, 5 July 1599, *CSPI, 1599–1600*, pp 78–9.

28 *Pacata Hibernia*, i, p. 2.

29 Carew to Cecil, 12 Feb. 1600, *CSPI, 1599–1600*, pp 469–70.

30 'A letter of reproof from Elizabeth I to the earl of Essex, then in Ireland', 14 Sept. 1599, BL, Cotton Julius F/VI, fo. 235.

31 [Anon.] to Sir George Carey, 23 May 1599, *CSPI, 1599–1600*, pp 43–5.

32 Sir Henry Harrington to Loftus, 29 May 1599, *CSPI, 1599–1600*, pp 58–9.

33 Essex to the privy council, 13 July 1599, *Cal. Salisbury MSS*, ix, pp 231–2.

34 Clifford to Burghley, 4 May 1597, TNA, SP 63/199, fo. 7.

35 A note on the army under the command of Sir Conyers Clifford at the Curlews, 5 Aug. 1599, TNA, SP 63/205, fo. 247.

36 Dymmock, *A treatise of Ireland*, p. 45.

37 Ibid.

38 *OSB*, pp 126–8.

39 Dymmock, *A treatise of Ireland*, p. 45.

40 Ibid.

41 *OSB*, p. 128.

42 Ibid., and Dymmock, *A treatise of Ireland*, p. 45.

43 Sir John Harington to Sir Anthony Standen in *Nugae Antiquae*, i, pp 266–7.

44 *OSB*, p. 128.

45 *AFM*, vi, p. 2133.

46 *AFM*, vi, p. 2137.

47 Essex to the privy council, 19 Aug. 1599, *CSPI, 1599–1600*, pp 125–6.

48 Comerford to Cecil, 27 Aug. 1599, *CSPI, 1599–1600*, pp 132–6.

49 Ibid.

50 Instructions by Essex to the Lord of Dunkellin [Richard Burke] and Sir Arthur Savage, 10 Aug. 1599, *Carew, 1589–1600*, pp 318–19.

51 Richard Weston to Essex, 28 Aug. 1599, *CSPI, 1599–1600*, pp 136–7.

52 Essex to Dunkellin and Savage, 10 Aug. 1599, *CSPI, 1599–1600*, pp 119–20.

53 Sir John Brooke to Cecil, 5 July 1599, *CSPI, 1599–1600*, pp 78–9.

54 *AFM*, vi, p. 2115.

55 Brooke to Cecil, 5 July 1599, *CSPI, 1599–1600*, pp 78–9.

56 Captain Francis Kingsmill to Cecil, 22 Aug. 1599, *CSPI, 1599–1600*, pp 128–30; Nolan, *Sir John Norreys*, pp 234–9.

57 'The opinions of the lords and colonels of the army, dissuading the journey northward', 21 Aug. 1599, TNA, SP 63/205, fo. 269.

58 Essex to the privy council, 30 Aug. 1599, TNA, SP 63/205, fo. 293. Later Cecil underlined this passage and sardonically wrote 'here was no sign of a parley toward [Tyrone]'.

59 Essex to the privy council, 31 Aug. 1599, CSPI, 1599–1600, pp 140–1.

60 Essex's journal from 28 Aug. to 8 Sept. 1599, CSPI, 1599–1600, pp 144–7.

61 Ibid.

62 Dymmock, A treatise of Ireland, p. 49.

63 OSB, p. 130.

64 Essex's journal from 28 Aug. to 8 Sept. 1599, CSPI, 1599–1600, pp 144–7.

65 Ibid. and OSB, p. 129.

66 Queen Elizabeth to Essex, 14 Sept. 1599, CSPI, 1599–1600, pp 150–3.

67 Queen Elizabeth to Essex, 17 Sept. 1599, Carew, 1589–1600, pp 325–7.

68 Ibid.

69 Report of the council of state to Philip III on letters brought from Ireland by Don Martin de la Cerda, 1 July 1600, Cal. S.P. Spain, 1589–1603, pp 662–3. The truth of this remains unclear as there were no other witnesses.

70 Queen Elizabeth to Essex, 17 Sept. 1599, Carew, 1589–1600, pp 325–7.

71 Chronicle, pp 161–2.

72 'Texts relating to Lord Essex in Ireland and the battle of the Yellow Ford, by John Pooley', 1638, TCD, MS 10837, p. 4.

73 Essex dismissed thirty-nine captains, many of whom had years of continental and Irish experience, including Captain Thomas Williams, who had stalwartly held the Blackwater fort in extreme conditions. See 'Captains cashiered in Ireland by the Lord Lieutenant and the present state of Ireland touching the rebellion' [no date], BL, Cotton Titus B/XII, fo. 637; Book of the cheque from 1 Mar. 1598–30 Sept. 1599, TNA, SP 63/207 pt 5, fos. 109–62.

74 Chronicle, p. 161.

75 'A journal of the occurrences of the camp from the 21 of May until the last of the same month and thence continued till the 22 of June 1599', 22 June 1599, Lambeth, MS 621, fo. 126.

76 Essex to the privy council, 14 Aug. 1599, CSPI, 1599–1600, pp 123–5.

77 Ibid.

78 L.W. Henry, 'The earl of Essex in Ireland, 1599', Bulletin of the Institute of Historical Research, 32:85 (1959), pp 4, 23.

79 Ibid., p. 13.

80 Lenman, England's colonial wars, p. 133.

81 Ibid.

82 David de Barry, fifth Viscount Buttevant to Cecil, 19 Feb. 1600, CSPI, 1599–1600, pp 492–3.

83 Lenman, England's colonial wars, p. 134.

84 'Memorandum by Captain Stafford on the state of Ireland' [May] 1598, CSPI, 1598–9, pp 165–7.

85 'The declaration of Sir William Warren touching my second journey to Tyrone, since the departure of the Lord Lieutenant, according to his Lordships former commission', 20 Oct. 1599, Lambeth, MS 617, fo. 336.

86 Warren to Cecil, 5 Dec. 1599, TNA, SP 63/206, fo. 202.

87 Sir Richard Bingham to Cecil, 5 Dec. 1598, TNA, SP 63/202 pt 4, fo. 2.

88 Fenton to Cecil, 13 Sept. 1598, CSPI, 1598–9, p. 260.

89 'A journal of the occurrences of the camp from the 21 May until the last of the same month and thence continued till the 22 June 1599', 22 June 1599, Lambeth, MS 621, fo. 126; Essex to the privy council, 14 Aug. 1599, CSPI, 1599–1600, pp 123–5.

90   'A journal of the occurrences of the camp from the 21 of May until the last of the same month and thence continued till the 22 of June 1599', 22 June 1599, Lambeth, MS 621, fo. 126.

91   Essex to the privy council, 13 July 1599, *Cal. Salisbury MSS*, ix, pp 231–2.

92   Essex to the privy council, 1 July 1599, *CSPI, 1599–1600*, pp 76–7.

93   Queen Elizabeth to Loftus and Carey, Ormond and the council, 6 Oct. 1599, *CSPI, 1599–1600*, pp 177–9.

94   Essex to the privy council, 13 July 1599, *Cal. Salisbury MSS*, ix, pp 231–2.

95   William Udall to Queen Elizabeth, *c.*Oct. 1599, HHA, CP 186/159.

96   Norman Dixon, *On the psychology of military incompetence* (London, 1994), pp 244–6.

97   Ibid.

98   Queen Elizabeth to Essex, 17 Sept. 1599, *CSPI, 1599–1600*, pp 150–3.

99   Privy council to Loftus and Carey, 17 Nov. 1599, *CSPI, 1599–1600*, pp 254–5.

100   Thomas Lee, *The discovery and recovery of Ireland with the author's apology*, BL Add. MSS, 33743, fos. 18–19, 64, 85–6, transc. John McGurk, viewed at http://www.ucc.ie/celt/published/E590001–005/index.html on 2 Feb. 2013.

101   *DSP*, fos. 316v–317.

102   The project for service by Sir Ralph Lane, 23 Dec. 1598, *CSPI, 1598–9*, pp 419–21.

103   Martin Van Creveld, *Supplying war: logistics from Wallenstein to Patton* (Cambridge, 1987), p. 6.

104   'Sir Henry Wallop's relation of the progress of Tyrone's rebellion', 1600, BL, Cotton Titus C/VII, fo. 156.

105   'A declaration of the present state of the English Pale of Ireland', 1598, TNA, SP 63/202 pt 4, fo. 200.

106   'A journal of the occurrences of the camp from the 21 May until the last of the same month and thence continued till the 22 June 1599', 22 June 1599, Lambeth, MS 621, fo. 126

107   'A journal of the Lord Lieutenant's proceedings from 22 June to 1 July 1599', Lambeth, MS 621, fo. 136.

108   Essex and the council to the privy council, 15 July 1599, *CSPI, 1599–1600*, pp 91–5.

109   The Maurician reforms transformed large infantry formations into smaller, more mobile units of 580–675 men. The new battalions were only ten ranks deep leading to broad, elongated deployments with pikes at the centre and shot placed at the wings. The shot used a counter-march whereby the front rank would fire then retire to the rear to reload, with the second rank taking their place to fire. This cycle continued until the initial front rank had returned to the front and ready to fire again with a now loaded weapon. The result was a unit that was flexible and made maximum use of its firepower. For a full description of the Maurician infantry reforms see J.A. de Moor, 'Experience and experiment: some reflections upon the military developments in 16th- and 17th-century Western Europe' in Marco Van der Hoeven (ed.), *Exercise of arms: warfare in the Netherlands, 1568–1648* (Leiden, 1997), pp 25–6.

110   Barnabe Riche, *A martial conference, pleasantly discoursed between two soldiers, the one Captain Skill, trained up in the French and Low Country services, the other Captain Pill* (London, 1598), pp 74–5.

111   Sir Thomas Norreys to the privy council, 9 Dec. 1599, *CSPI, 1598–9*, pp 399–401.

112   Dowdall to Cecil, 2 Jan. 1600, Lambeth, MS 614, fo. 267.

113   Webb, *Elizabethan military science*, p. 90.

114   Sir John Perrot quoted in Anon., *The history of that most eminent statesman, Sir John Perrott* (London, 1727), p. 53; Lord Lieutenant Sussex [Thomas Radclyffe, third earl of Sussex] cited in Mark C. Fissel, *English warfare, 1511–1642* (London, 2001), p. 208.

115   Russell and council to the privy council, 4 June 1595, TNA, SP 63/180, fo. 9.

116 Robert Osborne to Edward Reynolds, 13 Aug. 1599, HHA, CP 179/74.

117 'Texts relating to Lord Essex in Ireland and the battle of the Yellow Ford, by John Pooley', 1638, TCD, MS 10837, p. 44.

118 Mountjoy to the Lord Chancellor [Sir Thomas Egerton] and council, 14 July 1601, *CSPI, 1600–1*, pp 429–30; *Itinerary*, ii, pp 408–10; Dymmock, *A treatise of Ireland*, p. 49.

119 Russell and council to the privy council, 26 Jan. 1597, *CSPI, 1596–7*, p. 221.

120 See Chapter 1.

121 Bernadette Cunningham, 'The composition of Connacht in the lordships of Clanricard and Thomond, 1577–1641', *IHS*, 24:93 (1984), p. 5.

122 Ulick Burke to Russell, 16 Jan. 1597, TNA, SP 63/197, fo. 188.

123 'A note of the army under the command of Sir Conyers Clifford, at the Curlews', 5 Aug. 1599, TNA, SP 63/205, fo. 247.

124 Bernadette Cunningham, 'Donough O'Brien' in *DIB*, viewed at http://dib.cambridge.org/ viewReadPage.do?articleId=a6461&searchClicked=clicked&quickadvsearch=yes on 5 May 2013.

125 *OSB*, pp 51–2.

126 Russell to Burghley, 26 Jan. 1596, *CSPI, 1592–6*, pp 456–7.

127 *AFM*, vi, p. 1993.

128 Message delivered to Donough O'Connor Sligo from O'Donnell, Oct. 1596, TNA, SP 63/194, fo. 139.

129 'The circumstances of the Scots entry into parley with Sir John Chichester', 8 Dec. 1597, *CSPI, 1596–7*, pp 465–7.

130 'A part of Sir Conyers Clifford his letters of the 27 of February 1597[8]', 27 Feb. 1598, *CSPI, 1598–9*, p. 65.

131 Clifford to the privy council, 26 June 1598, *CSPI, 1598–9*, pp 192–3.

132 Thomás Ó Fiaich , 'The O'Neill of the Fews', *Seanchas Ardmhacha*, 7:1 (1973), p. 36.

133 Ibid., pp 39–41.

134 Sir Brian O'Rourke to Clifford, Jan. 1598, TNA, SP 63/202 pt 1, fo. 125.

135 *AFM*, vi, p. 2055.

136 *Life*, p. 171; *AFM*, vi, p. 2055.

137 Ormond to Cecil, 18 June 1598, *CSPI, 1598–9*, pp 187–8.

138 Lane to Burghley, 26 May 1594, TNA, SP 63/174, fo. 248; Russell to the privy council, 14 Oct. 1596, TNA, SP 63/194, fo. 39; Feagh MacHugh to Tyrone, 17 Aug. 1597, *Carew, 1589–1600*, p. 182.

139 Baron Delvin [Christopher Nugent] to Russell and council, 10 Oct. 1596, TNA, SP 63/194, fo. 101; 'The circumstances of the Scots entry into parley with Sir John Chichester', 8 Dec. 1597, *CSPI, 1596–7*, pp 465–7.

140 *DSP*, fo. 322v.

141 Ormond to [Sir Thomas Norreys], 9 Nov. 1597, *CSPI, 1596–7*, pp 446–7.

142 McCormack, *The earldom of Desmond*, p. 159.

143 The *sugán* or straw-rope earl of Desmond was a derogatory term used to describe the title accorded to James Fitzthomas by Tyrone. It is used here to differentiate this earl from James Fitzgerald, the queen's earl of Desmond.

144 'A discourse delivered by William Weever touching the proceedings of the rebels in Munster', Oct. 1598, TNA, SP 63/202 pt 3, fo. 278.

145 Sir Thomas Norreys to the privy council, 9 Dec. 1598, *CSPI, 1598–9*, pp 399–401.

146 'A discourse delivered by William Weever touching the proceedings of the rebels in Munster', Oct. 1598, TNA, SP 63/202 pt 3, fo. 278.

147 Ibid.

148 *OSB*, pp 114–15.
149 'Message delivered to O'Connor Sligo from O'Donnell', Oct. 1596, TNA, SP 63/194, fo. 139.
150 Hiram Morgan, 'Faith and fatherland in sixteenth-century Ireland', *History Ireland*, 3:2 (1995), p. 16.
151 'Tyrone's rebellion', 6 July 1596, *Carew, 1589–1600*, p. 179.
152 'A knavish letter to some nobleman in order to procure him to rebellion' [not dated], BL, Lansdowne vol. 96, fo. 93.
153 Morgan, 'Faith and fatherland in sixteenth-century Ireland', p. 16.
154 Hiram Morgan, 'Hugh O'Neill and the Nine Years War in Tudor Ireland', *Historical Journal*, 36:1 (1993), pp 26–7.
155 Ibid., p. 37.
156 Lennon, *Sixteenth-century Ireland*, pp 203–9.
157 Hiram Morgan, 'Faith and fatherland or queen and country?', *Dúiche Néill*, 9 (1994), pp 10–11.
158 Lennon, *Sixteenth-century Ireland*, p. 206.
159 Ruth Canning, 'War, identity and the Pale: the Old English and the 1590s crisis in Ireland' (PhD, University College Cork, 2010), pp 50–1.
160 K.W. Nicholls, 'Richard Tyrrell, soldier extraordinary' in Morgan (ed.), *The battle of Kinsale*, p. 163.
161 Tyrone to James Fitzpiers [James Fitzgerald, son of Sir Piers Fitzjames], 11 Mar. 1598, TNA, SP 63/202 pt 3, fo. 359.
162 Fitzpiers to Loftus and Gardiner, 18 Nov. 1598, *CSPI, 1598–9*, p. 359.
163 Canning, 'War and identity in the Pale', pp 96–7.
164 Henry Fitzgerald [12th earl of Kildare] to Russell, 13 July 1595, *CSPI, 1592–6*, p. 340.
165 Fenton to Burghley, 25 Nov. 1596, *CSPI, 1596–7*, pp 175–6.
166 Canning, 'War and identity in the Pale', pp 102–3.
167 'Opinions of sundry persons called before the council', 17 Feb. 1596, TNA, SP 63/186, fo. 227.
168 Fenton to Burghley, 7 Sept. 1595, TNA, SP 63/183, fo. 39.
169 *DSP*, fos. 318, 327.
170 Ibid., fos. 345r–346. Gossiprid was a formal ritualized kinship; a form of compaternity. See Peter Parks, 'Celtic fosterage: adoptive kinship and clientage in northwest Europe', *Comparative Studies in Society and History*, 49:2 (2006), p. 372; Fiona Fitzsimons, 'Fosterage and gossiprid in late medieval Ireland: some new evidence' in Patrick J. Duffy, David Edwards and Elizabeth FitzPatrick (eds), *Gaelic Ireland c.1250–c.1650: land, lordship, settlement* (Dublin, 2001), p. 143.
171 Bingham to Loftus and Gardiner, 27 Nov. 1598, TNA, SP 63/202 pt 3, fo. 390.
172 Wallop to Cecil, Nov. 1598, *CSPI, 1598–9*, pp 380–1.
173 Bingham to Loftus and Gardiner, 27 Nov. 1598, *CSPI, 1598–9*, pp 375–6.
174 'Paper on the condition of Ireland endorsed by Sir Robert Cecil', 1598, TNA, SP 63/204 pt 4, fo. 253.
175 Morgan, 'Faith and fatherland or queen and country?', pp 26–7.
176 Sir John Davies, *A discoverie of the true causes of why Ireland was never entirely subdued, nor brought under obedience of the crowne of England, until the beginning of his majesties happy reign* (Dublin, 1612), pp 160–1.
177 Mountjoy to Cecil, 7 Aug. 1601, *CSPI, 1601–3*, pp 7–8.
178 *Itinerary*, ii, p. 330.
179 'Advertisement from the north of Ireland', 20 July 1599, *CSPI, 1599–1600*, pp 103–4; *Life*, pp 269–71.

180 Sir John Bolles to Cecil, 16 Mar. 1601, *CSPI, 1600–1*, pp 229–31.

181 Mountjoy Carew, 28 July 1601, *Carew, 1601–3*, p. 113.

182 Kenneth Nicholls, *Gaelic and Gaelicized Ireland in the Middle Ages* (Dublin, 1972), pp 114–17.

183 Morgan, *Tyrone's rebellion*, p. 14.

184 *Lombard*, pp 37, 51.

185 'The description of the army which was defeated by the earl of Tyrone the [14] of August 1598', TCD, MS 1209/35.

186 Mountjoy to Cecil, 7 Aug. 1600, *CSPI, 1600*, pp 337–9; *Itinerary*, iii, p. 254.

187 George Beverly to Essex, 20 Sept. 1599, HHA, CP 73/101.

188 O'Dowd, 'Gaelic economy and society', pp 130–1.

189 Russell to Cecil, 22 Aug. 1596, TNA, SP 63/192, fo. 67.

190 'Memorandum, drawn up by James Nott for Cecil', July 1597, *CSPI, 1596–7*, p. 362.

191 'Articles of advertisements to be presented to the right honourable James [Fitzthomas] earl of Desmond' 1601, TNA, SP 63/209 pt 1, fo. 78.

192 Hall, *Weapons and warfare in Renaissance Europe*, pp 101–4.

193 Charles Edelman, *Shakespeare's military language: a dictionary* (London, 2004), p. 295.

194 *Lombard*, p. 33.

195 'Presumptions against the earl of Tyrone's loyalty', Aug. 1594, TNA, SP 63/175, fo. 300; Dowdall to Burghley, 9 Mar. 1596, *CSPI, 1592–6*, pp 484–8; 'Articles of advertisements to be preferred to the right honourable James [Fitzthomas], earl of Desmond', 13 Aug. 1601, TNA, SP 63/209 pt 1, fo. 78.

196 Jack Kelly, *Gunpowder: a history of the explosive which changed the world* (London, 2004), p. 35; Kris Lane (ed.) and Timothy F. Johnston (trans.), *The Indian militia and description of the Indies by Captain Bernardo de Vargas Machuca* (Durham, 2008), pp74–5. See also Brenda J. Buchanan, 'Saltpetre: a commodity of empire' in Brenda J. Buchanan (ed.), *Gunpowder, explosives and the state: a technological history* (Aldershot, 2006), pp 67–90.

197 *DSP*, fos. 300, 304, 307.

198 Dowdall to Burghley, 9 Mar. 1596, *CSPI, 1592–6*, pp 484–8.

199 Saxey to Essex, 9 Oct. 1599, *CSPI, 1599–1600*, pp 180–3.

200 'Intelligences for Her Majesty's services in the province of Leinster', 3 July 1600, TNA, SP 63/207 pt 4, fo. 9; Carew to the privy council, 18 July 1600, *Carew, 1589–1600*, pp 410–15; *Itinerary*, iii, pp 186–7.

201 Carew and the council of Munster to the privy council, 19 May 1600, *Carew, 1589–1600*, pp 390–1.

202 Russell to the privy council, 27 Feb. 1595, TNA, SP 63/178, fo. 136.

203 Dowdall to Burghley, 9 Mar. 1596, *CSPI, 1592–6*, pp 484–8; Carew the privy council, 19 May 1600, *CSPI, 1600*, pp 182–5.

204 'A discourse on Ireland.' [1601], *CSPI, 1601–3*, pp 250–5.

205 *Lombard*, p. 31.

206 'Instructions given by the Lord General Sir John Norreys to his brother Sir Henry Norreys', 27 July 1596, *CSPI, 1596–7*, pp 49–54.

207 'A letter to Sir Thomas Norreys, knight, governor of the province of Munster', 27 Nov. 1598, *APC*, xxix, pp 309–10.

208 'Paper on the condition of Ireland' [1598], *CSPI, 1598–9*, pp 443–5; Moryson, *Unpublished Itinerary*, p. 74.

209 Dowdall to Cecil, 2 Jan. 1600, Lambeth, MS 614, fo. 267.

210 'Intelligences for Her Majesty's services in the province of Leinster', 3 July 1600, TNA, SP 63/207 pt 4, fo. 9; Carew to the privy council, 19 May 1600, *CSPI, 1600*, pp 182–5.

211 The privy council to Mountjoy and the rest of the council', 29 Jan. 1601, *APC*, xxxi, pp 122–5.

212 'Warrant against illicit import of goods to Ireland', 22 Feb. 1601, *APC*, xxxi, pp 177–8.

213 'Intelligences for Her Majesty's services in the province of Leinster', 3 July 1600, TNA, SP 63/207 pt 4, fo. 9.

214 Moryson, *Unpublished itinerary*, p. 52.

215 Pauline Croft, 'Trading with the enemy, 1585–1604', *Historical Journal*, 32:2 (1989), p. 287.

216 Privy council to Carew, Sept. 1600, *APC*, xxx, pp 703–5.

217 Thomond to Cecil, 14 Sept. 1599, *CSPI, 1599–1500*, pp 153–4; Michael Lynch, mayor of Galway to Cecil, 27 Sept. 1600, TNA, SP 63/207 pt 5, fo. 168.

218 'Summary of the requests of O'Neill and O'Donnell to the king' [14 Apr. 1600], *Cal. S.P. Spain, 1589–1603*, p. 657; 'Report of the council of state to Philip III on a letter of 14 April, from O'Neill', 13 Aug. 1600, *Cal. S.P. Spain, 1589–1603*, p. 668.

219 This was demonstrated by Tyrone's destruction of his own castle at Dungannon and those of his followers. See Russell and council to the privy council, 20 July 1595, *CSPI, 1592–6*, pp 343–4. A letter to the *sugán* earl of Desmond advised him that the war was not to be one of defending castles but 'standing and upholding the field'. See 'Articles of advice to be preferred to the right honourable James [Fitzthomas], earl of Desmond', 13 Aug. 1601, TNA, SP 63/209 pt 1, fo. 78.

220 S.G.E. Lythe, *The economy of Scotland in its European setting, 1550–1625* (Edinburgh, 1960), p. 66.

221 £300 worth of gunpowder and the same in lead, then stored at Dunaneeny, Co. Antrim. See Dalway to the Russell, 28 Oct. 1594, TNA, SP 63/177, fo. 18.

222 'Supplies to the rebels in Ireland', July 1600, HHA, CP 80/99. See also 'Petition to the lord deputy [Mountjoy] of Sir Ralph Lane', 26 Oct. 1602, *CSPI, 1601–3*, pp 502–5, which referred to 20 Scottish ships in Strangford Lough.

223 Dowdall to Burghley, 9 Mar. 1596, *CSPI, 1592–6*, pp 484–8; Sir George Clifford, earl of Cumberland, to the lord admiral [Charles Howard, first earl of Nottingham] and Cecil, 21 Dec. 1595, HHA, CP 36/90.

224 Sir James MacSorley MacDonnell to Robert Bowes, 2 Nov. 1597, *Cal. S.P. Scot., 1597–1603*, pp 122–3.

225 Queen Elizabeth to James VI, 11 May 1601, *Cal. S.P. Scot., 1597–1603*, pp 820–2.

226 Bowes to Burghley, 6 Nov. 1597, TNA, SP 52/61, fo. 56.

227 George Nicholson to Cecil, 10 Sept. 1598, *Cal. S.P. Scot., 1597–1603*, pp 277–9.

228 Wallace T. MacCaffery, *Elizabeth I: war and politics, 1588–1603* (Princeton, 1992), pp 326–7; 'Proclamation against aiding Tyrone and his rebels in Ireland', 18 June 1595, *The register of the privy council of Scotland*, v, pp 223–4; 'Proclamation restraining the support of the rebels in Ireland', 8 Aug. 1598, *Cal. S.P. Scot., 1597–1603*, pp 253–4; 'Supplies to the rebels in Ireland', July 1600, HHA, CP 80/99.

229 James VI to Tyrone, 1597, BL, Lansdowne, vol. 84, fo. 79; James VI to Tyrone, 22 Dec. 1597, *Cal. S.P. Scot., 1597–1603*, p. 1138; Tyrone to James VI, 10 Apr. 1600, TNA, SP 52/66, fo. 28.

230 Cecil to George Nicholson, 27 Apr. 1598, *Cal. S.P. Scot., 1597–1603*, pp 196–9; Nicholson to Bowes, 2 May 1598, *Cal. S.P. Scot., 1597–1603*, pp 203–5.

231 'Supplies to the rebels in Ireland', July 1600, HHA, CP 80/99.

232 Docwra to the privy council, 2 Nov. 1600, *CSPI, 1600–1*, pp 7–12.

233 Privy council to Mountjoy, March 1602, HHA, CP 85/128.

234 By spring 1601, Cecil had engaged in secret correspondence with James VI to ensure the Scottish succession. See Pauline Croft, *King James* (Houndmills, 2003), p. 48; 'Actions against certain men of Glasgow and Irvine for transporting ammunition and goods to the rebels in Ireland', 22 Dec. 1601, *The register of the privy council of Scotland*, v, p. 324

235 Croft, *King James*, p. 44.

236 Ibid., p. 45.

237 Cecil to Nicholson, 1 Apr. 1600, *Cal. Salisbury MSS*, x, pp 93–4.

238 'Statement handed to the king by the archbishop of Tuam [William Ó Mullaly]' [1593], *Cal. S.P. Spain, 1589–1603*, pp 610–11; Matthew De Oviedo to Philip III, 24 Apr. 1600, *Cal. S.P. Spain, 1589–1603*, pp 655–6; O'Donnell to Philip III, 15 Apr. 1602, *Cal. S.P. Spain, 1589–1603*, pp 709–10.

239 Fenton to Cecil, 2 July 1599, *CSPI, 1599–1600*, pp 77–8.

240 'Report of the Council of State to Philip III on Irish affairs', 1 Oct. 1602, *Cal. S.P. Spain, 1589–1603*, pp 715–16.

241 John Lynn (ed.), *Feeding Mars: logistics in western warfare from the Middle Ages to the present* (Boulder, 1993), ix; Van Creveld, *Supplying war*, pp 2–3.

242 Stewart, 'The Irish road', pp 16–37; McGurk, *The Elizabethan conquest of Ireland*, pp 195–219.

243 Black, *European warfare 1494–1660*, p. 24.

244 'Memorandum concerning the plantation at Ballyshannon' [June] 1600, *CSPI, 1600*, pp 279–83.

245 'The examination of Dermond McMorris, taken before me, Sir Francis Barkley', 29 Apr. 1601, *CSPI, 1600–1*, pp 296–9.

246 Lane to Mountjoy, 26 Oct. 1602, *CSPI, 1601–3*, pp 502–5.

247 Identified as supply bases in McGleenon, 'The battle of Mullabrack', p. 91.

248 Captain John Morgan to Russell, 28 Feb. 1595–6, TNA, SP 63/187, fo. 10.

249 Mountjoy called them Maharylogchoo and Loghlurgan. See Mountjoy and the council to the privy council, 26 Nov. 1600, *CSPI, 1600–1*, pp 32–5.

250 *Itinerary*, ii, pp 372–3; T.G.F. Patterson, 'Lough Rorkan and the O'Lorkans', *Seanchas Ardmhacha*, 3:2 (1959), pp 263–4.

251 Docwra to the privy council, 2 Jan. 1602, *CSPI, 1601–3*, pp 261–3.

252 *Life*, pp 219–21.

253 *DSP*, fo. 296.

254 *Q&A*, pp 91–2.

255 Ibid., pp 97–8.

256 'Intelligences for Her Majesty's services in the province of Leinster', 3 July 1600, TNA, SP 63/207 pt 4, fo. 9.

257 Fenton to Cecil, 11 Oct. 1599, *CSPI, 1599–1600*, pp 185–6.

258 Ibid.

259 Sir George Thornton to Essex, 15 Oct. 1599, *CSPI, 1599–1600*, pp 188–9.

260 Captain John Lye to Fenton, 21 Oct. 1599, TNA, SP 63/205, fo. 413.

261 Thornton to Essex, 31 Oct. 1599, *CSPI, 1599–1600*, pp 188–9.

262 Sir Robert Napper to Cecil, 18 Nov. 1599, *CSPI, 1599–1600*, pp 258–60.

263 Cecil to Sir William Warren, 6 Nov. 1599, *CSPI, 1599–1600*, pp 236–8.

264 Ibid.

265 Articles intended to be stood upon by Tyrone [Nov.], TNA, SP 63/206, fo. 152.

CHAPTER 5

English milk for Irish blood: Mountjoy and English resurgence, 1600–1

1   Mountjoy and council to the privy council, 1 Mar. 1600, *CSPI, 1600*, pp 1–5.

2   Jones, *Mountjoy, 1563–1606*, p. 28.

3   Quoted in Falls, *Mountjoy: Elizabethan general*, p. 106.

4   Jones, *Mountjoy, 1563–1606*, pp 38–9.

5   John Stowe, *Annales; or, General chronicle of England* (London, 1631), p. 805; Nolan, *Sir John Norreys*, pp 240–8.

6   *Itinerary*, ii, p. 338.

7   Sir Robert Naunton, *Fragmenta Regalia or Observations on the late Queen Elizabeth, her times and favourites* (London, 1641), p. 38; McGurk, 'Terrain and conquest', p. 96.

8   H.J. Edwards (trans.), *Caesar: the Gallic wars* (London, 1917), p. 375.

9   Instructions for Mountjoy [Jan.] 1600, TNA, SP 63/207 pt 1, fo. 193.

10 Certain points necessary for the army in Ireland [Jan.] 1600, TNA, SP 63/207 pt 1, fo. 208.

11 Tyrone to Essex, 10 Nov. 1599, *CSPI, 1599–1600*, pp 240–1.

12 Copy of instrument signed by Ormond and other nobles, 1 Dec. 1599, TNA, SP 63/206, fo. 158.

13 Ormond to the privy council, 4 Dec. 1599, *CSPI, 1599–1600*, pp 297–300.

14 A note of the levy of 5,000 foot, 30 Dec. 1599, TNA, SP 63/206, fo. 270.

15 'Intelligences drawn out of several letters, lately written from the north to Sir Geffrey Fenton', 7 Jan. 1600, *CSPI, 1599–1600*, pp 388–90.

16 Intelligences brought to Fenton, 19 Jan. 1600, *CSPI, 1599–1600*, pp 405–6.

17 Loftus, Carey and council to the privy council, 4 Feb. 1600, *CSPI, 1599–1600*, pp 455–7.

18 William Jones, commissary in Munster to Cecil, 17 Feb. 1600, *CSPI, 1599–1600*, pp 483–4.

19 Dermot McCragh[e] [bishop of Cork and Cloyne] and Eugenius Heganius, vicar apostolic to viscount Buttevant, 2/12 Feb. 1600, TNA, SP 63/207 pt 1, fo. 329. In April 1600, a papal bull of indulgence was sent by Clement VIII, forgiving the sins of all those who sided with Tyrone. See Bull of indulgence by Clement VIII, 18 Apr. 1600, *Carew, 1589–1600*, p. 523.

20 Sir Henry Power to the privy council, 4 Mar. 1600, *CSPI, 1600*, pp 15–16.

21 William Meade [mayor of Cork], to the privy council, 4 Mar. 1600, *CSPI, 1600*, pp 18–19.

22 *OSB*, pp 130–1.

23 William Lyon [Anglican bishop of Cork, Cloyne and Ross] to Cecil, 5 Mar. 1600, TNA, SP 63/ 207 pt 2, fo. 38.

24 *AFM*, vi, p. 2165.

25 Service done by the garrison of the Newry [Feb. 1600], TNA, SP 63/207 pt 2, fo. 64.

26 'Extracts of several letters written to Sir Geffrey Fenton concerning the arch traitor Tyrone', Mar. 1600, *CSPI, 1600*, pp 38–9.

27 Mountjoy and council to the privy council, 17 Mar. 1600, *CSPI, 1600*, pp 41–3.

28 Ormond to Mountjoy, 8 Mar. 1600, TNA, SP 63/207 pt 2, fo. 111.

29 Fenton to Cecil, 15 Mar. 1600, *CSPI, 1600*, p. 40.

30 Mountjoy and council to the privy council, 17 Mar. 1600, *CSPI, 1600*, pp 41–3.

31 Mountjoy to Cecil, 18 Mar. 1600, *CSPI, 1600*, pp 45–7.

32 Mountjoy and the council to the privy council, 1 Mar. 1600, *CSPI, 1600*, pp 1–5.

33 'The heads of those things wherein I [Mountjoy] am touched by Her Majesty or the Lords in their several letters', 27 Oct. 1600, *CSPI, 1600*, pp 501–10.

34 Ibid.

35 *Itinerary*, ii, pp 268–9.

36 Mountjoy to Cecil, 15 Apr. 1600, *CSPI, 1600*, pp 93–4.

37 Henry Hardware [Mayor of Chester], to the privy council, 7 Aug. 1600, *Cal. Salisbury MSS*, x, pp 268–9.

38 Mountjoy to the privy council, 13 Aug. 1600, *CSPI, 1600*, pp 349–53.

39 'Laws and orders of war established for the good conduct of the service of Ireland, by Lord Mountjoy', 1600, Lambeth, MS 614, fo. 216.

40 Carew and the council of Munster to the privy council, 30 Apr. 1600, TNA, SP 63/207 pt 2, fo. 359.

41 Mountjoy and council to the privy council, 14 June 1601, *CSPI, 1600–1*, pp 381–5.

42 *Itinerary*, ii, pp 269, 394.

43 McGurk, 'Terrain and conquest 1600–1603', pp 95–9.

44 *Q&A*, p. 101.

45 Mountjoy and council to the privy council, 14 June 1601, *CSPI, 1600–1*, pp 381–5.

46 Sir Thomas Norreys to the privy council, 9 Dec. 1599, *CSPI, 1598–9*, pp 399–401; Dowdall to Cecil, 2 Jan. 1600, Lambeth, MS 614, fo. 267.

47 Captain Nicholas Dawtrey to Sir John Fortescue, 7 Sept. 1600, TNA, SP 63/207 pt 5, fo. 19; Dawtrey to Cecil, 9 Feb. 1601, *CSPI, 1600–1*, pp 182–3.

48 Captain Humphrey Covert to Cecil [Dec. 1600], TNA, SP 63/207 pt 6, fo. 285; 'Captain Greame's letter and the other captains and officers to the president of Munster', 17 Sept. 1600, TNA, SP 63/207 pt 5, fo. 78.

49 *Pacata Hibernia*, ii, pp 255–6

50 Sir Oliver Lambert to Mountjoy, 22 Apr. 1600, *CSPI, 1600*, pp 114–15.

51 'The journey into Queen's County', Aug. [1600], TNA, SP 63/207 pt 4, fo. 293.

52 Evans, *The works of Sir Roger Williams*, p. 39.

53 'Journal of the Lord Lieutenant's journey into Leinster', 9–19 May 1599, *CSPI, 1599–1600*, pp 37–40.

54 Essex and council to the privy council, 9 May 1599, *CSPI, 1599–1600*, pp 29–32.

55 *Itinerary*, ii, pp 334–6.

56 Aelianus [Capt. John Bingham], *The tactics of Aelian* (London, 1616), pp 153–6.

57 Parker, *The military revolution*, p. 20; Keith Roberts, *Pike and shot tactics, 1590–1660* (Oxford, 2010), p. 35; de Moor, 'Experience and experiment', pp 25–6.

58 Captain John Chamberlain to Essex, 14/24 Nov. 1598, HHA, CP 65/97.

59 'The points which Her Majesty is to afford him that shall be sent to recover Ireland', 7 Nov. 1598, TNA, SP 63/202 pt 3, fo. 336.

60 Prince Maurice to Essex, 16/26 Dec. 1598, *Cal. Salisbury MSS*, vii, p. 502.

61 John Derricke, *Image of Ireland* (London, 1581).

62 'Ordinances to be observed during the wars in Ireland, 1600', [Feb.] 1600, *Carew, 1589–1600*, pp 365–6.

63 'Letters to the lord lieutenants and commissioners for the musters of the several counties undernamed', 28 Apr. 1601, *APC*, xxxi, pp 311–13.

64 Evans (ed.), *The works of Sir Roger Williams*, pp 30–3.

65 Webb, *Elizabethan military science*, p. 121.

66 David R. Lawrence, *The complete soldier: military books and military culture in early Stuart England, 1603–1645* (Leiden, 2009), p. 268.

67 John Tincey, *The Armada campaign 1588* (Oxford, 1999), pp 62–3.

68 'The army at Lough Foyle', 29 Sept. 1600, *Carew, 1589–1600*, pp 455–6.

69 Mountjoy to the privy council, 13 Aug. 1600, *CSPI, 1600*, pp 349–53.

70 Mountjoy to the privy council, 1 Apr. 1600, *CSPI, 1600*, pp 66–7.

71 'Remembrances for the service of Ireland, taken at Mr Secretary's [Cecil's] house', 11 June 1600, TNA, SP 63/207 pt 3, fo. 256.

72 Ibid.

73 *Itinerary*, ii, p. 268.

74 Mountjoy and the council to the privy council, 1 Apr. 1600, *CSPI, 1600*, pp 66–7.

75 Mountjoy to the privy council, 15 Apr. 1600, *CSPI, 1600*, pp 91–3.

76 Ibid.; Fenton to Cecil, 8 Apr. 1600, *CSPI, 1600*, pp 81–3.

77 Mountjoy to Cecil, 9 Apr. 1600, *CSPI, 1600*, pp 85–7.

78 Fenton to Cecil, 20 May 1600, *CSPI, 1600*, pp 188–9.

79 Ibid.

80 Mountjoy to Cecil, 19 June 1600, *CSPI, 1600*, pp 252–4.

81 Plot by Captain William Piers, 6 Nov. 1594, TNA, SP 63/177, fo. 3.

82 Instructions from Mountjoy and council to Docwra, Mar. 1599 [1600], *Carew, 1589–1600*, pp 374–6.

83 Fenton to Cecil, 11 Jan. 1600, *CSPI, 1599–1600*, pp 400–1.

84 William Kelly (ed.), *Docwra's Derry: a narration of events on north-west Ulster, 1600–1604* (Belfast, 2003), p. 43.

85 Ibid., p. 44.

86 'Intelligence upon the designs of the arch traitor Tyrone with landing of the army at Lough Foyle', 12 Mar. 1598/9, HHA, CP 139/54; Fenton to Cecil, 1 Apr. 1600, *CSPI, 1600*, pp 67–8.

87 Mountjoy and the council to the privy council, 17 Mar. 1600, TNA, SP 63/207 pt 2, fo. 109.

88 William Hartpoole to Mountjoy, 11 Apr. 1600, TNA, SP 63/207 pt 2, fo. 246.

89 Mountjoy to Cecil, 12 Apr. 1600, *CSPI, 1600*, p. 87.

90 Extracts from diverse letters, 2 May 1600, TNA, SP 63/207 pt 3, fo. 26; Henry Bird to Cecil, 10 May 1600, *CSPI, 1600*, pp 171–3.

91 Captain [Edward] Blaney's report of the earl of Southampton's passing through the Moyry, 17 May 1600, *CSPI, 1600*, pp 190–2.

92 McGurk, *Sir Henry Docwra*, pp 68–9.

93 Kelly, *Docwra's Derry*, p. 51.

94 Hiram Morgan, 'The real Red Hugh' in Pádraig Ó Riain (ed.), *Beatha Aodha Ruaidh: the life of Red Hugh O'Donnell historical and literary contexts* (London, 2002), p. 4.

95 Quoted in Morgan, 'Mission comparable', p. 82.

96 Falls, *Elizabeth's Irish wars*, p. 136.

97 Terry Clavin, 'Sir George Carew', *DIB*, viewed at http://dib.cambridge.org/viewReadPage. do?articleId=a1464&searchClicked=clicked&quickadvsearch=yes, on 5 July 2011.

98 Treatise on Ireland by Sir George Carew, 13 Apr. 1594, TNA, SP 63/174, fo. 28.

99 Ibid.

100 Carew to Cecil, 2 May 1600, *CSPI, 1600*, pp 141–6.

101 Entry for James Fitzthomas Fitzgerald in *DIB*, viewed at http://dib.cambridge.org/view ReadPage.do?articleId=a3162&searchClicked=clicked&quickadvsearch=yes on 8 Apr. 2013.

102 Sheehan, 'The overthrow of the plantation of Munster', p. 15.

103 Terry Clavin, entry for James Fitzthomas Fitzgerald in *DIB* viewed at http://dib.cambridge. org/viewReadPage.do?articleId=a3162 on 6 July 2011.

104 Carew to Cecil, 2 May 1600, *CSPI, 1600*, pp 141–6; *Pacata Hibernia*, ii, pp 275–6.

105 *Pacata Hibernia*, i, pp 109–10

106 Ibid., pp 131–3.

107 'Memoranda on the state of affairs in Ireland' [19 Apr.] 1600, TNA, SP 63/207 pt 2, fo. 300.

108 Carew to the privy council, 17 June 1600, *CSPI, 1600*, pp 241–51.

109 *Pacata Hibernia*, i, p. 60.

110 *Pacata Hibernia*, i, pp 47–8; Carew to Cecil, 2 May 1600, *CSPI, 1600*, pp 141–6.

111 Cecil to Carew, 24 Sept. 1600, *Cecil–Carew Letters*, pp 29–33.

112 *Pacata Hibernia*, i, p. 28.

113 *Pacata Hibernia*, i, pp 37–8.

114 Carew to the privy council [12 Jan.?] 1601, *CSPI, 1600–1*, pp 143–5.

115 Daniel MacCarthy claimed there were 10,706 rebels pardoned. See Daniel MacCarthy (ed.), *The life and letters of Florence MacCarthy Reagh* (London, 1867), p. 315.

116 Ibid., pp 49–50.
117 Carew to the privy council, 15 Dec. 1600, *CSPI, 1600–1*, pp 59–63.
118 Sir Henry Power to the privy council, 30 Apr. 1600, *CSPI, 1600*, pp 131–4.
119 Carew to the privy council, 17 June 1600, *CSPI, 1600*, pp 241–6.
120 *Pacata Hibernia*, i, pp 27–8.
121 Carew to the privy council, 17 June 1600, *Carew, 1589–1600*, pp 399–403.
122 'Memoranda on the state of affairs in Ireland', 19 Apr. 1600, TNA, SP 63/207 pt 2, fo. 300.
123 Carew and council of Munster to the privy council, 19 May 1600, *CSPI, 1600*, pp 182–5.
124 Carew to the privy council, 17 June 1600, *CSPI, 1600*, pp 241–6.
125 Carew to the privy council, 25 Aug. 1600, *CSPI, 1600*, pp 366–71.
126 Carew to [Cecil], 6 Aug. 1601, *CSPI, 1601–3*, pp 5–7.
127 Carew to Cecil, 30 Aug. 1600, *CSPI, 1600*, pp 389–91.
128 Carew to Cecil [14] Jan. 1602, *CSPI, 1601–3*, pp 278–9.
129 Carew to the privy council, 15 Dec. 1600, *CSPI, 1600–1*, pp 59–63; *Pacata Hibernia*, i, pp 157–8.
130 Carew to Cecil, 29 May 1602, *CSPI, 1601–3*, pp 392–6.
131 *Pacata Hibernia*, ii, pp 276, 291.
132 Carew to the privy council, 12 Jan. 1601, *CSPI, 1600–1*, pp 143–5.
133 Mountjoy to Cecil, 12 Oct. 1602, TNA, SP 63/212, fo. 110.
134 *OSB*, p. 133.
135 Carew to Cecil, 27 June 1600, *CSPI, 1600*, pp 260–6.
136 *AFM*, vi, p. 2171.
137 *Pacata Hibernia*, i, p. 68.
138 Ibid., p. 67.
139 Ibid., pp 69–70.
140 Carew to Cecil, 27 June 1600, *CSPI, 1600*, pp 260–6.
141 *OSB*, p. 134; *AFM*, vi, pp 2173–5.
142 *AFM*, vi, p. 2175.
143 Carew to Cecil, 27 June 1600, *CSPI, 1600*, pp 260–6.
144 Miler Magrath, archbishop of Cashel, to Cecil, 31 Aug. 1600, *Cal. Salisbury MSS*, x, pp 297–300.
145 Captain Francis Kingsmill to Cecil, 22 Aug. 1599, *CSPI, 1599–1600*, pp 128–9.
146 *OSB*, p. 133.
147 'The copy of Captain Greame's letter and the other captains and officers to the president of Munster', 17 Sept. 1600, TNA, SP 63/207 pt 5, fo. 78.
148 *Pacata Hibernia*, i, p. 207.
149 Savage to Cecil, 3 July 1600, *CSPI, 1600*, pp 291–4.
150 Mountjoy to Cecil, 4 July 1600, *CSPI, 1600*, pp 299–302.
151 Carey to Cecil, 24 July 1600, *CSPI, 1600*, pp 329–30.
152 'The journey into the Queen's County [Laois]', Aug. [1600], *CSPI, 1600*, pp 394–7.
153 *OSB*, p. 133.
154 Donal Spaniagh [Kavanagh] to Ormond, 19 Aug. 1600, TNA, SP 63/207 pt 4, fo. 192.
155 'The journey into the Queen's County [Laois]', Aug. [1600], *CSPI, 1600*, pp 394–7.
156 The privy council to Mountjoy, 17 July 1600, *APC*, xxx, pp 506–15.
157 Queen Elizabeth to Mountjoy, 20 July 1600, *CSPI, 1600*, pp 324–7.
158 The privy council to Mountjoy, 10 Aug. 1600, *APC*, xxx, pp 572–5; Mountjoy to Cecil, 31 Aug. 1600, TNA, SP 63/207 pt 4, fo. 298.
159 The list as such are appointed for the northern service, 15 Sept. 1600, TNA SP 63/207 pt 5, fo. 44. This was accounted for by list, but the real number (by poll) was much lower.

Moryson recorded just 2,640 infantry by poll in the camp at Faughart. See *Itinerary*, ii, pp 340–6.

160 'Journal of Mountjoy's journey into the north' [28 Oct.] 1600, *CSPI, 1600*, pp 524–30.

161 Stafford to Cecil, 4 Oct. 1600, *CSPI, 1600*, pp 461–3.

162 'Journal of Mountjoy's journey into the north' [28 Oct.] 1600, *CSPI, 1600*, pp 524–30.

163 Sir Robert Lovell to Essex, 5 Oct. 1600, *CSPI, 1600*, p. 463.

164 See Lane to Cecil, 14 Nov. 1600, TNA, SP 63/207 pt 6, fo. 59.

165 'A brief journal of my Lord Deputy's second voyage into the north' [19 Nov.] 1600, TNA SP 63/207 pt 6, fo. 67. Sir Ralph Lane to Cecil, 14 Nov. 1600, TNA SP 63, 207 pt 6, fo. 59; H.G. Tempest, 'The Moyry Pass', *Journal of the County Louth Archaeological Society*, 14:2 (1958), pp 82–90.

166 Queen Elizabeth to Mountjoy, 3 Dec. 1600, *Carew, 1589–1600*, pp 481–2.

167 Mountjoy, Stafford and Sir Richard Wingfield to the council, 22 May 1600, *CSPI, 1600*, pp 205–7; St Leger to Cecil 28 July 1600, *CSPI, 1600*, pp 331–2; Mountjoy to Cecil, 7 Aug. 1600, *CSPI, 1600*, pp 337–9; *Itinerary*, ii, p. 350.

168 Willis to Cecil, 24 Jan. 1601, TNA, SP 63/208 pt 1, fo. 44.

169 Sir Theobald Dillon to Cecil, 25 Mar. 1601, *CSPI, 1600–1*, pp 239–40.

170 Carey to Cecil, 21 May 1601, *CSPI, 1600–1*, pp 351–2.

171 Docwra to the privy council, 24 May 1600, *CSPI, 1600*, pp 194–8.

172 Essex and the council to the privy council, 9 May 1599, *CSPI, 1599–1600*, pp 29–32.

173 Mountjoy and council to the privy council, 7 Feb. 1601, *CSPI, 1600–1*, pp 178–80.

174 *Itinerary*, ii, pp 270–1.

175 Docwra to the privy council, 24 May 1600, *CSPI, 1600*, pp 194–8.

176 *Itinerary*, iii, p. 178.

177 'Intelligence from the North; in the handwriting of Sir George Carey', 9 July 1600, *CSPI, 1600*, pp 305–6.

178 Sir William Warren to Cecil, 5 Dec. 1599, *CSPI, 1599–1600*, pp 305–7.

179 Mountjoy to Cecil, 4 July 1600, *CSPI, 1600*, pp 299–302.

180 Morgan, *Tyrone's rebellion*, p. 133.

181 Darren McGettigan, 'A house divided: the political community of the lordship of Tír Chonnaill and reaction to the Nine Years War' in Robert Armstrong and Tadhg Ó hAnnracháin (eds), *Community in early modern Ireland* (Dublin, 2006), pp 100–1.

182 Mountjoy to Cecil, 16 July 1600, *CSPI, 1600*, pp 306–7.

183 'Concordatums paid in the government of the Lord Mountjoy, between the 1 Feb. 1599 [1600] and 20 Apr.', 13 May 1600, TNA, SP 63/207 pt 3, fos. 92–4.

184 Stafford to Cecil, 28 Apr. 1600, TNA, SP 63/207 pt 2, fo. 352.

185 Mountjoy to Cecil, 7 Aug. 1600, *CSPI, 1600*, pp 337–9.

186 *Itinerary*, ii, p. 326.

187 Ibid.

188 Captain John Dowdall's riverine campaign in Fermanagh 1593–4 and Sir George Bingham's raid into Lough Swilly in 1595.

189 For an examination of English naval operations in Ireland see Tom Glasgow, 'The Elizabethan navy in Ireland', *Irish Sword*, 7:29 (1965–6), pp 291–307.

190 Willis to Cecil, 24 Jan. 1601, *CSPI, 1600–1*, pp 158–61.

191 Mountjoy and the council to the privy council, 28 Mar. 1601, *CSPI, 1600–1*, pp 244–6.

192 John McGurk, 'English naval operations at Kinsale' in Morgan (ed.), *The battle of Kinsale*, pp 155–7.

193 *Pacata Hibernia*, ii, pp 174–82.

194 'Copy, certified by Sir George Carew, of a letter from Hugh Roe O'Donnell to Florence McCarthy', Oct. 1600, *CSPI, 1600*, p. 539.
195 Captain George Thornton to Russell, 1 Oct. 1595, TNA, SP 63/183, fo. 253.
196 *Itinerary*, ii, p. 327.
197 Carew to the privy council, 17 June 1600, *CSPI, 1600*, pp 241–6.
198 Anthony Dawtrey to Sir Arthur Chichester, 14 May 1601, *CSPI, 1600–1*, p. 332.
199 Chichester to Cecil, 15 May 1601, *CSPI, 1600–1*, pp 332–5.
200 Mountjoy to Carey, 23 May 1601, TNA, SP 63/208 pt 2, fo. 288.
201 Chichester to the privy council, 8 July 1601, *CSPI, 1600–1*, pp 417–20.
202 Mountjoy and the council to the privy council, 17 Mar. 1600, TNA, SP 63/207 pt 2, fo. 109.
203 Carey to Cecil, 6 Oct. 1601, *CSPI, 1601–3*, pp 115–16. Unsurprisingly, Tyrone attempted to do the same thing in the Pale. See Loftus and council in Dublin to the English privy council, 6 Oct. 1601, TNA, SP 63/209 pt 2, fo. 37.
204 *Itinerary*, ii, p. 350.
205 Ibid., p. 270.
206 The use of subterfuge is often associated with the weak, as the strong have a more relaxed and overconfident approach to war with those they perceive to be much less powerful than themselves. See John Gooch and Amos Perlmutter (eds), *Military deception and strategic surprise* (London, 2007), p. 1
207 Joshua Aylmer to Cecil, 21 Apr. 1600, *CSPI, 1600*, pp 112–14.
208 'The copy of Captain Greame's letter and the other captains and officers to the president of Munster', 17 Sept. 1600, TNA, SP 63/207 pt 5, fo. 78.
209 Captain Nicholas Dawtrey to Cecil, 31 Jan. 1601, *CSPI, 1600–1601*, pp 168–71.
210 Pádraig Lenihan, 'Celtic warfare in the 1640s' in John R. Young (ed.), *Celtic dimensions of the British civil wars* (Edinburgh, 1997), pp 120–1. This was in response to an assertion that the Irish predilection for a charge into close combat was rooted in an ancestral style of warfare, based upon 'fury, strength and dexterity to overcome a lack of military sophistication'. See James M. Hill, *Celtic warfare, 1595–1763* (Edinburgh, 2003), p. 1.
211 Lenihan, 'Celtic warfare in the 1640s', p. 123.
212 At the end of 1598 when the Leinster forces under O'More were withdrawing from Munster, Captain Tyrrell remained to train those troops who were 'as yet unskilful'. See [Anon.] to Loftus and Gardiner, 1 Nov. 1598, TNA, SP 63/202 pt 3, fo. 297. Tyrone clearly intended for the Munster forces to be trained and equipped in the same manner as the rest of his armies.
213 Barret, *The theorike and practike of moderne warres*, p. 69.
214 Sir John Smythe, *Instructions, observations, and orders mylitarie* (London, 1595), pp 25–6. Thomas Douglas to Mountjoy [c.Apr. 1601], *Cal. S.P. Scot., 1597–1603*, part 2, pp 1138–43.
215 Referred to in Cuney to Essex, 28 Oct. 1598, HHA, CP 177/131. See Chapters 2 and 3.
216 'A brief declaration of the state wherein Ireland now standeth' [1599], *CSPI, 1599–1600*, pp 365–70.
217 Captain Francis Kingsmill to Cecil, 22 Aug. 1599, *CSPI, 1599–1600*, pp 128–30.
218 Donough O'Brien, earl of Thomond to Cecil, 14 Sept. 1599, *CSPI, 1599–1600*, pp 153–4.
219 Carew to the privy council, 30 Aug. 1600, *CSPI, 1600*, pp 387–9.
220 *Pacata Hibernia*, i, pp 189–90, 202–3.
221 'Note for Mr Secretary [Cecil] touching Leinster', Sept. 1600, TNA, SP 63/207 pt 5, fo. 220.
222 Mountjoy and council to the privy council, 11 Dec. 1600, *CSPI, 1600–1*, pp 55–7.
223 Mountjoy to Carew, 11 Mar. 1601, Lambeth, MS 615, fo. 117; Mountjoy and council to the privy council, 15 Mar. 1601, *CSPI, 1600–1*, pp 225–8.

224 *Life*, p. 201; *Q&A*, p. 96.
225 'A journal of Sir Thomas Norreys', 5 Apr. 1599, TNA, SP 63/205, fo. 21.
226 'Captain Richard Greame and other officers to Carew', 17 Sept. 1600, TNA, SP 63/207 pt 5, fo. 78.
227 Fenton to Cecil, 26 Oct. 1601, *CSPI, 1601–3*, pp 141–2.
228 Stafford to Cecil, 7 Dec. 1601, *CSPI, 1601–3*, pp 203–4. For a reference to Tyrone's sluggishness see *AFM*, vi, p. 2277.
229 *Q&A*, pp 91–2, 96–7.
230 *Life*, pp 219–21.
231 Sir Patrick Barnewall to Cecil, 29 Jan. 1601, TNA, SP 63/208 pt 1, fo. 58.
232 Mountjoy to Carew, 7 Feb. 1601, TNA, SP 63/208 pt 1, fo. 106.
233 Carew to Cecil, 11 Feb. 1601, *CSPI, 1600–1*, pp 186–8.
234 *Pacata Hibernia*, i, p. 190.
235 Carew to the privy council, 2 May 1601, *Carew, 1601–3*, pp 53–6.
236 Sir Francis Shane to Cecil, 22 Feb. 1601, *CSPI, 1600–1*, pp 195–8.
237 Mountjoy and council to the privy council, 15 Mar. 1601, *CSPI, 1600–1*, pp 225–8.
238 Chichester to Cecil, 12 Apr. 1601, *CSPI, 1600–1*, pp 268–72.
239 C.E. Challis, *The Tudor coinage* (Manchester, 1978), p. 268.
240 Ibid., pp 268–74. Research on the 1601 debasement has explored the issue of raising revenue, but the dual intent of the crown has not been made clear. See Joseph McLaughlin, 'What base coin wrought: the effects of the Elizabethan debasement in Ireland' in Morgan (ed.), *The battle of Kinsale*, pp 193–204.
241 'Proclamation concerning the new moneys for Ireland', 20 May 1601, TNA, SP 63/208 pt 2, fo. 231.
242 This could be viewed as an application of Gresham's Law which states that bad money drives out good money where both are legal tender. See J. Rolnick and Warren E. Weber, 'Gresham's law or Gresham's fallacy?', *Journal of Political Economy*, 94:1 (1986), pp 185–6, but in the case of the 1601 debasement, the previous monies were decried by the government and were declared bullion to be returned to the exchange.
243 This was the opinion of the English privy council who reported that 'the rebel hath more of the coin than the subject'. See privy council to Mountjoy, Gardiner, chief justices of Her Majesty's bench and Fenton, 3 Mar. 1601, *APC*, xxxi, pp 197–8.
244 'Discourse on the standard of Ireland', 1601, TNA, SP 63/209 pt 2, fo. 354.
245 McLaughlin, 'What base coin wrought', p. 195.
246 'Questions upon the benefits growing by making base money, with the objections thereunto' [Dec. 1600], *CSPI, 1600–1*, p. 127 and, TNA, SP 63/207 pt 6, fo. 335. The author goes on to dismiss the purported advantages of debasement as fallacies, but it is clear that the three reasons were given value at court.
247 'Proclamation concerning the new moneys for Ireland', 20 May 1601, TNA, SP 63/208 pt 2, fo. 231; The exchange: proclamation by the queen', 24 Jan. 1602[3], Lambeth, MS 607, fo. 244.
248 Carew to Cecil, 11 May 1601, Lambeth, MS 604, fo. 161.
249 Joseph McLaughlin, 'New light on Richard Hadsor II: Richard Hadsor "Discourse" on the Irish state, 1604', *IHS*, 30:119 (1997), p. 338; 'Proclamation concerning the new moneys for Ireland', 20 May 1601, TNA, SP 63/208 pt 2, fo. 231.
250 Docwra to the privy council of England, 2 Sept. 1601, *CSPI, 1601–3*, pp 45–6; Chichester to Cecil, 8 Oct. 1601, *CSPI, 1601–3*, pp 110–12.
251 'The mayor and sheriffs of Dublin to Cecil', 7 Jan. 1603, *CSPI, 1601–3*, p. 551.
252 Mountjoy and council to the privy council, 26 Jan. 1603, *CSPI, 1601–3*, pp 559–61.

253 'The exchange: proclamation by the queen', 24 Jan. 1602, Lambeth, MS 607, fo. 244.

254 'Proclamation by the lord deputy and council', 9 June 1602, Lambeth, MS 617, fo. 264.

255 Mountjoy and council in Dublin to the privy council [26] Feb. 1603, Lambeth, MS 615, fo. 450.

256 Carew to the privy council, 22 Jan. 1603, *Carew, 1601–3*, pp 403–9; 'A project for Ireland for coin by the lord deputy and council there' [Feb.] 1603, Lambeth, MS 621, fo. 141.

257 Challis, *The Tudor coinage*, pp 272–3.

258 *OSB*, pp 56–7.

259 Mountjoy to the privy council, 1 May 1601, *CSPI, 1600–1*, pp 303–5.

260 Chichester to Mountjoy, 14 May 1601, TNA, SP 63/208 pt 2, fo. 248.

261 *Itinerary*, ii, p. 391.

262 Ibid., pp 398–9.

263 Docwra to the privy council, 10 Aug. 1601, *CSPI, 1601–3*, pp 20–3.

264 *Itinerary*, ii, p. 396.

265 Mountjoy to Carew, 14 July 1601, *Carew, 1601–3*, pp 107–9.

266 Ibid., p. 408.

267 Mountjoy, Wingfield and Bourchier to the privy council, 19 July 1601, *CSPI, 1600–1*, pp 438–42.

268 Ibid. A note of such as were slain and hurt in winning our passage over the Blackwater, July 1601, TNA, SP 63/208 pt 3, fo. 203.

269 Sir Edward Fitzgerald to Cecil, 21 July 1601, TNA, SP 63/208 pt 3, fo. 245.

270 Armagh city and Mullin fort, 1602, NLI, MS 2656, iii.

271 Mountjoy, Wingfield and Bourchier to the privy council, 19 July 1601, *CSPI, 1600–1*, pp 438–42.

272 Proclamation signed by Mountjoy, Wingfield and Bourchier, 18 July 1601, *CSPI, 1600–1*, pp 442–3.

273 Mountjoy and council to the privy council, 9 Aug. 1601, *CSPI, 1600–1*, pp 10–12.

274 Sir Richard Greame to Cecil, 9 Aug. 1601, TNA, SP 63/209 pt 1, fo. 33.

275 Carey to Cecil, 10 Aug. 1601, TNA, SP 63/209 pt 1, fo. 46.

276 Mountjoy and council to the privy council, 3 Sept. 1601, *CSPI, 1601–3*, pp 49–51.

277 Mountjoy to Carey, 12 Sept. 1601, *CSPI, 1601–3*, p. 71.

278 John Meade [mayor of Cork] to Mountjoy, 21 Sept. 1601, TNA, SP 63/209 pt 1, fo. 228.

CHAPTER 6

The catastrophe of war and the road to Mellifont, 1601–3

1 Hayes-McCoy, *Scots mercenary forces in Ireland*; D.B. Quinn, *The Elizabethans and the Irish* (Ithaca, 1966); Canny, 'The ideology of English colonialism', pp 575–98. See also Alfred O'Rahilly, *The massacre at Smerwick, 1580* (Cork, 1938).

2 Bradshaw, 'Nationalism and historical scholarship in modern Ireland', pp 29–51.

3 Edwards et al. (eds), *Age of atrocity* (Dublin, 2007).

4 Carey, 'What pen can paint or tears atone?', p. 215.

5 Thanks to David Edwards for highlighting the effects of the deaths of kindred in a lineage-based society.

6 Clodagh Tait, David Edwards and Pádraig Lenihan, 'Early modern Ireland: a history of violence' in Edwards et al. (eds), *Age of atrocity*, pp 9–33.

7 Morgan, 'Mission comparable?', p. 78.

8 John J. Silke, 'Kinsale reconsidered', *Studies: An Irish Quarterly Review*, 90:360 (2001), p. 413.

9   Silke, *Kinsale*, p. 112.

10 *Pacata Hibernia*, i, pp 291–2.

11 Mountjoy and council to the privy council, 1 Oct. 1601, *CSPI, 1601–3*, pp 104–5.

12 *Pacata Hibernia*, i, p. 282.

13 *Itinerary*, iii, p. 14; Carew to Cecil, 24 Oct. 1601, *CSPI, 1601–3*, pp 139–40.

14 *Itinerary*, iii, p. 28.

15 Hiram Morgan, 'Disaster at Kinsale' in Morgan (ed.), *Battle of Kinsale*, p. 102.

16 Mountjoy to Loftus and the council in Dublin, 25 Oct. 1601, TNA, SP 63/209 pt 2, fo. 126.

17 A list of companies appointed to come to the camp near Kinsale, 25 Oct. 1601, TNA, SP 63/209 pt 2, fo. 128.

18 Silke, *Kinsale*, p. 125.

19 'Difficulties and impediments in our way since the discovery of the Spanish fleet before their entry into Kinsale' [Nov. 1601], *CSPI, 1601–3*, pp 211–12.

20 *Itinerary*, iii, p. 62.

21 Morgan, 'Disaster at Kinsale', p. 118.

22 *Itinerary*, iii, p. 62.

23 Ibid., p. 73.

24 Morgan, 'Disaster at Kinsale', p. 121.

25 Don Juan del Águila to General Pedro Lopez de Soto, 12 Feb. 1601, *CSPI, 1601–3*, pp 641–3.

26 Henry Power to Cecil, 27 Dec. 1601, *CSPI, 1601–3*, pp 241–2; also the erroneously titled 'An account of the proceedings of the lord deputy in Ireland (Essex) [no date], BL, Cotton Julius F/VI fo. 207.

27 Moryson, *Unpublished itinerary*, p. 69; Ciaran O'Scea, 'A newly discovered account of the battle of Kinsale, 1601–2' in Morgan (ed.), *Battle of Kinsale*, p. 371; Intelligence as to Tyrone's retreat, 13 Jan. 1602, *CSPI, 1601–3*, pp 283–4.

28 'An account of the proceedings of the lord deputy in Ireland (Essex) [Mountjoy] [no date], BL, Cotton Julius F/VI fo. 207.

29 Silke, *Kinsale*, p. 146.

30 C. Litton Falkiner, 'William Farmer's chronicles of Ireland from 1594 to 1613', *English Historical Review*, 22:85 (1907), p. 125.

31 *Pacata Hibernia*, ii, p. 63.

32 *Itinerary*, iii, pp 88–95.

33 Stafford to Cecil, 14 Jan. 1602, *CSPI, 1601–3*, pp 284–6.

34 Intelligence as to Tyrone's retreat, 13 Jan. 1602, *CSPI, 1601–3*, pp 283–4.

35 Fenton to Cecil, 5 Feb. 1602, TNA, SP 63/210, fo. 99.

36 *AFM*, vi, pp 2161–3.

37 Garrett Moore to Mountjoy, 15 Apr. 1600, TNA, SP 63/207 pt 2, fo. 286.

38 Stafford to Cecil, 28 Apr. 1600, TNA, SP 63/207 pt 2, fo. 352.

39 *The discovery and recovery of Ireland with the author's apology by Thomas Lee*, BL Add. MSS, 33743, fo. 10, John McGurk (transc.), viewed at http://www.ucc.ie/celt/published/E590001-005/index.html on 2 Feb. 2013.

40 Lennon, *Sixteenth-century Ireland*, p. 53.

41 Nicholls, *Gaelic and Gaelicized Ireland*, pp 41–3.

42 Fenton to Cecil, 6 Jan. 1602, *CSPI, 1601–3*, pp 205–6.

43 'Extraordinaries granted by lord Mountjoy and the council from 20 July to 30 September', 30 Sept. 1600, TNA, SP 63/207 pt 5, fo. 183.

44 As seen in a reference to Phelim MacFeagh O'Byrne in Ormond to Sir Thomas Norreys, 9 Nov. 1597, *CSPI, 1596–7*, pp 446–7.

45 Sir Francis Shane to Cecil, 8 Apr. 1600, TNA, SP 63/207 pt 2, fo. 238.

46 'Copies of Tyrone's letters', 22 Apr.–2 May 1600, *CSPI, 1600*, pp 122–3.
47 Ormond to Queen Elizabeth, 16 June 1600, TNA, SP 63/207 pt 3, fo. 275.
48 *Pacata Hibernia*, i, pp 50–1, 249–50.
49 Tyrone to Florence MacCarthy, 5 Feb. 1601, TNA, SP 63/208 pt 3, fo. 54.
50 Chichester to Mountjoy, 14 May 1601, *CSPI, 1600–1*, pp 355–8; Fenton to Cecil, 6 Jan. 1602, TNA, SP 63/210, fo. 11.
51 The entry of Mountjoy in the midlands precipitated the submission of the O'Molloys, O'Dempseys, O'Doynes, O'Carrolls who started cutting their passes for Mountjoy in September 1600. See 'Note for Mr Secretary [Cecil] touching Leinster', Sept. 1600, TNA, SP 63/207 pt 5, fo. 220.
52 Carew to Cecil, 26 Dec. 1601, TNA, SP 63/209 pt 2, fo. 394; Stafford to Cecil, 14 Jan. 1602, *CSPI, 1601–3*, pp 284–6.
53 Fenton to Cecil, 5 Feb. 1602, TNA, SP 63/210, fo. 99.
54 Stafford to Cecil, 14 Jan. 1602, TNA, SP 63/210, fo. 75.
55 Carew to Cecil, 14 Jan. 1602, *CSPI, 1601–3*, pp 275–8.
56 Minute from the privy council to Mountjoy, March [1602], HHA, CP 85/128.
57 Carew to Cecil, 14 Jan. 1602, *CSPI, 1601–3*, pp 275–8.
58 Fenton to Cecil, 6 Jan. 1602, *CSPI, 1601–3*, pp 265–6.
59 Carew to Cecil, 12 Mar. 1602, *CSPI, 1601–3*, pp 328–30.
60 Minute from the privy council to Mountjoy, March [1602], HHA, CP 85/128.
61 Chichester to Cecil, 22 Nov. 1601, *CSPI, 1601–3*, pp 174–5.
62 Docwra to the privy Council, 2 Jan. 1602, *CSPI, 1601–3*, pp 261–3.
63 McGurk, *Sir Henry Docwra*, p. 180.
64 Chichester to Cecil, 14 Mar. 1602, *CSPI, 1601–3*, pp 334–7.
65 *Pacata Hibernia*, ii, p. 149.
66 John Maclean (ed.), *Letters from Sir Robert Cecil to Sir George Carew* (London, 1864), pp 106–7.
67 Carew to Cecil, 13 Apr. 1602, *CSPI, 1601–3*, pp 361–2.
68 *Pacata Hibernia*, ii, pp 164–7.
69 Carew to Cecil, 19 Apr. 1602, *CSPI, 1601–3*, pp 370–1.
70 Carew to Cecil, 29 May 1602, TNA, SP 63/211, fo. 111.
71 *Pacata Hibernia*, ii, pp 156–7.
72 *Pacata Hibernia*, ii, pp 180–1.
73 *Pacata Hibernia*, ii, p. 199.
74 Examination of Anthony Ketley, 2 June 1602, *Cal. Salisbury MSS*, xii, p. 181; Declaration of John Burleigh of the Isle of Wight, 7 July 1602, HHA, CP 94/9.
75 *Pacata Hibernia*, ii, pp 183–4.
76 [Cecil], draft letter, July 1602, *Cal. Salisbury MSS*, xii, p. 271; Mountjoy and council to the privy council, 28 Apr. 1602, *CSPI, 1601–3*, pp 377–81.
77 Mountjoy and council to the privy council, 29 July 1602, *Carew, 1601–3*, pp 282–4.
78 Carew to the privy council, 13 July 1602, *Carew, 1601–3*, pp 265–7.
79 Mountjoy to Cecil, 12 Oct. 1602, TNA, SP 63/212, fo. 110; *Pacata Hibernia*, ii, p. 255.
80 *Pacata Hibernia*, ii, pp 212–13.
81 *Itinerary*, iii, p. 286
82 Lambert to Mountjoy, 18 June 1602, *CSPI, 1601–3*, pp 418–21.
83 *Itinerary*, iii, p. 166.
84 Mountjoy to Carey, 23 June 1602, TNA, SP 63/211, fo. 175.
85 Mountjoy to the privy council, 29 July 1602, *CSPI, 1601–3*, pp 458–9; *Itinerary*, iii, p. 182.
86 Mountjoy to Carew, 2 July 1602, *Carew, 1601–3*, pp 263–4.

87 Chichester to Cecil, 14 Mar. 1602, TNA, SP 63/210, fo. 188.
88 Fenton to Cecil, 15 July 1602, TNA, SP 63/211, fo. 232.
89 Sir Garrett Moore to Mountjoy, 27 July 1602, TNA, SP 63/211, fo. 245
90 Mountjoy to the privy council, 29 July 1602, *CSPI, 1601–3*, pp 282–4.
91 Mountjoy to the privy council, 9 Aug. 1602, *Carew, 1601–3*, pp 298–301; *Itinerary*, iii, p. 202.
92 Illustrated in 'Unidentified lake and crannog, Dungannon castle, the rath of Tullaghogue and the O'Neills' chair' by Richard Bartlett, NLI, MS 2656, v.
93 *Itinerary*, iii, p. 207.
94 *Itinerary*, iii, p. 260; Carew to Mountjoy and council, 31 Oct. 1602, *Carew, 1601–3*, pp 373–4.
95 *Itinerary*, iii, p. 208.
96 Ibid., p. 282.
97 Ibid., p. 283.
98 Mountjoy to Cecil, 20 Jan. 1603, *CSPI, 1601–3*, pp 555–7.
99 McGurk, 'The pacification of Ulster', pp 123, 127–8.
100 Carey, 'What pen can paint or tears atone?', pp 207–9.
101 Michael West, 'Spenser's art of war: chivalric allegory, military technology and the Elizabethan mock-heroic sensibility', *Renaissance Quarterly*, 41:4 (1988), p. 655.
102 Barbara Donagan, 'Halcyon days and the literature of war: England's military education before 1642', *Past and Present*, 147 (1995), p. 82.
103 Charles R. Shrader, 'The influence of Vegetius' *De re militari*', *Military Affairs*, 45:4 (1981), p. 168. It was translated and printed in London in 1572. See John Sadler (trans.), *The foure books of Flavius Vegetius Renatus* (London, 1572).
104 N.P. Milner (trans.), *Vegetius: epitome of military science* (2nd ed., Liverpool, 1996), p. 116.
105 After being recalled from France by the queen, Mountjoy was ordered to study military literature at court, most likely at Windsor castle as there was a mention of him formerly having lodgings there. See Robert Bennett, dean of Windsor to Cecil, 15 Sept. 1596, *Cal. Salisbury MSS*, vi, p. 387.
106 Edwards, 'Ideology and experience', p. 156; Edmund Spenser, *A view of the present state of Ireland*, ed. Andrew Hadfield and Willy Maley (Oxford, 1997), pp 101–2.
107 Mountjoy to Carew, 28 July 1601, *Carew, 1601–3*, p. 113.
108 Mountjoy to the privy council, 9 Aug. 1602, Lambeth, MS 604, fo. 206.
109 Carey, 'What pen can paint or tears atone', p. 213; *Itinerary*, iii, pp 272–7.
110 *Pacata Hibernia*, ii, pp 302–13.
111 Mountjoy to Carew, 2 July 1602, *Carew, 1601–3*, pp 263–4.
112 *Itinerary*, iii, pp 208–9.
113 Ibid.
114 *Q&A*, pp 111–12.
115 Chichester's description of his raid into Tyrone where 'we killed man, women, child, beast, and whatever else we found' has been used in most if not all articles relating to the end of the war. See Carey, 'What pen can paint or tears atone', p. 209 and McCavitt, *Sir Arthur Chichester*, p. 12.
116 Chichester to Cecil, 22 Nov. 1601, *CSPI, 1601–3*, pp 174–5.
117 Clifford J. Rogers, 'By fire and sword: bellum hostile and "civilians" in the Hundred Years War' in Mark Grimsley and Clifford Rogers (eds), *Civilians in the path of war* (London, 2002), p. 40.
118 Quentin Outram, 'The socio-economic relations of warfare and the military mortality crises of the Thirty Years' War', *Medical History*, 45 (2001), p. 157.
119 Chichester to Fenton, 22 May 1600, TNA, SP 63/207 pt 3, fo. 141.
120 Mountjoy to Cecil, 7 Aug. 1600, *CSPI, 1600*, pp 337–9.

121 In 1598, corn was 46s. per quarter. See Robert Arden to Burghley, 6 Mar. 1598, *CSPI*, *1598–9*, p. 81. In 1601 it was 50s. per quarter. See Captain Nicholas Dawtrey to Cecil, 9 Feb. 1601, *CSPI*, *1600–1*, pp 182–3.

122 Estimate of field productivity cited in Landers, *The field and the forge*, p. 59.

123 Mountjoy to Cecil, 7 Aug. 1600, *CSPI*, *1600*, pp 337–9. If it were possible Mountjoy's troops would surely have burnt the crops, but they did not on this occasion.

124 *Itinerary*, ii, pp 270–1.

125 Maurice Kyffin to Burghley, 18 May 1597, *CSPI*, *1596–7*, pp 291–2.

126 Falkiner, 'William Farmer's chronicles of Ireland', p. 129.

127 Mountjoy to Cecil, 20 Jan. 1603, *CSPI*, *1601–3*, pp 554–7.

128 Docwra to Cecil, 28 Sept. 1601, *CSPI*, *1601–3*, pp 97–8.

129 Carew to Cecil, 16 Nov. 1601, *CSPI*, *1601–3*, pp 517–18.

130 Mountjoy to Secretary Cecil, 23 June 1602, TNA, SP 63/211, fo. 161.

131 Mountjoy to Cecil, 12 Oct. 1602, TNA, SP 63/212, fo. 110.

132 *Itinerary*, iii, p. 260.

133 Carew to Mountjoy and council, 31 Oct. 1602, Lambeth, MS 624, fo. 239.

134 *Itinerary*, iii, p. 281; Mountjoy and council to the privy council, 26 Jan. 1603, *CSPI*, *1601–3*, pp 559–61.

135 Sir John Davies, solicitor general of Ireland to Cecil, 1 Dec. 1603, *CSPI*, *1603–6*, pp 111–13; *AFM*, vi, p. 2349.

136 *AFM*, vi, p. 2187.

137 *Pacata Hibernia*, ii, p. 213; *Itinerary*, iii, p. 202.

138 Chichester to the earl of Salisbury [Cecil], 2 Nov. 1605, *CSPI*, *1603–6*, pp 345–6.

139 *Itinerary*, iii, p. 283.

140 Sir John Norreys to Burghley, 25 Aug. 1595, TNA, SP 63/182, fo. 231.

141 Carew to Cecil, 6 Aug. 1601, *CSPI*, *1601–3*, pp 5–7.

142 Myler Magrath to Cecil, 12 Oct. 1600, *CSPI*, *1600*, pp 475–7.

143 Mountjoy and council to the privy council, 28 Apr. 1602, *CSPI*, *1601–3*, pp 377–81.

144 *Itinerary*, iii, p. 169.

145 'Suggestions [by Mountjoy] for the government of Ireland' [1602], HHA, CP 139/136. This appears to have been misattributed to Mountjoy by the archive in Hatfield House. The same letter appeared in *The works of Sir Francis Bacon*, v (London, 1826), pp 262–8.

146 *Itinerary*, iii, pp 172–6.

147 Ciaran Brady, 'Spenser's Irish crisis: humanism and experience in the 1590s', *Past and Present*, 111 (1986), p. 49.

148 Nicholas Canny, 'Comment on Spenser's Irish crisis: Humanism and experience in the 1590s', *Past and Present*, 120 (1998), pp 208–9; McGurk, 'The pacification of Ulster', p. 129.

149 David Edwards, 'Ideology and experience: Spenser's *View* and martial law in Ireland' in Hiram Morgan (ed.), *Political ideology in Ireland, 1541–1641* (Dublin, 1999), pp 155–6.

150 Hiram Morgan, 'Beyond Spenser? A historiographical introduction to the study of political ideas in early modern Ireland' in Morgan (ed.), *Political ideology in Ireland*, p. 18.

151 Edwards, 'The escalation of violence', pp 34–78; McGurk, 'The pacification of Ulster', pp 119–29.

152 David Edwards, 'Atrocities: "some days two heads some days four"', *History Ireland*, 17:1 (2009), p. 21.

153 *DSP*, fos. 307v–308.

154 One example was the murder of Gilbert Greene during Maguire's raid into Connacht in May 1593. See Sir George Bingham to Sir Richard Bingham, 25 May 1593, TNA, SP 63/170, fo. 13.

155 Preys and stealths committed by Tyrone, 1596–7, TNA, SP 63/198, fo. 27.

156 Mountjoy to Cecil, 2 June 1600, TNA, SP 63/207 pt 3, fo. 191.

157 Sir Richard Bingham to Cecil, 5 Dec. 1598, *CSPI, 1598–9*, pp 392–3.

158 Preys and stealths committed by Tyrone, 1596–7, TNA, SP 63/198, fo. 27.

159 Council of Ireland to the privy council, 2 July 1599, TNA, SP 63/205, fo. 189.

160 *Pacata Hibernia*, i, pp 35–6.

161 *Life*, p. 193.

162 Moryson, *Unpublished itinerary*, p. 48; Anon., 'The supplication of the blood of the English', pp 3–77.

163 *AFM*, vi, pp 2079–83; 'A discourse delivered by William Weever touching the proceedings of the rebels in Munster, and [their] creating an earl of Desmond, in September and October, 1598.' Oct. [1598], *CSPI, 1598–9*, pp 316–19.

164 *OSB*, pp 116–17.

165 'Information of William Saxey, chief justice of Munster [to Cecil] concerning the state of that province', 26 Oct. 1598, *CSPI, 1598–9*, pp 300–2.

166 'Portions of some manuscript history of the time' [Oct.] 1599, *CSPI, 1598–9*, pp 319–26.

167 The privy council to Carew, 18 June 1601, *APC*, xxxi, pp 437–8.

168 Brian MacCuarta, 'Religious violence against settlers in south Ulster, 1641–2' in Edwards et al. (eds), *Age of atrocity*, pp 154–75.

169 Captain Thomas Phillips to Cecil, Jan. 1599, *CSPI, 1598–9*, p. 470; [Anon.] to Loftus and Gardiner, 1 Nov. 1599, *CSPI, 1598–9*, pp 331–2.

170 Sheehan, 'The overthrow of the plantation in Munster', p. 18.

171 Henry Power to Essex, 6 Nov. 1598, *Cal. Salisbury MSS, viii*, pp 428–9.

172 *OSB*, p. 115.

173 Ibid., p. 116.

174 *AFM*, vi, pp 2137–9.

175 'Intelligences to Sir Geffrey Fenton', Feb. 1598–9 [1600], TNA, SP 63/203, fo. 80; *AFM*, vi, pp 2147–9. While the intelligence document sent to Fenton has been dated to 1599 in the calendar for 1598–9, the manuscript has no year recorded and the events described are dated in other documents as February 1600. The rumours of a Spanish peace mentioned in the Fenton document did not appear in Ireland until November 1599. See Queen Elizabeth to Loftus, Carey, Ormond and the rest of the council, 6 Nov. 1599, *CSPI, 1599–1600*, pp 229–33.

176 *Pacata Hibernia*, i, pp 35–6.

177 Nicholls, 'Richard Tyrrell', pp 161–78.

178 Carew to Mountjoy, 25 Oct. 1602, Lambeth MS 624, fo. 233.

179 Chichester to Cecil, 8 Oct. 1601, *CSPI, 1601–3*, pp 110–12.

180 Quinn, *The Elizabethans and the Irish*, pp 123–42; Edwards, 'The escalation of violence', pp 34–78; McGurk, 'The pacification of Ulster', pp 119–29; Carey, 'What pen can paint or tears atone', pp 205–16.

181 Joanna Bourke, *An intimate history of killing: face to face killing in twentieth-century warfare* (New York, 1999), pp 191–2.

182 Dave Grossman, *On killing: the psychology and cost of learning to kill in war and society* (New York, 1996), p. 208.

183 Ibid., pp 209–10.

184 During these periods the large-scale actions were focused on the midlands and southern Ulster borderlands. The core of the garrison in Carrickfergus were the survivors of the disastrous attack in 1597 in which Sir Arthur Chichester's brother (Sir John Chichester)

and over half the garrison were killed. This would have been fertile ground for animosity and resentment to flourish.

185 [Anon.] to Sir George Carey, 16 June 1599, *CSPI, 1599–1600*, pp 63–4; Commissioners of Munster to the privy council, 16 Feb. 1600, *CSPI, 1599–1600*, pp 480–2.

186 Grossman, *On killing*, p. 179.

187 McCavitt, *Sir Arthur Chichester*, pp 7–8.

188 McGurk, *Sir Henry Docwra*, p. 110.

189 Kelly, *Docwra's Derry*, p. 63.

190 Alexander B. Downes, *Targeting civilians in war* (Ithaca, 2008), pp 26–34.

191 Ibid., p. 176.

192 Ibid., p. 29; Grimsley and Rogers, *Civilians in the path of war*, xii.

193 Burgh and council to the privy council, 31 May 1597, *CSPI, 1596–7*, pp 301–3; Essex to the privy council, 11 July 1599, Lambeth, MS 621, fo. 141.

194 Downes, *Targeting civilians in war*, pp 26–7.

195 Ibid., pp 10, 26–9. There is an ongoing debate about the extent to which racism increases the likelihood of civilian mass killings, but it is clear that it is not a required element. For elaboration on this debate, see Benjamin Valentino, Paul Huth and Dylan Balch-Lindsay, '"Draining the sea": mass killing and guerrilla warfare', *International Organisation*, 58:2 (2004), pp 375–407.

196 'A brief of my [Captain George Flower] journey into Carbery' [Apr.] 1600, *CSPI, 1600*, pp 116–17.

197 Bagenal to Cecil, 13 Oct. 1597, *CSPI, 1596–7*, pp 417–19.

198 A certificate of English horse and foot, 12 July 1597, *CSPI, 1596–7*, p. 341.

199 Carew to the privy council, 24 Jan. 1600, *CSPI, 1600*, pp 161–5.

200 The bishop of Meath [Thomas Jones] to Carey, 27 Oct. 1601, *CSPI, 1601–3*, pp 145–6.

201 J.R. Hale, *War and society in Renaissance Europe, 1450–1620* (Leicester, 1985), pp 184–7.

202 Jeremy Black, *European warfare, 1494–1660* (London, 2002), pp 18–19.

203 Julius R. Ruff, *Violence in early modern Europe, 1500–1800* (Cambridge, 2001), pp 64–5.

204 Mountjoy to the privy council, 1 May 1601, *CSPI, 1600–1*, pp 303–5.

205 Mountjoy to Cecil, 25 Apr. 1603, *CSPI, 1603–6*, pp 24–7.

206 *Pacata Hibernia*, ii, p. 208.

207 'Observations of matters seeming to be out of order in Ireland', 3 Dec. 1596, *CSPI, 1596–7*, pp 180–2; John Danyell to Cecil, 12 Aug. 1598, HHA, CP 63/46.

208 *Lombard*, p. 65.

209 *Pacata Hibernia*, i, pp 131–2.

210 'Treatise on Ireland by Sir George Carew', Apr. 1594, TNA, SP 63/174, fo. 28.

211 Carew to the privy council, 31 Oct. 1602, *Carew, 1601–3*, pp 371–3.

212 Nicholls, 'Richard Tyrrell', p. 170.

213 *Pacata Hibernia*, ii, pp 268–9.

214 Carew to the privy council, 31 Oct. 1602, *Carew, 1601–3*, pp 371–3.

215 *Pacata Hibernia*, ii, pp 268–9.

216 Carew to the privy council, 31 Oct. 1602, *Carew, 1601–3*, pp 371–3.

217 *Pacata Hibernia*, ii, p. 280; Nicholls, 'Richard Tyrrell', p. 170.

218 Carew to Cecil, 16 Nov. 1602, TNA, SP 63/212, fo. 165.

219 *OSB*, p. 160.

220 *Pacata Hibernia*, ii, pp 281–2.

221 Ibid.

222 Carew to the privy council, 22 Jan. 1603, *Carew, 1601–3*, pp 403–9.

223 *OSB*, p. 160.

224 *Pacata Hibernia*, ii, pp 282–3.

225 *OSB*, pp 161–2; Carew to the privy council, 22 Jan. 1603, *Carew, 1601–3*, pp 403–9.

226 *Pacata Hibernia*, ii, pp 287–8.

227 *OSB*, pp 162–74.

228 *OSB*, p. 173.

229 Ibid., p. 166; *AFM*, vi, p. 2315.

230 *OSB*, p. 167.

231 Ibid., pp 168–9; *AFM*, vi, pp 2317–19.

232 Ibid., p. 173.

233 *OSB*, p. 175. Most likely anyone they found in the camp. The confederates' treatment of prisoners at this late stage in the war was as savage as anything perpetrated by the crown.

234 *OSB*, p. 175. See the entry for Cornashee earthworks in Northern Ireland Environment Agency, sites and monuments record (Ferm 246: 1, 2).

235 *OSB*, p. 176.

236 Ibid., pp 175–6.

237 Fenton to Cecil, 17 Dec. 1602, TNA, SP 63/212, fo. 207.

238 Fenton to Cecil, 11 Nov. 1602, *CSPI, 1601–3*, pp 516–17.

239 Mountjoy to Cecil, 8 Jan. 1603, *CSPI, 1601–3*, pp 551–2.

240 Carew has the same trouble in Munster when he sought James Fitzthomas, the *súgán* earl of Desmond.

241 *Itinerary*, iii, p. 230.

242 *Itinerary*, iii, p. 174.

243 Cecil to Mountjoy, 18 Feb. 1603, *Carew, 1601–3*, pp 417–18.

244 Ibid.

245 Tyrone to Mountjoy, 22 Dec. 1602, TNA, SP 63/212, fo. 273.

246 Walsh, *Destruction by peace*, p. 27.

247 Nicholas P. Canny, 'The treaty of Mellifont and the re-organization of Ulster, 1603', *Irish Sword*, 9:37 (1970), pp 255–6.

248 Ibid., pp 249–50.

249 Ibid., p. 250.

250 *Itinerary*, iii, pp 301–2; Canny, 'The treaty of Mellifont', pp 254–5.

251 *OSB*, p. 176.

252 Tyrone's submission, 8 Apr. 1603, TNA SP 63/215, fo. 40.

253 Ibid.

254 Walsh, *Destruction by peace*, pp 28–9.

255 Sir John Harington to Dr John Still, bishop of Bath and Wells, 1603, *Nugae Antiquae*, i, p. 340.

256 McCavitt, *The flight of the earls*, pp 55–6.

257 Jonathan Bardon, *The plantation of Ulster: the British colonisation of the north of Ireland in the seventeenth century* (Dublin, 2012), pp 55–6.

258 McCavitt, *The flight of the earls*, pp 57–60.

CHAPTER 7

Tyrone's military revolution

1 M. O'Báille, 'The buannadha: Irish professional soldiery in the sixteenth century', *Journal of the Galway Archaeological and Historical Society*, 22 (1946), p. 57.

2 Falls, *Elizabeth's Irish wars*, p. 72.

3 Ibid., pp 72–3.

4   Ibid., p. 74.
5   Hayes-McCoy, 'The army of Ulster', pp 105–17.
6   Ibid., p. 113.
7   Hiram Morgan, 'The end of Gaelic Ulster: a thematic interpretation of events between 1534 and 1610', *IHS*, 26:101 (1988), pp 8–32.
8   Nicholas Canny, 'Hugh O'Neill, earl of Tyrone, and the changing face of Gaelic Ulster', *Studia Hibernica*, 10 (1970), pp 7–35.
9   Hayes-McCoy, 'Strategy and tactics in Irish warfare, 1593–1601', pp 261–2.
10   Falls, *Elizabeth's Irish wars*; Silke, *Kinsale*, pp 54–5; Lennon, *Sixteenth-century Ireland*, p. 295; Ellis, *Ireland in the age of the Tudors*, p. 338; O'Carroll, 'Change and continuity in weapons and tactics 1594–1691', pp 211–56.
11   Hill, *Celtic warfare 1595–1763*, p. 22.
12   James M. Hill, 'Gaelic warfare, 1453–1815' in Jeremy Black (ed.), *European warfare, 1453–1815* (Houndmills, 1999), pp 201–23; Fissel, *English warfare*, p. 223; review by Ronald G. Haycock, '*Celtic warfare 1595–1763*, by James Michael Hill', *Military Affairs*, 51:4 (1987), p. 209; Wayne E. Lee, 'Using the natives against the natives: indigenes as "counterinsurgents" in the British Atlantic, 1500–1800', *Defence Studies*, 10:1–2 (2010), p. 88.
13   Seán Ó Domhnaill, 'Warfare in sixteenth-century Ireland', *IHS*, 5:17 (1946), p. 31.
14   Hayes-McCoy, *Scots mercenary forces in Ireland*, p. 78; Sir Henry Sidney to the privy council, 12 Nov. 1566, *CSPI, 1509–73*, p. 318.
15   Fitzwilliam to Cecil, 12 Sept. 1569, *CSPI, 1508–73*, p. 420.
16   Dean Gunther White, 'Henry VIII's Irish kerne in France and Scotland, 1544–1545', *Irish Sword*, 3:13 (1958), pp 213–25.
17   *Life*, pp 175–7; quoted in G.A. Hayes-McCoy, 'History of guns in Ireland', *Journal of the Galway Archaeological and Historical Society*, 18:1/2 (1938), p. 61.
18   Map showing the battle of the Erne fords, 10 Oct. 1593, BL Cottonian I/ii, fo. 38.
19   *OSB*, pp 80–1. The account by William O'Kennedy and Donough O'Shey in 1594 was careful to differentiate 'churls with darts and skeins' from Maguire's pike and shot. See 'Examination of William O'Kennedy and Donough O'Shey', 18 Apr. 1594, TNA, SP 63/174, fo. 60.
20   Black, *European warfare*, p. 38.
21   James M. Hill, 'Shane O'Neill's campaign against the MacDonalds of Antrim, 1564–5', *Irish Sword*, 18:71 (1991), p. 137; Hayes-McCoy, *Irish battles*, pp 68–86.
22   Parker, *The military revolution*, pp 1–5.
23   For examples of the complex formations devised by military writers see William Garrard, *The arte of warre* (London, 1591), pp 81–115, 177–95.
24   Gráinne Henry, *The Irish military community in Spanish Flanders, 1586–1621* (Dublin, 1992), pp 120–1.
25   [Anon.] to Adam Loftus and Sir Robert Gardiner, 1 Nov. 1598, TNA, SP 63/202 pt 3, fo. 297.
26   McCormack, *The earldom of Desmond*, pp 158–9.
27   Sir Henry Wallop to [Sir Francis] Walsingham, 23 Apr. 1581, *CSPI, 1574–85*, p. 300.
28   *DSP*, fo. 304.
29   'Henry Wallop's relation of the progress of Tyrone's rebellion', 1600, BL, Cotton Titus C/VII, fo. 153.
30   Spenser, *A view of the present state of Ireland*, p. 78; *DSP*, fo. 298.
31   *Q&A*, pp 92–3; *Itinerary*, ii, p. 189.
32   José Antonio De Yturriaga, 'Attitudes in Ireland towards the survivors of the Spanish Armada', *Irish Sword*, 17:67 (1990), p. 245.

33 Discourse of the Spanish wrecks, Sept. 1588, TNA, SP 63/136, fo. 236.

34 Captain Edward Bermingham to Sir Lucan Dillon, 31 Mar. 1589, *CSPI, 1588–92*, pp 146–7.

35 Sir Richard Bingham to Burghley, 6 Apr. 1589, TNA, SP 63/143, fo. 148.

36 'Act entered in the council', 5 Apr. 1589, TNA, SP 63/143, fo. 41.

37 'Answers of Sir Richard Bingham to the slanderous articles in the Burkes', 14 Sept. 1589, *CSPI, 1588–92*, p. 237.

38 Bingham to Fitzwilliam, 24 Apr. 1589, TNA, SP 63/151, fo. 228.

39 O'Connor Sligo to the archbishop of Tuam at Antwerp, 13 Aug. 1589, *CSPI, 1588–92*, p. 410.

40 Mountjoy to Cecil, 30 May 1603, HHA, CP 100/59.

41 William Waad to Cecil, 5 Nov. 1595, HHA, CP 35/104.

42 Ibid.

43 James Digges to Essex, 20/30 Oct. 1598, HHA, CP 177/138; John Danyell to Cecil, 16 Jan. 1598, HHA, CP 48/100.

44 In 1600, Tyrone requested that the archduke of Austria return all Irishmen serving in the armies of Flanders, but this was not countenanced by the archduke. See Henry, *The Irish military community in Spanish Flanders*, pp 123–4.

45 Lane to Burghley, 26 May 1594, TNA, 63/174, fo. 248.

46 Danyell to Cecil, 8 Oct. 1596, HHA, CP 45/53.

47 'Examination of Andrew Roche, taken before the lord lieutenant and others', 30 Mar. 1599, HHA, CP 69/35.

48 Bingham to the privy council, 28 June 1593, TNA, SP 63/170, fo. 47.

49 *Life*, pp 74–5; Duke and Herbert to Fitzwilliam, 10 Aug. 1594, TNA, SP 63/175, fo. 243; *AFM*, vi, p. 1951; *OSB*, pp 78–81.

50 Russell and council to the privy council, 4 June 1595, TNA, SP 63/180, fo. 9.

51 Lennon, *Sixteenth-century Ireland*, p. 259.

52 David Eltis, *The military revolution in sixteenth-century Europe* (London, 1998), p. 51; Capt. Edward Bermingham to Sir Lucas Dillon 31 Mar. 1589, *CSPI, 1588–92*, pp 146–7.

53 Ibid.

54 Hayes-McCoy, 'The army of Ulster', pp 105–17; Falls, *Elizabeth's Irish wars*, pp 72–4.

55 *Q&A*, pp 92–3.

56 *Itinerary*, ii, p. 189.

57 Gerrott Comerford to Cecil, 27 Aug. 1599, *CSPI, 1599–1600*, pp 132–3.

58 'A looking[-glass] for her majesty, wherein to view Ireland', May 1599, TNA SP 63/205, fo. 111. The problem of manpower shortages obliging the recruitment of native Irish was never fully solved. Even after the defeat of Tyrone at Kinsale and pursuit into Ulster, the crown still could not find sufficient troops in England. See Queen Elizabeth to [the justices of Northamptonshire], 26 Apr. 1602, HMC, *Report on the manuscripts of the duke of Buccleuch and Queensbury: preserved at Montague House, Whitehall* (vol. 3, London, 1926), pp 67–8.

59 John O'Donovan (ed.), 'Proclamation, in the Irish language, issued by Hugh O'Neill, earl of Tyrone, in 1601', *Ulster Journal of Archaeology*, 11 (1858), p. 63.

60 'An advertisement of the earl of Tyrone's forces', 11 Nov. 1594, *Carew, 1589–1600*, pp 101–2.

61 Falls, *Elizabeth's Irish wars*, p. 36.

62 O'Donovan, 'Proclamation … by Hugh O'Neill', p. 63.

63 Charles G. Cruickshank, 'Dead-pays in the Elizabethan army', *English Historical Review*, 53:209 (1938), pp 94–5.

64 Ibid., p. 96.

65 Cruickshank, *Elizabeth's army*, pp 114–15.

66 'A design upon Tyrone upon the landing of the army at Lough Foyle', 12 Mar. 1599, HHA, CP 139/54.

67 Captain Francis Croft to Cecil, 30 June 1597, TNA, SP 63/199, fo. 298.

68 Quoted in Geoffrey Parker, *The army of Flanders and the Spanish road, 1567–1659* (2nd ed., Cambridge, 2004), p. 10.

69 Stafford to Fenton, 4 June 1595, TNA, SP 63/180, fo. 66; A report of the service done by Sir Henry Bagenal in the relieving of Monaghan by Lieutenant Tucher Parkins, 1 June 1595, *Carew, 1589–1600*, pp 109–10.

70 Mountjoy and council in the camp to the lord chancellor and rest of the council in Dublin, 7 Oct. 1600, *CSPI, 1600*, pp 472–3.

71 Smythe, *Instructions, observations, and orders mylitarie*, pp 133–41.

72 *Chronicle*, p. 161; Mountjoy to the privy council, 1 May 1601, *CSPI, 1600–1*, pp 303–5.

73 Sir John Smythe, *Certain discourses military*, ed. J.R. Hale (Ithaca, 1964), p. 63.

74 Webb, *Elizabethan military science*, pp 89–90.

75 Evans, *The works of Sir Roger Williams*, p. 39.

76 'The description of the army which was defeated by the earl of Tyrone the 14 of August 1598', TCD, MS 1209/35. A second illustration of the battle was drawn by John Pooley, but it is less detailed. See 'Texts relating to Lord Essex in Ireland and the battle of the Yellow Ford, by John Pooley', 1638, TCD, MS 10837, iv–viii.

77 'The description of the army which was defeated by the earl of Tyrone the 14 of August 1598', TCD, MS 1209/35.

78 Captain Francis Kingsmill to Cecil, 22 Aug. 1599, *CSPI, 1599–1600*, pp 128–30.

79 Lane to Burghley, 28 June 1595, TNA, SP 63/180, fo. 179.

80 Sir Robert Salesbury to Burghley, 3 June 1595, TNA, SP 63/180, fo. 5.

81 Clifford to Burgh and council, 9 Aug. 1597, *CSPI, 1596–7*, pp 373–7.

82 Cuney to Essex, 28 Oct. 1598, HHA, CP 177/131.

83 Ignacio López and Iván López, *The Spanish tercios, 1536–1704* (Oxford, 2012), p. 39.

84 'The progress of my services since I arrived in Ireland on 17 March' [1602], *CSPI, 1601–3*, pp 338–42 and TNA, SP 63/210, fo. 192. This manuscript was erroneously dated to 1602 in the Irish calendar, but the Scottish calendars have identified the author as Thomas Douglas and more convincingly dated the letter to 1601. See Thomas Douglas to Mountjoy [*c*.Apr. 1601], *Cal. S.P. Scot., 1597–1603, part 2*, pp 1138–43.

85 Ibid.

86 Barret, *The theorike and practike of moderne warres*, p. 69.

87 Matthew Sutcliffe, *The practice and proceedings and laws of armes* (London, 1593), pp 185–6.

88 Mountjoy to Cecil, 7 Aug. 1600, *CSPI, 1600*, pp 337–9.

89 For the battle of the Ford of the Biscuits (1594) see *OSB*, pp 80–1 and O'Neill and Logue, 'The battle of the Ford of the Biscuits', pp 913–22; Clontibret (1595) see Salesbury to Burghley, 3 June 1595, TNA, SP 63/180, fo. 5 and Stafford to Fenton, 4 June 1595, TNA, SP 63/180, fo. 66; the battle of the Yellow Ford (1598) see Logue and O'Neill, 'The battle of the Yellow Ford', pp 62–83; for the battle of the Curlew Mountains (1599) in 1599 see *OSB*, pp 126–9; an account of the Moyry Pass battle can be found in G.A. Hayes-McCoy, 'The defence of the Moyry Pass', *Irish Sword*, 3:1 (1957–8), pp 32–8.

90 At the battle of the Ford of the Biscuits (1594), bogland was used to curtail the English cavalry. At the battle of the Yellow Ford (1598), pits were dug and a bank and trench used to cut off the English infantry from cavalry support. Barricades were used at the Curlew Mountains and the Moyry Pass to keep the English cavalry at bay.

91 'Instructions given by the Lord General Sir John Norreys to his brother Sir Henry Norreys', 27 July 1596, *CSPI, 1596–7*, pp 49–54.

92 Falls, *Elizabeth's Irish wars*, p. 69.

93 O'Carroll, 'Change and continuity in weapons and tactics, 1594–1691', p. 223.

94 Russell to Cecil, 22 Aug. 1596, TNA, SP 63/192, fo. 67; *Q&A*, p. 90.

95 G.A. Hayes-McCoy, 'Irish cavalry I: the sixteenth century', *Irish Sword*, 1:3 (1953), p. 317.

96 As the Scottish victories at Killiecrankie (1689) and Prestonpans (1745) demonstrated. See Hill, *Celtic warfare*, pp 70–5, 129–33.

97 'Advertisements from the camp', 7 Oct. 1594, TNA, SP 52/54, fo. 62iii; 'Certain notes by Sir John Norreys for the better explaining of a letter written from the lord deputy and council to my lords of the council of England', 16 July 1596, *CSPI, 1596–7*, pp 55–9.

98 James Michael Hill, 'The rift with Clan Ian Mor: the Antrim and Dunyveg MacDonnells, 1590–1603', *Sixteenth Century Journal*, 24:4 (1993), p. 868.

99 [Russell] to Cecil, 8 Oct. 1596, *CSPI, 1596–7*, pp 138–9; Fenton to Cecil, 14 Feb. 1597, TNA, SP 63/197, fo. 298.

100 *DSP*, fo. 349.

101 Stafford on the state of Ireland [May] 1598, *CSPI, 1598–9*, pp 165–8.

102 Carew and the council of Munster to the privy council, 15 Oct. 1602, *Carew, 1601–3*, pp 352–5.

103 Falls, *Elizabeth's Irish wars*, p. 74; William Palmer, *The problem of Ireland in Tudor foreign policy, 1485–1603* (Woodbridge, 1994), p. 137; Fissel, *English warfare*, pp 207–35; Simon Pepper, 'Aspects of operational art: communications, cannon, and small war' in Tallett and Trim (eds), *European warfare* (2010), p. 200; Wayne E. Lee, 'Keeping the Irish down and the Spanish out: English strategies of submission in Ireland, 1594–1603' in Williamson Murray and Peter R. Mansoor (eds), *Hybrid warfare: fighting complex opponents from the ancient world to the present* (Cambridge, 2012), pp 45–71.

104 Fenton to Burghley, 7 Sept. 1595, TNA, SP 63/183, fo. 39; Lambert to Mountjoy, 22 Apr. 1600, TNA, SP 63/207 pt 2, fo. 321; *Itinerary*, ii, p. 410.

105 Fenton to Burghley, 7 Sept. 1595, TNA, SP 63/183, fo. 39.

106 *Itinerary*, ii, p. 410.

107 Report of Walter Moore, constable of Ballinacor [Sept.?] 1596, TNA, SP 63/193, fo. 154.

108 *Life*, pp 91–2.

109 *OSB*, p. 152.

110 Ibid., p. 160.

111 A recent publication claimed the Irish had little use for fortifications or field works. See Eric Klingelhofer, *Castles and colonists: an archaeology of Elizabethan Ireland* (Manchester, 2010), pp 34–59.

112 Inishloughan fort, 1602, NLI, MS 2656, vi; G.A. Hayes-McCoy, *Ulster and other Irish maps c.1600* (Dublin, 1964), pp 11–12. For maps showing forts constructed by Tyrone see South-east Ulster, 1600, BL, Cotton Augustus I, ii, 37, Lough Neagh, 1601–2, TNA, MPF 1/133 and South-east Ulster, TNA, MPF 1/36.

113 *Itinerary*, iii, p. 200.

114 Ulick Burke, third earl of Clanricard to Essex, 25 Aug. 1599, *CSPI, 1599–1600*, pp 137–8; Mountjoy and council to the privy council, 15 Mar. 1601, *CSPI, 1600–1*, pp 225–7; *Pacata Hibernia*, ii, pp 127–8.

115 Captain John Bingham to Sir Richard Bingham, 21 Aug. 1596, *CSPI, 1596–7*, pp 91–2; Fenton to Cecil, 15 July 1597, TNA, SP 63/200, fo. 90; 'What the rebels of Munster have done to get Moghelly castle, since the beginning of the rebellion' [Sept. 1599], *CSPI, 1599–1600*, pp 161–5.

116 *AFM*, vi, p. 2057.

117 Dillon to Cecil, 2 Sept. 1600, *CSPI, 1600*, pp 409–10; Lambert to Mountjoy, 22 Apr. 1600, TNA, SP 63/207 pt 2, fo. 321.

118 'A journal of my [Sir Henry Bagenal] proceedings in the late pursuit of the traitor Maguire', 24 Oct. 1593, *CSPI, 1592–6*, pp 175–82; declaration of Piers Walsh, 1599, TNA, SP 63/205, fo. 125.

119 William Soare to Lane, 16 July 1597, *CSPI, 1596–7*, pp 344–5. This was illustrated in 'Lord Burgh assaults the Blackwater fort', 14 July 1597, TCD, MS 1209/34.

120 Mountjoy, Sir Richard Wingfield, and Sir George Bourchier to Cecil and the privy council, 14 July 1601, *CSPI, 1600–1*, p. 428.

121 *Pacata Hibernia*, ii, facing p. 141; 'Intelligence upon the designs of the arch traitor Tyrone with landing of the army at Lough Foyle', 12 Mar. 1598/9, HHA, CP 139/54.

122 Beatrice Heuser, *The evolution of strategy: thinking war from antiquity to the present* (Cambridge, 2010), pp 387–8; John Ellis, *A short history of guerrilla warfare* (London, 1975), p. 92.

123 Lawrence Rosinger, 'Politics and strategy of China's mobile war', *Pacific Affairs*, 12:3 (1939), pp 264–5; Harold Tanner, 'Mobile, and base warfare in communist military operations in Manchuria, 1945–1947', *Journal of Military History*, 67:4 (2003), pp 1217–18.

124 See M. de Jeney (trans.), *The partisan; or, The art of making war in detachment* (London, 1760).

125 Fenton to Cecil, 22 Dec. 1598, *CSPI, 1598–9*, pp 416–17.

126 See Chapter 5.

127 Ciaran Carson (trans.), *The Táin: translated from the old Irish epic Táin Bó Cúailnge* (London, 2007).

128 Marie Therese Flanagan, 'Irish and Anglo-Norman warfare in twelfth-century Ireland' in Bartlett and Jeffery (eds), *A military history of Ireland*, p. 52.

129 Ó'Domhnaill, 'Warfare in sixteenth-century Ireland', p. 30.

130 Katharine Simms, 'Gaelic warfare in the Middle Ages' in Bartlett and Jeffery (eds), *A military history of Ireland*, p. 107.

131 *DSP*, fo. 289.

132 These five men took 80 cattle and 400 sheep. See Ormond to the privy council, 4 Dec. 1599, *CSPI, 1599–1600*, pp 297–300.

133 Wallop to Cecil, 3 Feb. 1599, *CSPI, 1598–9*, pp 473–4.

134 Van Creveld, *Supplying war*, p. 7.

135 Chichester to Burghley, 16 Sept. 1597, TNA, SP/200, fo. 317; *Itinerary*, ii, p. 332.

136 'Examination of Walter Fitzgerald, alias Walter Reagh', 9 Apr. 1595, TNA, SP 63/179, fo. 48.

137 *DSP*, fo. 295.

138 Confession of James Fitzmorris Fitzgerald brother to Walter, 13 and 17 Feb. 1595, TNA, SP 63/178, fo. 124.

139 Burgh to Cecil, 10 Sept. 1597, *CSPI, 1596–7*, pp 394–5.

140 Clifford to Burgh and council, 9 Aug. 1597, *CSPI, 1596–7*, pp 373–7; *Life*, pp 159–61; *AFM*, vi, pp 2033–7.

141 Sir James MacSorley MacDonnell to Captain Charles Eggerton [Nov.] 1597, TNA, SP 63/201, fo. 138; 'Copy of a letter from Captains Charles Eggerton, Edward North, Charles Mansell, and Nicholas Merriman to [Sir Thomas Norreys]', 6 Nov. 1597, TNA, SP 63/201, fo. 140.

142 *Life*, pp 87–9.

143 Milner (trans.), *Vegetius: epitome of military science*, p. 116.

144 Donagan, 'Halcyon days and the literature of war', p. 82. The actions of Hannibal, Caesar and Spartacus are referred to by Barnabe Rich, and Matthew Sutcliffe cites Vegetius, Caesar, Livy and Xenophon. See Barnabe Riche, *A pathway to military practice* (London, 1587), h. 2–4; Matthew Sutcliffe, *The practice, proceedings and laws of arms* (London, 1593).

145 Privy council to Clifford, 23 Dec. 1598, *CSPI, 1598–9*, pp 418–19; *OSB*, pp 55–7.

146 Russell and council to the privy council, 9 Sept. 1596, *CSPI, 1596–7*, pp 100–1.

147 Sir John Norreys to Cecil, 21 Apr. 1597, *CSPI, 1596–7*, pp 274–5.

148 *Chronicle*, p. 121.

149 Dalway to Fitzwilliam, 8 Mar. 1594, *CSPI, 1592–6*, pp 220–1.

150 The O'Connors were preyed in 1596 after they defected to the crown. See *AFM*, vi, p. 2005. Theobald Dillon was spoiled for rejecting Tyrone's overtures in 1600. See Sir Arthur Savage to the Loftus and Carey and the council, 29 Jan. 1600, TNA, SP 63/207 pt 1, fo. 137.

151 Michael Savage [mayor of Carrickfergus] to Fitzwilliam, 7 Mar. 1594, TNA, SP 63/173, fo. 214.

152 Bagenal to Fitzwilliam, 20 Mar. 1594, TNA, SP 63/173, fo. 285.

153 Russell and council to the privy council, 10 July 1595, TNA, SP 63/181, fo. 48; Journal of Norreys' northern journey, 18 June–17 July 1595, TNA, SP 63/182, fo. 23.

154 Russell to Cecil, 15 Sept. 1595, TNA, SP 63/183, fo. 119.

155 Preys and stealths committed by Tyrone, 1595–6, TNA, SP 63/198, fo. 27.

156 Lennon, *Sixteenth-century Ireland*, p. 174.

157 Brady, *The chief governors*, p. 217.

158 Ibid., p. 224.

159 Nicholls, *Gaelic and Gaelicized Ireland*, pp 31–6.

160 Lennon, *Sixteenth-century Ireland*, p. 37; See also Quinn, *The Elizabethans and the Irish*, p. 49.

161 Nicholls, *Gaelic and Gaelicized Ireland*, pp 42–3.

162 Anon., 'The supplication of the blood of the English', p. 61. While this is essentially a polemic against the reform policies of earlier governments, the accusation is borne out by other sources.

163 Patrick Plunkett [Baron Dunsany] to Cecil, 2 Jan. 1600, *CSPI, 1599–1600*, pp 373–5.

164 Moryson, *Unpublished itinerary*, pp 44–5.

165 Saxey [Chief to Viscount Cranborne (Cecil)], 'A Discovery of the decayed state of the kingdom of Ireland, and of means to repower the same' [1604], *CSPI, 1603–6*, pp 217–28.

166 For references to opportunistic score settling and criminality see *AFM*, vi, p. 2009; *DSP*, fo. 309.

167 *DSP*, fo. 295.

168 'Preys, stealths, and spoils committed by the earl of Tyrone', 1596–7, TNA, SP 63/198, fo. 27.

169 *DSP*, fo. 334.

170 *DSP*, fo. 300.

171 'Account of the messages brought by two men sent to the state by O'Connor Sligo', 27 Sept. 1599, TNA, SP 63/205, fo. 341.

172 Bingham to Cecil, 5 Dec. 1598, *CSPI, 1598–9*, pp 393–4.

173 Mountjoy to Cecil, 7 Aug. 1600, *CSPI, 1600*, pp 337–9. In this one raid, Mountjoy estimated that £10,000 of corn was destroyed.

174 Black, *European warfare, 1494–1660*, p. 28; Pádraig Lenihan, *Confederate Catholics at war, 1641–49* (Cork, 2001), p. 124.

175 'Brian Reogh O'More to Teig M'Mortogh and Lysagh oge and their followers', 20 May 1598, *CSPI, 1598–9*, p. 150; 'copies of letters from the earl of Tyrone to his son, Conn O'Neill', 3 Apr. 1599, TNA, SP 63/205, fo. 11.

176 'Preys, stealths, and spoils committed by the earl of Tyrone', 1597, TNA, SP 63/198, fo. 27.

177 *Life*, p. 139.

178 Dowdall to Cecil, 2 Jan. 1600, Lambeth, MS 614, fo. 267.

179 Proclamation by Mountjoy and council, 9 June 1602, Lambeth, MS 617, fo. 264.

180 Bingham to Cecil, 5 Dec. 1598, *CSPI, 1598–9*, pp 392–3; 'A brief declaration of the state wherein Ireland now stands', 1599, TNA, SP 63/206, fo. 332.

181 Landers, *The field and the forge*, p. 225.

182 Ibid.

183 Expanding the area of influence to increase the potential tax revenue was also a feature of war in the 1640s. See Lenihan, *Confederate Catholics*, pp 120–5.

184 Discourse of the mere Irish of Ireland, Hiram Morgan (transc.), ECO, MS 154, fos. 55–74, viewed at http://www.ucc.ie/celt/published/E600001–004/index.html on 26 Apr. 2010.

185 Thomas Arnold, 'War in sixteenth-century Europe: revolution and Renaissance' in Jeremy Black (ed.), *European warfare, 1453–1815* (New York, 1999), pp 40–1.

CHAPTER 8

Tyrone's rebellion: a European war?

1 Barnabe Rich, *A new description of Ireland* (London, 1610), pp 94–5.

2 Cruickshank, *Elizabeth's army*, pp 207–79.

3 Parker, *The military revolution, 1500–1800*, pp 1–5.

4 'Advertisements out of Ireland', 1599, BL, Harleian 292, fo. 165; 'an estimate of the estate of Ireland', 17 Apr. 1599, TNA, SP 63/205, fo. 37.

5 Russell to Burghley, 24 May 1595, TNA, SP 63/179, fo. 233; 'an estimate of Tyrone's forces upon the relation of Thomas Barnewall', 22 Nov. 1599, TNA, SP 63/206, fo. 80; Carew to Cecil, 2 May 1600, *CSPI, 1600*, pp 141–6; 'The main strengths of the rebels in Ireland', 1600, ULC, MS Kk.1. 15, no. 147, fo. 503.

6 Sir George Carey to Henry Cuffe, 3 Apr. 1600, *CSPI, 1600*, p. 74; Bruckhurst to Cecil, 13 Aug. 1600, *CSPI, 1600*, pp 346–9.

7 Jan Glete, *War and the state in early modern Europe: Spain, the Dutch Republic and Sweden as fiscal-military states, 1500–1660* (London, 2006), pp 32–3.

8 Ibid., pp 34–5, 39.

9 Fissel, *English warfare*, pp 209, 216.

10 John France, 'Close order and close quarter: the culture of combat in the West', *International History Review*, 27:3 (2005), p. 502.

11 Ibid., p. 507.

12 Robert C. Stacy, 'The age of chivalry' in Michael Howard, George J. Andreopoulos and Mark R. Shulman (eds), *The laws of war: constraints on warfare in the western world* (London, 1994), p. 35.

13 Sean McGlynn, *By sword and fire: cruelty and atrocity in medieval warfare* (London, 2009), p. 81.

14 Heuser, *The evolution of strategy*, p. 89.

15 Quoted in ibid., p. 91.

16 Bernardino de Mendoza, *Theorique and practise of warre written to Don Philip Prince of Castil*, (trans.) Sir Edward Hoby (Middleburg, 1597), p. 109.

17 Sir Calisthenes Brooke to Cecil, 13 Aug. 1597, *CSPI, 1596–7*, pp 381–2; Anthony Fletcher and Diarmaid MacCulloch, *Tudor rebellions* (4th edn, Harlow, 1997), p. 114; Falls, *Elizabeth's Irish wars*, p. 75.

18 McGurk, 'Terrain and conquest', p. 86; O'Carroll, 'Change and continuity in weapons and tactics 1594–1691', p. 225. Eoin Ó Néill criticized some historians' predilection for defining the Irish war in battles. He thought this approach was too Clausewitzian and produced a

very limited view of the war which obscured the less glamorous aspects of the conflict, such as logistics or desertion rates. See Ó Néill, 'Towards a new interpretation of the Nine Years War', pp 245–50.

19 Quoted in Heuser, *The evolution of strategy*, p. 93.

20 William S. Maltby, *Alba: a biography of Fernando Alvarez de Toledo, third duke of Alba, 1507–1582* (Berkeley, 1983), pp 177–8.

21 Captain John Ogle to Cecil, 12 July 1602, HHA, CP 94/26.

22 Robert Devereux, *An apology of the Earl of Essex. Against those which falsely and maliciously tax him to be the only hinderer of the peace and quiet of his country* (London, 1603), E1ᵛ.

23 Evans, *The works of Sir Roger Williams*, cxliii, pp 72, 77, 87–8, 93, 109, 11, 113, 137.

24 Sir John Smythe, *Certain discourses military*, ed. J.R. Hale (Ithaca, 1964), p. 6.

25 Henk van Nierop, *Treason in the Northern Quarter: war, terror, and the rule of law in the Dutch Revolt* (Princeton, 2009), p. 76.

26 Henri Drouot, *Mayenne et la Bourgogne* (Paris, 1937), p. 333.

27 Quoted in Parker, *The military revolution*, p. 41. This phrase was on the title page of Henry Brome, *The commentaries of Messire Blaize de Montluc, marshal of France* (London, 1674).

28 Robert J. Knecht, *The French religious wars, 1562–1598* (Oxford, 2002), p. 60.

29 Lorraine White, 'The experience of Spain's early modern soldiers: combat, welfare and violence', *War in History*, 9:1 (2002), p. 33; Charles Carlton, *Going to the wars: the experience of the English civil wars, 1638–1651* (London, 1992), pp 206–7.

30 Parker, *The army of Flanders and the Spanish road*, p. 10, fn. 17.

31 McGurk, 'Terrain and conquest', p. 110.

32 L.L. Doedens, '"The day the nation was born": the battle of Heiligerlee, 1568' in Van der Hoeven, *Exercise of arms: warfare in the Netherlands*, pp 63–4.

33 Charles Oman, *A history of the art of war in the sixteenth century* (New York, 1979), pp 555–8.

34 Nolan, *Sir John Norreys*, p. 99.

35 'A brief journal of my Lord Deputy's [Mountjoy] second voyage into the north' [19 Nov.] 1600, CSPI, *1600–1*, pp 27–31.

36 Ben Cassidy, 'Machiavelli and the ideology of the offensive: gunpowder weapons in "The art of war"', *Journal of Military History*, 67:2 (2003), p. 394.

37 Hall, *Weapons and warfare in Renaissance Europe*, pp 175–6.

38 Maltby, *Alba*, pp 174–5.

39 Smythe, *Certain discourses military*, pp 55–6.

40 Józef Kelenik, 'The military revolution in Hungary' in Pal Fodor and David Geza (eds), *Ottomans, Hungarians, and Habsburgs in central Europe: the military confines in the era of Ottoman conquest* (Leiden, 2000), p. 118.

41 Ibid., p. 130.

42 Brian L. Davies, 'The development of Russian military power, 1453–1815' in Black (ed.), *European warfare, 1453–1815*, p. 164.

43 Arnold, 'War in sixteenth-century Europe', pp 40–1.

44 Hall, *Weapons and warfare in Renaissance Europe*, pp 178–9.

45 Keith Roberts, *Pike and shot tactics, 1590–1660* (Oxford, 2010), p. 36.

46 Hayes-McCoy, *Scots mercenary forces in Ireland*, pp 15–24; Seán Duffy, 'The pre-history of the galloglass' in Seán Duffy (ed.), *The world of the galloglass: kings, warlords and warriors in Ireland and Scotland, 1200–1600* (Dublin, 2007), pp 1–23.

47 Dowdall to Burghley, 9 Mar. 1596, CSPI, *1592–6*, pp 484–8.

48 Oman, *A history of the art of war in the sixteenth century*, p. 51.

49 Ibid., p. 62; Parker, *The army of Flanders and the Spanish road*, p. 9.

50 Morgan, 'Disaster at Kinsale', pp 129, 131–2.

51   Cruickshank, *Elizabeth's army*, p. 102.

52   Smythe, *Certain discourses military*, pp 81–102.

53   Cruickshank, *Elizabeth's army*, p. 114.

54   Brendan Scott and Kenneth Nicholls, 'Landowners of the late Elizabethan Pale: the general hosting appointed to meet at ye Hill of Tarrah on the 24 September 1593', *Analecta Hibernica*, 43 (2012), pp 4–15.

55   Gavin White, 'Firearms in Africa: an introduction', *Journal of African History*, 12:2 (1971), p. 174.

56   Michael C. Paul, 'The military revolution in Russia, 1550–1682', *Journal of Military History*, 68:1 (2004), p. 24.

57   Ibid., pp 20–1.

58   Marshall Poe, 'The consequences of the military revolution in Muscovy: a comparative perspective', *Comparative Studies in Society and History*, 38:4 (1996), p. 609.

59   Paul, 'The military revolution in Russia', p. 23.

60   John Keep, *Soldiers of the Tsar: army and society in Russia, 1462–1874* (Oxford, 1985), pp 80–1.

61   Colin Imber, *Ottoman Empire, 1300–1650: the structure of power* (Basingstoke, 2002), pp 282–3.

62   Thomas Arnold, *The Renaissance at war* (London, 2001), pp 119–20.

63   Fissel, *English warfare*, pp 207–37 and Lenman, *England's colonial wars*, pp 125–43.

64   William S. Maltby, *The black legend in England: the development of anti-Spanish sentiment, 1558–1660* (Durham, 1971), pp 50–1.

65   Fenton to Cecil, 24 Mar. 1597, TNA, SP 63/198, fo. 10; Stafford to Cecil, 14 Jan. 1602, *CSPI, 1601–3*, pp 284–6.

66   Fenton to Cecil [23] Jan. 1601, *CSPI, 1600–1*, pp 156–7.

67   Morgan, *Tyrone's rebellion*, p. 210; Morgan, 'Hugh O'Neill and the Nine Years War', pp 21–37.

68   Herbert H. Rowens, 'The Dutch Revolt: what kind of revolution?', *Renaissance Quarterly*, 43:3 (1990), p. 580.

69   Ibid., p. 582.

70   Ibid.

71   Van Creveld, *Supplying war*, pp 7–8.

72   James B. Wood, *The king's army: warfare, soldiers, and society during the wars of religion in France, 1562–1579* (Cambridge, 2002), pp 226–8.

73   Matthew C. Waxman, 'Strategic terror: Philip II and sixteenth-century warfare', *War in History*, 4:3 (1997), p. 342.

74   Evans, *The works of Sir Roger Williams*, p. 137.

75   Van Nierop, *Treason in the Northern Quarter*, pp 147–8.

76   John C. Theibault, *German villages in crisis: rural life in Hesse-Kassel and the Thirty Years War, 1580–1720* (Brill, 1995), p. 138.

77   F. Redlich, 'Contributions in the Thirty Years' War', *Economic History Review*, 12:2 (1959), pp 247–8.

78   Myron P. Gutmann, *War and rural life in the early modern Low Countries* (Princeton, 1980), p. 41.

79   'A declaration of the state of the English Pale of Ireland' [15 June] 1600, TNA, SP 63/207 pt 3, fo. 267. See also Canning, 'War, identity and the Pale', pp 153–60.

80   Gutmann, *War and rural life in the early modern Low Countries*, p. 42.

81   Geoffrey Parker, *The Dutch Revolt* (London, 1979), p. 254.

82   Theibault, *German villages in crisis*, p. 151.

83   Gutmann, *War and rural life in the early modern Low Countries*, pp 166–7.

84   Ibid., p. 164–5.

85   Quentin Outram, 'The demographic impact of early modern warfare', *Social Science History*, 26:2 (2002), pp 245–6.

86   Clodagh Tait et al., 'Early modern Ireland: a history of violence', pp 9–33; Edwards, 'Atrocities: "some days two heads some days four"', pp 18–21; Carey, 'Elizabeth I and state terror', pp 201–6.

87   Nolan, *Sir John Norreys*, p. 115.

88   Sir Thomas Digges, *England's defence; or, A treatise concerning invasion* (1588), comp. Thomas Adamson (London, 1680), pp 2–3.

89   Hale, *War and society in Renaissance Europe*, p. 184.

90   Jordan Fantosme cited in McGlynn, *By sword and fire*, pp 198–9.

91   Clifford J. Rogers, 'The age of the hundred years war' in Maurice Keen (ed.), *Medieval warfare: a history* (Oxford, 1999), p. 136.

92   Ibid., pp 136–7.

93   Rogers, *By fire and sword*, pp 38–9.

94   Waxman, 'Strategic terror', p. 340.

95   Ibid., pp 342–6.

96   Van Nierop, *Treason in the Northern Quarter*, pp 82, 89.

97   Ibid., pp 88–9.

98   Maltby, *The black legend in England*, pp 48–9.

99   Maltby, *Alba*, p. 156. Parker estimated this figure to be c.60,000. See Parker, *The Dutch Revolt*, p. 119.

100 Maltby, *Alba*, pp 241–55.

101 Waxman, 'Strategic terror', p. 342.

102 Charles Cotton (trans.), *The commentaries of Messire Blaize de Montluc* (London, 1674), p. 218.

103 Knecht, *The French religious wars*, p. 70.

104 Quoted in Parker, *The Dutch Revolt*, p. 161.

105 Maltby, *The black legend in England*, pp 48–9.

106 Parker, *The Dutch Revolt*, p. 297.

107 Evans, *The works of Sir Roger Williams*, pp 141–2.

108 Geoffrey Parker, 'Early modern Europe' in Michael Howard et al. (eds), *The laws of war*, p. 44.

109 Parker, *The Dutch Revolt*, p. 160.

110 Maltby, *Alba*, pp 238–9.

111 Van Vierop, *Treason in the northern quarter*, p. 76.

112 Chamberlain to Essex, 20 Jan. 1597, HHA, CP 59/7.

113 Docwra to the Essex, 6 Oct. 1598, *Cal. Salisbury MSS*, vii, p. 380.

114 Ralph Winward to Cecil, 31 Mar. 1604, HHA, CP 104/112.

115 *OSB*, p. 88; 'Certain instructions conceived by the queen's majesty to be imparted to her deputy and council in Ireland', June 1600, *CSPI, 1600*, pp 272–8; 'An extract of a letter sent unto me [Mountjoy] … from the army', 12 Mar. 1601, *CSPI, 1600–1*, pp 247–8; *AFM*, vi, p. 2239.

116 *OSB*, p. 71; *Pacata Hibernia*, ii, p. 287.

117 'Memorandum concerning the plantation at Ballyshannon' [June] 1600, *CSPI, 1600*, pp 279–83.

118 Mountjoy to Cecil, 20 Jan. 1603, *CSPI, 1601–3*, pp 555–7.

119 Advertisements sent to Sir Henry Duke, 20 Feb. 1595, TNA, SP 63/178, fo. 122.

120 Map of southern part of Ulster … by Richard Bartlett, 1602–3, TNA, MPF 1/36.

121 Site report for Ardboe high cross and abbey, NIEA, SM7 TYR 4:3.

122 Captain Paul Gore to Docwra, 24 Sept. 1601, TNA, SP 63/209 pt 1, fo. 285.

123 *OSB*, pp 139–40; Niall Garbh to Docwra, 24 Sept. 1601, TNA, SP 63/209 pt 1, fo. 287.

124 Rowens, 'The Dutch Revolt: what kind of revolution?', pp 573–4.

125 The Sea Beggars were privateers given letters of marque by the Dutch stadholder, William I, to operate against Spanish naval interests and coastal towns in the Low Countries.

126 Pieter Geyl, *The revolt in the Netherlands, 1555–1609* (London, 1932), pp 127–8.

127 Parker, *The Dutch Revolt*, pp 258–9.

128 James B. Wood, 'The impact of the Wars of religion: a view of France in 1581', *Sixteenth Century Journal*, 15:2 (1984), pp 139–41.

129 Mack P. Holt, *The French wars of religion, 1562–1629* (Cambridge, 1995), pp 62, 88–9.

130 Ibid., pp 88–9.

131 Mary O'Dowd, 'Women and war in Ireland in the 1640s' in Margaret MacCurtain and Mary O'Dowd (eds), *Women in early modern Ireland* (Edinburgh, 1991), p. 101.

132 Anon., 'The supplication of the blood of the English', pp 12, 51.

133 'A draft answer to Tyrone's libel by the honest Catholic lords of the Pale' [Dec.] 1600, TNA, SP 63/207 pt 6, fo. 338. Morgan suggested that this document was written by a government official. See Morgan, 'Faith and fatherland or queen and country?', pp 21–2.

134 Thomas Jones [bishop of Meath] to Burghley, 22 Mar. 1598, TNA, SP 63/202 pt 1, fo. 225; Plan for the reformation of Ireland [Anon.], 1603, *Carew, 1601–3*, pp 457–63.

135 Jones to Burghley, 22 Mar. 1598, TNA, SP 63/202 pt 1, fo. 225.

136 Ibid.

137 William Palmer, 'Gender, violence and rebellion in Tudor and early Stuart Ireland', *Sixteenth Century Journal*, 23:4 (1992), p. 704.

138 Ibid., p. 712.

139 Holt, *The French wars of religion*, p. 62.

140 Ibid., pp 86–7.

141 Robert O'Connell, *Of arms and men: a history of war, weapons and aggression* (Oxford, 1989), p. 133.

142 Van Nierop, *Treason in the Northern Quarter*, p. 148.

143 Penny Roberts, 'Peace, ritual, and sexual violence during the religious wars', *Past and Present*, 214 (suppl. 7, 2012), p. 97.

144 Philip G. Dwyer, '"It still makes me shudder": memories of massacres and atrocities during the Revolutionary and Napoleonic wars', *War in History*, 16:4 (2009), p. 383.

145 Barbara Donagan, 'Atrocity, war crime, and treason in the English Civil War', *American Historical Review*, 99:4 (1994), p. 1146.

146 Outram, 'The demographic impact of early modern warfare', p. 246.

147 Ibid., p. 247.

148 Ibid., p. 259.

149 Barbara Donagan, 'Codes of conduct in the English Civil War', *Past and Present*, 118 (1988), p. 76.

150 Outram, 'The demographic impact of early modern warfare', p. 266.

151 Canning, 'War, identity and the Pale', pp 205–6.

Bibliography

MANUSCRIPT SOURCES

British Library
Additional MSS: 4728
Cottonian MSS: Augustus I, Julius F VI, Titus B XII, Titus B XIII, Titus C VII
Harleian MSS: 35,292
Lansdowne MSS: 84, 96

Hatfield House Archives
The Cecil papers

Lambeth Palace Library, London
MSS 604, 607, 612, 614, 615, 617, 620, 621, 624, 627, 632

The National Archives, Kew, London
MPF 1: Maps and plans extracted to flat storage from various series of records of the State
     Paper Office
SP 52: State papers Scotland Series 1, Elizabeth I, 1558–1603
SP 63: State papers Ireland, Elizabeth I to George III, 1558–1782

National Library of Ireland
Manuscript Maps MS 2656

Northern Ireland Environment Agency: sites and monuments record
SM7 TYR 4:3: Report for Ardboe high cross and abbey

Somerset Heritage Centre
Carew of Crowcombe MSS DD/TB

Trinity College, Dublin
MSS 1209, 4457, 10,837

University Library Cambridge
Additional MSS Kk 1 15: Letters and state papers relating to the rebellion in Ireland in the
     reign of Elizabeth.

PRIMARY PRINTED SOURCES

Acts of the privy council of England, ed. J.R. Dasent, 32 vols (London, 1890–1907).
Aelianus [Capt. John Bingham], *The tactiks of Aelian* (London, 1616).
Annals of the kingdom of Ireland by the Four Masters from the earliest period to the year 1616,
     ed. and trans. John O'Donovan, 7 vols (3rd ed., Dublin, 1990).
Anon., 'The supplication of the blood of the English most lamentably murdered in Ireland,
     crying out of the earth for revenge (1598)', ed. Willy Maley in *Analecta Hibernica*, 36
     (1995), pp 3–77.

Anon., *Discourse of the mere Irish of Ireland*, Hiram Morgan (transc.) (ECO, MS 154, ff 55–74), viewed at http://www.ucc.ie/celt/published/E600001–004/index.html on 26 Apr. 2010.

Anon., *The government of Ireland under the honourable, just and wise Sir John Perrot knight, one of the privy council to Queen Elizabeth, beginning 1584, and ending 1588* (London, 1626).

Bacon, Francis, *The works of Francis Bacon*, 10 vols (London, 1826).

Barret, Robert, *The theorike and practike of modern warres* (London, 1598).

Beacon, Richard, *Solon his follie; or, A politique discourse touching the reformation of the common-weales conquered, declined or corrupted*, ed. Clare Carroll and Vincent Carey (Binghamton, 1996).

Braun, Georg, & Franz Hogenberg, *Civitates Orbis Terrarum (Cites of the World, 1572–1617)*, ed. Stephan Fussel (Cologne, 2011).

Brome, Henry, *The commentaries of Messire Blaize de Montluc, mareschal of France* (London, 1674).

Calendar of the Carew manuscripts preserved in the archiepiscopal library at Lambeth, 1551–1642, ed. J.S. Brewer & William Bullen, 6 vols (London, 1867–73).

Calendar of letters and state papers relating to English affairs preserved principally in the archives of Simancas, ed. Martin Hume, 4 vols (London, 1892–9).

Calendar of the manuscripts of the most honourable the marquess of Salisbury: preserved at Hatfield House, Hertfordshire, ed. R.A. Roberts, E. Salisbury, G. Montague & O. Geraint Dyfnallt, 24 vols (London, 1883–1976).

Calendar of the records of the borough of Haverfordwest, 1539–1660, ed. B.G. Charles (Cardiff, 1967).

Calendar of state papers relating to Ireland, 1509–1670, ed. H.C. Hamilton, E.G. Atkinson, & R.P. Mahaffy, 24 vols (London, 1860–1912).

Calendar of the state papers relating to Scotland and Mary, queen of Scots, 1547–1603, ed. J. Bain, W.K. Boyd, A.I. Cameron, M.S. Giuseppi, H.W. Meikle & J.D. Mackie, 13 vols (Glasgow, 1898–1969).

Callot, Jacques, *Les Misères et les Malheurs de la Guerre* (Paris, 1633).

Camden, William, *Britain; or, A chorographicall description of the most flourishing kingdoms, England, Scotland, and Ireland, and the islands adjoining, out of the depth of antiquity beautified with maps of the several shires of England: written first in Latin by William Camden Clarenceux K. of A. Translated newly into English by Philémon Holland Doctour in Physick: finally, revised, amended, and enlarged with sundry additions by the said author* (London, 1610).

Carleton, George, *A thankful remembrance of God's mercy* (London, 1630).

Charters relating to the city of Glasgow, ed. J.D. Marwick, 2 vols (Glasgow, 1894–1906).

Collier, Hugh, *The Dialogue of Silvynne and Peregrynne* (TNA, SP 63 /203, fo. 283), transc. Hiram Morgan, viewed at http://www.ucc.ie/celt/online/E590001–001.html on 16 Sept. 2010.

Cotton, Charles (trans.), *The commentaries of Messire Blaize de Montluc* (London, 1674).

Davies, Sir John, *A discovery of the true causes of why Ireland was never entirely subdued, nor brought under obedience of the crown of England, until the beginning of his majesties happy reign* (Dublin, 1612).

Dawtrey, Nicholas, 'A booke of questions and answars concerning the wars or rebellions of the kingdome of Irelande', ed. Hiram Morgan in *Analecta Hibernica*, 36 (1995), pp 79, 81–132.

de Gheyn, Jacob, *The exercise of armes* (The Hague, 1607).

de la Vega, Captain Luis Guntierras, *A compendious treatise entitled, De re military*, trans. Nicholas Lichfield (London, 1582).

Derricke, John, *The image of Ireland with a discovery of wood kerne, wherein is most lively expressed, the nature, and quality of the said wild Irish wood kerne, their notable aptness, celerity, and proness to rebellion* (London, 1581).

Devereux, Robert, 2nd earl of Essex, *An apology of the Earl of Essex. Against those which falsely and maliciously tax him to be the only hinderer of the peace and quiet of his country* (London, 1603).

Digges, Sir Thomas, *England's defence; or, A treatise concerning invasion ... 1588*, comp. Thomas Adamson (London, 1680).

Dymmok, John, *A treatise of Ireland*, ed. Richard Butler (Dublin, 1842).

Edwards, H.J. (trans.), *Caesar: the Gallic wars* (London, 1917).

Evans, J.X. (ed.), *The works of Sir Roger Williams* (Oxford, 1972).

Farmer, William, 'William Farmer's chronicles of Ireland from 1594 to 1613', ed. C.L. Falkiner, *English Historical Review*, 22 (1907), pp 104–30 and 527–52.

Gainsford, Thomas, *A true exemplary, and remarkable history of the earl of Tyrone* (London, 1619).

Garrard, William, *The arte of warre* (London, 1591).

Harrington, John, *Nugae Antiquae: being a miscellaneous collection of original papers, in prose and verse / written during the reigns of Henry VIII, Edward VI, Queen Mary, Elizabeth and King James by Sir John Harington, Knt. and others who lived in those times*, 3 vols (London, 1804).

Irish faints of the Tudor sovereigns in the reigns of Henry VIII, Edward VI, Philip & Mary, and Elizabeth I, ed. K.W. Nichols, 4 vols (Dublin, 1994).

Jeney, M. de (trans.), *The partisan; or, The art of making war in detachment* (London, 1760).

Kelly, William, *Docwra's Derry: a narration of events in north-west Ulster, 1600–1604* (Belfast, 2003).

Lee, Thomas, *Information given to Queen Elizabeth against Sir William Fitzwilliam, his government in Ireland*, transc. Hiram Morgan (BL, Harley MS 35, fos. 258–65), viewed at http://www.ucc.ie/celt/published/E590001–002/index.html on 3 Aug. 2012.

Lee, Thomas, *The discovery and recovery of Ireland with the author's apology*, transc. John McGurk (BL Add. MSS, 33743), viewed at http://www.ucc.ie/celt/published/E590001–005/index.html on 2 Feb. 2013.

Lombard, Peter, *The Irish war of defence, 1598–1600: extracts from the De Hibernia Insula commentaries*, ed. and trans. M.J. Byrne (Cork, 1930).

MacCarthy, Daniel (ed.), *The life and letters of Florence MacCarthy Reagh* (London, 1867).

Maclean, John (ed.), *Letters from Sir Robert Cecil to Sir George Carew* (London, 1864).

Manchuca, Captain Bernardo de Vargas, *The Indian militia and description of the Indies* (1599), ed. Kris Lane and trans. Timothy F. Johnston (Durham, 2008).

Marcus, Leah S., Janel Mueller & Mary Beth Rose (eds), *Elizabeth I: collected works* (Chicago, 2000).

de Mendoza, Bernardino, *Theorique and practise of warre written to don Philip Prince of Castil*, trans. Sir Edward Hoby (Middleburg, 1597).

Milner, N.P. (trans.), *Vegetius: epitome of military science* (2nd ed., Liverpool, 1996).

Morales, Óscar Recio, 'Florence Conroy's memorandum for a military assault on Ulster, 1627', *Archivium Hibernicum*, 56 (2002), pp 65–72.

Moryson, Fynes, *An itinerary: containing his ten yeeres travel through the twelve dominions of Germany, Bohmerland, Sweitzerland, Netherland, Denmarke, Poland, Italy, turkey, France, England, Scotland and Ireland*, 4 vols (Glasgow, 1907–8).

—, *The Irish sections of Fynes Moryson's unpublished itinerary*, ed. Graham Kew (Dublin, 1998).

Naunton, Sir Robert, *Fragmenta Regalia; or, Observations on the late Queen Elizabeth, her times and favourites* (London, 1641).

Ó Clérigh, Lughaidh, *The life of Aodh Ruadh O' Domhnaill*, ed. and trans. Paul Walsh (London, 1948).

O'Donovan, John (ed.), 'Proclamation, in the Irish language, issued by Hugh O'Neill, earl of Tyrone, in 1601', *Ulster Journal of Archaeology*, first series, 11 (1858), pp 57–65.

O'Sullivan Beare, Philip, *Ireland under Elizabeth: chapters towards a history of Ireland under Elizabeth*, trans. M.J. Byrne (Dublin, 1903).

Perrot, Sir James, *The chronicle of Ireland 1584–1608*, ed. Herbert Wood (Dublin, 1933).

Register of the privy council of Scotland [1st ser.], ed. J.H. Burton & D. Masson, 14 vols (Edinburgh, 1877–98).

Report on the manuscripts of the duke of Buccleuch and Queensbury: preserved at Montague House, Whitehall, ed. R.E.G. Kirk, 3 vols (London, 1899–1926).

Rich, Barnabe, *A pathway to military practice* (London, 1587).

—, *A new description of Ireland* (London, 1610).

Sadler, John (Trans), *The four books of Flavius Vegetius Renatus* (London, 1572).

Scott, Brendan, & Kenneth Nicholls, 'Landowners of the late Elizabethan Pale: "the general hosting appointed to meet at Ye Hill of Tarrah on the 24 September 1593"', *Analecta Hibernica*, 43 (2012), pp 1–15.

Smythe, Sir John, *Certain discourses military* (1590), ed. J.R. Hale (Ithaca, 1964).

—, *Instructions, observations, and orders mylitarie* (London, 1595).

Spenser, Edmund, *A view of the present state of Ireland*, ed. Alexander B. Grosart (1894), viewed at http://www.ucc.ie/celt/published/E500000–001/index.html, 16 Aug. 2010.

—, *A view of the state of Ireland*, ed. Andrew Hadfield & Willy Maley (Oxford, 1997).

Stafford, Thomas, *Pacata Hibernia: Ireland appeased and reduced; or, A history of the late wares of Ireland, especially in the province of Munster under the command of Sir George Carew*, ed. Standish O'Grady, 2 vols (London, 1896).

Stowe, John, *Annales; or, General chronicle of England* (London, 1631).

Styward, Thomas, *The pathwaie to martiall discipline* (London, 1582).

Sutcliffe, Matthew, *The practice and proceedings and laws of armes* (London, 1593).

SECONDARY SOURCES

Andrews, K.R., N.P. Canny, & P.E.H. Hair (eds), *The westward enterprise: English activities in Ireland, the Atlantic and America, 1480–1650* (Liverpool, 1978).

Anon., *The history of that most eminent statesman, Sir John Perrott* (London, 1727).

Armstrong, Robert, & Tadhg Ó hAnnracháin (eds), *Community in early modern Ireland* (Dublin, 2006).

Arnold, Thomas, 'War in sixteenth-century Europe: revolution and Renaissance' in Black (ed.), *European warfare, 1453–1815* (1999), pp 23–44.

Arnold, Thomas, *The Renaissance at war* (London, 2001).

Bagwell, Richard, *Ireland under the Tudors*, 3 vols (London, 1885–90).

Bardon, Jonathan, *The plantation of Ulster: the British colonisation of the north of Ireland in the seventeenth century* (Dublin, 2012).

Bartlett, Thomas, 'The academy of warre': military affairs in Ireland, 1600 to 1800, 30th O'Donnell lecture 2002 (Dublin, 2002).

—, & Keith Jeffery (eds), A military history of Ireland (Cambridge, 1996).

Beckett, F.W., 'War, identity and memory in Ireland', Irish Economic and Social History, 36 (2009), pp 63–84.

Berleth, Richard, The twilight lords (London, 1978).

Black, Jeremy, A military revolution? Military change and European society, 1550–1800 (London, 1991).

—, 'A military revolution? A 1660–1792 perspective' in Rogers (ed.), The military revolution debate (1995), pp 95–116.

— (ed.), European warfare, 1453–1815 (New York, 1999).

—, European warfare, 1494–1660 (London, 2002).

Boazio, Baptista, & R. Dunlop, 'Sixteenth-century maps of Ireland', English Historical Review, 20:78 (1905), pp 309–37.

Bottigheimer, Karl S., 'Kingdom and colony: Ireland and the westward enterprise, 1536–1660' in Andrews et al. (eds), The westward enterprise (1978), pp 45–64.

Bourke, Joanna, An intimate history of killing: face to face killing in twentieth-century warfare (New York, 1999).

Bradshaw, Brendan, 'Native reaction to the westward enterprise: a case study in Gaelic ideology' in Andrews et al. (eds), The westward enterprise (1978), pp 66–80.

—, 'The Elizabethans and the Irish: a muddled model', Studies: an Irish Quarterly Review, 70:278/279 (1981), pp 233–44.

—, 'Nationalism and historical scholarship in modern Ireland', IHS, 26:104 (1989), pp 329–51.

Brady, Ciaran, & Raymond Gillespie (eds), Natives and newcomers: the making of Irish colonial society, 1534–1641 (Dublin, 1986).

Brady, Ciaran, 'Court, castle and country: the framework of government in Tudor Ireland' in Brady and Gillespie (eds), Natives and newcomers (1986), pp 22–49.

—, 'Spenser's Irish crisis: humanism and experience in the 1590s', Past and Present, 111 (1986), pp 17–49.

—, The chief governors: the rise and fall of reform government in Ireland, 1536–1588 (Cambridge, 1994).

—, 'The captain's games: army and society in Elizabethan Ireland' in Bartlett and Jeffery (eds), A military history of Ireland (1996), pp 136–59.

Brewster, Scott, Fiona Beckett, David Alderson & Virginia Crossman (eds), Ireland in proximity: history, gender, space (London, 1999).

Buchanan, Brenda J. (ed.), Gunpowder, explosives and the state: a technological history (Aldershot, 2006).

—, 'Saltpetre: a commodity of empire' in Buchanan (ed.), Gunpowder, explosives and the state (2006), pp 67–90.

Canny, Nicholas, 'The ideology of English colonialism: from Ireland to America', William and Mary Quarterly, 30:4 (1973), pp 575–98

—, The Elizabethan conquest of Ireland: a pattern established, 1565–1576 (Hassocks, 1976).

—, From Reformation to Restoration: Ireland, 1534–1660 (Dublin, 1987).

—, 'Comment on Spenser's Irish crisis: humanism and experience in the 1590s', Past and Present, 120 (1998), pp 201–9.

—, 'Taking sides in early modern Ireland: the case of Hugh O'Neill, earl of Tyrone' in Carey and Lotz-Heumann (eds), Taking sides? (2004), pp 94–115.

Carey, Vincent, & Ute Lotz-Heumann (eds), *Taking sides: colonial and confessional* mentalities
    in early modern Ireland: essays in honour of Karl H. Bottigheimer (Dublin, 2003).
—, '"What pen can paint or tears atone?": Mountjoy's scorched earth campaign' in Morgan
    (ed.), *The battle of Kinsale* (2004), pp 205–16.
—, 'Elizabeth I and state terror in sixteenth-century Ireland' in Stump at al. (ed.), *Elizabeth
    I and the 'sovereign arts'* (2011), pp 201–6.
Carson, Ciaran (trans.), *The Táin: translated from the old Irish epic Táin Bó Cúailnge* (London,
    2007).
Cassidy, Ben, 'Machiavelli and the ideology of the offensive: gunpowder weapons in "The
    art of war"', *Journal of Military History*, 67:2 (2003), pp 381–404.
Challis, C.E., *The Tudor coinage* (Manchester, 1978).
Chase, Kenneth, *Firearms: a global history to 1700* (Cambridge, 2008).
Connolly, Sean (ed.), *The Oxford companion to Irish history* (Oxford, 1998).
—, *Contested island: Ireland, 1460–1630* (Oxford, 2007).
Croft, Pauline, 'Trading with the enemy, 1585–1604', *Historical Journal*, 32:2 (1989), pp
    281–302.
—, *King James* (Houndmills, 2003).
Cruickshank, Charles G., 'Dead-pays in the Elizabethan army', *English Historical Review*,
    53:209 (1938), pp 93–7.
—, *Elizabeth's army* (2nd ed., Oxford, 1966).
Cunningham, Bernadette, 'The composition of Connacht in the lordships of Clanricard
    and Thomond, 1577–1641', *IHS*, 24:93 (1984), pp 1–14.
Davies, Brian L., 'The development of Russian military power 1453–1815' in Black (ed.),
    European warfare (1999), pp 145–79.
Davis Biddle, Tami, 'Military history, democracy and the role of the academy', *Journal of
    American History*, 93:4 (2007), pp 1143–5.
De Moor, J.A., 'Experience and experiment: some reflections upon the military
    developments in 16th and 17th century Western Europe' in Van der Hoeven (ed.),
    Exercise of arms (1997), pp 17–32.
De Yturriaga, José Antonio, 'Attitudes in Ireland towards the survivors of the Spanish
    Armada', *Irish Sword*, 17:67 (1990), pp 244–54.
Doedens, L.L., '"The day the nation was born": the battle of Heiligerlee, 1568' in Van der
    Hoeven (ed.), *Exercise of arms* (1997), pp 57–68.
Donagan, Barbara, 'Codes of conduct in the English Civil War', *Past and Present*, 118
    (1988), pp 65–95.
—, 'Atrocity, war crime, and treason in the English Civil War', *American Historical Review*,
    99:4 (1994), pp 1137–66.
—, 'Halcyon days and the literature of war: England's military education before 1642', *Past
    and Present*, 147 (1995), pp 65–100.
Downes, Alexander B., *Targeting civilians in war* (Ithaca, 2008).
Drouot, Henri, *Mayenne et la Bourgogne* (Paris, 1937).
Duffy, Patrick J., David Edwards & Elizabeth FitzPatrick (eds), *Gaelic Ireland, c.1250–
    c.1650: land, lordship, settlement* (Dublin, 2001).
Duffy, Seán (ed.), *The world of the galloglass: kings, warlords and warriors in Ireland and
    Scotland, 1200–1600* (Dublin, 2007).
—, 'The pre-history of the galloglass' in Duffy (ed.), *The world of the galloglass* (2007), pp
    1–23
Dwyer, Philip G., '"It still makes me shudder": memories of massacres and atrocities during
    the Revolutionary and Napoleonic wars', *War in History*, 16:4 (2009), pp 381–405.

Edelman, Charles, *Shakespeare's military language: a dictionary* (London, 2004).
Edwards, David, 'In Tyrone's shadow: Feagh McHugh O'Byrne, forgotten leader of the Nine Years War' in O'Brien (ed.), *Feagh McHugh O'Byrne* (1998), pp 212–48.
—, 'Ideology and experience: Spenser's *View* and martial law in Ireland' in Morgan (ed.), *Political ideology in Ireland* (1999), pp 127–57.
—, Pádraig Lenihan & Clodagh Tait (eds), *Age of atrocity: violence and political conflict in early modern Ireland* (Dublin, 2007).
—, 'The escalation of violence in sixteenth-century Ireland' in Edwards et al. (eds), *Age of atrocity* (2007), pp 34–78.
—, 'Atrocities: "some days two heads some days four"', *History Ireland*, 17:1 (2009), pp 18–21
—, *Campaign journals of the Irish wars* (Dublin, 2014).
Ellis, John, *A short history of guerrilla warfare* (London, 1975).
Ellis, Steven, *Ireland in the age of the Tudors, 1447–1603: English expansion and the end of Gaelic rule* (London, 1998).
Eltis, David, *The military revolution in sixteenth-century Europe* (London, 1998).
Falls, Cyril, 'Neill Garve: English ally and victim', *Irish Sword*, 1:1 (1949), pp 2–7.
—, *Elizabeth's Irish wars* (London, 1950, repr. London, 1996).
—, 'Mountjoy as a soldier', *Irish Sword*, 2:1 (1954), pp 1–5.
—, 'The growth of Irish military strength in the second half of the sixteenth century', *Irish Sword*, 2:1 (1954–6), pp 103–8.
—, *Mountjoy: Elizabethan general* (London, 1955).
—, 'Black Tom of Ormonde', *Irish Sword*, 5:18 (1961–2), pp 10–22.
—, 'Hugh O'Neill the great', *Irish Sword*, 6:23 (1963–4), pp 94–102.
Fissel, Mark C. (ed.), *War and government in Britain, 1598–1650* (Manchester, 1991).
—, *English warfare, 1511–1642* (London, 2001).
Fitzsimons, Fiona, 'Fosterage and gossiprid in late medieval Ireland: some new evidence' in Duffy et al. (eds), *Gaelic Ireland* (2001), pp 138–52.
Flanagan, Marie Therese, 'Irish and Anglo-Norman warfare in twelfth-century Ireland' in Bartlett & Jeffery (eds), *A military history of Ireland* (1996), pp 52–75.
Fletcher, Anthony, & Diarmaid MacCulloch, *Tudor rebellions* (4th ed., Harlow, 1997).
Fodor, Pal, & David Geza (eds), *Ottomans, Hungarians, and Habsburgs in central Europe: the military confines in the era of Ottoman conquest* (Leiden, 2000).
Foley, Claire, & Ronan McHugh, *An archaeological survey of County Fermanagh*, 2 vols (Newtownards, 2014).
France, John, 'Close order and close quarter: the culture of combat in the West', *International History Review*, 27:3 (2005), pp 498–517.
García-Hernán, Enrique, 'Philip II's forgotten armada' in Morgan (ed.), *The battle of Kinsale* (2004), pp 45–57.
Geyl, Pieter, *The revolt in the Netherlands, 1555–1609* (London, 1932).
Glete, Jan, *War and the state in early modern Europe: Spain, the Dutch Republic and Sweden as fiscal-military states, 1500–1660* (London, 2006).
Gooch, John, & Amos Perlmutter, *Military deception and strategic surprise* (London, 2007).
Grimsley, Mark, & Clifford J. Rogers (eds), *Civilians in the path of war* (Lincoln, 2002).
Grossman, Dave, *On killing: the psychological cost of learning to kill in war and society* (New York, 1996).
Gutmann, Myron P., *War and rural life in the early modern Low Countries* (Princeton, 1980).
Hale, J.R., *War and society in Renaissance Europe, 1450–1620* (Leicester, 1985).
Hall, Bert S., *Weapons and warfare in Renaissance Europe: gunpowder, technology and tactics* (Baltimore, 1997).

Hammer, Paul E., *The polarisation of Elizabethan politics: the political career of Robert Devereux, 2nd earl of Essex, 1585–1597* (Cambridge, 1999).

—, *Elizabeth's wars: war, government and society in Tudor England, 1544–1604* (Houndmills, 2003).

Hayes-McCoy, G.A., 'History of guns in Ireland', *Journal of the Galway Archaeological and Historical Society*, 18:1/2 (1938), pp 43–65.

—, 'Strategy and tactics in Irish warfare, 1593–1601', *IHS*, 2:7 (1941), pp 255–79.

—, 'The tide of victory and defeat: I. The battle of Clontibret, 1595', *Studies: an Irish Quarterly Review*, 38:150 (1949), pp 158–68.

—, 'The army of Ulster, 1593–1601', *Irish sword*, 1:2 (1949–53), pp 105–17.

—, 'Irish cavalry I: the sixteenth century', *Irish Sword*, 1:4 (1953), pp 316–17.

—, 'The defence of the Moyry Pass', *Irish Sword*, 3:1 (1957–8), pp 32–8.

—, *Irish battles: a military history of Ireland* (London, 1969).

— (ed.), *Ulster and other Irish maps c.1600* (Dublin, 1964).

—, *Scots mercenary forces in Ireland (1565–1603)* (Dublin 1937, repr. Dublin, 1996).

—, 'The completion of the Tudor conquest and the advance of the counter-reformation, 1571–1603' in Moody et al. (eds), *A new history of Ireland; iii, early modern Ireland, 1534–1691* (2009), pp 94–140.

Henry, Gráinne, *The Irish military community in Spanish Flanders, 1586–1621* (Dublin, 1992).

Henry, L.W., 'The earl of Essex as a strategist and military organizer (1596–7)', *English Historical Review*, 68:268 (1953), pp 363–93.

—, 'The earl of Essex in Ireland, 1599', *Bulletin of the Institute of Historical Research*, 32:85 (1959), pp 1–23.

Herron, Thomas, & Michael Potterton (eds), *Ireland in the Renaissance, c.1540–1660* (Dublin, 2007).

Heuser, Beatrice, *The evolution of strategy: thinking war from antiquity to the present* (Cambridge, 2010).

Hill, James M., 'Shane O'Neill and the campaign against the MacDonalds of Antrim, 1564–5', *Irish Sword*, 18:71 (1991), pp 129–38.

—, 'The rift with Clan Ian Mor: the Antrim and Dunyveg MacDonnells, 1590–1603', *Sixteenth Century Journal*, 24:4 (1993), pp 865–79.

—, 'Gaelic warfare, 1453–1815' in Black (ed.), *European warfare* (1999), pp 201–23.

—, *Celtic warfare, 1595–1763* (Edinburgh, 2003).

Holt, Mack P., *The French wars of religion, 1562–1629* (Cambridge, 1995).

Houston, R.A., *The population history of Britain and Ireland, 1500–1750* (Cambridge, 1992).

Howard, Michael, George J. Andreopoulos & Mark R. Shulman (eds), *The laws of war: constraints on warfare in the western world* (London, 1994).

Hunter, R.J., *Ulster transformed: essays on plantation and print culture, c.1590–1641* (Belfast, 2012).

—, *Men and arms: the Ulster settlers, c.1630* (Belfast, 2012).

Imber, Colin, *Ottoman Empire, 1300–1650: the structure of power* (Basingstoke, 2002).

Jones, F.M., *Mountjoy, 1563–1606: the last Elizabethan deputy* (Dublin, 1958).

Kane, Brendan, & Valerie McGowan-Doyle (eds), *Elizabeth I and Ireland* (Cambridge, 2014).

Keen, Maurice (ed.), *Medieval warfare: a history* (Oxford, 1999).

Keep, John, *Soldiers of the Tsar: army and society in Russia, 1462–1874* (Oxford, 1985).

Kelly, Jack, *Gunpowder: a history of the explosive which changed the world* (London, 2004).

Kelenik, József, 'The military revolution in Hungary' in Fodor & Geza (eds), *Ottomans, Hungarians, and Habsburgs* (2000), pp 117–59.

Kiernan, Ben, *Blood and soil: a world history of genocide and extermination from Sparta to Darfur* (New Haven, 2007).

Klingelhofer, Eric, *Castles and colonists: an archaeology of Elizabethan Ireland* (Manchester, 2010).

Knecht, Robert J., *The French religious wars, 1562–1598* (Oxford, 2002).

Lacey, Robert, *Robert, earl of Essex: an Elizabethan Icarus* (London, 1971).

Lawrence, David R., *The complete soldier: military books and military culture in early Stuart England, 1603–1645* (Leiden, 2009).

Lee, Wayne E., 'Using the natives against the natives: indigenes as "counterinsurgents" in the British Atlantic, 1500–1800', *Defence Studies*, 10:1–2 (2010), pp 88–105.

—, 'Keeping the Irish down and the Spanish out: English strategies of submission in Ireland, 1594–1603' in Williamson and Mansoor (eds), *Hybrid warfare* (2012), pp 45–71.

Lenihan, Pádraig, '"Celtic" warfare in the 1640s' in Young (ed.), *Celtic dimensions of the British civil wars* (1997), pp 116–40.

—, *Confederate Catholics at war, 1641–49* (Cork, 2001).

— (ed.), *Conquest and resistance: war in seventeenth-century Ireland* (Leiden, 2001).

—, 'Conclusion: Ireland's military revolution(s)' in Lenihan (ed.), *Conquest and resistance* (2001), pp 345–70.

Lenman, Bruce, *England's colonial wars, 1550–1688: conflicts, empire and national identity* (Harlow, 2001).

Lennon, Colm, *Sixteenth-century Ireland: the incomplete conquest* (Dublin, 2005).

Loeber, Rolf, & Geoffrey Parker, 'The military revolution in seventeenth-century Ireland' in Ohlmeyer (ed.), *Ireland from independence to occupation* (1995), pp 66–88.

Logue, Paul, & James O'Neill, 'The battle of the Yellow Ford', *Dúiche Néill*, 16 (2007), pp 62–83.

Lynn, John A. (ed.), *Feeding Mars: logistics in western warfare from the Middle Ages to the present* (Boulder, 1993).

Lyons, Mary Ann, 'French reaction to the Nine Years War and the Flight of the Earls, 1594–1608', *Seanchas Ardmhacha*, 19:1 (2002), pp 70–90.

Lythe, S.G.E., *The economy of Scotland in its European setting, 1550–1625* (Edinburgh, 1960).

MacCaffrey, Wallace T., *Elizabeth I: war and politics, 1588–1603* (Princeton, 1992).

MacCionnaith, Seamus, 'Beal Atha ns mBriosgadh. Srath Fer Lurg Loch lamrugan', *Clogher Record*, 1:3 (1955), 111–17.

MacCuarta, Brian, 'Religious violence against settlers in south Ulster, 1641–2' in Edwards et al. (eds), *Age of atrocity* (2007), pp 154–75.

MacCurtain, Margaret, & Mary O'Dowd (eds), *Women in early modern Ireland* (Edinburgh, 1991).

Maley, Willy, 'Nationalism and revisionism: ambiviolences and dissensus' in Brewster (ed.), *Ireland in proximity* (1999), pp 12–27.

Maltby, William S., *The black legend in England: the development of anti-Spanish sentiment, 1558–1660* (Durham, 1971).

—, *Alba: a biography of Fernando Alvarez de Toledo, third duke of Alba, 1507–1582* (Berkeley, 1983).

McCabe, Richard, 'Fighting words: writing the "Nine Years War"' in Herron and Potterton (eds), *Ireland in the Renaissance* (2007), pp 105–21.

McCavitt, John, *Sir Arthur Chichester, lord deputy of Ireland* (Belfast, 1998).
—, *The flight of the earls* (Dublin, 2002).
McCormack, Anthony, *The earldom of Desmond, 1463–1583: the decline of a feudal lordship* (Dublin, 2005).
McGettigan, Darren, *Red Hugh O'Donnell and the Nine Years War* (Dublin, 2005).
—, 'A house divided: the political community of the lordship of Tír Chonaill and reaction to the Nine Years War' in Armstrong and Ó hAnnracháin (eds), *Community in early modern Ireland* (2006), pp 91–102.
McGleenon, C.F., 'The battle of Mullabrack, 5 September 1595', *Seanachas Ardmhacha*, 13:2 (1989), pp 90–101.
McGlynn, Sean, *By sword and fire: cruelty and atrocity in medieval warfare* (London, 2009).
McGurk, John, *The Elizabethan conquest of Ireland: the 1590s crisis* (Manchester, 1997).
—, 'Terrain and conquest, 1600–1603' in Lenihan (ed.), *Conquest and resistance* (2001), pp 87–114.
—, 'English naval operations at Kinsale' in Morgan (ed.), *The battle of Kinsale* (2004), pp 147–60.
—, *Sir Henry Docwra, 1564–1631: Derry's second founder* (Dublin, 2006).
—, 'The pacification of Ulster, 1600–3' in Edwards et al. (eds), *Age of atrocity* (2007), pp 119–29.
McLaughlin, Joseph, 'New light on Richard Hadsor II: Richard Hadsor "Discourse" on the Irish state, 1604', *IHS*, 30:119 (1997), pp 337–53.
—, 'What base coin wrought: the effects of the Elizabethan debasement in Ireland' in Morgan (ed.), *The battle of Kinsale* (2004), pp 193–204.
Moody, T.W., F.X. Martin & F.J. Byrne (eds), *A new history of Ireland; iii, early modern Ireland, 1534–1691* (Oxford, 2009).
Morgan, Hiram, 'The end of Gaelic Ulster: a thematic interpretation of events between 1534 and 1610', *IHS*, 26:101 (1988), pp 8–32.
—, 'Hugh O'Neill and the Nine Years War in Tudor Ireland', *Historical Journal*, 36:1 (1993), pp 21–37.
—, *Tyrone's rebellion: the outbreak of the Nine Years War in Tudor Ireland* (Dublin, 1993).
—, 'Faith and fatherland or queen and country?', *Dúiche Néill*, 9 (1994), pp 9–65.
—, 'Faith and fatherland in sixteenth-century Ireland', *History Ireland*, 3:2 (1995), pp 13–20.
— (ed.), *Political ideology in Ireland, 1541–1641* (Dublin, 1999).
—, 'Beyond Spenser? A historiographical introduction to the study of political ideas in early modern Ireland' in Morgan (ed.), *Political ideology in Ireland* (1999), pp 9–21.
—, 'The real Red Hugh' in Ó Riain (ed.), *Beatha Aodha Ruaidh* (2002), pp 1–35.
— (ed.), *The battle of Kinsale* (Bray, 2004).
—, 'Mission comparable? The Lough Foyle and Kinsale landings of 1600 and 1601' in Morgan (ed.), *The battle of Kinsale* (2004), pp 73–90.
—, 'Disaster at Kinsale' in Morgan (ed.), *The battle of Kinsale* (2004), pp 101–46.
—, 'Never any realm worse governed: Queen Elizabeth and Ireland', *Transactions of the Royal Historical Society*, 6th series, 14 (2004), pp 295–308.
—, '"Slán Dé fút go hoíche": Hugh O'Neill's murders' in Edwards et al. (eds), *Age of atrocity* (2007), pp 95–118.
—, '"Tempt not God too long, O Queen": Elizabeth and the Irish crisis of the 1590s' in Kane and McGowan-Doyle (eds), *Elizabeth I and Ireland* (2014), pp 209–38.
Morillo, Stephen, & Michael Pavkovic, *What is military history?* (Cambridge, 2008).
Nicholls, K.W., *Gaelic and Gaelicized Ireland in the Middle Ages* (Dublin, 1972).
—, 'Richard Tyrrell, soldier extraordinary' in Morgan (ed.), *The battle of Kinsale* (2004), pp 161–78.

Nolan, John S., *Sir John Norreys and the Elizabethan military world* (Exeter, 1997).

Ó Báille, M., 'The Buannadha: Irish professional soldiery in the sixteenth century', *Journal of the Galway Archaeological and Historical Society*, 12:1/2 (1946), pp 49–94.

O'Brien, Conor (ed.), *Feagh MacHugh O'Byrne: the Wicklow firebrand* (Rathdrum, 1998).

O'Byrne, Emmet, *War, politics and the Irish of Leinster, 1156–1606* (Dublin, 2003).

O'Connell, Robert L., *Of arms and men: a history of war, weapons and aggression* (Oxford, 1989).

O'Carroll, Donal, 'Change and continuity in weapons and tactics 1594–1691' in Lenihan (ed.), *Conquest and resistance* (2001), pp 211–56.

Ó Doibhlin, Éamon, 'Ceart Uí Néill: a discussion and translation of the document', *Seanchas Ardmhacha*, 5:2 (1970), pp 324–58.

Ó'Domhnaill, Seán, 'Warfare in sixteenth-century Ireland', *IHS*, 5:17 (1946), pp 29–54.

O'Donnell, Timothy, *Swords around the cross: the Nine Years War* (Font Royal, 2001).

O'Dowd, Mary, 'Gaelic economy and society' in Brady and Gillespie (eds), *Natives and newcomers* (1986), pp 120–47.

—, 'Women and war in Ireland in the 1640s' in MacCurtain and O'Dowd (eds), *Women in early modern Ireland* (1991), pp 91–11.

Ohlmeyer, Jane (ed.), *Ireland from independence to occupation, 1641–1660* (Cambridge, 1995).

O'Faolain, Seán, *The Great O'Neill* (Dublin, 1986).

Ó'Fiaich, Thomás, 'The O'Neills of the Fews', *Seanchas Ardmhacha*, 7:1 (1973), pp 1–64.

O'Grady, Standish, *Red Hugh's captivity: a picture of Ireland, social and political, in the reign of Queen Elizabeth* (London, 1889).

Oman, Charles, *A history of the art of war in the sixteenth century* (New York, 1979).

Ó Mearáin, Lorcan, 'The battle of Clontibret', *Clogher Record*, 1:4 (1956), pp 1–28.

Ó Néill, Eoin, 'Towards a new interpretation of the Nine Years' War', *Irish Sword*, 26:105 (2009), pp 241–62.

O'Neill, James, 'The cockpit of Ulster: war on the river Blackwater, 1593–1603', *Ulster Journal of Archaeology*, 74 (2013–14), pp 184–99.

—, & Paul Logue, 'The battle of the Ford of the Biscuits, 7 August 1594' in Foley and McHugh (eds), *An archaeological survey of County Fermanagh* (2014), pp 913–22.

—, 'Three sieges and two massacres: Enniskillen and the outbreak if the Nine Years War, 1593–5', *Irish Sword*, 30:121 (2016), pp 241–50.

O'Rahilly, Alfred, *The massacre at Smerwick, 1580* (Cork, 1938).

Ó Riain, Pádraig (ed.), *Beatha Aodha Ruaidh: the life of Red Hugh O'Donnell historical and literary contexts* (London, 2002).

O'Riordan, Michelle, *The Gaelic mind and the collapse of the Gaelic world* (Cork, 1990).

Outram, Quentin, 'The socio-economic relations of warfare and the military mortality crises of the Thirty Years War', *Medical History*, 45 (2001), pp 151–84.

—, 'The demographic impact of early modern warfare', *Social Science History*, 26:2 (2002), pp 245–72.

Palmer, Patricia, '"An headless Ladie" and "a horses loade of heads": writing the beheading', *Renaissance Quarterly*, 60:1 (2007), pp 25–57.

Palmer, William, 'Gender, violence, and rebellion in Tudor and early Stuart Ireland', *Sixteenth Century Journal*, 23:4 (1992), pp 699–712.

—, *The problem of Ireland in Tudor foreign policy, 1485–1603* (Woodbridge, 1994).

Parker, Geoffrey, *The Dutch Revolt* (London, 1979).

—, 'Early modern Europe' in Howard et al. (eds), *The laws of war* (1994), pp 40–58.

—, 'The "Military Revolution, 1560–1660" – A myth?', *Journal of Modern History*, 48:2 (1976), pp 196–214.

—, *The military revolution: military innovation and the rise of the West, 1500–1800* (2nd ed., Cambridge, 1999).

—, *The army of Flanders and the Spanish road, 1567–1659* (2nd ed., Cambridge, 2004).

—, 'The "military revolution", 1955–2005: from Belfast to Barcelona and the Hague', *Journal of Military History*, 69:1 (2005), pp 205–9.

Parks, Peter, 'Celtic fosterage: adoptive kinship and clientage in northwest Europe', *Comparative Studies in Society and History*, 49:2 (2006), pp 359–95.

Paul, Michael C., 'The military revolution in Russia, 1550–1682', *Journal of Military History*, 68:1 (2004), pp 9–45.

Patterson, Nerys, 'Gaelic law and the Tudor conquest of Ireland: the social background of the sixteenth-century recensions of the pseudo-historical prologue the Senchas Már', *IHS*, 27:107 (1991), pp 193–215.

Patterson, T.G.F., 'Lough Rorkan and the O'Lorkans', *Seanchas Ardmhacha*, 3:2 (1959), pp 261–7.

Pepper, Simon, 'Aspects of operational art: communications, cannon, and small war' in Tallett & Trim (eds), *European warfare* (2010), pp 181–203.

Poe, Marshall, 'The consequences of the military revolution in Muscovy: a comparative perspective', *Comparative Studies in Society and History*, 28:4 (1996), pp 603–18.

Quinn, D.B., *The Elizabethan's and the Irish* (Ithaca, 1966).

Rapple, Rory, *Martial power and Elizabethan political culture: military men in England and Ireland, 1558–1594* (Cambridge, 2009).

—, 'Writing about violence in the Tudor kingdoms', *Historical Journal*, 54:3 (2011), pp 829–54.

Redlich, F., 'Contributions in the Thirty Years' War', *Economic History Review*, 12:2 (1959), pp 247–54.

Roberts, Keith, *Pike and shot tactics, 1590–1660* (Oxford, 2010).

Roberts, Michael, 'The military revolution, 1560–1660' in Rogers, *The military revolution debate* (1995), pp 13–36.

Roberts, Penny, 'Peace, ritual, and sexual violence during the religious wars', *Past and Present*, 214, suppl. 7 (2012), pp 75–99.

Rogers, Clifford J. (ed.), *The military revolution debate: readings on the military transformation of early modern Europe* (Oxford, 1995).

—, 'The military revolution in history and historiography' in Rogers (ed.), *The military revolution debate* (1995), pp 1–12.

—, 'The military revolutions of the Hundred Years War' in Rogers (ed.), *The military revolution debate* (1995), pp 55–94.

—, 'The age of the Hundred Years War' in Keen (ed.), *Medieval warfare* (1999), pp 136–62.

—, 'By fire and sword: *bellum hostile* and "civilians" in the Hundred Years War' in Grimsley & Rogers (eds), *Civilians in the path of war* (2002), pp 33–78.

Rolnick, J., & Warren E. Weber, 'Gresham's law or Gresham's fallacy?', *Journal of Political Economy*, 94:1 (1986), pp 185–99.

Rosinger, Lawrence, 'Politics and strategy of China's mobile war', *Pacific Affairs*, 12:3 (1939), pp 263–77.

Rowens, Herbert H., 'The Dutch Revolt: what kind of revolution?', *Renaissance Quarterly*, 43:3 (1990), pp 570–90.

Rowse, A.L., *The expansion of Elizabethan England* (London, 1973).

Ruff, Julius R., *Violence in early modern Europe, 1500–1800* (Cambridge, 2001).

Ryan, Patrick J., *Archbishop Miler McGrath: the enigma of Cashel* (Roscrea, 2014).

Sheehan, A.J., 'The overthrow of the Plantation of Munster in October 1598', *Irish Sword*, 15:58 (1982), pp 11–22.

Shrader, Charles R., 'The influence of Vegetius' *De re militari*', *Military Affairs*, 45:4 (1981), pp 167–72.

Shy, John, 'History and the history of war', *Journal of Military History*, 72:4 (2008), pp 1033–46.

Silke, John J., 'Spain and the invasion of Ireland, 1601–2', *IHS*, 14:56 (1965), pp 295–312.

—, *Kinsale: the Spanish intervention in Ireland and the end of the Elizabethan wars* (Liverpool, 1970, repr. Dublin, 2000).

—, 'Kinsale reconsidered', *Studies: an Irish Quarterly Review*, 90:360 (2001), pp 412–21.

Simms, Katharine, *From high kings to warlords: the changing political structures of Gaelic Ireland in the later Middle Ages* (Woodbridge, 1987).

—, 'Gaelic warfare in the Middle Ages' in Bartlett & Jeffery (eds), *A military history of Ireland* (1996), pp 99–115.

Stacy, Robert C., 'The age of chivalry' in Howard et al. (eds), *The laws of war* (London, 1994), pp 27–39.

Stewart, Richard W., 'The "Irish road": military supply and arms for Elizabeth's army during the O'Neill rebellion in Ireland, 1598–1601' in Fissel (ed.), *War and government in Britain* (1991), pp 16–37.

Stump, Donald V., Linda Shenk & Carole Levin (eds), *Elizabeth I and the 'sovereign arts': essays in literature, history and culture* (Temple, 2011).

Sugden, John, *Sir Francis Drake* (London, 2006).

Tait, Clodagh, David Edwards & Pádraig Lenihan, 'Early modern Ireland: a history of violence' in Edwards et al. (eds), *Age of atrocity* (2007), pp 9–33.

Tallett, Frank, & D.J.B. Trim (eds), *European warfare, 1350–1750* (Cambridge, 2010).

Tanner, Harold M., 'Mobile, and base warfare in communist military operations in Manchuria, 1945–1947', *Journal of Military History*, 67:4 (2003), pp 1177–222.

Tempest, H.G., 'The Moyry Pass', *Journal of the County Louth Archaeological Society*, 14:2 (1958), pp 82–90.

Theibault, John C., *German villages in crisis: rural life in Hesse-Kassel and the Thirty Years War, 1580–1720* (Brill, 1995).

Tincey, John, *The Armada campaign, 1588* (Oxford, 1999).

Treadwell, Victor, 'Sir John Perrot and the Irish parliament of 1585–6', *Proceedings of the Royal Irish Academy, section C: archaeology, Celtic studies, history, linguistics, literature*, vol. 85c (1985), pp 259–308.

van Creveld, Martin, *Supplying war: logistics from Wallenstein to Patton* (Cambridge, 1987).

van der Hoeven, Marco (ed.), *Exercise of arms: warfare in the Netherlands (1569–1648)* (Leiden, 1997).

van Nierop, Henk, *Treason in the Northern Quarter: war, terror, and the rule of law in the Dutch Revolt* (Princeton, 2009).

Valentino, Benjamin, Paul Huth & Dylan Balch-Lindsay, '"Draining the sea": mass killing and guerrilla warfare', *International Organisation*, 58:2 (2004), pp 375–407.

Walsh, M.K., *Destruction by peace: Hugh O'Neill after Kinsale* (Armagh, 1986, repr. 2015).

—, 'Archbishop Magauran and his return to Ireland, October 1592', *Seanchas Ardmhacha*, 14:1 (1990), pp 68–79.

Walsham, Alexandra, *The Reformation of the landscape: religion, identity and memory in early modern Britain and Ireland* (Oxford, 2011).

Waxman, M.C., 'Strategic terror: Philip II and sixteenth-century warfare', *War in History*, 4:3 (1997), pp 339–47.

Webb, Henry J., *Elizabethan military science: the books and practice* (Madison, 1965).

West, Michael, 'Spenser's art of war: chivalric allegory, military technology, and the Elizabethan mock-heroic sensibility', *Renaissance Quarterly*, 41:4 (1988), pp 654–704.

White, Dean Gunther, 'Henry VIII's Irish kerne in France and Scotland, 1544–1545', *Irish Sword*, 3:13 (1958), pp 213–25.

White, Gavin, 'Firearms in Africa: an introduction', *Journal of African Studies*, 12:2 (1971), pp 173–84.

White, Lorraine, 'The experience of Spain's early modern soldiers: combat, welfare and violence', *War in History*, 9:1 (2002), pp 1–38.

Williamson, Murray, & Peter R. Mansoor (eds), *Hybrid warfare: fighting complex opponents from the ancient world to the present* (Cambridge, 2012).

Wood, James B., 'The impact of the wars of religion: a view of France in 1581', *Sixteenth Century Journal*, 15:2 (1984), pp 131–68.

—, *The king's army: warfare, soldiers, and society during the wars of religion in France, 1562–1576* (Cambridge, 2002).

Young, John R. (ed.), *Celtic dimensions of the British civil wars* (Edinburgh, 1997).

UNPUBLISHED SECONDARY SOURCES

Canning, Ruth, 'War, identity and the Pale: the Old English and the 1590s crisis in Ireland' (PhD, University College Cork, 2010).

WEBSITES USED

British History Online at, http://www.british-history.ac.uk
Corpus of Electronic Texts at, http://celt.ucc.ie/index.html
Dictionary of Irish Biography at, http://dib.cambridge.org/home.do
Oxford Dictionary of National Biography at, http://www.oxforddnb.com
The State Papers Online by Gale Cengage Learning at, http://www.galeuk.com/state papersonlineII/

Glossary

arquebus   a long-barrelled firearm, dating from the fifteenth century, smaller than a caliver or musket.

barque   a square-rigged sailing ship with three masts.

bastion   a projecting work in a fortification designed to permit flanking fire along the face of the wall.

battalia or battle   a large body of soldiers in array.

blackrent   extorted money or goods, normally by Irish chiefs off English neighbours in return for 'protection' from raiding.

bonnaght/   wages and provisions of a mercenary levied as a tax on regions, by
  buannacht   extension also the name given to said mercenaries.

buying   protection money paid to Gaelic chief to avoid depredations of raiding troops.

cabaset   a type of steel helmet, normally worn by infantry.

caliver   a light long-barrelled firearm introduced in the sixteenth century, half the weight of a musket making it more mobile but less powerful with a shorter effective range.

camisado   an attack on an enemy at night.

cashier   to disband or break up bands of soldiers, or to dismiss from a position of command.

cess   a range of government impositions used to maintain the garrisons.

cessation   a temporary truce or ceasefire.

churl   a peasant or rural labourer.

citadel   a fortress commanding a city that served both to protect and keep in subjugation.

composition   a formal contract or arrangement for tax purposes.

corselet   plate armour covering the front and back of the torso.

coyne and livery   a range of Gaelic exactions allowing the free quartering of a lord's dependants on his tenantry.

crannog   a lake dwelling, normally a small artificial island.

cromster   a small flat-bottomed ship designed for inshore operations.

cuirass   plate armour worn on the torso covering the chest. Can have a back but then becomes similar to a corselet. The terms are sometimes interchangeable in contemporary accounts.

debasement   the lowering of the value of a currency by reducing the quantity of valuable metal contained in the coinage.

fastness   a secure or fortified place, normally in forests or mountains.

fosterage	Gaelic custom where nobles commit the upbringing of their children to others to promote political connections.
gallowglass	mercenary heavy infantry, originally from Scotland, generally armoured with a helmet and mail, armed with swords and distinctive long-handled axe.
garran	a small workhorse, normally used to carry loads.
gossiprid	a formal pledge of fraternal association.
half-moon	a crescent- or v-shaped fortification that is open to the rear, also known as a demi-lune.
hargulatier	cavalry armed with firearms such as the petronel or carbine
horse	cavalry or troops mounted on horses.
hosting	a military expedition usually including militia forces, also an obligation of all able-bodied men for unpaid military service to defend the kingdom. In Gaelic lordships this was known as the rising out.
jinete	a Spanish light horseman armed with javelins, lance and small shield, primarily used for reconnaissance, foraging and skirmishing.
kerne	un-armoured Gaelic light infantry, armed with sword, bow and javelin, later equipped with firearms.
match	hemp cord soaked in saltpetre. When lit it burned slowly and was used in ignition system for firearms, for example, Matchlock.
musket	a heavy firearm, weighed 16–20 pounds, fired a larger bullet than a caliver. More powerful and longer range than a caliver but it had a slower rate of fire and had to be fired from a forked rest.
the Pale	area of English domination in Ireland comprising the four medieval counties of Dublin, Kildare, Meath and Louth.
palisade	a barrier of wooden stakes set in the ground.
parley	a conference between enemies at war.
petronel	a firearm carried by cavalry, sometimes fired while braced against the shooter's chest, sometimes known as a horseman's piece.
pike	a weapon with a long wooden staff, normally 15–18 foot in length tipped with an iron spike.
pinnace	a small sailing ship.
plashing	a barricade or hedge made of interwoven branches of trees and bushes.
preying	a raid to gather goods, money, hostages or intimidate. Spoiling attack to commandeer or destroy property.
proofing	the test firing of a gun barrel to ensure it can withstand the high pressures generated when gunpowder ignites to propel a bullet down the barrel.

push of pike	this occurred when two opposing blocks of pikemen meet and their interleaving pikes become locked along their front as both sides push the other back, while stabbing with pikes and swords.
reiter	from the German for horse rider, they were armoured cavalry armed with swords, pistols and sometime carbines.
rising out	military service given to Irish lords from dependant districts. In the Pale this was an assembly of able-bodied men who were obliged to perform up to forty days military service. Only those recognized as subjects were required to attend.
saker	a cannon firing shot weighing six pounds.
saltpetre	potassium nitrate was the key ingredient in gunpowder. It occurs as efflorescence in barnyards and similar places, primary as a product of animal urine in soil.
sconce	a small detached fort or defensive work.
shot	soldiers equipped with firearms.
spoil	the action or practice of pillaging and plundering, also the goods taken during these actions.
tánaiste	a designated successor to a Gaelic lordship
target	a small shield; troops equipped with targets and swords were called *targeteers*.
tassets	plate armour fastened to the bottom of a corselet to protect the thighs.
tercio	A Spanish infantry unit, often associated with dense formations of mutually supporting pike, shot and swordsmen, sometimes up to 3,000 strong.
trace italienne	polygonal fortifications appearing in the fifteenth century and developed thereafter in response to the destructive power of cannon. They were low and thick with complex systems of bastions mounting defensive artillery sited to provide mutual protection to adjacent defences and maximize defensive firepower against besieging forces.
uirríthe	sub-kings or lords of districts over whom other more powerful lords claimed suzerainty.
undertaker	persons granted land by the state that had been confiscated from Irish lords. This was conditional on their agreement to establish settlers from England and later Scotland on smaller parcels of land within these estates.
vambraces	plate armour for the upper and lower arms.
van	the foremost division of an army.
victual	food supplies, provisions.
ward	the guards or custodians of a castle, keep or fort.

Index